Building Power, Breaking Power

Building Power, Breaking Power

The United Teachers of New Orleans, 1965–2008

JESSE CHANIN

THE UNIVERSITY OF NORTH CAROLINA PRESS

Chapel Hill

Designed by Jamison Cockerham
Set in Scala and Futura Now
by Jamie McKee, MacKey Composition

Manufactured in the United States of America

Cover art: "Victory," 1978, American Federation of Teachers
Archives, Walter P. Reuther Library, Archives of Labor and Urban
Affairs, Wayne State University, Detroit, Michigan.

LIBRARY OF CONGRESS CATALOGING-IN-PUBLICATION DATA
Names: Chanin, Jesse, author.
Title: Building power, breaking power : the United Teachers of New Orleans,
1965–2008 / Jesse Chanin.
Description: Chapel Hill : The University of North Carolina Press, [2024] |
Includes bibliographical references and index.
Identifiers: LCCN 2023047518 | ISBN 9781469678214 (cloth) | ISBN 9781469678221
(paperback) | ISBN 9781469678238 (epub) | ISBN 9798890887054 (pdf)
Subjects: LCSH: United Teachers of New Orleans—History. | Teachers' unions—
Louisiana—New Orleans—History. | Labor movement—Louisiana—New Orleans—
History. | African American teachers—Louisiana—New Orleans—History. | Charter
schools—Louisiana—New Orleans—History. | BISAC: HISTORY / United States /
State & Local / South (AL, AR, FL, GA, KY, LA, MS, NC, SC, TN, VA, WV) |
SOCIAL SCIENCE / Ethnic Studies / American / African American & Black Studies
Classification: LCC LB2844.53.U62 N464 2024 | DDC 331.88/1137110976335—dc23/
eng/20231204
LC record available at https://lccn.loc.gov/2023047518

This book will be made open access within three years of publication thanks to Path
to Open, a program developed in partnership between JSTOR, the American Council
of Learned Societies (ACLS), the University of Michigan Press, and the University
of North Carolina Press to bring about equitable access and impact for the entire
scholarly community, including authors, researchers, libraries, and university
presses around the world. Learn more at https://about.jstor.org/path-to-open/.

For

Nat LaCour

And for all the educators who were fired
in the wake of Hurricane Katrina

CONTENTS

ILLUSTRATIONS

ACKNOWLEDGMENTS

So many people supported me through the process of researching and writing this book. I would like to thank the professors at Tulane who encouraged and supported me through graduate school: Rosanne Adderley, Fred Buttell, Xiaojin Chen, Kevin Fox Gotham, J. Celeste Lay, Laura McKinney, Carol Reese, and Allison Truitt. Special thanks to Camilo Leslie and Stephen Ostertag. I am especially grateful to Patrick Rafail and Jana Lipman, who guided me through the research process, read every chapter I wrote, and always pushed me to think more analytically. The book is much stronger, and better written, thanks to their feedback.

Thanks also to my colleagues in the City, Culture, and Community program who influenced and challenged my thinking: Danica Brown, Annie Freitas, Chloe Tucker, Sarah Woodward, and Tait Kellogg. I am especially grateful to Ari King, who talked through my arguments with me and helped edit the manuscript. Thanks to my comrades in Solidarity Tulane—some day I hope Tulane will have a graduate student union.

I was fortunate to work at two institutions that sharpened my research skills as a graduate student. Thanks to everyone at the Education Research Alliance, especially Christian Buerger, Doug Harris, Nathan Barrett, and Jane Lincove, for mentoring me. Special thanks to Huriya Jabbar for inviting me to collaborate on a research project and for introducing me to many of the tools of qualitative research. Thanks to Samantha Francois, who hired me as a research assistant at the Louisiana Public Health Institute and shared with me her many insights about the city and the schools.

This work would have been much more difficult without a generous dissertation fellowship from the Spencer Foundation. Thanks to Maria Gahan and Angie Harmon for their work coordinating the fellowship. I am grateful also to the mentors I met through the program, specifically Jon Shelton and Ansley Erickson. Thanks to Walter Stern who met with me both at the Spencer

Foundation conference and a couple years before, when I had no idea where this research was going.

Thanks to Dan Golodner, American Federation of Teachers (AFT) archivist at Wayne State, who was warm and welcoming when I visited and then fielded quite a few requests over email once I had left. Thanks also to Connie Phelps and James Hodges at the University of New Orleans special collections, who went above and beyond to assist me, despite less-than-ideal funding conditions. I had the great fortune of getting connected to Al Kennedy, who shared with me his reflections on the school system as well as guiding me through working with uncatalogued archives. I am also indebted to the many Tulane librarians who assisted me in finding books, reading microfilm, and accessing government data.

Thanks to my editors at the University of North Carolina Press, Andrew Winters and Brandon Proia. Thanks to the two reviewers whose insightful comments improved the manuscript incalculably.

My family and friends were endlessly supportive of the project. Thanks to Kevin Connell, Theo Hilton, and Rosamund Looney for reading drafts and giving me feedback. Thanks to Nicky Gillies for her unwavering belief that I was doing something worthwhile. And thanks, of course, to Oscar and Silas for ensuring that I was never tempted to work too much.

Last, and most importantly, I want to thank all the United Teachers of New Orleans (UTNO) members who fought to make the union successful as well as those who shared their stories with me. I hope I did those stories justice. Thanks to Colette Tippy and the union activists today who continue to fight for equity in our schools. Thanks to the former and current union presidents who participated in the study, read drafts, and connected me to other educators: Dave Cash, Wanda Richard, Jim Randels, and Brenda Mitchell. And thanks, especially, to the late Nat LaCour, whose leadership inspired so many, and whose razor-sharp memory contributed significantly to this project. I will be forever grateful that I had the chance to meet and work with all of you.

ABBREVIATIONS

ACORN Association of Community Organizations for Reform Now
AFL-CIO American Federation of Labor and Congress
of Industrial Organizations
AFSCME American Federation of State,
County and Municipal Employees
AFT American Federation of Teachers
A&M Alvarez and Marsal (a New York–based consulting firm)
APRI A. Philip Randolph Institute
(AFL-CIO constituency group focused on civil rights)
ASCA Algiers Charter Schools Association
BESE Board of Elementary and Secondary Education
CBA collective bargaining agreement
CBTU Coalition of Black Trade Unionists (AFL-CIO's Black caucus)
CIO Congress of Industrial Organizations
CMO Charter Management Organization
COPE Committee on Political Education (UTNO committee)
CTU Chicago Teachers Union
ILA International Longshoremen's Association
JFT Jefferson Federation of Teachers
(Jefferson Parish neighbors Orleans)
LABI Louisiana Association of Business and Industry
LAE Louisiana Association of Educators
(NEA state organization, integrated in 1975)
LaTEP Louisiana Teacher Evaluation Program

LDOE Louisiana Department of Education

LEA Louisiana Education Association
(Black NEA local and state organization)

LFT Louisiana Federation of Teachers (state-level AFT-affiliate)

Local 527 Majority-Black AFT local (changed its name to
UTNO when it merged with the OEA)

LTA Louisiana Teachers Association
(white NEA local and state organization)

NAACP National Association for the Advancement of Colored People

NALC National Association of Letter Carriers

NCLB No Child Left Behind Act of 2001 (in effect 2002–2015)

NEA National Education Association

NLRB National Labor Relations Board

NOCCA New Orleans Center for Creative Arts

NOCTF New Orleans Classroom Teachers Federation
(the white AFT local expelled from the organization
in 1958 for refusing to integrate)

NTE National Teacher Examination

OEA Orleans Educators Association (integrated but
majority-white NEA local formed when the
LTA and LEA merged in Orleans Parish)

OPSB Orleans Parish School Board

QuEST Quality Educational Standards in Teaching
(UTNO's annual conference)

RSD Recovery School District

SCLC Southern Christian Leadership Conference

SEIU Service Employees International Union

SNCC Student Nonviolent Coordinating Committee

SUNO Southern University at New Orleans

TFA Teach for America

UFCT United Federation of College Teachers

UFT United Federation of Teachers (New York City)

UFW United Farm Workers

UNO University of New Orleans

UTNO United Teachers of New Orleans

CHRONOLOGY

1937 AFT Local 527 chartered

1960 New Orleans school integration crisis

1965 Local 527 launches collective bargaining campaign

1966 Local 527 holds unsuccessful strike, the
      first teachers' strike in the South

1969 Local 527 holds second unsuccessful strike

1969 Eugene Didier elected Local 527 president

1971 Nat LaCour elected Local 527 president

1972 Overnight faculty desegregation transfers

1972 Local 527 and OEA merge to form UTNO

1974 UTNO teachers win collective bargaining

1975 UTNO paraprofessionals win collective bargaining

1978 UTNO disaffiliates from the NEA

1978 UTNO holds successful eight-day strike

1982 UTNO clerical workers win collective bargaining

1990 UTNO holds successful fifteen-day strike

1995 Louisiana legislature passes law
      permitting charter schools

1999 Brenda Mitchell elected UTNO president

2003 Voters approve constitutional amendment that
      allows the state to take over failing schools

2005 OPSB allows outside turnaround company (A&M)
      to take over major school district functions

2005 Hurricane Katrina hits New Orleans

2005 7,500 educators fired, including 4,000 teachers

2008 Larry Carter elected UTNO president

2016 Jim Randels elected UTNO president

2019 Wanda Richard becomes UTNO president
      when Randels steps down

2022 Dave Cash elected UTNO president

Building Power, Breaking Power

The Union Is People

When we elected a board to the union, we ran a ticket against whoever our opponents were within the union and our ticket was always integrated. For somebody like me that was a pro-union, liberal democrat, never voted for a Republican in my life, believed in integration, believed in teachers' rights and that unions could make schools better and did not hurt students, UTNO was like heaven. Everything I believed in and supported, there it was. We were integrated. We wanted better education. We wanted teachers' rights. We believed in Civil Rights.

Mike Stone, retired New Orleans teacher

Interviewer:

"Do you think the teachers were supported by the community?"

Kalamu ya Salaam, community activist:

"Of course. They *were* the community."

HISTORY REPEATS

In November 2005, just three months after Hurricane Katrina flooded the city of New Orleans, the Orleans Parish School Board (OPSB) fired more than 7,500 educators, including nearly 4,000 teachers.[1] Reflecting the city's population, 71 percent of the fired educators were Black.[2] The move devastated the city's Black middle class, nearly destroyed the teachers' union, and laid the groundwork for

a complete overhaul of the Orleans Parish school district. These dismissals ultimately resulted in a complete reinvention of public education in the city, replacing public schools with charter schools and an experienced, union-organized,
native New Orleanian educational workforce with one that is younger, whiter,
less experienced, and less likely to be from the city.[3] Today, New Orleans is
the only major US city with a district composed entirely of publicly funded
and privately governed charter schools—institutions renowned for eschewing
union activity. Fewer than one-third of the dismissed teachers returned to teach
in Orleans Parish and, by 2013, only 22 percent remained employed by the
district.[4] As a result of the post-Katrina dismissals, the United Teachers of New
Orleans (UTNO), which had been a powerful force in education since teachers
won collective bargaining in 1974, was crippled, losing the vast majority of its
membership dues as well as its clout as a voice advocating for democratic and just
educational policies. In 2006, the OPSB allowed UTNO's contract to expire. By
that time, the contract covered only four schools, compared to the more than 100
it covered before the storm, and the union had a mere sliver of its former power.[5]

Though catastrophic, these dismissals were not unprecedented. The post-
Katrina layoffs were, in fact, the second mass firing of Black educators in the
South. The first occurred after the 1954 *Brown v. Board of Education* ruling mandated the integration of public schools. The ruling resulted in the termination of
more than 38,000 Black educators in seventeen southern and border states—a
calculated effort by white politicians and parents to shift the burden of desegregation to Black families and to limit interactions between white children and Black
professionals and authority figures.[6] For example, in Nashville, which unlike
many districts achieved significant statistical desegregation, Black students were
bused longer distances and for more grades than their white counterparts.[7]
Across the South, white families often refused to enroll their children in formerly
Black institutions or in schools led by Black principals, resulting in the closure
of historically Black schools and the dismissal of Black educators and administrators.[8] Today, public schools remain largely segregated, both economically
and racially, in part because so many white families have withdrawn from the
public schools and have never returned.[9]

Louisiana emerged as a leader in post-*Brown* attempts to maintain segregated
schooling and white educational power. A 1970 report by the National Education
Association (NEA) detailed concerted efforts by districts throughout the state
to dismiss and demote Black educators and administrators and replace them
with less-qualified white educators as well as to close public schools and open
"hastily established" all-white private schools. In addition, a policy mandating
one-way transfers for Black students to white schools resulted in the eventual
closure of many Black institutions. The report acknowledges that "the terms of

desegregation have been determined unilaterally by whites without involvement of black educators, students, or parents."[10] Though Black educational advocates won school integration, at least on paper, there was an immense cost to this victory, paid by the loss of Black schools, Black principals, and Black teachers.

However, due in part to the work of New Orleans's two majority-Black teachers' unions—the American Federation of Teachers (AFT) Local 527 and the Louisiana Education Association (LEA)—educators in New Orleans dodged most of the post-*Brown* layoffs and school closures.[11] The commitment of Black political leaders and teachers to school integration, and their careful consideration of its burden on Black students and educators, changed the racial power balance in the schools and in the city through the 1960s and 1970s. Though white families fled the city and abandoned the public school system—the city went from 37 percent Black in 1960 to 55 percent Black in 1980,[12] while the schools went from 58 percent to 84 percent Black over the same time period[13]—the most prominent educator labor shift occurred when approximately 300 white teachers quit in protest after being forced to transfer to formerly Black schools.[14] Though genuine school integration was fleeting in New Orleans, the majority-Black unions in the city created a thriving landscape for Black educational labor in the city.

Yet nearly fifty years later, in the aftermath of Katrina, teachers, school leaders, and union activists were unable to stymie layoffs that disproportionately affected Black educators. The dismissal of more than 5,000 Black educators in late 2005 undermined Black political power in the city and effectively dismantled the same teachers' union that had protected Black jobs in the 1960s and 1970s. Longtime teacher and union member Grace Lomba, like many other educators, was shocked when she got her pink slip in the mail in late 2005:

> [The mass dismissal] totally interrupted [educators'] lives, there are some who have never come back. There are some who have gone to other states and settled their lives. They became teachers over there. Everywhere that our teachers went, that I know of, they were welcomed as educators because they were qualified educators, many of them were more qualified than some of the people in the districts they went to. When I went to Lafayette, I was only one of a few people who had a master's plus thirty, and that happened with a lot of our teachers. Many of the districts, they begged them to stay. Had you put the resources into this district that you put in there now, after that storm, we would have been the district you wanted it to be. But you didn't want that. And the question is, why?[15]

Firing the UTNO educators and dismantling the union were key steps to transforming the Orleans Parish school district into a laboratory for school choice reforms. This book examines why, what was at stake, and the role the union played in fighting for democracy and equity in the decades leading up to the storm.

LESSONS FROM THE UTNO STORY

The rise and fall of UTNO (AFT Local 527) complicates common narratives about unions in the South. It demonstrates the dynamic relationship between professional unions and the families they serve and illuminates the effects of the privatization of public education on the educator workforce. The UTNO story offers four main takeaways:

> 1. Teachers unions in the South have been largely overlooked due to the dearth of collective bargaining agreements (CBAs) in the region, resulting in an incomplete understanding of the role that Black teachers and majority-Black unions have played in the teacher organizing landscape.
>
> 2. UTNO demonstrates how teachers brought lessons and skills from the civil rights movement into their organizing, creating a conceptual and strategic bridge between the civil rights unionism of the 1940s–60s and the social movement unionism that emerged in the late 1990s.
>
> 3. These strategies, in which labor organizers tackle economic and racial justice in tandem, also open up new possibilities for democratic participation and civic engagement.
>
> 4. School privatizations and neoliberal education reforms are anti-democratic, anti-union, anti-Black and anti-educator; whatever gains are made in test scores are offset by the harm done to communities and teachers.

TEACHER UNIONISM IN THE SOUTH

First, UTNO demonstrates the potential for successful teacher unionism in the South, particularly in the immediate post-*Brown* era. This has been largely overlooked by researchers due to the comparatively small number of CBAs throughout the region.[16] Yet research that focuses on teachers' unions in the Northeast, Midwest, and West, all relative labor strongholds, tends to exclude Black teachers, who are concentrated in the South, from narratives of union activism and teacher power (see table 0.1). Moreover, it categorizes occurrences of southern union activism as exceptional and anomalous rather than as a constitutive part of movements for social, racial, and educational justice. Historian Jacquelyn Dowd Hall highlights the relationship between union participation and the struggle for

Table 0.1. Number of Black and white public school
teachers in selected states, 2011–2012

REGION	STATE	TOTAL NUMBER OF TEACHERS	BLACK TEACHERS (%)	WHITE TEACHERS (%)
United States		3,385,200	6.8	81.9
South	Alabama	45,000	18.6	78.8
	Arkansas	37,700	13.6	82.3
	Georgia	123,300	17.1	76.2
	Louisiana	44,500	19.9	74.4
	Mississippi	37,600	25.0	73.3
	North Carolina	104,300	10.4	84.1
	South Carolina	51,800	15.5	81.3
	Tennessee	76,500	5.2	91.3
	Texas	350,800	9.0	65.3
West	California	285,500	3.2	70.5
	Oregon	31,800	N/A*	88.6
	Washington	55,500	N/A	87.0
Midwest	Illinois	140,900	7.1	83.3
Northeast	Massachusetts	79,200	N/A	96.6
	New Jersey	125,200	6.6	82.2
	New York	241,400	8.6	76.3
	Pennsylvania	148,800	N/A	95.7

Source: U.S. Department of Education, National Center for Education Statistics,
Schools and Staffing Survey (SASS), "Public School Teacher Data File," 2011–12.
* "N/A" indicates that reporting standards were not met,
at least in part because the numbers were so low.

civil rights, arguing that the civil rights movement started in the 1940s, when racial and economic activism were deeply intertwined, and lasted through the Black Power–era of the 1970s—a period that coincided with enormous gains in public sector unionism.[17] This framework emphasizes the pivotal role that workplace activism played in achieving civil rights goals, and it recontextualizes the backlash against organized labor in the 1970s and 1980s as a reaction to civil rights gains. Similarly, Hall's framework illuminates how the absence of teacher CBAs in the South is a legacy of racial exploitation in the region.

Though UTNO was perhaps the strongest teachers' union in the South from 1965 to 2005, its work is not the only significant instance of teacher activism. For example, Black educators were central to the "Black Monday" protest in Memphis in 1969, in which parents boycotted the city's schools to demand student desegregation, a greater Black administrative voice in the district, culturally inclusive textbooks, and free or reduced-price lunches for students living in poverty.[18]

Similarly, a multiracial teacher coalition in Florida helped win statewide collective bargaining in 1974; and Mississippi teachers engaged in a successful wildcat strike in 1985, winning a significant pay raise.[19] These examples demonstrate that a lack of educator CBAs does not necessarily indicate the absence of teacher activism. According to a study by historian Lane Windham, just as many private sector workers sought collective bargaining in the 1970s as in the previous two decades, yet fewer of them won collective bargaining elections.[20] The efficacy of employer counteroffensives and state governments hostile to labor stymied organizing across the South—and would ultimately hobble UTNO. However, the dearth of powerful unions with CBAs does not indicate a lack of labor activism from southern educators.

UTNO's collective bargaining victories garnered widespread community support by explicitly combining the struggles for racial and economic justice. This approach diverged from that of the national AFT, which privileged a color-blind, meritocratic ideology in its organizing.[21] Though the AFT supported the civil rights movement and initiatives like Freedom Summer with both money and members, many union leaders, including AFT president Al Shanker, eventually saw due process and seniority protections as being in tension with civil rights goals[22]—as did most AFL-CIO (American Federation of Labor and Congress of Industrial Organizations) unions. The labor movement wanted full employment and a redistribution of wealth; instead, the government offered affirmative action processes that unions felt penalized workers for the discriminatory practices of their employers, especially once jobs became scarce in the 1970s.[23]

For the AFT, these tensions reached a crossroads in 1968 when Shanker led the New York City teachers in a months-long strike to protest the transfer of mostly white and Jewish teachers accused of racism by Black district administrators; the strike effectively destroyed the Black community's experiment in community controlled schools.[24] In the subsequent decade, more conflicts between majority-white teachers' unions and Black communities emerged, with Black leaders often accusing the unions of deprioritizing the needs of Black students.[25] Though other major locals had Black presidents—for example, the Newark Teachers Union elected its first Black president in 1968, and the Chicago Teachers Union (CTU) elected its first in 1984—these Black leaders had fought to assume the leadership of historically white institutions and struggled to unify the Black community behind the unions' demands.[26] In contrast, UTNO was a historically Black institution connected to broader civil rights organizing in New Orleans. Under the leadership of Black presidents, UTNO fought integration-related teacher dismissals, stood in solidarity with Black parents and students mistreated in schools, and advanced an agenda that prioritized not only collective bargaining and educator salary and workplace demands but also racial justice goals. The union's organizing, at least at the time of its collective bargaining campaign (1965–74), was seen as part of the civil rights movement rather than as separate from it. Moreover, its organizing and activism were effective because of the overwhelming support it received from the Black community.

FROM CIVIL RIGHTS TO SOCIAL MOVEMENT UNIONISM

In part, UTNO's focus on racial justice came from its leaders' grounding in the civil rights movement. The union's collective bargaining campaign and early militancy demonstrate the power of civil rights unionism and provide a conceptual bridge to the "social movement unionism" of today. Historian Robert Korstad uses the term "civil rights unionism" to refer to the 1940s organizing efforts of a coalition of early civil rights activists and CIO trade unionists—as well as communists—who sought to combine working-class insurgency with the Black freedom struggle.[27] While the strikes and union growth of the 1940s stagnated due to aggressive employer counteroffensives, the beginning of urban deindustrialization, and the anticommunist backlash of the Cold War years,[28] civil rights unionism reemerged with the 1960s wave of public sector Black protest—most famously through the activism of Memphis sanitation workers. The sanitation workers' strike, which earned the support of Dr. Martin Luther King Jr., was to demand that the city recognize the union, implement more rigorous safety standards, and pay workers a higher wage.[29] Protests such as this reinvigorated the struggle for civil rights as well as the Black Power movement that followed, and they inspired new labor organizing, more militant union action, and the integration and democratization of existing unions.[30] As part of this organizing wave, UTNO educators, many of whom were civil rights movement veterans, connected their struggle for collective bargaining to the rights and dignity of Black people.

Though UTNO became less radical and more bureaucratic over time, the union continued to demonstrate qualities consistent with the social movement unions of today. Social movement unions strategically link union initiatives to a broader economic justice agenda intended to improve the life chances for women and people of color, and these unions are often based in the service sector, which expanded exponentially in the 1990s.[31] UTNO, for example, prioritized the interests of its least powerful members by waging a strike in 1990 to demand raises for paraprofessionals (school aides), and it used its leadership role in the local labor movement to bolster less powerful unions across the education sector and in neighboring parishes. It collaborated with community organizations in the city, including churches, to fight for meaningful citywide reforms, such as a higher minimum wage. It consistently advocated for more funding for public schools, drawing attention to the many challenges educators faced, including poor building conditions, lack of teaching materials, and large class sizes. It also expressed early opposition to the unregulated expansion of charter schools, which has emerged as a key issue for powerful unions across the country, most notably in Chicago and Los Angeles.[32]

In addition to fighting more broadly for economic and racial equity, UTNO employed the tactic of linking educator struggles to the quality of education accessible to students. In the 2018 "Red for Ed" teacher uprisings in six conservative, right-to-work states in the West and South, educators modeled UTNO's approach, demonstrating the tactical power in combining educator struggles— rising health care costs, stagnant salaries, and proposed pension changes—to educational quality.[33] In this way, UTNO provided a bridge between civil rights union struggles and the social movement unions of today, re-centering the analytic focus on Black-led southern activism.

DEMOCRACY AND CIVIC ENGAGEMENT

At the center of UTNO's success was its decision to incorporate strategies popularized by civil rights and post–civil rights Black organizing, which emphasized the importance of democracy and civic engagement. Specifically, leaders fostered a strong internal culture of union democracy and regularly participated in disruptive actions including work stoppages, strikes, sick-outs, and rallies. Additionally, and in part through these actions, the union developed a powerful political machine that garnered community support and anchored a left-leaning Black middle-class political agenda. It drew inspiration from civil rights activists such as Ella Baker and Septima Clark, who developed theories of power and democracy staunchly opposed to the status quo, pushing for working-class leadership, consensus-building, and mass mobilization.[34] For example, Ella Baker and the Student Nonviolent Coordinating Committee (SNCC) used nonhierarchical participatory decision-making to ensure that members were willing to literally put their bodies on the line, demonstrating that strong, male, autocratic leadership is not the only "efficient" way to run an organization.[35] UTNO developed an internal structure that created numerous pathways to active participation and helped train and uplift working-class and women leaders. The union's commitment to democratic decision-making—or "rank-and-file unionism"—created an organization that empowered workers and developed the type of transparent and participatory system union members hoped to see in the school board and the city.

Unfortunately, UTNO's democratic power structure was part of its undoing after Katrina, as longtime teacher Gwendolyn Adams explains: "The union is made up of people, the union is not a building, the union is not a name, the union is people. And at that point, when they fired all the teachers, people were displaced all over the country. So there really wasn't a union, because people were not back home yet, and they took advantage of that."[36] Union leaders, such as building representatives, and especially members of the executive council, spoke about their work in UTNO as some of the most profoundly participatory and democratic experiences of their lives. Some described four-hour meetings where everyone was given a chance to speak before the president would express his opinion for the first time.[37] The experience of participating actively in such a democratic project had a profound effect on union members, but it also undermined UTNO's power after the storm. With members evacuated throughout the country, the few UTNO elected leaders who remained found themselves largely powerless and easily sidelined by reform advocates determined to remake the public school district along neoliberal lines.

UTNO was also committed to using disruptive action to achieve its goals, which further opened spaces for rank-and-file participation and democratic decision-making. UTNO held three strikes in the 1960s and 1970s, the heyday of teacher job actions,[38] and then a longer strike in 1990, when strikes were less frequent nationwide (see graph 0.1).[39] Strikes declined precipitously in the United States after President Reagan fired the striking air traffic controllers in 1981 and a business backlash against organized labor put unions on the defensive;[40] but strikes and successful unionization drives remain strongly linked.[41] In addition to UTNO's strikes, it also held marches, rallies, sick-outs, and protests—alternative forms of disruptive action that contributed to meaningful victories for the educators. For example, in 1997 the union forced the district to close schools for the day so that teachers could attend a rally in Baton Rouge for increased education spending.[42] Each of these actions required the mobilization of a network of rank-and-file union members, organized by local building representatives, who themselves were directed by "area coordinators." UTNO members, including clerical workers and paraprofessionals, took pride in their contributions to the union as area coordinators. They recalled their fear and excitement giving speeches at strike rallies and the challenge of ensuring everyone in their buildings participated. Disruptive actions directed at the level of the school board and state frequently garnered mass participation within the union, creating new feelings of solidarity and loyalty to UTNO.

However, from 2000 to 2005, shortly before Katrina, fewer of these actions took place, and active participation in union activities declined. This was due to several factors—a new UTNO president who was less open to democratic decision-making, bureaucratic ineptitude and instability at the district level, escalating attacks on the teachers and the schools, and the retirement of members who had lived through the civil rights era and collective bargaining campaign—but it certainly left UTNO more vulnerable when the storm struck the city. Fewer members participated in union activities, including elections, and the union often opted for procedural rather than disruptive tactics to solve the issues they faced.

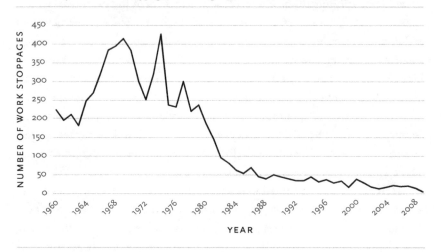

Graph 0.1. Work stoppages involving more than 1,000 workers, 1960–2008

Source: US Bureau of Labor Statistics, "Annual Work Stoppages Involving 1,000 or More Workers, 1947–2019," accessed December 1, 2020, www.bls.gov/web/wkstp/annual-listing.htm.

For example, in 2003, when the state legislature created the Recovery School District (RSD)—the mechanism that would eventually be used to take over the Orleans school district and dismiss the educators after Katrina—UTNO offered only tepid opposition and neglected to hold a strike or rally to protest the plan.[43] Similarly, the Black community's support for UTNO waned over the 1990s and 2000s as class divisions within New Orleans's Black population grew and as it became clear that the election of Black mayors and other political leaders would not necessarily improve the lot of the Black poor.[44] With that said, UTNO continued to garner significant support from the Black community, union participation remained relatively high, and the union held some disruptive public events, such as protesting the district's chronic inability to issue employees their correct paychecks and provide teachers with classroom supplies.[45] Though there were signs of growing weakness, the union remained a robust and powerful force in the city until Hurricane Katrina hit.

In addition to strikes and work stoppages, UTNO developed member-led institutions that allowed for extensive rank-and-file participation and cultivated leadership skills among its members. Union members built a Health and Welfare Fund that provided comprehensive healthcare benefits to members, and they established a credit union that gave members access to loans to purchase their first houses or cars. They also developed a teacher center that helped teachers improve their practice and stay up-to-date with innovations in the field. These institutions were run and staffed by UTNO members with funding from UTNO's contract negotiations. Such systems helped members take on leadership roles and encouraged them to mentor and train one another. Moreover, the rank-and-file members who worked at these institutions or served on their boards felt essential to the union's day-to-day functioning. They saw the union as a product of the people involved, rather than as an independent organization created to serve teachers' needs. These internal organizational structures helped UTNO maintain its democratic ideals and avoid the pitfalls of becoming a "service union," that is, one in which members see the union as an external organization that exists to meet their needs. Instead, UTNO members recognized their union as a vibrant collective fueled by the voices and energy of its participants.

As a well-organized collective of invested members, UTNO was also able to develop strong community support and create space for other activism in the city and state. The union worked closely with the broader community to elect left-leaning candidates at the municipal and state levels, providing an anchor for Black middle class economic power in the city. UTNO's political machine was well-known, and candidates throughout the state solicited the union's endorsement. The union sent buses full of educator-volunteers to canvass on behalf of UTNO-endorsed candidates, and it monitored polls on Election Day, coordinating get-out-the-vote efforts in target neighborhoods. UTNO played a significant role in defeating David Duke, the former grand wizard of the Ku Klux Klan, in his 1991 gubernatorial campaign, helping prevent the spread of a statewide atmosphere of greater repression and fear.[46] The union also supported Black candidates for mayor, city council, and the state legislature, helping to diversify a political system that had been exclusively white since Reconstruction. Yet, as a union, members also worked to avoid the trap of blindly supporting Black candidates regardless of their political position on relevant issues. Instead, UTNO focused on endorsing pro-Black, pro-worker candidates who espoused a redistributive agenda.

Though UTNO did not always support the most progressive candidates or causes, in the context of Louisiana, representing mostly Black constituents was a significant political lift. By representing Black people, women, and labor interests in mainstream electoral politics, UTNO created space for others to engage in more radical campaigns outside of the union's purview, such as fighting against police brutality or for a higher minimum wage.[47] At the same time, the teachers anchored a Black economic base in the city, living in economically diverse neighborhoods and leveraging their financial and social capital for infrastructural improvements and neighborhood amenities.

Of course, middle- and upper-class Black residents, like many UTNO teachers, did not always align themselves with their working-class Black neighbors and could instead contribute to their criminalization and displacement.[48] For example, in the words of one Black teacher:

A lot of people don't like gentrification, [but] I do . . . it's pretty quiet right here. But several streets over and if you go about three miles back, there's little wars, you can hear gunshots. People that didn't come back in these beautiful homes like this, Section 8, and they're not the nicest people. We have some young people that stay down there, and another house that's Section 8, and they're different. They put their cars on the grass, they're loud. This is a subtle neighborhood. Pretty much on this side, everybody is professional.[49]

New Orleans's Black teachers occupied (and continue to occupy) a liminal space, both supporting and potentially pathologizing their poorer neighbors. As sociologist Mary Pattillo describes, Black people also often have a more tenuous relationship to middle-class status than their white peers, since due to ongoing discrimination and lack of intergenerational wealth, it is easier for them to lose status.[50] The New Orleans teachers experienced this phenomenon first hand when they were fired *en masse* after Katrina and were suddenly faced with destroyed homes, no source of income, and skyrocketing health insurance costs. Along with constituting a personal tragedy for many members, these dismissals diminished the power of the city's Black political machine, further marginalizing Black political voices in larger discussions about governance and reform.

It is also notable that UTNO obtained its collective bargaining agreement and achieved the heights of its power under the leadership of Nat LaCour, an almost universally beloved president, staunchly committed to integration, and presented as unflappably calm and reasonable. Male leadership of a union whose members were predominantly women undoubtedly gave UTNO additional clout in the patriarchal political system—the union could not win collective bargaining under longtime president Veronica Hill, and it was during the tenure of LaCour's successor, Brenda Mitchell, that the union was eviscerated. Historian Jon Shelton argues that teachers' unions and their strikes were seen as subversive because women were expected to conform to ideals of service and sacrifice—not demand rights.[51] That was especially true of Black women, who were frequently accused of being angry or unfeminine when they protested unfair conditions.

LaCour also embodied a Blackness that the power structure could tolerate; he was rarely emotional, always considered. The most negative, and racialized, depiction of him in the press came from white columnist Iris Kelso: "A big, imposing-looking man, he is a natural leader—charismatic and articulate. He is aggressive, a hard bargainer. But he also is reasonable."[52] By contrast, school officials and some teachers saw Mitchell as polarizing and angry: "[Brenda was] almost like having Hillary Clinton become president. There'll be some who will love her and some who are going to hate her."[53] Mitchell certainly had a less democratic style than LaCour, and she lacked his connections—which had been cultivated during his nearly thirty years of building political and institutional relationships—but LaCour was also palatable to political leaders in a way that Mitchell could never be. Though UTNO was not a textbook example of a radical teachers' union, and while its members' gender, racial, and class politics were certainly not above reproach, UTNO's commitment to democracy and civic engagement grounded its politics in progressivism and helped the union become one of the few powerful voices advocating for school equity at the local and state level for forty years.

NEOLIBERAL EDUCATION REFORM HARMS
TEACHERS AND COMMUNITIES

Finally, rather than interpreting the charterization of public schools in New Orleans as an exceptional scenario and the dissolution of the union as an anomaly of disaster capitalism, I argue that UTNO was specifically targeted and weakened in order to limit Black political power and stymie a redistributive agenda in the name of color-blind neoliberalism. Though the flooding of the city provided policymakers with the opportunity to wipe out the union and the educators overnight, similar processes of educational privatization are occurring nationwide on a school-by-school basis.[54] Analyzing the New Orleans case, then, elucidates the mechanisms of school reform and how they promote an anti-labor, anti-Black, and antidemocratic agenda. This is true even when some school reform proponents include Black administrators, educators, and parents.[55] UTNO's evisceration also highlights union busting as a central project of neoliberal reform in education as well as in other sectors. The educator dismissals were not an unintentional side effect of the privatization agenda; they were instead a crucial step toward creating the system that exists in New Orleans today. This all-charter district is significantly whiter and less local than before the storm, and it is characterized by a lack of labor power and scant avenues for democratic participation or oversight.

Neoliberalism emerged in the late 1970s and early 1980s as a supposedly color-blind ideology of individual freedom and economic rationality in response to shifts toward economic equality, a robust and somewhat interracial labor movement, and the first steps toward workplace and school integration. Economist Milton Friedman's 1962 *Capitalism and Freedom* became the roadmap for policymakers who wanted to take this neoliberal turn. Portraying himself as an anti-racist, Friedman wrote that the unregulated market would best eliminate discrimination, as bigotry is irrational and thus disadvantages people in the free market. He advocated for the rollback of government services, including the elimination of public education, suggesting that mandating that families pay the cost of educating their children would help regulate family size.[56] He hailed the importance of schools competing for students (to improve the quality of education) and the importance of parental "choice," two hallmarks of the contemporary charter movement. This ideology is an example of what critical theorist Jodi Melamed calls "neoliberal multiculturalism," a state-sanctioned antiracist discourse in support of free market capitalist values, such as property rights and competition.[57] School choice reformers cast education as a personal rather than a collective good; education, these reformers maintained, should be in the domain of the free market, not the government.[58] The New Orleans school reformers incorporated the language of racial equity, diversity, and closing the achievement gap for Black students, even though the project itself was predicated on the firing of 7,500 mostly Black educators.

Education theorist Pauline Lipman argues that neoliberal reforms within education are largely about controlling the city and promoting gentrification. Closing traditional public schools, dismissing veteran educators, opening privately run charters, and providing parents with vouchers to attend private and parochial schools all create new avenues for development, such as opening high-end markets in shuttered schools. These processes also transfer wealth from local government to private education entrepreneurs and developers.[59] This strategy echoes the ways in which city planners used segregated schools to promote residential redlining and encourage white middle-class development under Jim Crow.[60] Lipman demonstrates the ways in which these reforms are antidemocratic and elite-led and how they replace the participatory citizen with the "consumer" who must compete with others to choose the right school for their children, rather than organize for quality schools for all children.[61] Such policies also explicitly target teachers unions, which remain a labor stronghold: by 2007, teachers were second only to the postal service in terms of union density.[62] Teachers today represent "the single largest body of union members in the country."[63] The mass firing of the UTNO educators, and their replacement by mostly out-of-town young, white educators, many recruited through programs such as Teach for America, played a role in the post-Katrina gentrification of New Orleans.[64]

Policymakers targeted UTNO and the educators it represented after the storm because of UTNO's persistent resistance to a neoliberal development agenda. With one of the largest constituencies in the state, UTNO was a political force to be reckoned with in the state legislature, and it worked tirelessly to protect union benefits, such as tenure, health insurance, and pension plans. UTNO also publicly opposed free-market education reforms, especially those borrowed from business that foregrounded the rhetoric of "accountability" and "choice." Within education, accountability has become nearly synonymous with high-stakes standardized testing, and choice generally refers to a family's ability to select a school through the introduction of new charter schools or voucher programs. New Orleans instituted its first high school exit exam in 1989, despite UTNO's objections, and the Louisiana Association of Business and Industry (LABI), one of the union's staunchest opponents, advocated for vouchers as early as 1985, though the state's first voucher law was not passed until 2008.[65]

The state passed a law permitting charters in 1995, but before Hurricane Katrina, only eight charter schools existed in Orleans Parish.[66] UTNO played a significant role in preventing the introduction of a voucher system and limiting the growth of charters, as evidenced by their successful 1995 campaign against the for-profit school takeover group, Educational Alternatives, Inc.[67] The union also opposed a 2003 constitutional amendment that allowed the state to take over failing schools—a policy widely understood to be targeting New Orleans.[68] The law threatened the union directly by stipulating that a state takeover would negate any CBAs in effect while also allowing for the privatization of school services.[69] The union suggested, instead, that administrators and policymakers work with teachers to develop successful research-based education programs, claiming that state takeovers rarely result in increased achievement.[70] The conflict highlighted the strategic importance of union busting to advancing the neoliberal agenda in education. Although attempts to privatize the New Orleans school system and remove local democratic control had occurred before the storm, UTNO's strength, as well as the power of the Black voting bloc in the city, prevented drastic changes—until the power vacuum emerged in the wake of Hurricane Katrina. However, the pathway of neoliberal reform was clear: drastically cut city and school funding, implement strict accountability measures, and then posit privatization, union busting, and layoffs as the only solution for a failing district. UTNO's long-standing resistance to these reforms demonstrates the real threat that powerful unions pose to the neoliberal agenda. Today, teachers' unions continue to provide some of the only substantive opposition to educational privatization nationwide.[71]

Scholars often portray the case of New Orleans schools as exceptional—exceptionally bad before the storm, boasting a strong teachers' union against the logic of the South, and then privatized overnight, with an exceptionally harsh program of educator dismissals. Yet New Orleans demonstrates instead the future that may await other districts and other unions across the country that are already struggling. Cities in right-to-work states in the South have demonstrated the potential to organize powerful, anti-racist, redistributive teachers unions and have also shown that even apparent union strongholds can be summarily destroyed through processes of privatization and school reform. Historian Nancy MacLean argues that the federal government and other regional blocs have exported the fiscal and social policies of the Deep South to create national programs of austerity, social control, and pro-business regulation: "As the South's conservative elites have amassed power, they have succeeded in imposing more and more of their historic model of political economy on the nation as a whole, indeed, on the wider world."[72] The privatization agenda that devastated the once strong and connected community of New Orleans teachers is similarly dismantling public school districts nationwide. Through the piecemeal introductions of charter schools and vouchers and an accompanying reduction in public accountability, traditional public school districts are being undone. UTNO's destruction after the storm shows the strength of the neoliberal school-reform movement, yet UTNO also offers a story of hope and resistance, neighborhood-based organizing, and strategies that, for a time, held that well-funded movement at bay.

CONCLUSION: THE AFT, RACE, AND UTNO'S LEGACY

The role of southern, majority-Black, and feminized unions and the work that their rank-and-file members have undertaken to combat economic and racial injustice have been comparatively overlooked. Unions are often portrayed as conservative institutions, and many have long histories of racism and exclusion; the AFT in New Orleans, for example, maintained segregated local chapters until 1958.[73] Classic social movement theorists Frances Fox Piven and Richard Cloward, citing sociologist Robert Michels's 1911 "iron law of oligarchy," argue that once organizations are established, they will inevitably become antidemocratic. As leadership becomes more deeply entrenched in organizational hierarchy, its tactics become more conservative and less effective.[74] As large, powerful bureaucracies, unions often exemplify this law. For example, the AFT emerged in the early 1900s out of working-class, mostly women-led, teacher and student strikes in Chicago. The radical collective led defiant strikes throughout the Great Depression and supported socialist, pacifist, and civil rights agendas through the 1960s. Yet by 1983, the AFT publicly supported President Reagan's *A Nation at Risk* report, which provided justification for education reform, privatization, and the extensive use of standardized testing to measure student learning and monitor teacher efficacy as well as the many other measures of "accountability" that were accompanied by major cutbacks in federal funding.[75] Like most other major unions at the time, the AFT also embraced a race-blind and meritocratic ideology, which reflected a strategy intended to protect union gains, such as pensions and seniority protections, and to unite working- and middle-class people along economic justice lines.[76] However, this strategy was easily co-opted by neoliberal and, later, by neoconservative agendas, and often caused unions to fail to acknowledge and address long histories of racial discrimination.

Communities of color critiqued the AFT for failing to develop systems to support the targeted recruitment and retention of teachers of color to meaningfully address white overrepresentation in the teaching corps. As a result, some claimed that the union's rhetoric in support of civil rights was not backed up by significant structural changes that might have resulted in the loss of privileges for middle-class white educators.[77] The overrepresentation of white people in the teaching force led communities of color to perceive teacher strikes across northern cities in the 1970s and early 1980s as being in opposition to the interests of Black students and families, including the 1968 confrontation between unionists and Black educators that resulted in the end of the Black community–controlled schools experiment in New York City.[78] Leftist educators also critiqued the AFT for adopting international programs that appeared uncomfortably aligned with US imperialist interests abroad.[79]

Though UTNO certainly supported more conservative agendas at times, the union persistently demonstrated a commitment to participatory democracy, economic redistribution, and the improvement of students' educational outcomes and social mobility.[80] The union's original campaign for collective bargaining, which ran from 1965 to 1974, emerged directly from the civil rights movement and was a successful attempt to create an integrated, democratic organization in the face of racial exploitation and repression. Along with fighting for a collective bargaining agreement, UTNO promoted community-driven demands, such as ending the disproportionate suspension and expulsion of Black students and the right to teach a curriculum that reflected Black history.[81] Though the New York City strikes—and similar racialized strikes in Newark, Philadelphia, Detroit, and Chicago—demonstrated that teachers' unions, as professional, middle-class organizations, are not always aligned with the children and families who use their schools, UTNO came closer to being so. Up until Hurricane Katrina, UTNO had Black presidents and a majority-Black membership and was seen by the public, for better and worse, as a Black union.[82] As the union grew, paraprofessionals (sometimes referred to as "paras") and clerical workers became a sizable constituency, tying the middle-class members of the teaching workforce directly to the parents and children attending their schools. Moreover, in the "flattened class structure of Black America"[83] relatively low-paying public-service jobs, such as teaching or working at the post office, conveyed middle-class status without significantly distancing people from their working-class peers. Many middle-class UTNO educators lived in mixed-income neighborhoods and had family and friends who were working class or working poor. Aside from the radical Teachers Union in New York City, which was destroyed by the Red Scare and folded in 1964, scholars have claimed an "absence of a model of teacher unionism that stresses building strong alliances with the local community."[84] Particularly in the 1960s and 1970s, UTNO built those alliances, and also, in the words of activist Kalamu ya Salaam, "They *were* the community."[85]

Once UTNO negotiated a collective bargaining agreement in 1974, the union stayed politically engaged by endorsing and campaigning for progressive pro-labor candidates, but it lost some of its radical edge. Its militancy was mostly seen through "job actions," according to ya Salaam, rather than through deep collaboration with activist groups pushing for systemic or redistributive change.[86] It also began to advocate for harsher disciplinary policies and more security in schools, reforms that ultimately contributed to disproportionate suspension and expulsion rates for Black children as well as to the rise of mass incarceration. In 2004, for example, 19 percent of Black students served out-of-school suspensions in Orleans Parish, compared to only 5 percent of white students.[87] In the 1980s and 1990s, distance grew between the union-organized educators and the communities using the schools, especially as middle-class families left Orleans Parish or enrolled their children in private or parochial schools in greater numbers. In a 1989 *Times Picayune* exposé of parish superintendents and school board members who put their own children in private or parochial schools, UTNO president Nat LaCour revealed that "a large number" of teachers sent their children to private schools as well.[88] The trajectory of the union also mirrored the trajectory of Black politics in the city. Black political claims in the civil rights and Black Power eras were much more radical and subversive than the claims of the Black establishment two decades later.

Though UTNO's story mirrors that of many other urban teachers' unions, the union's struggles also offer insight into the mechanisms of southern organizing and the devastating effects of neoliberal school reform on educators and communities. It is a story that highlights the role that racism and white supremacy have played, and continue to play, in determining the contours of school reform, despite images of diversity and co-opted language of racial justice. UTNO, during the 1990s and early 2000s, was not a radical organization, though it has become more radical, by necessity, since Katrina. Pre-Katrina, the union was, however, an organization that prioritized democracy, member participation, and disruptive organizing, and it used its power to improve the schools for both educators and students. UTNO challenged systems of power; but it also acquiesced to them and made strategic sacrifices that allowed their influence to grow. The union's evisceration after the storm reveals the deeper transformative impact of what it had built, and all the educators, children, and schools it helped nurture.

ORGANIZATION OF THE BOOK

Although this story starts in 1965, during AFT Local 527's first campaign for collective bargaining, and ends in 2008, when Brenda Mitchell stepped down as president of UTNO, it could have started much earlier. Activist Black educators first chartered New Orleans AFT Local 527 in 1937, and the struggle for equitable schooling for Black children and fair working conditions for Black teachers extends to the city's founding.[89] It could also continue through today: though UTNO lost most of its membership after the storm, it has continued to fight to organize New Orleans teachers, and it has successfully won CBAs at seven independent charter schools over the past decade (see table 6.1). The union's rise to prominence in the early 1970s, its struggles and achievements in the intervening decades, and finally its fall from power after the storm, demonstrate that Black-led labor unions have the potential to promote a democratic and redistributive agenda, and that the loss of these organizations renders vulnerable populations more susceptible to the ravages of white supremacy and neoliberal reforms.

Chapter 1 examines the union's campaign for collective bargaining (1965–74). When AFT Local 527 launched its collective bargaining campaign in 1965, it was one of five mostly segregated teachers' locals in New Orleans and represented a minority of the system's educators. In 1966, spurred on by the national AFT, which saw Local 527 as the lynchpin to organizing the South, it held the first teachers' strike in the South—a three-day job action—followed in 1969 by a nine-day strike. These mobilizations connected Local 527's demand for collective bargaining to racial and economic equity agendas in the schools, and helped align union membership with Black students, parents, and lower-paid support workers.

In the early 1970s, the Orleans Parish school district underwent an ambitious faculty desegregation program that transformed the schools and led to the merger between AFT Local 527 and the majority-white NEA local (the Orleans Educators Association; OEA) to form UTNO. Though faculty desegregation was a top-down reform, the union capitalized on teacher integration to form intentional alliances across race, while mobilizing new members. Following the merger, UTNO renewed its call for collective bargaining, eventually pressuring the board to approve an election in 1974. I argue that by positioning racial justice at the center of its organizing agenda, by prioritizing participatory democracy among its membership, and by engaging in civil rights unionism, UTNO succeeded in achieving a collective bargaining agreement where so many other southern cities failed.

Chapter 2 discusses the ways that UTNO promoted participatory democracy (especially within the union), developed member-leaders, and created institutions that advocated for quality education and economic justice (1975–82). I analyze how UTNO's structure allowed for the meaningful participation of rank-and-file members, mirroring a larger vision for participatory democracy that promoted equity and shared leadership in the city writ large. UTNO members created responsive institutions that met their needs as professionals, parents, and citizens. These included a mentor network, a full-service teacher center, scholarship programs, professional development seminars, and a Health and Welfare Fund. Through these programs, teachers new to the middle class were able to secure low-cost health insurance, improve their teaching pedagogy, and debate pertinent education issues of the time. All these services were run or coordinated by UTNO members, contributing to a genuine feeling of participation and empowerment.

I end by analyzing the union's 1978 strike, which promoted democratic leadership and demonstrated the efficacy of disruptive collective action by members and supporters. The strike led to the inclusion of clerical workers among UTNO's ranks and inspired labor mobilizations throughout the sector. These collective actions included two 1979 teacher strikes—one in neighboring Jefferson Parish, and one in East Baton Rouge. I argue that throughout this period, UTNO deviated from the more widely studied teachers' unions in the North and Midwest by continuing to promote civil rights–era goals and foster union democracy, even as it gained power and moved toward institution building.

Chapter 3 analyzes the state and national turn toward neoliberal policymaking and UTNO's attempts to resist that agenda (1976–98). I look at the ways in which business organizations, policymakers, and education leaders attempted to reverse labor gains and advance school reforms ostensibly intended to increase accountability, competition, and choice. The exodus of middle-class residents through processes of white flight, in addition to national and state budget cuts and austerity measures, left New Orleans in dire financial straits, further weakening UTNO's position. At the same time, neoliberal educational policy at the federal level, exemplified by the *A Nation at Risk* (1983) report, impacted the ways that union members and policymakers thought about education and its goals, subtly pushing the discussion to the right. UTNO resisted many of these reforms—often successfully—slowing the neoliberal agenda in the city and the state. However, the union acquiesced to other reforms, such as increased standardized testing—a move that would later help justify the state takeover of the school system and the mass teacher dismissals. Over and over, UTNO argued that the solution to struggling schools was not privatization but, instead, increased funding and resources to meet the needs of the poor student population. They campaigned and lobbied repeatedly for new millages and taxes as a means to increase educational spending.

In this chapter, I also examine the outsized role UTNO played in city and state politics, and the impact of the union's strong, progressive, anti-racist perspective on the local labor movement. UTNO built a mighty political operation and contributed to the coalescing of Black and women's political power in the city. The union collaborated with community organizations and coordinated voter turnout initiatives. As it gained power, it remained aligned with the city's working class. This period of UTNO's history features the 1990 strike, in which educators joined the picket lines to demand raises for their low-paid paraprofessional colleagues. This strike occurred at a moment when the labor movement was on the defensive and teachers' strikes were rare on the national level, demonstrating UTNO's ongoing commitment to disruptive activism. It also radicalized members and helped them participate more actively in UTNO's, and the city's, democratic processes. I argue that despite external factors threatening the union, UTNO remained committed to an agenda that was deeply enmeshed in the Black community, rejected discourses of "neoliberal multiculturalism," and looked to improve the schools and the city. UTNO looked, in short, much like a social movement union.[90]

Chapter 4 examines the years leading up to Hurricane Katrina, the leadership of new president Brenda Mitchell, and the ongoing attempts of city and state leaders to push through neoliberal education reforms (1999–2005). I analyze both the external and internal challenges that UTNO faced. Along with the "hollowing out of government" on national, state, and local levels,[91] the union had to contend with several challenges. These included the school board's ongoing incompetence and occasional corruption, a string of short-lived superintendents, apparent financial mismanagement, and the state's repeated threats to take over the district. UTNO also wrestled with the federal government's growing commitment to neoliberal reforms as codified in the No Child Left Behind (2001) legislation. Internally, Mitchell had a more authoritarian style than previous UTNO president LaCour. While some members saw her leadership style as "tough love" mentorship that helped them realize their own power and potential, others felt dismissed and alienated.

The union's bureaucracy, beyond its president, had also become more entrenched, and critics accused UTNO of protecting bad teachers, enforcing arcane regulations, and stymieing attempts to improve the district. These critiques gained salience as the divisions between the middle-class teachers and the poor and working-class students attending the schools grew. I examine the validity of the accusations of board corruption and the state's takeover threat as well as the internal union complaints described above. I argue that despite very real attempts to dismantle the union and privatize the district before Katrina, UTNO's power combined with the Black political machine in New Orleans prevented any drastic overhaul. Reformers needed Hurricane Katrina to disperse residents throughout the country; only in the absence of any semblance of democracy could they fully actualize their agenda.

Chapter 5 begins with Hurricane Katrina and ends with Brenda Mitchell's retirement (2005–8). I analyze the impact of the storm and the mass dismissals on educators, the union, and the schools. I argue that UTNO was intentionally targeted and almost destroyed, not because the union had become weaker, but because it wielded so much political and economic power and represented a significant Black power-base in the city. I examine the ways in which the privatization of the school system was part of a larger neoliberal attempt at the federal, state, and local levels to remake the city by disciplining organized labor, reorganizing public employment, and promoting gentrification and shifting city demographics. I discuss the impact of the storm and the dismissals on educators and what the loss of their expertise means for students and families.

Finally, I look at UTNO's attempts to rebuild after the storm and analyze why these efforts fell short. Ultimately, UTNO's democratic structure was both its greatest strength and its undoing. With its members scattered throughout the country and dealing with their own personal disasters, the union became a shell of its former self. When OPSB voted to allow UTNO's contract to expire in 2008, the only attendees at the meeting were two security guards, a *Times Picayune* reporter, and one man reading a newspaper.[92] I reflect on what UTNO's loss of power means for schools, politics, and organized labor in the state.

I conclude by considering the post-Katrina school landscape through the lens of the dismissed educators. I look at UTNO's mostly failed attempts to rebuild after the storm and the possibilities and limitations of its work organizing charter school unions. I argue that despite claims of renewal and reform, the schools have returned in many ways to the working conditions and lack of democracy that existed in the 1960s, before the union had a contract: teacher voice is minimal, work hours vary wildly, and teachers are paid inequitably, often along lines of race and gender. Moreover, Black teachers and other teachers of color remain especially marginalized in a city that still serves a majority-Black student body. I argue that analyzing school reform with a focus on educators reveals community-wide impacts that extend far beyond traditional measures of student outcomes. Schools are part of neighborhood and citywide ecosystems, providing jobs, spaces for democracy and debate, and opportunities for community collaboration and activism. These ecosystems have been destroyed in New Orleans. Geographer Clyde Woods argues that economic and social crises spur shifts in the methods of exploitation by and mobilization of elite white powerbrokers.[93] However, this is then met with countermobilizations by communities that continue to fight for redistributive social democracy.[94] Activists both within and outside of UTNO continue to fight to make the city and its schools more just, community-led, and effective for students, teachers, and families. The results of these struggles will determine the contours of the educational landscape in New Orleans, while the current state of education in the city provides lessons for reformers and union organizers nationwide.

1

The Collective Bargaining Campaign, 1965-1974

We were the first teachers in the South, white or Black, who ever walked off the job. We were the real saints because we didn't know whether we were going to have a job or not.

Veronica Hill, 1994

In 1965, when AFT Local 527, first launched its collective bargaining campaign, it was one of five mostly segregated teachers' locals in New Orleans and represented a minority of the system's educators. In 1966, drawing on the legacy of civil rights organizing in New Orleans, it held a three-day job action—the first teachers' strike in the South—followed by a nine-day strike, three years later in 1969. Through these mobilizations, union members and leaders demonstrated their solidarity with the Black community, displaying vocal support for Black students and parents who decried discriminatory school conditions and demanded fair treatment, particularly at Wilson Elementary and Fortier High School, two schools in the throes of student integration. And, in aligning themselves with Black students, parents, and lower-paid support workers, union members also connected their demand for collective bargaining to the broader movement for racial and economic equity in the schools.

As their campaign for collective bargaining progressed, in the early 1970s, New Orleans underwent an ambitious faculty desegregation program that transformed the schools and led to the merger between AFT Local 527 and the majority-white NEA local OEA to form UTNO. Although faculty deseg-regation was a top-down reform, the union leveraged the pivotal moment of teacher integration to form intentional alliances across race and mobilize new members. After the merger, a larger and more diverse UTNO, now repre-senting a majority of the district's teachers, redoubled its pursuit of collective bargaining, launching a massive community effort and eventually pressuring the New Orleans school board to approve an election in 1974. Teachers voted overwhelmingly to be represented by UTNO and thus became the first educa-tors in Louisiana to win collective bargaining. By positioning racial justice at the center of its union organizing, by emphasizing participatory democracy within their membership, and by engaging in civil rights unionism, UTNO achieved a collective bargaining agreement when so many other teachers' unions in southern cities failed.

THE INITIAL CAMPAIGN AND THE FIRST
TEACHERS' STRIKE IN THE SOUTH

In 1937, Veronica Hill was a founding member of Local 527,[1] a segregated Black AFT affiliate, and she served twenty-three years as its president.[2] The AFT required all its locals to integrate by January 1958 but New Orleans's white local (#353) refused to do so and was expelled from the organization. This made Local 527 the only AFT affiliate in the city—"integrated" by its charter but in reality composed nearly entirely of Black teachers, as white teachers continued their own independent group (the New Orleans Classroom Teachers Federation [NOCTF]) or joined the segregated, white NEA affiliate (the Louisiana Teachers Association [LTA]).[3] When Hill led Local 527 into its first collective bargaining campaign, in 1965, there were five teachers' organizations in the city, none of which could claim a majority of the approximately 3,600 teachers in the system.[4] In addition to three white locals—NOCTF, LTA, and the nearly defunct New Orleans Public School Teachers Association—Local 527 was also competing for members with the Black NEA affiliate, the LEA. However, the locals also had a history of collaboration. Most famously, in an event that spurred the formation of Local 527, Hill and the longtime president of NOCTF, Sarah T. Reed, climbed up a fire escape and entered the OPSB offices through a window to demand the restoration of Black teachers' pay. The two locals also shared an office and, for a while, the services of executive secretary Hasket Derby.[5]

In 1965, when Local 527 launched its collective bargaining campaign, the New Orleans schools remained largely segregated and severely underfunded.[6] Though *Brown v. Board of Education* mandated school desegregation in 1954, and the first four Black girls attended white schools under military escort in 1960, by the spring of 1965, only 873 Black students and one white student attended

Veronica Hill was born in New Orleans in 1903. She was a founding member of Local 527 and served as its president from 1946 to 1969. During her tenure, teachers won increased salaries, improved terms of maternity leave, and the right of women teachers to stay employed when married, among other gains. In 1966, Hill led the first teachers strike in the South. *Courtesy of United Teachers of New Orleans.*

schools historically of the opposite race in a district with a total enrollment of over 100,000 students (see graph 1.1).[7] The district was 63 percent Black, and white enrollment was declining slightly before its precipitous decline in the 1970s and 1980s.[8] Due to court orders, much more rapid student and faculty desegregation was on the horizon, creating a contentious and ever-changing school environment that resulted in important openings for the educators. The work of Local 527 was closely aligned with the civil rights movement, and many movement veterans were involved in the schools, both through the union and through advocacy for desegregation and educational justice for Black students. The politicization of the Black community around school integration contributed momentum and urgency to the educators' struggle.

In May 1965, Hill formally requested that the OPSB hold an election by "secret ballot" for teachers to select an exclusive bargaining agent (see table 1.1 for a timeline of the collective bargaining campaign). Along with her request, she submitted petitions signed by nearly 2,000 teachers in the district, slightly less than half the total teacher population.[9] It was clear that Local 527 had the national AFT's support; AFT president Charles Cogen described the New Orleans local as "on the threshold of achieving collective bargaining" and reaffirmed that "the AFT has given first priority to Louisiana in its southern organizing program."

Graph 1.1. Black students in historically white schools in New Orleans, 1961–1972

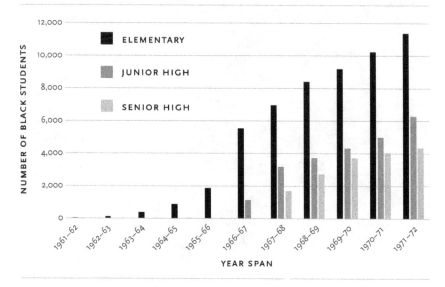

Source: "Facts and Finances," 1960–72. Orleans Parish School Board Collection
(MSS 147), Financial Records, boxes 7 and 8, Louisiana and Special Collections,
Earl K. Long Library, University of New Orleans, New Orleans.
Note: The only historically white high school to accept Black students before the 1967–68
school year was the magnet school Benjamin Franklin. Very few white students attended
historically Black schools. For example, in the 1968–69 school year, just twenty-nine white
elementary school students, nine junior high students, and two high school students
attended historically Black schools. That same year, there remained forty-five schools that
were 100 percent Black, and eight schools that were 100 percent white. By the 1972–73
school year, twenty-five historically white schools had become majority-Black, some of them
over 90 percent Black. Thus, the numbers stop reflecting "integration" in any meaningful way.

Already the idea that Louisiana was the lynchpin for organizing in the South had traction: "We regard Louisiana as our prime hope for teacher unionism below the Mason-Dixon line," Cogen told Louisiana teachers.[10] Since President Kennedy signed Executive Order 10988 in 1962, permitting public sector collective bargaining for federal employees, teachers had been struggling nationwide for binding contracts. From 1960 to 1974, there were more than 1,000 teacher strikes in the United States, involving over 823,000 teachers, and 72 percent of public teachers were covered by CBAs by the end of the decade.[11] The Louisiana campaign was part of a nationwide movement.

Though the OPSB said it would study the request, in November it voted down the proposal 4–1, the one dissenting vote coming from a board member who had previously been an attorney for the longshoremen's union (International Longshoremen's Association; ILA).[12] The racial implications of the all-white board voting down a request from the majority-Black teachers' union was not lost on the teachers.[13] The following February, Louisiana Federation of Teachers

Table 1.1. Major events in the history of AFT Local 527, 1965–1974

DATE	EVENTS
1965	May: Local 527, led by Veronica Hill, launches collective bargaining campaign.
1966	March: Local 527 holds a three-day strike, the first teachers' strike in the South.
1968	May: New Orleans locals of the LTA (white) and LEA (Black) merge to form the integrated OEA.
	May/June: Local 527 supports protesting parents at Wilson Elementary.
1969	January: Local 527 supports suspended students at Fortier High.
	April: Local 527 holds a nine-day strike.
	June: Eugene Didier becomes president of Local 527.
	November: State LTA (white) refuses to merge with the LEA (Black) and is expelled from the NEA. Many white members of the OEA (integrated) leave that group as well.
1971	June: Nat LaCour becomes president of Local 527.
	September: Gene Geisert appointed superintendent of Orleans Parish schools.
1972	June: Merger between Local 527 and the OEA forms UTNO.
	Summer: Overnight faculty desegregation transfers.
1974	April: OPSB approves collective bargaining election.
	November: Teachers overwhelmingly choose UTNO to be their exclusive bargaining agent.

(LFT; the state-level AFT affiliate) president Ed Fontaine told the board that Local 527 would call a "work stoppage" unless the board granted them a collective bargaining election and met five additional demands related to racial justice: hiring a Black assistant superintendent, appointing Black supervisory staff in proportion to the number of Black teachers, appointing Black teachers to the personnel department, hiring Black clerical workers in OPSB offices, and using more Black bus drivers and maintenance workers.[14] These demands drew on civil rights goals and allied the teachers with lower-paid support workers in their united fight for racial and economic justice. Fontaine told the school board that if the demands were not met, he would ask the federal government to investigate whether OPSB should continue to receive federal funds.[15] The New Orleans NAACP (National Association for the Advancement of Colored People) issued a statement in support of the demands—with the exception of the use of "ratios" because of their "un-American flavor"—and the local held a rally to generate support.[16] Yet again, national AFT representatives were in town to assist Local 527 AFT organizer Howard Hursey told the audience that a strike was necessary: "There's no alternative. You can't get what you want by being nice."[17]

The board was outraged by Local 527's strike threat and found its demands around race to be specious. The superintendent of schools Dr. Carl Dolce, who was white,[18] claimed that the real issue was "not a racial one" and that the board "has had the proposals under consideration for some time."[19] One board member was more blunt: "If you need a recommendation [on what to do with the demands], I propose we file them in the wastebasket."[20] The board accused the local of using the racial demands to obscure their real goal, collective bargaining, and noted that OPSB hired people based on merit, not race—a claim belied by the de facto faculty segregation that would continue into the early 1970s.[21]

To further pressure the board, Veronica Hill wrote a letter announcing that Local 527 would not support OPSB's one-cent sales tax at the next election (the tax was intended to generate more revenue for the schools), until they granted the teachers the right to collective bargaining.[22] This left the local vulnerable to attacks that it was not genuinely concerned about students' education, which rival groups were happy to make. At the time, the NEA considered itself a professional organization and, as remains true today, it did not affiliate with the more militant AFL-CIO, arguing that both collective bargaining and strikes were the purview of private sector labor unions—not teachers.[23] The executive secretary of the integrated Orleans Parish NEA local claimed that the AFT was deceiving Orleans Parish residents and announced that his group planned to work with OPSB to pass the one-cent sales tax increase, which had already been earmarked to increase teacher salaries.[24] The president of the Orleans Principals' Association similarly pledged his support to the board members and the superintendent, whom he believed were trying to address the problems of the school system: "We do not believe that Mr. Fontaine's views represented more than a small minority of the loyal teachers of the system."[25] The white NOCTF urged educators and the public to have patience and to support the board and superintendent as they worked to solve educational issues, a statement that ignored the reality that Black community members were still being denied jobs and promotions twelve years after *Brown v. Board of Education*.[26]

Despite a growing coalition of groups announcing their opposition to the strike, Local 527 forged ahead. It held a rally in early March—shortly before the March 11 strike deadline—and supporters from the AFL-CIO addressed the crowd, including state AFL-CIO president Victor Bussie.[27] Bussie, who served as president of the state AFL-CIO for forty-one years, was a powerful force in state politics and a perennial supporter of Local 527.[28] He certainly did not cultivate the "professional" status desired by members of the NEA. One teacher remembered that when she told her father she was going with the teachers to a state AFL-CIO conference, he said, "Oh my goodness, my daughter is going to be with the mafia."[29] Bussie was seen as a blue-collar union boss, and his AFL-CIO was implicated in the occasional use of violent tactics to win union shops.[30] Ed Fontaine (the LFT president) announced that Local 527's membership had voted "overwhelmingly" in favor of the work stoppage, with thirty-four teachers, each representing one of thirty-four buildings, voting in support.[31] Fontaine's leadership during this strike was unorthodox for the AFT, as he was the state president and not a member of the local. Later, Local 527 accused Fontaine of calling the strike "without any consultation with Executive Board or with membership of Local 527. [The] Executive Board induced membership to fulfill his commitment to save face."[32] Though it is unclear whether this claim is true—it appears in only one document—it hints at tension between Local 527's Black leadership and white statewide leaders such as Fontaine. However, publicly demonstrating a united front, Local 527 claimed a membership of 1,400 teachers and said it expected upward of 1,500 teachers to strike—it planned to picket every school in the city as well as the OPSB offices and hoped to shut down several schools. Meanwhile, the board announced that nearly 3,000 teachers had signed a "no-strike pledge," and the LEA said it would escort all teachers intimidated by pickets into their buildings, demonstrating the lack of union solidarity.[33]

On Friday, March 11, 1966, the first day of the strike, the school board reported that 507 teachers participated—though the union claimed more than 1,000 participants—and classes were canceled at only one school.[34] The vast majority of striking teachers were Black, and the schools with picket lines were overwhelmingly majority-Black schools.[35] The bus drivers, represented by the Teamsters local, crossed the picket lines to bring children to school, though AFT organizer Hursey claimed that some delivery truck drivers honored the lines.[36] Strike participation was slightly higher on Monday, March 14, but it dropped again on Tuesday and Local 527, which two days earlier had pledged their intention to continue the strike "indefinitely," voted to return to the classroom.[37] While the strike had lasted only three days, Hill praised the membership for conducting the first teachers' strike in the South: "[It was] eye opening to the teachers to see what was going on. It had never happened before. Nobody in the South, white or Black, had ever gone on a strike. Teachers up North had gone on strike, but nobody in the South. Even in big cities like Atlanta, no teachers, white or Black, had defied their bosses and walked off the job."[38] Superintendent Dolce announced that striking teachers would be docked pay for days missed but would face no other disciplinary action, and Local 527 emerged mostly unscathed from the unsuccessful strike.[39] AFT president Charles Cogen wrote, "While no tangible gain was achieved, I feel that it has added to the union's standing as a militant group ready to fight for its rights."[40]

The strike did, however, reveal fissures in the Black community. "When we went back to school," Hill recalls, "the other people looked at us like we were dirt, like we had committed some crime. They didn't want to speak to us."[41] Rev. Avery Alexander, head of the local NAACP chapter and renowned for his civil rights work, expressed his support for the strikers, as did Representative John Conyers of Detroit, another civil rights activist, who spoke to the local while visiting New

Orleans.[42] Black-led organized labor campaigns were viewed as an offshoot of the civil rights movement, and locals in New Orleans, especially those of the longshoremen and the letter carriers (National Association of Letter Carriers; NALC), had been crucial to relatively recent Black economic gains. At the same time, some parents counterprotested the picketers in anger. The *Times Picayune* published a photograph of a Black mother outside Carver High holding a sign that reads "1st BETSY / NOW STRIKE / WHAT NEXT," noting that students had already lost instructional time due to the impact of Hurricane Betsy that past fall.[43] Paraprofessional Susie Beard recalls, "Some of the parents were out there cold picketing against the union for that first strike, saying you were taking away teaching time, quality education from their kids and it went national . . . it was all over the media."[44] This bad press was exacerbated by attacks by Local 527's competitors for union members. However, it was Don Pierce with the local NEA affiliate who delivered the most scathing critique: "The strike against the children of New Orleans . . . is a deliberate attempt to defeat the passage of the proposed sales tax increase, which is the only means available to solve the educational problems of this parish."[45] This argument—that the union was prioritizing its own narrow interests over those of New Orleans's schoolchildren—would be one levied against the local for years to come. It also has a gendered element, suggesting that the striking educators, most of them women, were harming children instead of fulfilling their natural role as caretakers.[46]

Despite Pierce's words, the one-cent sales tax campaign helped to unite teachers and heal some of the wounds from the failed strike. Superintendent Dolce earmarked 62 percent of the funds generated for raising teacher salaries, a move guaranteed to quell some of the teacher unrest, and Local 527 retroactively announced its support of the measure after it had passed. The local published a somewhat disingenuous advertisement suggesting that the teachers' strike led to the earmarking of the funds as well as to the public's support for the sales tax and omitting its own failure to endorse the tax. However, the strike did dramatize the plight of New Orleans's teachers, whose starting salaries ranked near the bottom of the nation's largest school systems.[47] And the members of Local 527 indicated their support for the strike action by reelecting Veronica Hill president and electing Eugene Didier, a prominent white strike supporter, to the union's executive board later that May.[48] Only Victor Bussie, state AFL-CIO president, remained firm in his stance against the sales-tax increase, saying it was a regressive tax: "It is that we just do not believe it is fair to ask extremely poor people to bear the cost of this educational program."[49] Sales taxes, unlike income or property taxes, apply to everyone equally regardless of their wealth, and thus place a disproportionate burden on the poor. The 1966 sales tax election would be the last time voters would approve a tax increase to allocate more funding to the Orleans Parish schools until 1980.

In the late 1960s, the school board began taking its first reluctant steps toward student and faculty desegregation, which gave Local 527 ample opportunities to demonstrate its support for racial justice. In the 1966–67 school year, fourteen teachers, three Black and eleven white, voluntarily transferred as the first teachers to integrate school faculties in the district.[50] For the next three years, the OPSB continued to rely on voluntary transfers and, as a result, the district saw little faculty integration.[51] By 1969, fifteen years after *Brown v. Board of Education*, 13.4 percent of students attended schools that historically served students of the opposite race, almost all of them Black students who had integrated formerly white schools—only twenty-five white students were attending formerly Black schools.[52] Racial conflict arose at schools with mixed student bodies, and Local 527 frequently took a prominent stance on these issues, demonstrating its commitment to a civil rights unionism that looked beyond workplace rights.

At the same time, Local 527 chose not to endorse Mack J. Spears in his campaign for school board in 1968. Spears was a former teacher and longtime principal of McDonogh 35, the preeminent—and, for many years, sole—Black public high school in the city. He ran on a platform of "equal education" for all students and pointed out that a school district that was two-thirds Black should have some Black representation on the board.[53] However, Spears was also a past president of the LEA and staunchly opposed collective bargaining for teachers. Local 527 endorsed a pro-union Black candidate in the primary and, when he lost, Veronica Hill issued a statement explaining that the local could not endorse anyone in the general election because statements made by candidates had "caused concern among membership."[54] Spears was supported by both the Black *Louisiana Weekly*—which often lauded LEA efforts—and the more conservative, white-owned *Times Picayune*, and he won the election to become the first Black member of the school board.[55] He served on the board, several times as its president, until 1986, and was a persistent adversary to Local 527, frequently causing public relations issues for the union by accusing them of prioritizing their own economic interests over the well-being of the mostly Black schoolchildren. However, due to the union's racial activism, these accusations often fell flat.

Local 527 took a prominent stand on several racial justice issues in the late 1960s. In spring 1968, it became involved with a parent group at Wilson Elementary who accused its principal of discriminating against Black students and parents. The school had previously been all-white, but by 1968 it had a majority-Black student body, though the principal and teaching staff remained white. Parents reported that the principal arbitrarily and frivolously disciplined Black students, suspended them for trivial offenses, and gave them inadequate lunch food.[56] Local 527 sponsored parent meetings, advocated for the parents in front of the school board, and threatened to picket OPSB meetings on behalf of the parents and students at Wilson.[57] The racial elements of the situation were clear; the parents published a press release demanding a public hearing for the principal that read, "[The OPSB] should not conduct its business as if the school system were its privately owned southern plantation."[58] Similarly, Local 527 blamed the school board for fomenting racial conflict in a polemical press release of their own, stating: "THE ANTEBELLUM DAYS of white being right was evidenced when a group of Black Parents questioned THE LEADERSHIP and quality of EDUCATION their children were receiving."[59] The union, though nominally integrated, was aligning itself with Black Power–era politics, a reflection of the long connection between Black labor and civil rights activism in the city.

By the 1960s, the civil rights movement in New Orleans was well-established and had been grounded in the work of churches, the powerful ILA, and Black community organizations.[60] For example, Clarence "Chink" Henry, longtime president of the ILA Local 1419, allowed Congress of Racial Equality activists and other civil rights leaders to meet at the ILA hall and pledged his support to the Southern Christian Leadership Conference (SCLC) as they worked to fight segregation in New Orleans.[61] Such activism also reflected the Local 527's own history. Local 527 had long advocated for improvements in Black school facilities and educational programs and won a hard-fought battle for racial salary equalization in 1943.[62] Similarly, the statewide Black NEA affiliate, the LEA, had fought battles for Black educational justice, including pushing for school integration before *Brown v. Board of Education*.[63] Due to the success of civil rights efforts as well as to an influx of money and resources from federal Great Society programs, the tides finally seemed to be turning for Black workers seeking leadership positions and stable jobs, many of which had been previously only open to white workers.[64] Brenda Mitchell, later president of UTNO, recalled that few choices were available for Black people when she started college in 1964: "I got into teaching because when I was a youngster, the options were teaching, the post office, and the welfare office, in social work, or a nurse. I don't like blood, I wasn't going to walk around the city to deliver mail and I liked the feeling of working with kids."[65] As one of the few middle-class jobs open to Black people, especially Black women, teaching was used as a means of both individual and social uplift by the Black community—teachers were expected to use their social position to advocate for opportunities and rights for Black children and families. Historian Philip Rubio argues that Black postal workers mediated between the civil rights, labor, and leftist movements as well as between the middle and working classes, and Black teachers played a similar mediation role in New Orleans, with their student-centered advocacy connecting them directly to their working-class peers.[66] By involving themselves with the protesting parents at

Wilson, Local 527 members reaffirmed their commitment to racial activism. Eventually, the principal of Wilson was transferred to another school—a solution that would become a common practice in dealing with incompetent employees at all levels of the school system. Parents and teachers were unsatisfied, and after the transfer was announced, they held up placards that read, "A Segregationist Principal Gets a Promotion."[67]

Despite the outcome, Local 527 earned some positive press for its participation in the protest, especially important at a moment when its collective bargaining campaign seemed to have stalled. Though an AFT national representative announced in late 1967 that New Orleans would be the union's next target site—"We will be here for as long as it takes and know from past experience how to get the right of collective bargaining"—the school board's attorney, in early 1968, ruled that it would be illegal for the board to recognize an exclusive bargaining agent.[68] The union was especially disappointed by this result because it had campaigned on behalf of several school board candidates who had indicated they would be open to collective bargaining before they were elected and then voted against the collective bargaining election once they became members of the board.[69] Superintendent Dolce was concerned that this decision would spark teacher unrest and proactively sent a letter to all staff detailing improvements made under his tenure—smaller class sizes, additional counselors in schools, the reduction of nonteaching duties, and the construction of more buildings to relieve over-crowding—and also pledged his support in advocating for a raise for teachers to come from the state legislature.[70]

Meanwhile, the local and regional chapters of the NEA continued to attack the New Orleans local. The Southeast regional director for the NEA said that "feeble attempts" by the AFT to organize teachers in New Orleans and three other southern cities were one of the main reasons that the NEA refused to merge with the AFT at the national level. The AFT, said NEA director, "has failed miserably at protecting educators in New Orleans."[71] Internally, some AFT representatives were "disappointed" with how the local was running the collective bargaining campaign; Charles Cogen reported that staff believed "the local could do more" to make the campaign a success.[72] The local was also in debt, both to the LFT and to the national AFT, and its co-organizing funds with the national AFT had "been depleted by improper transfers and improper expenditures." Because of underpayment of dues, the LFT suspended the local's membership in the LFT, AFT, and AFL-CIO effective December 1, 1968.[73]

This latter dispute was political as much as it was economic. The local had been on poor terms with the state organization since the failed 1966 strike, which had been ordered by the state president Ed Fontaine, over the heads of Hill and other Local 527 leaders.[74] Moreover, the New Orleans teachers almost singlehandedly bankrolled the state organization with their 1,328 dues-paying members; the next largest local was the Jefferson Federation of Teachers (JFT), which claimed only 141 members in December 1968.[75] Internal discord between the state federation and the local continued through the early 1970s. In November 1969, Hill attempted to disband the state federation altogether and, although she was prevented from doing so, the organization essentially ceased to function until it was resurrected in summer 1972 with assistance from the national AFT.[76] Local 527's conflict with the state organization reflects the ways in which the local faced racism and additional hurdles even from its allies in the AFT.

As Local 527 worked to sort out its financial and organizational woes, it continued to advocate for Black students. In January 1969, 300 Black students at Fortier, an integrated but still majority-white high school, signed a petition demanding Black history courses, revision of discriminatory discipline codes, and permission to start a Black student union. Administrators refused to meet with the students, so they held a protest in which fifty-four students were arrested and many more were suspended; in the altercation, police sprayed the students with mace.[77] The students were backed by both the local NAACP chapter and Local 527.[78] Yet again, the Local 527 accused the board of sowing racial disharmony. In a speech before the board, Veronica Hill critiqued the board's delay in desegregating the schools and its failure to implement programs to facilitate smooth and peaceful integration: "The Fortier students by their action have pointed up a festering wound that has lingered all too long in our school system."[79] The OPSB president issued a long statement saying that students do not have the right to protest, and eventually eight students were suspended for the entire school year because of their "failure to acknowledge that disruptive activities like singing and chanting in the vicinity of the school while classes are being held are both illegal and improper."[80] Local 527 lauded the students' efforts and touted the union's own history in advocating for multiracial textbooks, the incorporation of Black history, and programs to eliminate prejudice among students and teachers.[81] In a pattern that would repeat for years to come, the union and school board member Mack Spears clashed. Spears said the students should return to class and called the request for a Black student union essentially a desire for resegregation. The board blamed the Fortier protests on outside agitators—referring specifically to members of the SNCC and Tulane's chapter of Students for a Democratic Society, but likely also intending to criticize the involvement of Local 527.[82]

Spurred on by pressure from the national AFT and the laudatory press it received in response to its racial justice activities, Local 527 members yet again threatened to strike if the school board refused to grant a collective bargaining election. This time, the union solicited more community and parent support and obtained more funding and personnel from the national AFT. As predicted, school board member Mack Spears strongly opposed the strike, and he did so in explicitly racialized language: "Most of the teachers involved are black. And it is paradoxical that an organization would call a strike of predominantly black teachers against black kids."[83] Spears's language emphasizes the ways in which the public still saw educators' labor as feminized caretaking and viewed their job actions as harming children rather than as a legitimate tactic to put pressure on public officials. Spears also alleged that teachers had been coerced into signing the petition and that the AFT was holding "nightly cocktail parties at a Gentilly motel" to solicit signatures.[84] By contrast, Local 527 tried to frame the strike as a means to fight apathy and frustration in the district and to improve conditions for both students and teachers. Black families had taken significant risks in their multigenerational struggle for quality education,[85] so segments of the Black community understandably felt concerned by the threats to close the schools. However, unlike in contentious teacher strikes in the Northeast and Midwest,[86] Local 527 neutralized this opposition and earned the support of most of the Black community by continuously demonstrating its commitment to racial justice and equitable Black education.

Yet the union continued to face significant opposition as well. By 1969, the local LTA and LEA chapters had merged in New Orleans to form the integrated, but majority-white, Orleans Educators Association (OEA). Both the OEA and the LTA, made up of white segregationists, opposed the strike.[87] The OEA, diverging from the NEA's traditional opposition to collective bargaining, said that it would seek to change state law to allow collective bargaining, believing that a legal solution was a better strategy than a strike.[88] The OEA also published a series of escalating leaflets attacking the AFT strike threat and encouraging teachers to join the OEA instead, painting itself as a more professional choice. They drew on teachers' memories of the 1966 strike to discourage them from participating again: "You remember the last AFT strike—how pitiful it turned out to be! Strikes by teachers are *illegal* in every school district in the land!"[89] The *States-Item* also published an editorial that strongly critiqued the AFT and urged teachers to join the OEA instead. The editorial argued that Local 527 was working against the school system by opposing the one-cent sales tax, putting their efforts toward strikes instead of increased school funding, and firing up racial discord to accomplish its goals: "[Local 527] was willing to exploit race relations for reasons of union power."[90] This critique misinterpreted Local 527's ongoing commitment to civil rights unionism that viewed racial and economic justice as inseparable. The editorial also claimed that voters had rebuffed Local 527's agenda by electing Spears to the school board, as he ran an explicitly anti–collective bargaining campaign.

However, Local 527's efforts in community outreach and its work presenting its campaign as a continuation of the Black freedom struggle also bore more fruit this time around. The Urban League held a forum on the strike, the Mayor's Human Rights Committee passed a resolution supporting collective bargaining for teachers, the SCLC telegrammed its support, and the NAACP announced its full support of striking teachers.[91] The Black City Council, a coalition of organizations that included the NAACP Youth Council and the National Welfare Rights Organization, went a step further to call for a two-day citywide strike in support of the teachers, indicating the local's success in presenting itself as an organization working for racial justice.[92] Community activist Kalamu ya Salaam was then part of a student group that took over Southern University at New Orleans to demand lower fees and the establishment of a Black Studies department, among other concerns. His mother was a striking schoolteacher, and he saw these struggles as connected: "We went to the teachers and offered any support we could give. At that time, as I remember it, they wanted the picket line to be maintained by teachers and not 'outsiders,' so they wouldn't have that."[93] Local 527's rejection of the students' support reflects growing tension in the Black community between those rooted in civil rights politics and a growing, more militant, Black Power contingent. The racial justice framing was unintentionally aided by the release of a report by a committee assigned by Superintendent Dolce to investigate the situation at Fortier in the middle of the strike buildup. Notwithstanding the pepper spray, arrests, suspensions, and continued racial violence at the campus, the committee found "no clear overt act of bias."[94]

Despite the community support, there was a sense of foreboding leading into the strike. Though the teachers had voted to strike on April 3, union leaders later said they would be willing to postpone the strike if the school board would hold a closed meeting with them, which the board refused.[95] Nat LaCour was not in a leadership position at that time, nor was he privy to union decision-making, but he participated in both the 1966 and 1969 strikes: "I think the union thought that they could get the teachers actually to come out, and that even just the threat of a strike would cause the board to vote yes on bargaining. But they went to the board with that petition, the board voted no. So, they were then in a bind. They had to strike because they had claimed they were going to strike."[96] Dave Selden, then national AFT president, came to town to support the teachers and predicted, incorrectly, that the coming strike would cut across racial lines.[97] Shortly before the strike deadline, AFT officials attempted unsuccessfully to secure Mayor Schiro's backing, and, yet again, the Teamsters announced that they would not honor the teachers' picket lines.[98] This was likely both a racial and a sectoral divide as the bus drivers were still majority-white and did not see their fight as aligned with that of the middle-class, public sector schoolteachers.

Kenneth Miesen, an AFT national representative in town to support the local, told parents to keep their children home because "the AFT will not be responsible for their health or safety in or near school buildings . . . we are cautioning parents not to allow the school board and administration to use children as tools in this battle."[99] Despite the irony of this statement, parents did seem more active in support of the 1969 strike than they had been in 1966. For example, at the public OPSB meeting held midway through the strike, parents attended in significant numbers, helped fill the auditorium to capacity, booed the school board, and joined teachers in singing "We Shall Overcome."[100] Miesen, exaggerating the union's power to draw support, claimed the strike would close 70 to 90 of the district's 130 schools. Controversially, the night before the strike, Superintendent Dolce announced the preemptive closure of twenty-nine of the city's majority-Black schools, and the reassignment of non-striking teachers to other schools to fill in for striking teachers. The closures impacted 33,806 Black children and only 16 white children; the non-striking teachers were thus transferred to ensure the uninterrupted education of white students while many Black students had nowhere to go.[101] Rev. Percy Simpson of the SCLC said that to close the schools was to "flirt with total community disaster," while community member Samuel Bell stated his displeasure more strongly: "This is a revolution—a black revolution. The action to close 29 schools was to pit black teachers against black parents. The board is not fighting collective bargaining, but the black community of New Orleans."[102] He said the board should either send white teachers to closed schools or it should bus Black children to open, white schools.

Local 527 joined the critiques of Dolce's school closures, accusing him of trying to divide the city along racial lines. Dolce responded that "outside organizers" were to blame for the strike and that he had closed the schools in which AFT membership was highest—all of which were majority-Black schools because the union's membership was predominantly Black.[103] Though this argument may sound logical, when the teachers went on strike again, in 1978, then Superintendent Geisert was able to keep every school open despite approximately 70 percent of the district's teachers participating—far more than in 1969.[104] The community thus saw the school closures in 1969 as indicative of a larger devaluation of Black education, a critique Local 527 used to reinforce its own demands.

According to the school board, 826 teachers struck on Thursday, April 3, the first day of the strike, and 900 on the following day.[105] From there, numbers began to wane. The OPSB held its regularly scheduled meeting on Monday, April 7, and more than 600 people attended, most of them in support of the striking teachers.[106] At that meeting, the board threatened to fire striking teachers, and the following day Superintendent Dolce announced that the board was advertising to fill posts left vacant by those on strike.[107] The *Times Picayune* weighed in on the racial implications of the strike and school closures, blaming the union for trying to turn Black families and students against the board by asking parents to keep students home during the strike.[108] The Black-run *Louisiana Weekly* refrained from critiquing the union, but it noted that those most affected by the strike were Black students treated as "innocent pawns."[109] Though Local 527 enjoyed significant support, the Black community was not united in its backing of confrontational tactics, especially by mostly middle-class women teachers.

Carver High School, where LaCour was a teacher, was a stronghold for the union and had a student population active in Black rights. The school was located adjacent to the Desire Housing Project, where just one year later the Black Panthers would have a "showdown" with local police.[110] On Wednesday, April 9, the fourth day of the strike, only seniors had been admitted into the school; but other students showed up to demand entry and to protest in solidarity with the teachers. Police barred the students from entering the building, but some broke in and wrote on the blackboards, "We Want School" and "Don't Lock Me Out," before being expelled from school grounds. Several students threw bricks at the officers. Two officers were injured, and three youths were arrested in the incident. Yet again, Local 527 connected its struggle for collective bargaining to larger struggles for educational equity and racial justice. Saunders, the local's strike chairman, said the violence at Carver was "another sign that the issues go far deeper than collective bargaining . . . there's a sense of disturbance in the community."[111]

Though drawing on the power of the civil rights movement—and on the rage of a Black community still denied equal participation in education and society—was a useful tactic for the union, it also genuinely reflected the beliefs of much of its membership. The *Louisiana Weekly* ran a story interviewing striking teachers and union leaders, and while many talked about the importance of democracy and improving conditions for children, they also discussed the role of race: "I feel very happy today to see MANY black teachers finally beginning to turn black and to begin to identify with their black brothers and sisters. Fellow teachers, let us never forget that in our dark hour of need the black community has come to aid us and now we shall win." Strike chairman Saunders said to the paper, "The real issue is a neglected black community."[112] Again, Local 527 sought to link its activism to ongoing civil rights struggles. Though there was some student integration by 1969, the majority of Black students still attended segregated and subpar institutions—which is also where most Black teachers taught. The teachers' and the students' interests were aligned.

As numbers dwindled on the picket lines, Local 527 tried other strategies to force the board's hand. Veronica Hill led a delegation of teachers to the city council to ask for its assistance in resolving the strike; but the council declined to get involved.[113] On Friday, April 11, striking teachers occupied the OPSB board room and staged a mock debate, with an empty chair that represented absent Superintendent Dolce, in which they accused him of using parents and students as pawns. Meanwhile, approximately 200 teachers and students picketed outside the school board offices, marching and singing.[114] While the protests continued outside, Alfred Hebeisen, the schools' personnel director, was videotaped interviewing replacement teachers. He announced that the board had hired fifteen new teachers to replace those on strike.[115] The AFT reported that principals were calling striking teachers, threatening to give away their jobs and to create a statewide blacklist to prevent them from being hired elsewhere, and "the intimidation, most of it by whites against Blacks, began to work."[116] On Sunday, April 13, picketers returned to the school board offices, hoping to deter potential applicants, and at least two individuals protested in front of the home of school board president Lloyd Rittiner. Rittiner's wife offered them iced tea and folding chairs, but they declined.[117] The following day, April 14, the seventh day of the strike, picketers once again walked in front of the school board office, and approximately eighty-five protesters held a sit-in inside the building. Fourteen people were arrested including AFT national representatives Miesen and Robert Bates, and local strike chairman Saunders.[118] The sit-in and the publicized arrests, clearly tactics borrowed from the civil rights movement, garnered support from the Interfaith Social Justice Committee but not from civil rights leader Rev. A. L. Davis,[119] who repeated OPSB's argument that collective bargaining for public sector employees was illegal.[120]

Despite their escalation in tactics, it was clear that teachers' solidarity with the protest was dwindling and the local ended the strike on April 16. Teachers had been on strike for nine school days.[121] Peter Saunders, strike chairman, met with Rittiner at his house to negotiate a settlement, and they held a joint press conference. Rittiner chided the union: "The strike was ill-advised and unnecessary, and, unfortunately, will leave certain scars and animosity among our teachers that I can only hope will be healed with the passing of time."[122] Though union leadership was under the impression that there would be no reprisals, the contract they drew up was never signed by school board representatives.[123] Some teachers who returned found substitutes or new permanent hires still in their classrooms and, although the substitutes were reassigned, teachers who had been replaced by new hires were reassigned or demoted to substitutes themselves.[124] Later that month, the school board fired fourteen temporary teachers who had participated in the strike.[125] Mike Johnson was a temporary, uncertified teacher at the time, attending night school to obtain his certification; he went on strike in solidarity with his coworkers. He woke up on the morning of April 29 to see his name in the paper and learned he had been fired.[126] Other teachers were luckier. Brenda Mitchell was advised by her union building representative to call in sick because "they might not [otherwise] be able to protect my job"; and she was not penalized for her absences.[127] Connie Goodly, who later became a union employee, was a substitute teacher in 1969: "One of the teachers told me, 'We're going on strike so you better not cross that picket line.'" Goodly was pregnant and had little protection as a substitute, so she called out sick instead of joining her colleagues on the picket lines.[128] Grace Lomba was a probationary teacher but went on strike, nonetheless. She said her principal wrote "on strike" on the top of her tenure evaluation, but she earned tenure anyway. "My attitude at the time was, I'm a certified person, I have my degree and I passed the test. Get rid of me and I'll go someplace else because I've got the qualifications."[129] Teachers knew that they were taking risks by going on strike, especially young Black women teachers in a mostly segregated school system, but many of them walked out anyway.

The local tried to convince the school board to return striking teachers to their positions both through public pressure and through legal means. Saunders urged the board to return teachers to their original classrooms since they already had built positive rapport with their students, but the board was unmoved.[130] Local 527 also sued the board, claiming it had violated the contract by reclassifying strikers as "relief teachers" and having them perform nonteaching duties including yard duty, hall monitoring, and clerical tasks.[131] This was especially egregious as the reclassified teachers were often experienced, certified teachers, while thirty-four of their replacements were uncertified.[132] The judge ruled in favor of the school board, saying that the teachers had abandoned their duties and had been given multiple warnings to return to their classrooms.[133] Unable to protect its teachers, and reeling from the unsigned no-reprisals agreement, Local 527 was wracked with internal discord. The union's secretary, Hasket Derby, wrote an open letter critiquing Veronica Hill and other members of the executive board who, Derby claimed, ended the strike without properly consulting its membership or the national representatives and had failed to secure an authentic agreement.[134] Hill and the executive board then fired Derby, who responded by suing them for backpay.[135] Meanwhile, the union was conducting its semiannual elections for president and executive board; the *Times Picayune* speculated that Derby's open letter was intended to—and succeeded in—affecting the results of that election.[136] Hill was retiring from both the New Orleans Public Schools and the union,[137] so the contest was between Eugene Didier, Maxine Copelin, and strike chairman Peter Saunders, who was closely associated with the failed strike agreement.[138] The membership elected Didier, the first white president in the local's history, with LaCour as vice president from Copelin's ticket.[139]

Didier's election brought to the fore questions of race, power, and integration. Support for the strike was certainly divided along racial lines, though Didier was a strong strike supporter. At the late April OPSB meeting in which the board decided to fire the probationary teachers, "an outspoken segregationist" urged the board not to pay teachers who had gone on strike and alleged that Black people were trying to take over the school system.[140] Selden, president of the national AFT, then stirred up significant controversy when he suggested that the AFT hold a demonstration against the "white, racist power structure" of the city during its annual convention scheduled for August in New Orleans.[141] Ed Fontaine wrote to him, "Our racial problems in New Orleans are not, and never have been, as severe as they are in other parts of the nation. . . . Let me further point out that Mrs. Hill, and the ousted ruling oligarchy of Local 527, for years pursued Black racism and politics calculated to discourage white membership in the local."[142] A. P. Stoddard, president of the Greater New Orleans AFL-CIO, similarly denied that a white, racist power structure existed and pointed to Mack Spears as evidence: "[Spears] has yet to vote for anything that Local 527 sponsors and if he ever does, in my opinion, it will be by accident."[143] Both Stoddard and Victor Bussie blamed the Black membership of the local for the defeated strike efforts: "It's unfortunate that they, apparently, do not see the importance of giving strong support to their own organization."[144] Notably, no Black labor organizers or members of the local contradicted Selden's statement about New Orleans's racial politics; indeed, Hill portrayed the failed strike in clearly racial terms: "[Local 527] had the difficulty of [being] a predominantly black local facing a mighty white power structure. Teachers in New Orleans have not given up. We firmly believe that 'Some Day, We Shall Overcome.'"[145] The white Louisiana labor movement's failure to recognize the dual battles Local 527 was fighting against racism and against economic exploitation speaks both to the challenges facing the union and its status as an outlier in the state, misunderstood even by its allies. Selden acquiesced to these white leaders' demands and canceled the planned demonstration, but he continued to maintain the truth of his original analysis: "There is no doubt at all in my mind that if a majority of teachers were white and that if those teachers had shown the same degree of militancy that the members of Local 527 have shown, we would now have collective bargaining in Orleans Parish."[146]

The local's choice of Didier as president, however, does speak to the membership's desire for a change and to a growing commitment to integration. Didier was a popular and charismatic physical education teacher from Fortier High. Brenda Mitchell recalls his election—she ran for executive board on his ticket in 1971—and maintains she would not have been thinking about Didier's election as a racial issue: "My concern would have been can you make a difference for us? Can you make it better for the kids and for the teachers and other school employees? It wasn't about race, we wanted the best person."[147] LaCour, on the other hand, suggests that teachers had seen the negative outcome of the 1969 strike and believed they needed to have more access to power in order to reach their goals in a city that still maintained an all-white city council and that was run by mayor Victor Schiro, who did little to challenge segregation: "I assume the teachers felt that Ms. Hill had been around a long time, they needed a male, and that a white male would probably lead them to success."[148] Didier promised to increase member participation, fight for integrated education, and build a

From left to right: Unknown individual, **Ed Fontaine, Nat LaCour, and Eugene Didier.** Eugene Didier won the UTNO presidency in 1969, only to be ousted by his vice president, Nat LaCour, two years later. Didier was the only white president of the union until Jim Randels was elected in 2016. Ed Fontaine ran the struggling state organization (the LFT) during this period, until he became president of the Jefferson Federation of Teachers (JFT) in 1972. Jefferson Parish is adjacent to Orleans. *Courtesy of United Teachers of New Orleans.*

broader base of community support for teachers. Perhaps most importantly, Didier predicted there would not be another teacher strike in the near future.[149]

The strikes had taken a toll on teachers and on the community. Louise Alford, a national representative who had worked both strikes, recalled with some hyperbole: "What a mark these strikes left on me . . . jailings by the busload, combat troops to break up a 'sit-down' in the administration building, screams, crying babies, etc."[150] Parents and students were frustrated from two weeks of interrupted classes, particularly in the Black community, and the *Louisiana Weekly* editorialized that nothing had been gained from the strike.[151] The AFT tried to develop a positive spin by arguing that many were impressed with the teachers' courage and that community groups had been mobilized to a greater extent than ever before.[152] Teachers returned to school with their colleagues who had walked through the picket lines, leaving their striking coworkers to bear the consequences. And despite the election of Didier, both the union and the school system remained racially polarized. An executive board member of Local 527 wrote an article in which he lauded the "group of predominantly black teachers starting at 1,200 and dwindling to two hundred sixty-nine—who for ten hectic days with sore feet, wet eyes, and fallen hopes courageously endured threats and fear tactics of every conceivable denomination. The question is: why did they persevere? Was this the beginning of something new—the prime step in demonstrating to the white power structure that black teachers are determined to solve their own problems and, moreover, plan, shape, and direct their own destiny?"[153] Yet, as Didier's election portended, change was on the horizon. The following two years would include liberal Moon Landrieu winning the mayoral election with over 90 percent of the Black vote, two new superintendents in succession, and the true beginning of faculty integration.[154] Local 527 would be transformed in the process.

FACULTY DESEGREGATION AND THE FORMATION OF UTNO

Though the OPSB had permitted limited and voluntary staff desegregation since 1966—in order to avoid losing federal funds—two prominent court rulings in 1969 led the board to fear they would be sued if they did not ramp up their faculty desegregation efforts.[155] The board proposed that for the 1970–71 school year, no more than 75 percent of teachers at each school could be from one race. For the first time, the plan approved by the board for the 1970–71 school year included forced transfers of teachers to achieve the 75/25 balance.[156] Though representatives from Local 527 participated in the advisory committee that developed the plan and although the union supported teacher desegregation, members worried that the process would result in the loss of Black teaching positions.[157] The local sponsored a motion that required that the board protect the current Black-white teacher ratio, but the motion was voted down, leading the union to accuse the board of only paying "lip service to protecting the jobs of black teachers."[158] The local also sent a letter to the superintendent asking him to initiate desegregation in the school board's central offices, which had previously employed almost entirely white personnel. For example, among a maintenance force of 240 individuals, only four were Black.[159]

Local 527's fears about the loss of Black jobs were not unfounded. In April 1970, the NEA released a report critiquing the processes of desegregation in Louisiana. The NEA found that faculty desegregation had resulted in educator displacement "of crisis proportions" throughout the state. Black administrators in desegregated schools were routinely demoted to teaching positions, and Black teachers transferred to white schools were not given classrooms to use.[160] Typically, the most highly qualified Black teachers were transferred to white schools, while the least-qualified white teachers were transferred to Black schools.[161] The following year, the LEA filed a lawsuit to stop the "indiscriminate" firing of Black teachers and principals throughout the state. It found that from 1968 to 1970, the number of Black teachers had decreased by 1,072, and the number of white teachers had increased by 5,575 across Georgia, Alabama, Louisiana, Mississippi, and Florida.[162] Local 527 sought to prevent a similar phenomenon in New Orleans. In November 1970, three months after the 75/25 policy was initiated, the AFT released a report critiquing the plan and alleging a drain of Black teacher talent from predominantly Black schools. Meanwhile, more than 300 teachers had resigned since the beginning of the year, most of them white people who chose to leave the system rather than teach in Black schools.[163]

The board continued to rely mostly on volunteers and, by the following year, still had not achieved the 75/25 goal. Faced with the possibility of losing almost $9 million in federal funding, in July 1972 the OPSB announced it would integrate faculties completely.[164] Approximately 800 teachers were transferred in order to achieve close to a 50/50 Black/white ratio in all the schools.[165] Although Local 527 had originally opposed the proposal, it supported the initiative once the new superintendent, Gene Geisert, assured members that the current Black/white teaching ratio would be maintained and that no teachers would be fired.[166] Nonetheless, many members felt ambivalent about the transfers. Connie Goodly was "devastated" when she was transferred from the school she taught at, which served the Desire Housing Project, to Sherwood Forest Elementary, which served mostly middle-class white children: "I felt that my children needed me. I love children, but I felt my greatest need was with those kids who were from single-family homes, didn't know their fathers, and I wanted to try to make a difference with them. To show them that they could be anything that they wanted to be."[167] Other teachers avoided the transfers; Grace Lomba was reassigned to a majority-white school, but an older friend offered to take the transfer instead of her, since Lomba was still new at her school.[168] Laverne Kappel moved to New Orleans in 1969 after having taught in rural Alabama through the National Teacher Corps. She took a job at majority-Black Lawless High School in the Lower 9th Ward and recalls that, at the time, she was the only white person in the building. When the 1972 transfers occurred, suddenly many more white teachers appeared: "They were mostly just out of college and very nice people. No experience." Kappel believes her Black coworkers were skeptical about faculty desegregation: "They hated that some of the best young teachers, Black teachers, were being sent to Behrman. And they felt like pawns. . . . But they wanted colleagues, they liked their colleagues. And most of them had gone to segregated schools, they belonged to segregated clubs and churches, and the whole thing. So it was part of the social contract that got broken."[169]

Wilson Boveland started teaching in 1973, shortly after the transfers occurred: "I didn't see much racial tension between the faculty. Because, really, what kind of happened was that the Black teachers did their thing and the white teachers did their thing."[170] The faculty being socially separated by race, however, did not protect paraprofessionals who often worked inside teachers' classrooms. Susie Beard had mixed experiences with the white teachers who were transferred into her school: "Some were good teachers and some were racist because it was during segregation time. You did the best you could working with them. I worked with teachers who wouldn't even communicate verbally. They would write notes and have the notes written when you walked in in the morning, just give you the notes and tell you what your duties were."[171] Still, many of the most intolerant white teachers had left the system rather than teach in integrated schools, so the faculty was more racially liberal than it had been in prior years, aiding the local's campaign.[172]

Though there were ongoing issues around the implementation of faculty desegregation—teachers complained about lack of preparation and being assigned to subjects they were not qualified to teach—the process was crucial to the union's growth.[173] Shortly before the mass transfers, in the spring of 1972, Local 527 and the majority-white OEA announced that they were merging to form UTNO.[174] The new union would affiliate with both the NEA and the AFT, only the sixth such merger in the nation, and UTNO's first priority would be obtaining collective bargaining for teachers.[175] The merger was possible because of a significant shift in the NEA, which at the national level had merged with the majority-Black American Teachers Association in 1966, devoted itself fully to the cause of school desegregation, and by the early 1970s, embraced collective bargaining as a core strategy.[176] Following the AFT's lead, the NEA threatened to expel all southern locals that refused to integrate and, making good on that promise, expelled the all-white LTA in 1970. This resulted in an exodus of segregationist white teachers from the OEA, rendering its membership smaller, more diverse, and more liberal—as well as more receptive to a merger with Local 527. Thus, the merged group would have more than 2,000 members, close to a majority of the teachers in the system.[177] Ken Ducote, a teacher who later worked in planning and facilities for the district, recalls: "I was told . . . that when Alfred Hebeisen, who was the HR person for the school system, when he got the phone call that said the two unions [Local 527 and OEA] had merged, the story was he turned white as a ghost and dropped the phone."[178] Nat LaCour, who was then president of Local 527—having defeated Eugene Didier in the 1971 union elections[179]—became president of UTNO, and Cheryl Epling, a white teacher from the OEA, became vice president. Over 90 percent of the OEA and Local 527 membership voted in favor of the merger, which union leaders argued indicated widespread teacher support for collective bargaining.[180]

Though merger talks occurred in the spring of 1972, the two organizations had been moving ideologically closer together for several years already. Ahead of the 1969 strike, the OEA released a flyer saying that it believed in both collective bargaining and the right to strike—though not "at this time."[181] Both unions served on the committee to plan faculty desegregation, and they both had worked together on a coalition at the state level to get a pay raise for teachers. Also, at the time, it seemed likely that the AFT and NEA were going to merge on the national level, and LaCour had sat in on merger talks in New York. LaCour recalls that an OEA staffer, Bob Crowley, put out a flyer asking for the two groups to merge, and at first LaCour did not take it seriously—he responded that any OEA members were welcome to fill out Local 527 membership cards and join. But then the members of Local 527 asked him to reconsider.[182] Brenda Mitchell believes the merger was a key shift: "We were diverting our energies by fighting each other. Because we all wanted the same thing, we wanted better working conditions, we wanted to have input on, for example, book selection, we wanted a limit on class size. There were certain things that we wanted, all of us wanted, it wasn't Black or white but all of us."[183] The merger that formed UTNO was extraordinary not only because it was a rare joining of NEA and AFT forces but also because it was clear that Local 527, with LaCour at the helm, was leading the direction of the united organization:

> I think UTNO was really the first institution in New Orleans to merge where whites joined a majority Black organization. That had not happened. Integration in the South had been a movement where Blacks integrated into white situations. Blacks went to white churches, Blacks moved into white neighborhoods, Blacks went into white restaurants, but it was never whites moving into a majority Black setting. I think UTNO was the first institution I know where that happened, and that was because people understood that race was not the big factor in our progress, that we needed to be together. So, we didn't have to love each other, socialize with each other, but we could come together and campaign for our mutual interests. And that's what happened.[184]

Though the merger was a key shift, the new group was less powerful than it appeared at the outset because, according to then OEA staffer Bob Crowley, the OEA was misrepresenting its membership. Though it had once claimed 900 members, the majority of its white constituency had left the group when the LTA voted not to integrate at the state level. "Cheryl [Epling] knew a guy that worked in the computer department at Tulane. . . . He forged a printout for us and I told him to just put 700 names on there and you can get them out of the directory."[185] Conveniently for the OEA, the board then required that the new group, UTNO, sign every member up anew, a move intended to stymie its organizing. By the time the membership drive ended, it was clear that the OEA had underrepresented its membership, but the merger was already in place.[186] The

OEA-AFT merger negotiating team, early 1970s. Included are Leon Felix, president of the OEA (*seated, fourth from left*); Cheryl Epling, vice president of the OEA (*seated, third from left*); Bob Crowley, OEA organizer (*standing, left*); Nat LaCour, president of AFT Local 527 (*standing, middle*); and Fred Skelton, Local 527 organizer (*standing, right*). *Courtesy of United Teachers of New Orleans.*

merger allowed the New Orleans teachers to avoid the pitfalls of split organizational allegiance, which had stymied collective bargaining campaigns in other cities, such as Atlanta. Though the NEA affiliate there held a one-day strike in 1975 for collective bargaining, it lost momentum as more radical teachers flocked to the growing AFT affiliate in the city instead, and the Atlanta educators never won a CBA.[187]

The faculty desegregation process also helped facilitate the merger in New Orleans. White and Black teachers working in the same schools in large numbers for the first time were able to build relationships and friendships and no longer saw the need for separate teacher organizations. Moreover, especially once UTNO had formed, faculty desegregation enabled the mass recruitment of teachers: "[Faculty desegregation] really did help UTNO because when we got the Black teachers into the white schools, they were able to talk to their white colleagues about collective bargaining. And so, from '72 to '73, our membership really grew."[188] In the 1969–70 school year, forty-one elementary schools had no teachers of the minority race; but by 1971–72, there was only one school, all-white Lakeview Elementary, that had not achieved even token integration (see table 1.2).[189] In anticipation of conflict arising from the desegregation transfers, schools had instituted special professional development days to orient new teachers. Ducote, then a teacher at Lawless High, said those meetings revealed more commonalities between the teachers than differences: "Then, one of the things that came out of our desegregation workshops, it became [clear] that it was less and less a racial thing and more an administration thing. The faculty was kind of united in opposing the governance structure that the principal had."[190] The teachers found the principal at Lawless to be "oppressive" and working conditions to be intolerable: "There was a story that I heard . . . that he kept the teacher's bathroom locked and you had to go to him for the key. . . . Even if it is apocryphal, it gives you some insight into how we saw him."[191] Lawless became one of UTNO's strongest buildings.

In the early 1970s, working conditions for teachers were difficult, and they had little recourse when they felt mistreated. This was particularly a problem along lines of class and race. Black women, for example, were vulnerable both to sexual harassment and to all manner of false or demeaning accusations from racist white parents and coworkers. Brenda Mitchell experienced both. Before she was hired by the district, she was told she had to lose a certain amount of weight before it would sign the contract—she ended up bringing a doctor's note certifying that she had lost the weight. Later, a white child in her class whom she had disciplined told his mother that she had hit him on the head with a ruler: "The principal calls me to the office and tells me I hit a kid with a . . . I said, 'Think about what you're saying. No, I didn't.' She then had the ranking teacher to go talk to my class while I was in the office and they told her that never happened but the parent made a charge and she just wanted her kid out of my class because I was Black."[192] Another Black woman teacher recalls that when she first started, her principal wanted to date her: "The principal tried to date me and I had just married, right after I got out of college. I married my childhood sweetheart who I had a child for. And so I wasn't into anything like that. I came to teach. But he would stand and watch and when I'd look up, he'd stand and watch and be peering around a corner and stuff like that made me very uncomfortable."[193] When she refused, the principal rated her "unsatisfactory" and eventually she transferred to another school. Men were also victims of discriminatory and capricious hiring practices. Leoance Williams graduated from a program at Xavier University designed to bring more men into early childhood education, but when he applied for a kindergarten position, he was told by the principal, "Oh no, you cannot teach kindergarten, you are a man. . . . I could see you working with the little boys, but what are you going to do with the little girls?"[194] As Ken Ducote remembers: "The thing is, the climate was such that you had a lot of craziness. You had retaliation. You had no due process. The other teachers, especially the Black teachers, told me that there was resentment.

**Table 1.2. Percentage of minority teacher population
in New Orleans schools, 1969–1973**

	1969–70	1970–71	1971–72	1972–73
All elementary (grades K–8)	7.6	18.5	22.9	39.5
All secondary (grades 9–12)	6.7	18.0	21.1	43.2
Total	7.2	18.3	22.0	40.6

Source: Sam Scarnato, "Informational Report on Staff Desegregation," 1969–73,
Sam Scarnato folder, Orleans Parish School Board Collection (MSS 147), box 16, Louisiana
and Special Collections, Earl K. Long Library, University of New Orleans, New Orleans.
Note: Minority teacher population includes both white teachers working at formerly
Black schools and Black teachers working at formerly white schools.

There was feelings of if you were darker than a certain skin tone, then you were written up more than others, or that some principals had the thing that they would write all first-year teachers as unacceptable . . . to kind of control them or something."[195] Other teachers told stories of being unfairly assigned to duties, of being forced to pay for their own photocopies, and of having successful grants and programs they had started taken away by jealous and controlling administrators. Teachers felt like collective bargaining would increase their voice and their protection in a district that often afforded them neither.

THE FINAL PUSH TO COLLECTIVE BARGAINING

In the summer and fall of 1971, the OPSB was once again searching for a new superintendent.[196] Many in the Black community, including the editorial board of the *Louisiana Weekly*, wanted Mack Spears appointed to the position, and he was endorsed by the LEA, the organization he used to lead, as well as by the Orleans Principals Association, the local historically Black colleges and universities (HBCUs)—including Dillard, Xavier, and Southern University at New Orleans (SUNO)—and various other organizations.[197] However, despite the school district being two-thirds Black, school board member Robert Smith was quoted saying, "the community [is] not ready for a Black superintendent."[198] The NAACP accused the selection committee of racism, and there were rumors that the white members of the school board were trying to appoint a superintendent from a neighboring parish as a favor.[199] When the dust settled, the board approved Dr. Gene Geisert, a white educator originally from the Midwest, for the position—with Spears abstaining.[200]

Geisert had grown up poor, and neither of his parents had attended high school. He joined the Navy and then, through the G.I. Bill, was able to attend college and eventually earn his master's and PhD. He worked as superintendent of tiny Alpena, Michigan—"as far north as you can go without hitting Canada, 35 degrees below zero in the winter, 10 feet of snow . . ."—for five years until he secured the superintendency in Wilmington, Delaware, in 1967.[201] Wilmington had a school district that was 79 percent Black, and the city was wracked by race riots. Geisert stayed there for four years and earned a reputation for turning the district around. However, there were also rumors that he had been under pressure from "so-called activist members of a Black community" in Wilmington who believed Black people should have more control over the school district.[202]

For the union, Geisert was a promising, if complicated, choice. He had worked extensively negotiating early teacher contracts in Michigan and was comfortable with collective bargaining as a concept. UTNO staffer Fred Skelton recalls: "[Geisert] was a superintendent in a collective bargaining school system, was familiar with it, didn't have any apprehension about it. Didn't have any misgivings. And so he, I don't know, whether consciously or unconsciously, made it comfortable for us."[203] On the other hand, Geisert was famous for an article he had published that argued that the superintendent's responsibility was to directly lead the management of schools—not to be a middleman or "Mr. Nobody" between the teachers and the board: "In the final analysis, [the superintendent] must represent the board of education and the administrative viewpoint in all matters concerning negotiations with the staff."[204] He had also experienced a strike from the school custodians during his time in Wilmington, and he had defeated the union there: "I organized the administrators and had them pick up all the rubbish and everything and we beat the union. . . . My supervisors, they sent me a great big plaque . . . and it said, *Yea, though I walk through the valley of death, I will fear no evil because I'm the meanest son of a bitch in the valley.* And they all signed it. And I thought that was really neat."[205] Geisert, then, would not be an ally to the union, but neither was he ideologically opposed to collective bargaining. Louise Alford, an AFT national representative who had worked in both Wilmington and New Orleans, knew Geisert on a first-name basis: "Although Dr. Geisert fought us tooth and toenail in Wilmington, he honestly believed in Collective Bargaining as a process and did all in his power to enforce the contract once it was hammered out."[206]

In another positive sign for the union, starting in the early 1970s, union organizing would gain momentum, both in the country and in New Orleans. New Orleans experienced several prominent and successful strikes, many of them geared toward obtaining greater rights for Black workers. The longshoremen (ILA) went on strike in both 1969 and 1971 and the city sanitation workers held a strike in January 1969.[207] UTNO had support from both the AFT and the NEA, which would expel its administrators in 1973 and commit itself further to union organizing.[208] Riding the momentum from the merger and newly empowered by faculty desegregation during this period, UTNO returned to their campaign for collective bargaining.

LaCour knew that to be successful in obtaining collective bargaining, the union needed more support from teachers, community groups, and the press. He had his staff bring doughnuts and coffee into schools and discuss the benefits of collective bargaining with teachers. He also used UTNO's existing network of building representatives to recruit new teachers. Paraprofessionals formed their own UTNO chapter in June 1973, further boosting UTNO's numbers.[209] United across race, educators felt empowered to stand up to principals and the school board. Skelton recalls educators' enthusiasm for the union: "It was a great time to go to school meetings. You know, we'd come in and we'd say, 'We're the United Teachers of New Orleans!' And they'd be saying, 'Can I have a membership card?' Interrupting you as you spoke! So it was a heady time."[210] In an attempt to prioritize internal democracy and member leadership, the union also developed a survey to send to all teachers and paraprofessionals so they could express what they wanted to see in a collective bargaining contract, helping to increase educators' enthusiasm and involvement.[211] Even as teachers rallied behind the new organization, LaCour and the other leaders of UTNO knew from the failed strikes of the 1960s that they needed a broad base of support: "We met with all kinds of groups in the city. Civic organizations, political organizations. I brought Mr. Shanker in to meet with the editorial board of the *Times Picayune*. We met with The League of Women Voters. Every entity that was out there, we met with to ask them to not oppose our efforts."[212] UTNO bought large billboards advocating for collective bargaining that depicted teachers and students at work and read, "HELP THE TEACHERS TEACH."[213]

The *Times Picayune* remained hostile and wrote an editorial condemning UTNO's campaign, accusing "out-of-town strategists" of manipulating teachers, and claiming the union was putting children in danger.[214] UTNO was more successful on talk shows and radio shows, often sparring with members of the school board, making collective bargaining for teachers a popular topic for conversation.[215] The *Louisiana Weekly* wrote a strong editorial in support of the campaign, at times echoing UTNO's own press release: "Teachers in New Orleans have no voice in formulating the policies, regulations and conditions under which they work. These are decided and arbitrarily enforced by the Orleans Parish School Board."[216] The union also had success generating support among community groups, especially in the Black community. It set up a "Speakers' Bureau" to solicit endorsements from civic organizations, churches, and other unions.[217] Connie Goodly recalls that a lot of this work was done by members, who were asked to speak to groups they belonged to:

Because so many of our teachers and members belong to sororities and fraternities and churches. We had to develop relationships with the churches, the faith-based community. . . . And sometimes they would allow us to go into the churches and talk, if you were a member of Greater St. Steven's Baptist Church, sometimes the reverend would let you stand up and say, 'This is why we're doing this.' If you were a member of Alpha Kappa Alpha sorority, you would explain to your sorority girls, this is what we're gonna do and this is why we're gonna do it.[218]

Relying on grassroots member-based organizing reinforced the sense of participation and democracy within the union. Eventually, at least twenty-four community groups endorsed the campaign.[219]

UTNO organizers also worked hard to secure the support of organized labor. Though the AFL-CIO had always backed the union in theory, some AFL-CIO affiliates, such as the Teamsters who represented bus drivers, had crossed Local 527 picket lines in both of its failed strikes. UTNO also struggled, as a middle-class union, to ensure that blue-collar workers would see it as an ally and support its campaign. In June 1973, in a show of interunion solidarity, UTNO joined the United Farm Workers (UFW) to picket outside the A&P grocery store that was selling non-UFW lettuce.[220] "It took lots of meetings to convince [other unions] to stick their neck out for teachers and paras who had scored zero in two strikes," recalls national representative Alford.[221] Skelton said that the ILA (the longshoremen's union) frequently allowed UTNO to use its office for meetings, perhaps at the urging of Victor Bussie: "Public employee unions are a little bit looked on, and they are a little bit different than industrial unions. You're a longshoreman, it's different than you're a college graduate teacher and you wear a suit. There was never a moment when Victor Bussie did not support us. He was on call, came down to meet with our bargaining team . . . just to encourage us and tell us how important what we were doing was for the labor movement in this state and how he wanted to help us."[222] Eventually, most local unions signed on; Chuck Winters, the president of the Teamsters local, even spoke at one of UTNO's rallies.[223]

As the community campaign wore on, UTNO attempted to secure the three votes it needed from OPSB, which ultimately would decide whether to permit the collective bargaining election. The board had voted the union down 4–1 both times it had petitioned in the 1960s, but its one supporting member retired in November 1970. UTNO endorsed and helped elect William Reeves to the board in November 1972, so the union could count on his vote, but two other board members would need to be convinced.[224] UTNO met individually with school board members and also convinced Superintendent Geisert "to secretly take all Board Members across Lake Pontchartrain to a cabin and talk CB [collective bargaining] sense to them. The Chairman [Mack Spears] didn't show up."[225] Geisert liked the challenge of collective bargaining, which was one of his main activities before moving to New Orleans: "I spent five years going up and down the State of New Jersey negotiating, weekends, evenings, rain or snow, running into all kinds of interesting problems. . . . I enjoyed it a lot."[226] He also respected Nat LaCour and, despite their positions as adversaries across the negotiating table, they struck up a professional friendship. LaCour argued that collective bargaining had the potential to reduce friction between teachers and administrators because it forced them to sit down together and work out their differences.[227] That was certainly true for LaCour and Geisert; years later, LaCour flew down from Washington, DC, to attend Geisert's ninetieth birthday celebration.[228] Despite individual and group meetings with board members, by both the superintendent and the union, UTNO was certain only of two votes—Reeves's and Mildred Blomberg's—as it started to ramp up its campaign in the spring of 1974.[229]

UTNO also faced vocal opposition from the LTA—the all-white local that had been expelled from the NEA for refusing to integrate. The LTA had sued the school district over faculty desegregation—arguing that it was illegal to transfer more than 100 teachers at one time—and lost.[230] It had 430 members in New Orleans in January 1974, far fewer than UTNO's 2,600, and LTA members knew that they would lose an election for collective bargaining if the board approved it, further diminishing their union's power.[231] They argued, in racially coded language, that unions rendered teaching less professional: "The teacher union disavows the professional status of teachers and urges teachers to think in terms of 'the worker vs. the boss.'"[232] This argument was repeated by board member Edward Knight, who said that unions put the "concept of professionalism in danger."[233] Some members of the business community also opposed collective bargaining and made their views clear to the board, yet there was no cohesive resistance at the time: "We heard of information that business leaders had talked to the school board about, 'You'll bankrupt the school system' and all that sort of stuff. 'It's going to result in higher taxes' . . . but by and large, the white community, while not overly supportive—there was no protest."[234] By the mid-1970s, with Moon Landrieu as mayor integrating city hall, fewer people wanted to be publicly affiliated with segregationist groups such as the LTA.

Dave Selden, the national AFT president, came to New Orleans again, in February 1974, and reiterated his belief that a contract in New Orleans would serve as impetus for further organizing throughout the South.[235] In sharp contrast to his speech in 1969, he said that since "this city is different from others in that racial antagonisms have apparently been resolved, it seems like a logical place to make a breakthrough."[236] Selden was likely thinking about the integrated union and the somewhat-smooth process of faculty desegregation, but it was a strange comment to make at a moment when white families were rapidly exiting the public schools.[237] UTNO also, as an intentionally integrated union at every level, from its officers to its staff to its executive board, offered a sharp contrast to AFT unions in New York and Newark that had experienced racially divisive strikes in 1968 and 1971, respectively.[238] In both of these cases, the strikes had been perceived as majority-white, middle-class teachers striking against the Black community—and, in Newark, which had a more diverse teaching force, the strike also divided the union internally along racial lines.[239] These racial dynamics were mirrored in cities throughout the Northeast.[240] New Orleans presented a more promising scenario, in that white and Black union factions appeared aligned, and the majority-Black union had earned strong community support. The rarity of genuine interracial collaboration at the time led both union members and the public to feel positively about UTNO: "And the fortunate thing about the place and time was that New Orleans was still very segregated and here, we have the Blacks and the whites coming together. I mean, we got all the ink, we got all the TV we wanted. 'How's the merger coming? How's it working, whites and Blacks together?' And it was very fortunate that at that time that we were perceived as a progressive force, an enlightened force. And it was well taken and it was very popular that we had integrated the organizations."[241]

In March 1974, approximately twenty-five UTNO officers and staff picketed OPSB offices to promote the collective bargaining campaign; they anticipated asking the board, yet again, to consider a collective bargaining election at their upcoming meeting.[242] UTNO sent out a press release enumerating issues in the schools it believed collective bargaining would help resolve, focusing not only on teacher salaries and benefits but also on conditions for students: "Most of our schools have an inadequate supply of textbooks, teaching materials, and equipment. Most of our classes are over-crowded and our buildings dilapidated and in need of repair. Our schools are failing to meet the need of thousands of students with social, emotional, and learning difficulties."[243] In connecting members' workplace demands to the quality of education the schools provided, the union cast itself as a proto-social movement union, organizing for the public good.[244] UTNO presented over 4,000 petitions for collective bargaining from teachers and paraprofessionals to the board at its March 25 meeting.[245] Teachers packed the auditorium—more than 1,000 teachers attended and picketed outside—and they sat grouped by school, identified by placards, as if attending a political convention.[246] The board members took the matter under advisement and said they would vote at their following meeting, on April 15. Meanwhile, the LTA challenged the veracity of the petitions and insisted that they be checked by a second accounting firm.[247]

In addition to the 4,000 teacher petitions, UTNO collected petitions of support from community members by standing on street corners or at the mall.[248] Businesses across the city put up UTNO posters, depicting an apple and the

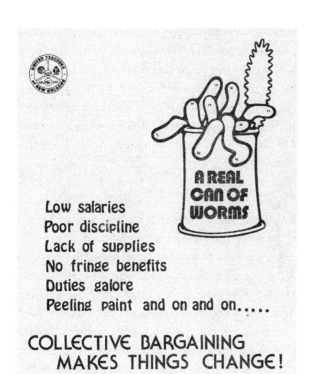

Low salaries
Poor discipline
Lack of supplies
No fringe benefits
Duties galore
Peeling paint and on and on......

A REAL
CAN OF
WORMS

COLLECTIVE BARGAINING
MAKES THINGS CHANGE!

"A Real Can of Worms" broadside from UTNO's 1973–74 collective bargaining campaign. Note the logo at the top left indicating that UTNO was affiliated with both the AFT and the NEA. *Courtesy of United Teachers of New Orleans.*

statement, "We Support Collective Bargaining for New Orleans Schools." The posters were ubiquitous because members put them in their windows as well.[249] Skelton remembers that the energy and enthusiasm in the community and among teachers was overwhelming:

> Now part of it also was that Geisert was in support of it. And when you've hired this superintendent, he's done a nice job of keeping the staff together with integration. He says he can handle this collective bargaining stuff. And we've got community support. We've got mothers here, we've got fathers here, we've got community leaders. I remember we walked down the aisle with these cardboard boxes and laid them out in front of the school board. And we said, "We've got 20,000 signatures on these petitions and more coming." Well, I'm sure it was controversial. I'm sure the business community, I'm sure there were portions who said, "Do not do this." But we created an atmosphere where it was popular.[250]

When the Louisiana attorney general issued an opinion that teachers had the legal right to collective bargaining, in early April 1974, it seemed that the campaign could not be stopped.[251] Though Louisiana offered no protection for public sector employees engaging in collective bargaining, the process remained implicitly legal in the state, and unlike in any other southern state today, teachers' strikes in Louisiana were (and remain) legal.[252] Moreover, there was some precedent in the state for public employee collective bargaining. Though no teachers had won CBAs, workers at public hospitals and universities, such as Charity Hospital and Southern University, had won CBAs through the American Federation of State, County, and Municipal Employees (AFSCME).[253] The landscape faced by UTNO organizers was not as dire as it could have been.

VICTORY

On the evening of April 15, 1974, 1,000 New Orleans teachers and para-professionals packed into the auditorium at Cohen High School to hear the school board's vote on whether the educators would be permitted to choose an exclusive collective bargaining agent.[254] The educators were poised to become the first teachers' union in Louisiana with a collective bargaining agreement and one of a select few in the South. As the board members announced their votes, approving collective bargaining 3–2, the auditorium erupted in cheers. Edward Knight, the board member who had questioned the professionalism of union affiliation, provided the third vote that the union needed. UTNO's president, Nat LaCour, proclaimed the vote a "100 percent victory."[255]

The teachers' hero of the day was undoubtedly LaCour, who had quickly risen to prominence both in UTNO and with the national AFT.[256] Even the *Times Picayune*, in a scathing anti–collective bargaining editorial published the following day, could find little harsh language for the union leader, describing him as "low-keyed" and using "the mildest of threatening tone[s]."[257] LaCour, perhaps more than anybody else in the audience, understood both what had been accomplished and the work still to come. LaCour had graduated from Cohen High just eighteen years earlier, two years after *Brown v. Board of Education* made de jure segregation illegal and four years before the New Orleans schools took their first halting steps toward integration.[258] He graduated with a master's from Southern University, an HBCU in Baton Rouge, in 1960, and moved back to New Orleans to teach high school biology. However, in an attempt to obstruct the federal desegregation order, the Louisiana state legislature had stripped the OPSB of its authority. As a result, teachers in Orleans Parish taught without pay for four months and LaCour could not get hired; he worked instead as a substitute until the spring semester.[259]

Looking forward, LaCour had visited Al Shanker's United Federation of Teachers (UFT) in New York City and understood how far New Orleans had to go to gain benefits, salaries, working conditions, and professional development opportunities comparable to those enjoyed by UFT educators.[260] "Nat's attitude to us was that we deserved as much as the teachers in New York deserved. So we fought to get whatever they had in New York," recalls longtime teacher and UTNO member Grace Lomba.[261] Yet, on the eve of collective bargaining, some New Orleans teachers worked in schools with no air conditioning, leaking roofs, and toilets in the school yard instead of inside the buildings—far from the working conditions enjoyed by educators in strong union cities in the Northeast and Midwest.[262]

LaCour would go on to lead UTNO for twenty-eight years, until leaving for the national AFT in 1998. But the initial years were the most transformational. "In hindsight, what he did was remarkable. His leadership changed a city and changed a teaching corps for decades. At the time, we didn't know what the hell we were doing. I mean, we were just, 'Okay, this is what the book says, okay, we'll do this.' I'm not sure that there's a lot of Nat LaCour around."[263] Though teachers focused on LaCour's skill and magnetism in explaining the union's success, key to his strategy was his ability to draw meaningful member participation, make democratic decisions, and ensure everyone felt heard. LaCour, as a dynamic Black leader committed to integration, represented for many their hopes for a new era of racial reconciliation and labor power. Unlike longtime president Veronica Hill, LaCour could move successfully in male-dominated political circles, and his calm demeanor appealed to white people fearful of Black radicalism. Teacher Leoance Williams saw LaCour as a mentor. "I liked his style. I had never seen him angry, and I'm somewhat like that myself, I'm kind of mellow. And he was always diplomatic."[264] LaCour had a civil rights history, having participated in student protests while at Southern,[265] and he was known as a strong and fair teacher.[266] His leadership during this early period united Black parents and the Black community behind the union, and the union's victories were part of larger working-class and Black struggles for equality and economic justice.

Following the OPSB vote, the LTA again tried to stop UTNO, this time by sponsoring a bill in the state legislature that would have made collective bargaining illegal; but UTNO joined with the state AFL-CIO to defeat the bill.[267] The board set November election dates for teachers, paraprofessionals, custodians, and maintenance workers to choose collective bargaining agents—the latter two groups were selecting either the Teamsters or AFSCME.[268] The LTA sued to prevent the election from occurring but lost at the civil court level; they appealed and were denied.[269] The *Times Picayune* wrote an editorial encouraging teachers to vote "no representation" instead of choosing UTNO on the ballot, as "it is necessary to realize that the school board is the duly constituted voice of the people; the union is a voice of a private, special interest group."[270] Schools closed early on November 12, 1974, the day of the election, and UTNO won the vote overwhelmingly. Of 4,800 eligible teachers, 4,252 voted and 3,308 chose UTNO.[271] Superintendent Geisert said, "Today's election enabled teachers to democratically express their desire for collective bargaining . . . [that] has the

UTNO president Nat LaCour oversees New Orleans teachers' first collective bargaining election, November 12, 1974. Teachers overwhelmingly chose UTNO as their exclusive bargaining agent. *Courtesy of United Teachers of New Orleans.*

potential for positive improvements in teaching conditions and educational advantages."[272] Later that month, the custodians voted to be represented by the Teamsters, the maintenance workers voted for AFSCME, and an election for the paraprofessionals was set for March 1975.[273] UTNO's fight had galvanized the sector, but it was still unclear what impact the unions would have on public schools and what gains for teachers could be made through their nascent CBAs.

CONCLUSION

The union that won collective bargaining in 1974 looked very different from the union that started the first campaign in 1965. UTNO was one of few locals nationwide affiliated with both major teacher organizations, the AFT and the NEA, at a moment when it seemed as though a merger on the national level was imminent.[274] In November 1974, Al Shanker heralded: "For too many years [the South's] power has been dissipated by racial divisions and organizational rivalries. The United Teachers of New Orleans has made a major contribution toward healing these divisions and ending these rivalries, first by the merger two years ago between locals of the AFT and the NEA, and now with their effort to win the first major collective bargaining victory in the South."[275] That merger, which brought unionized white and Black teachers together in large numbers for the first time, was both key to UTNO's successful collective bargaining campaign and served to blunt some of its earlier racial activism. The union became significantly whiter, larger, and more powerful, and its successful election signaled its relatively mainstream acceptance. However, its overwhelming community support, particularly from Black churches and political organizations, demonstrates its ongoing allegiance to Black working-class politics and civil rights unionism.

Not only were UTNO members an integral part of the Black community, they were also aligned politically with Black and working-class issues; members connected their struggle for collective bargaining to ending segregation and racial oppression. By standing in solidarity with Black parents and students, union members affirmed their role as middle-class mediators, promoting racial and economic justice for both themselves and the students they taught. The union achieved its success by orchestrating a merger that maintained Black union leadership within an intentionally integrated governing body, consolidating the white support it needed while continuing to ally itself with the Black community. It also effectively relied on member activists to recruit their colleagues, speak to community groups, mobilize parents, and rally support. The union offered a place where both Black and white teachers could experience a genuine sense of interracial democracy and decision-making, in a way that city and state politics often did not.

UTNO won collective bargaining because of the skills and commitment of its members and leaders but also because of the shifting political and social climate in New Orleans. White board members in the late 1960s had no reason to grant the majority-Black local bargaining rights, as Local 527 represented only a fraction of the segregated schools and educators. Yet Local 527's strikes and protests during this period earned it the respect and devotion of the Black community and connected it in the public imagination to the struggles of the civil rights movement. By the early-1970s, the racial tides were shifting, both at the federal and local levels. The school board was forced to integrate, threatened by the loss of federal funds if it did not, and Mayor Moon Landrieu worked to desegregate other institutions in the city. White liberals, including Landrieu and Superintendent Geisert, saw the integrated union as a hopeful harbinger of interracial harmony and rallied behind UTNO to help the union win a collective bargaining election without a strike. The Local 527 gained the NEA's support through the merger with the OEA, and the public quickly began to see UTNO's main opposition, the segregationist LTA, as a relic of the past, no longer relevant in the changing city. UTNO members and leaders capitalized on this atmosphere, connecting collective bargaining rights for educators to the city's new turn toward progressivism and the unrealized hopes of the civil rights movement. UTNO emerged victorious not by turning away from its earlier racial activism and embracing color-blind rhetoric about a shared economic struggle, but by maintaining its identity as a progressive, Black-led organization for which economic and racial justice, collective bargaining, and the desegregation of the school system, were inseparable.

Though UTNO was one of the most successful teachers' unions in the South, its members certainly were not the only teachers engaged in labor organizing. Teachers and students in Memphis, Tennessee, collaborated with the NAACP to hold a series of "Black Monday" protests in 1969 that resulted in changes to the discriminatory processes of faculty and student desegregation in the city.[276] Florida teachers held an unsuccessful statewide strike in 1968, and the teachers' activism eventually led to the enactment of a statewide collective bargaining law for public sector workers in 1974.[277] The law makes Florida an outlier in the South, where no other state protects public workers' right to collective bargaining. The integrated Alabama Education Association, led by Paul Hubbert and civil rights veteran Joe Reed, used its clout to defeat Gov. George Wallace's attempt to take money away from the state's Education Trust Fund in 1971—and that union today continues to play an outsized role in state politics.[278] Finally, in 1985, Mississippi teachers went on strike statewide for nearly a month to demand pay raises. More than 9,000 teachers participated across 55 school districts, eventually winning pay raises of over $4,300 (over $10,000 in 2023 dollars).[279] Educators in the South were willing to fight for improved teaching and learning conditions, yet they did so in consistently hostile political environments, with city and state governments determined to limit the power of organized labor. As historian Lane Windham demonstrates, a dearth of successful collective bargaining contracts does not necessarily indicate that workers do not want a union or are not attempting to organize.[280] UTNO's success, though remarkable, hints at the possibility for powerful teacher organizing in the South, both historically and today.

As the union continued to grow and consolidate power over the subsequent decade, it would build meaningful programs and institutions and win crucial raises and benefits that would begin to distance its members economically from the students they taught. At the same time, the union would expand to incorporate paraprofessionals and clerical workers, both groups of working-class school employees, who would connect the union more intimately to families and communities across the city. UTNO also would become a powerful progressive political force in the city and the state, pushing for legislation that centered the needs of its constituency, who remained overwhelmingly Black women, and helping move political discourse to the left. Though UTNO would continue to prioritize fighting for both racial and economic justice, it would also make compromises in response to its diverse membership, such as advocating for harsher school discipline, which disproportionately affected Black students.

Critics would accuse the union of becoming too powerful and using its influence to protect ineffective teachers and enforce arcane bureaucracy, such as seniority transfers, that did nothing to benefit students and families. It transitioned from operating clearly in the tradition of the civil rights movement to looking much more similar to the social movement unions heralded today. Yet the tension between growth and institutionalization versus active protest, democracy, and racial justice would follow the union until Hurricane Katrina.

2

Educating Our Own People

Union Democracy and Leadership Development, 1975–1982

She would sit there and she would literally almost let a meeting fall apart. People were at each other before she would intervene, because she wanted the decision to come out of the group and not be hers.

A colleague describing Ella Baker, in Barbara Ransby,
Ella Baker and the Black Freedom Movement

Union power *requires* democracy.

Mike Parker and Martha Gruelle, *Democracy Is Power*

Growing up on a farm in rural Georgia, Susie Beard learned the value of belonging to a union from her father, who worked at a paperware plant in Augusta. Starting on an assembly line and eventually moving his way up, Beard observed the power of her father's loyalty to the collective and its ability to effect real change in their lives. "He was strong in unionism, so I had seen all he had done and how he moved up from just common labor to become the chef making the food."[1] Beard and her husband moved to New Orleans in 1955; they had one young child and she was eight months pregnant with a second. They were unable to find an apartment due to segregation and lived for months in a motel; once they were settled, Beard became involved in voting rights activism in the city: "To vote, you had to dot an I, cross a T. If you didn't do all those things, they wouldn't even swear you in. You had to know your birthday by years, month, dates, weeks and time, all of that." After eventually securing a position as a paraprofessional, Beard joined UTNO. She saw her membership in the union as an extension of her civil rights work and as a means to demand rights for Black professionals, children, and families.[2] For the Black working class, democratic participation and the fight for economic and racial justice went hand in hand, forming the backbone of civil rights unionism.[3]

In this chapter, I examine how white flight and divestment from the New Orleans school system, combined with a national turn toward austerity, created challenges for the nascent teachers' union. As corporations lashed out against recent union gains on both the state and national levels, UTNO faced new threats and attempts to curtail its power. I argue that UTNO's strategic focus on participatory democracy and disruptive protest helped empower and mobilize rank-and-file members, which allowed the union to gain momentum and grow despite the hostile climate of the time. Moreover, as UTNO expanded to cover more working-class employees, including paraprofessionals and clerical staff, union leadership and members remained steadfast in their allegiance to the larger Black community. During this time, UTNO also created institutions to meet its members' needs as professionals and as people. These institutions included a mentoring program, a full-service teacher center, scholarship programs, professional development seminars, and a Health and Welfare Fund. Through these member-run programs, educators had access to affordable health insurance, resources to improve their teaching pedagogy, and opportunities to engage in action-oriented dialogue about pertinent education issues of the time. Run or coordinated by members themselves, these programs contributed to a genuine feeling of participation and empowerment among educators. As conservative and business interests attempted to portray the union and the district as engaged in a zero-sum game, in which every victory for UTNO resulted in a loss for the city's schoolchildren, the union consistently espoused a shared vision for quality education that included both well-supported educators and fully funded services for children. In modeling collaboration, democratic decision-making processes, and a spirit of mutual assistance, the union challenged the district and the city to reject the ideology of austerity and rally to support the schools and families who used them.

This chapter starts in 1975, shortly after UTNO won its collective bargaining agreement, and ends in 1982, when UTNO added clerical workers to its bargaining unit. Though UTNO became more bureaucratic during this period and its leadership became more entrenched, it still supported a democratic and redistributive agenda for the city of New Orleans and the state of Louisiana. Both internally and externally UTNO's leadership fostered a culture of participatory democracy, while also engaging in political struggles that required compromise and the strategic endorsements of imperfect candidates. UTNO pushed the labor movement and the state legislature to the left and created meaningful space within New Orleans for more progressive activism by anchoring the Black middle class. In all these areas, UTNO members contributed to a meaningful shift in the balance of power toward Black and working-class ideas of equity and justice. In addition, the union provided a space of genuine racial integration, collaboration, and deliberative conversation that many members did not encounter elsewhere in their lives. These spaces helped union members develop a framework to imagine a social and economic world outside of the schemas of racial and economic exploitation that continued to define the region.

PARTICIPATORY DEMOCRACY IN UTNO

The dominant narrative of the civil rights movement typically begins with *Brown v. Board of Education* and culminates with the 1964 passage of the Civil Rights Act. Yet as historian Jacquelyn Dowd Hall demonstrates, this story erases both early civil rights activism, which was deeply enmeshed with organized labor, as well as the post–Civil Rights Act struggle for economic justice. The late 1960s and early 1970s brought a significant rise in employment opportunities for Black Americans, and, "Once on the job, black workers became the most avid of new union members, and the understanding of workplace rights they brought with them inspired a surge of organizing in the public sector, which became one of the brightest spots in an otherwise-bleak landscape for organized labor."[4] UTNO ascended to power at just this moment, and it did so by drawing on the tactics and legacy of civil rights organizing: galvanizing community support, engaging in disruptive actions, building Black and working-class leadership, and promoting a culture of democracy and participation.

Participatory democracy is both an organizing strategy and a potential outcome; it is an alternative political structure with a radical redistribution of power and control. It has a long history. Sociologist Francesca Polletta traces its use from pacifists organizing against World War I to early labor movement educators in the 1920s who were working to produce organizers who would move beyond business unionism to push for fundamental change. Veterans of these movements then taught the strategy to early civil rights organizers, such as Septima Clark and Ella Baker, who brought the ideas to SNCC.[5] Later, participatory democracy became more associated with majority-white groups, such as Students for a Democratic Society and women's liberation collectives. Polletta demonstrates how all these groups—with varying success—used participatory democracy to foster cultures that uplifted working-class leadership, taught organizers to value individuals' different skill sets, promoted "deliberative talk," created buy-in to group decisions, and gave participants a feeling of political efficacy.[6] Democracy is also one of the keys to union success. In the words of a hospital workers' organizing manual: "The union is not a fee for service; it is the collective experience of workers in struggle."[7]

UTNO created space for participatory democracy both internally, within the union, and externally, in the education sector more broadly. Nat LaCour, UTNO's president from 1971 to 1999, though certainly a traditional leader in many respects, created a culture of deliberative talk within the union and worked to democratize and demystify the processes of collective bargaining. He developed worker leaders, seriously considered everyone's ideas, and built consensus. Moreover, the union itself was structured to foment participatory democracy. Union members at each school would elect a building representative ("a building rep") to handle their grievances and represent their needs at larger assembly meetings. These building reps were then managed by experienced "area coordinators," who were educators, union members, and mentors to the building reps. Members also directly elected union officials and members of the executive board, which was structured to represent all constituencies; thus, these elected officials included paraprofessionals, teachers, clerical workers, and support staff, who taught at various grade levels and various subjects, including teachers of special education and gifted students, geographically distributed across the city. Not only were executive board members elected by the membership, but the board also reflected the union's membership in terms of job categories as well as race, gender, and experience in the classroom.

Like many paraprofessionals—the school aides and assistant teachers vital to classroom instruction—Susie Beard started as a volunteer at the school her children attended and then was hired as a paraprofessional by the school. Over her more than thirty-year career in the classroom, she worked closely with students with special needs and their families, and she advocated for policies she believed would best serve them. On the side, she served on the Desire/Florida community board (the Florida Housing Project was adjacent to the Desire Projects), as a resident of the Desire Housing Project, and later on the Lower 9th Ward community board, fighting for the needs of her neighbors.[8] Within UTNO, she became the first paraprofessional area coordinator, responsible for servicing a network of schools, and the first paraprofessional staff person hired by the union in 1999. LaCour convinced her to apply for the job when he was leaving the city for a job in Washington, DC, with the AFT. "I got a call and they said I was hired," Beard recalls. "I was thankful, but I was a little fearful." In her new position, she built coalitions with local universities to provide educational programs for paraprofessionals that would result in increased salaries and state certification. The trajectory of Beard's life—from rural Georgia to New Orleans, educating her five children in segregated and then nominally integrated schools, from parent volunteer to UTNO staffer—demonstrates not only the possibilities provided by the union but also the challenges members had to confront. The thread of democracy and participation also follows Beard, both personally, in her own growth and activism, as well as politically, in her efforts to support her community, work for the union, and register people to vote.

Beard's trajectory demonstrates that those individuals at the intersection of multiple oppressions—in Beard's case, as a Black working-class woman from the rural South—develop the knowledge necessary to overcome them and to imagine a more equitable world.[9] After Hurricane Katrina, when the state had dismissed over 7,500 UTNO educators and was just beginning to privatize the schools, Beard received a call from UTNO president Larry Carter. "Ms. Beard," she remembers him saying, "we need you in Baton Rouge. You have testified before in the legislature about conditions for para educators and the schools' conditions." When she received the call, Beard was in the process of moving back to New Orleans from Maryland—where her daughter lived and to whom she fled when she had to evacuate—but Carter convinced her to stop in Baton Rouge on the drive home to testify. She spoke to the legislature about the trauma of being fired in the wake of the storm and the loss of health insurance, moves that hit her especially hard because her husband had passed away the year before. She remembers saying, "If your mother was a teacher and was terminated, would you want to remove every benefit from her [while she's] at her worst? Have some compassion and help us get some legislation passed to help us get reorganized and get our schools back."[10] Throughout her life, Beard had fought for political emancipation and justice for Black and working-class families and children, and much of that was channeled through the union and the schools. The democratic structure of UTNO, as well as UTNO leaders' commitment to developing working-class members, helped Beard develop her voice and ascend into leadership.

UTNO's commitment to participatory democracy derived from its connection to the civil rights movement as well as from Nat LaCour's leadership style, and it was key to its strength and success. Most members did not just join UTNO, they also worked for the union, sang its virtues, coordinated its programs, campaigned for the candidates it endorsed, and participated in its protests, rallies, and events. Through their involvement in these activities, members honed their political analysis, grew into leadership roles, and became fiercely loyal to the union. Many of these leaders were women: "We may not have been president, but it was women who did the work."[11] The union created a leadership pipeline that primed members to organize their peers, take on additional union roles, and become politically engaged in their communities more generally. UTNO was successful in pushing back against austerity and neoliberal education reforms because it had so many members willing to commit their time and even put their jobs on the line to fight for what they saw as just.

Twenty years after *Brown v. Board of Education*, processes of white flight were well underway in New Orleans. Though segregationists had delayed school integration significantly, limiting it to only four Black children in 1960 and slowing its growth to a snail's pace in the years that followed, court orders sped up the process in the late 1960s, and faculty integration was complete by 1974.[12] Meanwhile, liberal white mayor Moon Landrieu (1970–78) had desegregated city hall, while quieter struggles resulted in the desegregation of the public libraries, parks, and pools.[13] Just as Black candidates began to experience electoral success—with New Orleans electing its first Black city council member in 1976 and its first Black mayor in 1978—and schools experienced a few brief years of genuine integration, white people began to leave the city, taking their economic resources and taxable incomes with them. Nearly 100,000 white people left New Orleans between 1970 and 1980, a loss of approximately 30 percent of the white population. Another 100,000 white residents left by 2000; they went from constituting 62.6 percent of the city's population in 1960 to only 22.6 percent in 2000 (see graph 2.1).[14] The white public school population declined even more rapidly, as white parents placed their children in private and parochial schools, some of which had been set up specifically to preserve segregation.[15] The white population in the public schools declined by over 60 percent, so that by the 1979–80 school year, there were only 14,079 white children enrolled in the public schools. In a district that was nearly 85 percent Black, its few white students clustered mostly into selective-admission magnet schools, and most Black public school children continued to attend deeply segregated schools.[16] Yet the 1970s and early 1980s remained times of hopeful growth for UTNO, as the city and its schools had yet to feel the full impact of white departure and programs of fiscal austerity.

In the early 1970s, Jim Randels attended Beauregard Junior High—named after the Confederate general—in the brief years that it was genuinely integrated. Though he experienced his first Black teacher at his all-white elementary school, the result of faculty integration, at Beauregard he attended classes alongside Black and Latino peers. "It was very much a working-class school. So I was very fortunate. It was one of the few times in the city when you could go to a neighborhood school and have it be integrated just by the residential patterns . . . and so there were a lot of interesting lessons in that."[17] Gene Geisert, the white superintendent of schools from 1971 to 1980, felt that the Black community was

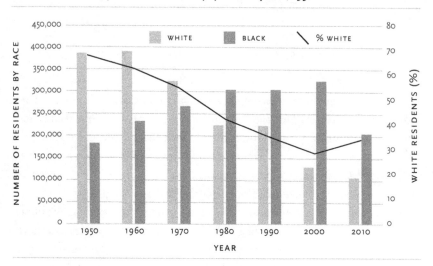

Graph 2.1. New Orleans population by race, 1950–2010

Source: US Census Bureau, *Profile of General Demographic Characteristics: Race and Hispanic Origin*, Decennial Census: 1950, 1960, 1970, 1980, 1990, 2000, 2010, https://data.census.gov/.

much more supportive of the public schools: "We had a terrible time keeping white teachers and parents. They did not want to integrate."[18] However, he believed that in order to keep white parents sending their children to the public schools, he had to maintain a 50–50 racial balance among the faculty—a difficult mission when white teachers who had been transferred to Black schools kept leaving the district: "I lost most of my white teachers. They left for Jefferson Parish and elsewhere. The Catholic schools picked them up. I had a very difficult time trying to keep a balance in my schools because I didn't want to go all Black. So I went all over the country. I went to San Francisco and New Jersey and all over trying to recruit teachers to come to New Orleans. And I had a set-up for them. If they'd come, I'd find them a house and get them settled and have them work here."[19] Along with failing to keep white students enrolled in the public schools, Geisert's recruitment efforts angered some Black teachers, who alleged that "incompetent teachers are being hired to fulfill race requirements" and "good black teachers with degrees are being displaced to achieve racial balance." They further complained that out-of-town teachers were "not very friendly."[20] Geisert did, however, open two selective-admissions schools that successfully retained some white students: McMain, which operated on a racial quota system, and the New Orleans Center for Creative Arts (NOCCA), which accepted students who were judged gifted in an artistic medium.

As white people fled the city and the schools, Black political power began to coalesce. The 1970 election of Moon Landrieu demonstrated the growing influence of Black voters and, in 1978, the city had its first serious Black candidate for mayor in Creole lawyer and politician Dutch Morial. Morial had a long civil rights history: he was the first Black graduate of Louisiana State University (LSU) Law School,[21] litigated civil rights cases with A. P. Tureaud, and had been president of the local NAACP.[22] Though Morial successfully brought more Black people into government jobs and assisted the Black middle class, like many Black mayors at the time, he was constrained by economic and legal limitations and did little to improve the condition of the Black poor.[23] By 1985, toward the end of Morial's eight-year tenure, Black median family income was only $10,516 (approximately $29, 800 in 2023 dollars), less than half that of white families. With the percentage of Black families rapidly increasing in the parish, this meant a declining tax base for city services.[24] Political scientist Adolph Reed argues that a politics of racial advancement tends to rely on nonparticipatory and undemocratic "elite custodianship" that does not reflect the diversity of Black life or center the Black poor and working class.[25] Morial opened up new opportunities for UTNO and generally supported the union's efforts, but his election did little to stymie growing issues of poverty and inequity in the city and the schools.

However, UTNO's collective bargaining campaign inspired other labor activism that directly improved conditions for Black workers. As the largest union in the area, UTNO played a significant role in the local AFL-CIO's central body. In this realm, it pushed the labor movement to the left, toward campaigns benefiting Black and working-class people, and away from the less radical concerns of the building trades, whose constituency was mostly white men. UTNO prompted labor leaders at both the city and the state levels to take seriously the concerns of women, Black people, and public sector workers, the demographics they represented.[26] Moreover, UTNO's success inspired organizing in other parishes—several of which later secured teacher CBAs of their own—as well as in other industries, especially those connected to education. In November 1974, just eight months after OPSB granted UTNO its collective bargaining election, school maintenance workers and bus drivers won collective bargaining with the Teamsters and school custodians organized with AFSCME.[27] AFSCME was one of the main unions organizing public sector workers and, especially under the leadership of Jerry Wurf (1964–81), was a leftist union committed to interracial organizing and civil rights. Wurf, for example, was in Memphis supporting the sanitation workers' strike when Martin Luther King Jr. was assassinated. Though AFSCME was a powerful national union and the fastest growing public sector union in the country, the AFSCME locals in New Orleans remained relatively weak and mostly piggybacked on UTNO's campaigns.[28]

UTNO encouraged this organizing and, after the successful elections, LaCour proclaimed, "The vote should also extend collective bargaining rights to other employees, such as paraprofessionals, secretaries, clerks and cafeteria workers."[29]

Before UTNO's first teacher contract was even ratified, Nina Marchand, the paraprofessionals' representative to UTNO, officially petitioned the board for a collective bargaining election of their own. When the board delayed, insisting that they needed to first resolve the teachers' contract, Marchand defiantly announced, "I don't think the paraprofessionals are going to stand by and let the board push them aside."[30] Many paraprofessionals had been active in the teachers' collective bargaining campaign and had even participated in "sick-outs" to support them.[31] OPSB set the paraprofessionals' election for March 1975, and they voted 898 to 40 for UTNO to represent them—months before the teachers' first contract was finalized.[32]

The paraprofessionals, as a feminized workforce, were particularly marginalized in the school system prior to their 1975 contract. They worked on at-will, year-long contracts, accrued no sick time, and were fired if they became pregnant. All paraprofessionals made $300 per month regardless of their level of education or years of experience. In some schools, they were required to wear uniforms. According to an UTNO brochure, "Many paras served as errand girls, running personal errands for the principal and teachers."[33] The same document laments that some paraprofessionals were forced to recruit children for pre-K, which ironically became part of educators' job descriptions again after Hurricane Katrina. Even once they won a contract, paraprofessionals earned less than half the salary of teachers. In fall 1977, a teacher with a bachelor's degree and 0 years of experience made $10,096 ($28,630 in 2023 dollars), while a para with 0 years of experience made $4,790 ($13,583 in 2023 dollars).[34] Despite their continued low pay, the UTNO contract significantly improved the paraprofessionals' salaries, benefits, and working conditions, and perhaps most importantly, it gave them a means of redress when they were mistreated in the workplace. They became some of the union's most active and loyal members and benefited immensely from ongoing union victories.

Less than a year after the paraprofessionals won their election, school cafeteria workers also secured collective bargaining, choosing AFSCME as their bargaining agent.[35] Though these locals were smaller and less powerful than UTNO, union density tends to create a "moral economy" of fair pay and working conditions, which improves workers' salaries across the sector, even for nonunionized employees.[36]

In December 1974, teachers in Jefferson Parish announced they would launch a campaign for collective bargaining that spring. Jefferson Parish neighbors Orleans Parish; but, especially at that time, it had a much whiter student and teacher population as it had absorbed many of the white families fleeing Orleans Parish following integration. Jan Skelton, who was then a teacher in Jefferson Parish and who later became JFT president, described the parish as "very conservative . . . much more conservative than it is now, although it still is."[37] Though the JFT had successfully worked to elect pro-union school board candidates, they represented fewer than 50 percent of the teachers in the parish and would face the all-white LTA in the upcoming election.[38] Nonetheless, the JFT persevered in the election that April, making Jefferson the second parish in the state to obtain collective bargaining.[39] In no small part due to UTNO's influence, New Orleans still had the highest union density of any southern city in 2004, at 8.5 percent.[40] A strong labor movement serves to counteract the influence of business elites, mobilize the working class, and democratize political decision-making.

Though UTNO successfully inspired others, getting its own contract ratified proved to be a struggle. However, the union used this process to increase member involvement and develop new leaders. Its original demands were a mixture of bread-and-butter union asks, such as improved pay and benefits and a workable grievance procedure as well as improvements intended to assist children and teachers in the classroom, such as a librarian and a counselor in each school and teacher voice in developing the reading curriculum.[41] LaCour assembled a bargaining team of ten teachers, three union staff members, and one professional negotiator from the AFT: "We had a bargaining team of probably ten to twelve people, high school teachers, elementary teachers, young, old, Black, white. Nat made it—this was not going to be the Nat LaCour or the Nat and staff show. This was going to be the teachers' union. And so he had everything from first-year teachers to veterans. Now, he just didn't pick them at random. He knew what he was doing."[42] The *Times Picayune* latched onto UTNO's salary demands and desire for duty-free lunch and planning periods and blasted the union for wanting to "erect a wall between teachers and children," suggesting that the paper saw teachers more as feminized caretakers than as professional workers.[43] Karen Walk Geisert was a teacher added to the negotiating team when another member fell ill. She remembers those first negotiations as chaotic and exciting:

> We had a lot of time to prepare. We had notebooks, like binders, this big [gestures] with all of the articles that we wanted to negotiate. So we had the specific disciplines [i.e., math, science, etc.] writing things, and then we had just the general ones like the grievance procedure, and all those things. We would study them from all the other places, and then we'd write it up, and then we'd bring it in there, and they'd critique it. . . . And so [the binder] was just massive because we were starting from scratch. It wasn't like a renegotiation where you already had the basics. And we were covering paraprofessionals as well as teachers. So we had a paraprofessional bargaining team, and some of us would go in with them too to help. It was all new. Nobody had ever done it before.[44]

Walk Geisert and other teachers who participated remembered sleepless nights in a shared hotel room, trying to hammer out the details of the contract.

The bargaining process was drawn out and slow and, to apply additional pressure, UTNO membership voted to strike if the contract was not ratified by the beginning of the 1975–76 school year.[45] Yet again, the union used the threat of disruption and protest to move management on their demands—a threat that was taken seriously because of the massive member participation UTNO had previously demonstrated. School board president Lloyd Rittiner said the vote "makes no difference," but the board threatened reprisals against striking employees, suggesting that they were actually rattled by strike possibility.[46] The strike vote led the *Times Picayune* to accuse the union of being led by outside agitators from the AFT, as if in disbelief that such union militancy could be homegrown: "One of the characteristics of the AFT is that its negotiator always insists on complete control of the local bargaining conditions. One of the characteristics of teacher unionization in New Orleans has been that the national AFT has had entirely too much control, as if New Orleans were a colony, and called two unsuccessful strikes in 1966 and 1969."[47] Though the union had certainly been inspired by AFT militancy in New York and across the country, it had no shortage of examples of local activism from civil rights veterans born and raised in New Orleans.[48]

Opposition to the union would repeatedly project this framework: insistence that UTNO's decisions were made unilaterally by the national AFT, or even by LaCour alone, despite the union's ongoing commitment to participatory democratic decision-making. UTNO staffer Fred Skelton recalls the first contract negotiations: "The AFT sent someone in . . . [who] stayed with us, and gave us good advice, wasn't dictatorial, came to the bargaining table, but basically said to Nat, 'You're the talker here. I'll sit here and give you advice if you need it. But you're the spokesman for this organization.' And we grew to really, really like that, that this wasn't somebody coming in and telling us what to do."[49] Teacher Patti Reynolds, who was on the bargaining team in later UTNO negotiations, recalls a similar phenomenon:

UTNO is the most direct democratic thing I have ever been in in my life. . . . [The 1990 strike] meeting is another example of where we took a break and some of us came out of the meeting to use the restroom or whatever, and there were people from the administration who were sitting in a lounge area outside of where we were meeting. Some of them, probably most of them, were people that were on the negotiating team that we had been negotiating with in the prior days. One of them, who was a principal, asked me as we were walking by, "What are you all doing in there? You all have been in there for hours," and was aghast when I said, "We are trying to decide what to do." Again, his assumption was that Nat was going to tell people what to do.[50]

By involving teachers in the process, LaCour helped develop their leadership skills and increase their buy-in to the union. Moreover, the collaborative bargaining team ensured that decisions were authentic and came from members themselves.

Beth Butler, who moved to New Orleans in 1980 to work for the community organization ACORN (Association of Community Organizations for Reform Now),[51] recalls that many of the working-class leaders in the New Orleans chapter were UTNO paraprofessionals, including longtime ACORN president Geraldine Bell. Butler says that the paraprofessionals' presence in ACORN was advantageous: "They already had tremendous training because they're used to running a classroom, and understood the dynamics of that. . . . And also that Nat had trained them in how to do negotiations. . . . Certainly they knew that you had to be organized and you had to get everybody on the same page, and that you had to move people from a point of either fear or lack of comfort into direct action, so that they could experience becoming stronger and working together as a group."[52] These skills, which developed paraprofessionals into leaders in the union and in their classrooms, also proved indispensable in their work fighting for economic and racial justice in their communities. LaCour was committed to this model of negotiating, even when it slowed the process down. Frank Fudesco became chief negotiator for the school board in the mid-1980s and was responsible for negotiating contracts with all the different groups that had collective bargaining. He recalls that he would assemble a team with a few principals that stayed mostly the same regardless of the group he was negotiating with, "But Nat's team was constantly changing. I'm sitting with teachers; he's got all teachers. I'm talking about secretaries, he's got all the secretaries, I'm sitting with paraprofessionals, he's got all paraprofessionals on his team. He had a bigger job, trust me."[53] Not only did this strategy ensure that LaCour was prioritizing the issues most important to the constituents in each group, it also provided a forum for consensus-building and group decision-making.

LaCour also prioritized "deliberative talk" and fostered a culture in which everyone was encouraged to participate. Deliberative talk is a method used by organizers to allow participants to reach mutually agreed-upon decisions, gain a better understanding of the issue in question, and avoid reproducing inequalities, and it leads to heightened trust in the organization or outcome.[54] Joe DeRose, a teacher who became communications director for the union, recalls that this was an explicit strategy: "Even at executive council meetings, [Nat] made a point of never speaking first. He would lay out the situation, allow everybody who wanted to have their input, he said, 'Because you never know what ideas are going to come, even from the person who you think is least likely to have a good idea. They might have a good idea that comes out, and maybe that will change my thinking.'"[55] This strategy might have taken longer than LaCour simply stating his opinion from the outset, but it also encouraged participatory decision-making and prevented the organization from becoming an oligarchy. Mike Stone remembers this technique more bluntly: "He could sit for hours with every wacko person on the council or in a committee or whatever and listen to what they had to say and take a little bit of this, a little bit of that, and come up with something that was satisfactory to everybody."[56] LaCour was a visionary in his own right, yet had the patience to insist on a democratic practice that ultimately increased the union's strength: "He might have had it in his mind where he wanted to go, but he made everybody feel empowered that what they had to say could maybe change his viewpoint on how he was going to approach something."[57] Juanita Bailey started teaching in 1995, just four years before LaCour left for the national AFT. Even at this point, twenty-four years into his presidency, LaCour made sure that people felt comfortable questioning and participating: "He wielded a lot of respect. I say that because when he spoke, you could hear a pin drop in the room. It was after meetings, like you asked the perfect question. He went up and had conversations with people, and he shook people's hands. 'How's it going for you?'"[58] Rank-and-file members, as well as building reps and members of the executive council, genuinely felt like LaCour cared about them, valued their opinions, and would prioritize the issues they valued. This was key to the union's strength, as labor educators Mike Parker and Martha Gruelle explain: "Democracy with its mistakes and inefficiencies works better than any other arrangement."[59]

By June 1975, it became clear that one major sticking point for the union and the board in reaching a contract was over "binding arbitration," or a clause that would mandate that the board submit to outside judgment on disputes rather than simply taking that judgment "under advisement."[60] LaCour explains, "What makes a contract strong is to have a good grievance procedure. And a grievance procedure is strong if, in the final step, you can submit a grievance that hasn't been resolved to binding arbitration."[61] However, UTNO also still had to resolve issues around pay as well as several other policies. Orleans Parish teachers remained woefully underpaid; they earned less than their peers in most other major southern cities and less than their peers in other parishes in Louisiana.[62] Though the union had originally asked for a 37 percent pay raise, which would have brought teachers to the national average in terms of pay at the cost of $15.7 million, it expected to negotiate around the issue. The union was often lambasted in the press for making seemingly outrageous demands that it intended to use only as bargaining chips. Teacher and union leader Brenda Mitchell explains: "One of the main things that people forget is that collective bargaining is not just the union getting what it wants. Collective bargaining is a negotiation between the union and the school board. It's like for any good marriage, it's two people coming together. Sometimes you get along, you might have a little argument but here's a way to ameliorate that, you know. . . . But it is a mutual negotiation between two parties and some of your issues you win and some you lose on both sides."[63] Though the process was inherently adversarial, Geisert, LaCour, and the members of their negotiating teams developed good working relationships. Geisert enjoyed negotiating with LaCour: "[Nat] had very little experience as a negotiator, but he was real. There was nothing sneaky about him. He laid it out."[64]

In June 1975, over the objections of board president Rittiner, the school board passed a budget that left room to potentially offer teachers pay raises. Rittiner was outraged by the board's decision to cut student services to enable teacher pay raises, but even the usually anti-union *Times Picayune* pointed out that a teachers' strike would rob students in order to *not* pay teachers.[65] The board's united front fell apart, and they succumbed to infighting. Rittiner later said that supporting his fellow board member Woody Koppel was "one of the biggest mistakes of my life."[66] The budget the board passed did not include money desperately needed to repair dilapidated and unsafe schools, leading some to speculate that the facilities might be closed by the state due to inadequate conditions.[67] The board—and the teachers, to some extent—were in a bind: they needed more money from the city or the state to adequately fund both their educational programming and employee salaries and benefits, but they had trouble getting residents to vote for an increase in taxes to fund education, and the state's funding formulas did not allocate extra money to districts struggling to serve students living in poverty. Despite the board's budget, the slow pace of negotiations led the union to believe that a late-August strike was a real possibility. UTNO sent out a bulletin to teachers with advice on how to prepare, such as preemptively applying for food stamps: "Hints for summer are: . . . Divest yourself of as many debts as possible . . . Cut your expenses to the minimum . . . Write your creditors explaining that there is a possibility you may be on strike come September and arrange for a postponement of payments . . . Establish credit with grocers and butchers . . . Take a job during the summer months."[68]

Later that June, UTNO formally requested that an outside mediator join the negotiations as the board was refusing to negotiate at all around salary and fringe benefits, binding arbitration, or working conditions for employees in special categories such as coaches or librarians.[69] Though negotiations had been moved out of school board offices and to a neutral location and a federal mediator had been called in, by early August, a strike looked "almost certain."[70] UTNO began painting picket signs and assigning strike captains and announced to the press that ninety-eight issues remained to be resolved.[71] The *Times Picayune* seemed most upset at the public's apathy about the upcoming strike, noting that although 30 percent of families send their children to private or parochial schools, public schools are still vital to the city's future.[72] They bemoaned the middle-class transfer of loyalties away from the public schools, resulting in a poor student population that "will have to be funded by a taxpaying public with no direct stakes in the public schools."[73] Amid this buildup, OPSB signed a contract with the Teamsters (covering bus drivers and maintenance workers) that included an 8 percent raise and advisory—not binding—arbitration. As part of the contract, the Teamsters promised to report to work even if UTNO went on strike.[74] Geisert claimed that the Teamsters' contract demonstrated OPSB's willingness to bargain in good faith, and Rittiner said, more pointedly, "This will be the first labor contract in the history of the Orleans Parish School Board and demonstrates reasonableness and equity in the ability of the Board to reach accord with an experienced Union. . . . I am especially pleased that . . . we can also report a firm commitment by these employees to be on the job regardless of an effort by any other Union to strike the school system."[75] The next day, the board ratified their contract with AFSCME, who then represented just school custodians, also with a "no-strike" clause; however, an AFSCME representative said, "I don't think our people are going to cross picket lines."[76]

As the August 25 strike deadline approached, the board sent letters to teachers threatening to fire them if they went on strike and alleging that strikes by public sector workers were illegal. The day before the deadline, the union and the school board finally agreed on a contract. Teachers and paraprofessionals had packed the municipal auditorium, waiting to hear the report from LaCour about whether they would strike the next morning. "At 4:30 p.m., the UTNO bargaining team made a dramatic late entrance into the auditorium. Teachers tried to read their faces but could not. Tension mounted. . . . Finally, [LaCour] announced that at 4:15 the contract had been settled. The cheer that greeted the announcement was one of relief as much as anything else."[77] Though teachers won a modest raise, most of it actually came from the state, as Democratic governor Edwin Edwards had passed a statewide teacher pay raise earlier that year. The teachers' most notable achievement was binding arbitration. Also guaranteed in the first contract were a thirty-minute duty-free lunch break, a classroom supplies fund for individual teachers, five-dollar-per-hour extracurricular pay, and an increase in the board's share of hospitalization insurance. Though they did not succeed in winning a reduction in class sizes, the board promised not to increase them.[78] Paraprofessionals won a pay raise, greater job security, and the ability to accrue sick leave. The two contracts were approved overwhelmingly by UTNO membership.[79] The threat of disruption had played no small role in the eventual contract resolution.

Both UTNO and OPSB seemed happy and relieved with the contracts.[80] Though UTNO would be accused of fighting narrowly for teachers' interests, sometimes at the expense of the students they served, the *Times Picayune* editorialized that students and parents were well-served in the contract. Drawing on the legacy of civil rights unions, UTNO had fought for changes that would benefit both educators and families who used the schools. The board had agreed to set up a citywide committee to study discipline that would offer parents and students spots, giving them voice in district-wide discipline procedures. UTNO also argued for reforms to special education services that would benefit students and involve parents, including mandatory parent conferences every three years. All kindergarten classes would be guaranteed a play area, the confidentiality of student-counselor relationships would be maintained, and the use of the public address system would be reduced. The *Times Picayune* piece ends with the following: "When one compares the contract to the original demands, it is surprising how many student and community benefits are allowed in the final product. It is also surprising how few of the working conditions and fringe benefits demanded by the union were won."[81] The student-centered demands described above also reflect the ways in which LaCour and the negotiating team solicited input and took seriously the concerns of different constituencies within the union. Clearly, school counselors, coaches, special education teachers, and kindergarten teachers were consulted and invited to share suggestions that would improve their working conditions and improve education for their students. UTNO formalized this by setting up a committee for each special group. UTNO staffer Fred Skelton recalls: "We would get together with [each group] and say to them, what would you like to get in the contract? 'Well, we don't know.' We'd show them contracts from other places. And they would then discuss among themselves."[82] This structure allowed UTNO to maintain the involvement of a significant number of members, even when they were not directly participating on the negotiating team.

The contract was controversial because it repurposed money from facilities and educational programming to fund employee salaries—though this had not been UTNO's intention—and it also demonstrated a shift in the union's framework on discipline. In the late 1960s, UTNO had joined community groups to protest the "frivolous" discipline of Black students as well as the disproportionately harsh punishments they received for legitimate protests.[83] However, in part due to the influence of white teachers who had joined the union, in the first contract negotiation, UTNO argued for harsher discipline policies, including establishing a teacher's right to remove disruptive students from the classroom, mandating that the removed child be held in the office for at least an hour, and setting up special classes or schools to handle chronically disruptive students.[84] At one point, the union also asked for a policy that would mandate that administrators call the police for a list of serious offenses, regardless of the child's age.[85] Though these demands were not finalized in the contract, they speak to UTNO's shift toward viewing student discipline as a serious problem facing teachers and schools, without serious consideration of the impact of such policies on Black children vulnerable to incarceration.

In its shift toward more punitive school discipline, UTNO was mirroring a national trend. The federal Safe Schools Act of 1971 encouraged districts to create school security plans and included funding for policing and surveillance in schools. Al Shanker, then president of the New York City UFT and soon-to-be president of the national AFT, testified in Congress in support of the bill. Shanker's AFT went on to support the zero tolerance policies of the 1980s that contributed to the creation of a racially discriminatory school-to-prison pipeline that still exists today.[86] LaCour argued that UTNO put a discipline policy in the contract in order to make sure that it was consistently enforced, not to create a more punitive environment for students, but he later explained, "It was a period of time around the country with the unions engaging in what they called 'zero tolerance.'"[87] Mack Spears—a staunch anti-unionist and in 1975 still the only Black school board member—voted against the contract in part because he thought tougher discipline guidelines would hurt Black and poor students.[88] This concern was warranted; legal scholar James Forman has traced the ways in which Black communities—especially middle class ones—helped drive the rise in mass incarceration. Though UTNO did not support some of the more controversial programs Forman describes, such as stop and frisk policing or mandatory minimum sentences, the union did advocate for policies that sought to push disruptive children out of mainstream classrooms.[89]

Racialized reports on the lack of discipline in schools had ramped up since faculty integration. For example, a March 1975 letter to the *Times Picayune* reads, "They don't need security guards only [at my school], but just about everywhere. Teachers are beaten up and have to stay in the hospital for several months; a garbage can full of garbage is thrown in the classroom; the students refuse to pay attention and read magazines. White teachers are used to being addressed as 'you white b—.' A teacher cannot reprimand students."[90] Similarly, in response to a 1973 survey produced by Superintendent Geisert to assess the success of faculty integration, teachers wrote comments such as, "the usual methods of discipline don't work in an all-Black school"; "this school draws students from a federal project where children have nothing to keep them occupied except to learn to commit crimes"; and "Blacks constantly harass white children."[91] These reports, though racially biased, reflect national studies that found an uptick in violence and assaults against teachers.[92] Such complaints, from both within and outside of the union, pushed UTNO to take action on discipline that diverged from its earlier alliances with Black students and families. Growing its membership allowed UTNO to exercise renewed political strength and win a strong contract, but it also required compromises in its commitment to supporting the larger working-class Black community.[93]

While UTNO's leadership worked to counteract external opposition to the union, it also had to address internal dissent. Though the first contract had been a victory in many respects, especially the union's win on binding arbitration, the raises for teachers and paraprofessionals had not been significant and both still earned less than many of their peers in other cities and parishes. "Actually, the first contract was not much of a contract. We didn't know what we were doing. I mean, it was okay, but I don't think it provided a raise. And we got some backlash from some of the rank and file that you go out to the schools and you're talking, but we didn't get a raise. And so we knew that this next contract we had to deliver."[94] The following year, in 1976, UTNO demanded a 7 percent raise along with increased board contributions to hospitalization insurance; but the board insisted it had no money.[95] To increase pressure, approximately 1,000 teachers attended an OPSB meeting demanding pay raises and theatrically demonstrating their displeasure. LaCour compared New Orleans's salaries to other major cities and then announced, "We would like to present the board with something indicating our opinion of its position at the negotiating table," whereupon teachers released hundreds of balloons filled with hot air. Next, he said, "We would like to present you with something indicating what we think of our pay," and the teachers handed the board members packets of peanuts.[96] The *Times Picayune*, unamused by the union's tactics, said that teachers had behaved like "unruly children" and should "expect dire consequences."[97] Though these tactics were intended to be humorous, they also displayed the union's ongoing commitment to disruptive action that challenged the status quo. Following the meeting, UTNO briefly hinted at a strike but decided against it, and instead launched a public campaign to promote the salary demands, which included picketing schools and educating the public.[98]

By early 1977, both the union and the board knew that they needed to find new revenues for the upcoming contract renegotiation. Superintendent Geisert threatened to cut academic or athletic programs to fund teacher raises if additional funds were not found, and LaCour bemoaned the state of the schools, "The economic condition of this school district presents an unusually difficult bargaining climate. Inadequate revenues have resulted in budget cuts in personnel, programs, supplies, and student services."[99] LaCour asked the board to call a millage election to produce additional funding, but the board refused.[100] Even the *Times Picayune* seemed sympathetic to the teachers' pay woes, running a profile piece about teacher in her fifth year who worked a summer job and was still eligible for food stamps.[101] As the start of the 1977–78 school year drew near, the union started hinting yet again that it might strike, and it also ran a series of advertisements in the paper intending to influence public opinion in

UTNO members attend an **OPSB** meeting in 1976 carrying balloons filled with "hot air." They released the balloons when Nat LaCour asked the room what they thought about the board's position at the negotiating table. *Courtesy of United Teachers of New Orleans.*

its favor. The ads argued that people mistakenly believed that the schools had gotten worse, but actually more middle- and upper-class parents had taken their children out of the schools, resulting in declining test scores.[102] This had been combined with campaigns mounted by "die-hard segregationists who want to see public education fail" and newspapers that focused only on the negative aspects of education.[103] UTNO asked the public to support greater funding for the schools and to get involved in positive ways: "Some people express the feeling that the white citizens in our community will not support a public school system with predominantly black students. Others say parents of children in parochial and private schools will not vote to raise taxes for public schools . . . as dedicated teachers we do not believe these stories hold true for a majority of the people in New Orleans. We still believe you care."[104] While UTNO rallied for more school funding and higher salaries, OPSB proposed salary cuts, including taking away the extra compensation paid to coaches and special education teachers.[105]

The union ramped up its strike talk, marched to city hall, and held a rally at the municipal auditorium that was attended by more than 2,000 educators.[106] However, when Governor Edwards gave teachers a statewide $1,500 pay raise, the union abandoned its salary demand.[107] UTNO settled the contract with a promise that the OPSB would hold a millage election in the spring, an increase in the board's contribution to employee hospitalization insurance, and most

Table 2.1. Comparison of teachers' and superintendents' salaries, 1977

	TEACHERS' SALARY ($)		
CITY	BEGINNING (WITH BACHELOR'S DEGREE)	MAXIMUM (WITH MASTER'S DEGREE)	SUPERINTENDENTS' SALARY ($)
Atlanta	8,832	15,168	42,000
Boston	10,358	18,685	51,000
Chicago	11,000	21,075	56,000
Columbus, OH	9,540	18,317	44,500
Dallas	9,336	21,006	47,500
Hartford, CT	9,831	17,054	45,000
Houston	9,300	15,000	53,000
Memphis	9,080	14,820	40,248
Miami	9,164	16,867	47,250
Nashville	9,150	15,372	40,000
New Orleans	8,596	13,058	47,088
New York City	9,700	18,500	53,000
Philadelphia	9,390	20,987	46,000
St. Louis	9,000	17,100	48,000
Washington, DC	11,045	21,546	44,000

Source: UTNO compilation based on research sources provided by the American Association of School Administrators, Educational Research Service, and the American Federation of Teachers Research Department Teacher salaries in June 1977, prior to Governor Edward's $1,500 pay raise. "Teacher Salaries . . . Why the Big Difference?" (advertisement), *Times Picayune*, August 21, 1977.

importantly, the creation of a $50,000 Health and Welfare Fund, the first of its kind in the South.[108] This fund, which provided medical and vision insurance as well as other benefits for UTNO members, was an attempt by the union to create a more meaningful social safety net through the bargaining process. Though UTNO had pressured the board into calling the millage election, it remained unclear if that strategy would result in additional funds for teachers or the schools. Voters had not passed a millage for the schools in the previous twenty-five years, and a board-sponsored survey of voters' attitudes concluded, "The New Orleans public schools continue to be financially dependent on a majority of voters who have no personal investment with the schools."[109] Despite their successes, UTNO left the 1977 bargaining session without having secured significant raises for its members in either of its first two contracts. Moreover, those members remained underpaid compared to their counterparts in other major cities (see table 2.1).

Between the 1977 and 1978 bargaining sessions, Dutch Morial was elected mayor, UTNO disaffiliated from the NEA—to cut members' dues in half and also because a merger on the national level now looked unlikely—and substitute teachers, who were not represented by a union, successfully petitioned the board for a three-dollar-per-day raise.[110] But the board did not call the promised millage election, setting itself up yet another contract showdown with the union. Generally, attitudes were pessimistic about the state of the schools. Superintendent Geisert wrote a letter to the *Times Picayune* bemoaning the public's "low-grade hostility" toward the school system as well as the public's tendency "to expect the public schools to do poorly and discount their achievements."[111] Meanwhile, LaCour noted that Black schools remained racially segregated and now were becoming economically segregated as well, as the Black middle class had moved their children to private schools or integrated magnet schools.[112] OPSB held public hearings about its budget and received suggestions such as "becoming more effective in its use of the funds it already has."[113] The board had little to bargain with, a new mayor in the mix, and a teachers' union that was tired of delays.

Leading into the 1978 bargaining session, the board claimed it had no money for pay raises, and UTNO, again, threatened to strike. There were early hints that public opinion was shifting in its favor; the *Times Picayune* critiqued the board's refusal to negotiate on salaries at all and said it was "inviting a strike."[114] However, UTNO still had to convince its membership: "You remember this is a city where the teachers had gotten their behinds whipped in a strike seven years ago. Most of the staff had been there then, most of them, if they went on strike, they knew what it was like to lose, if they didn't go on strike, they knew what it was like to lose. So we didn't know what was going to happen when we went out."[115] Nonetheless, the board's financial offers remained far from UTNO's demands—UTNO asked for 9 percent raises at a cost of $5 million, and the board offered in return less than 1.5 percent raises, or $800,000. The board eventually raised its offer to $1 million, which the teachers called, "totally unacceptable, ridiculously low and far, far from being accepted."[116] Though the board offered significantly more, 4 percent raises, on the morning of the strike vote, the protest had already been set in motion and, for the first time since 1969, the teachers went on strike.

The beginning of the strike, as told by Geisert, portended ominous outcomes for the board:

> I met with Nat at the hotel, neutral ground. And we had an agreement, 5 percent raise, solid, no problems. But I couldn't do that without getting permission from the president of the board. So I called Dr. Mack Spears, who was the president of the board, and I said, "We have a contract agreement, all I need is your approval." [Spears' secretary] said, "He doesn't want to talk to you." And I said, "You go back and tell him that if he does not settle this, we're going to have a strike and it's not going to

be good." He came back and he said, "Dr. Spears said do not bother with another telephone call." So I didn't. And Nat struck and we had a terrific teachers' strike. I had a lot of experience on my side and Nat had a lot of experience and also had the community behind him pretty much. So it was a really tough battle between two people who really liked each other. But there was no alternative because the teachers had to strike. They couldn't get pay. The board didn't know what they were doing.[117]

Following this experience, Geisert advocated for the elimination of school boards altogether.[118] The landscape for teachers was very different than it had been in 1969, in large part due to the union—and specifically due to LaCour's political work. AFSCME, which represented custodians and cafeteria workers, had already settled its contract with the board and told its members to report to work but not to cross picket lines if they were set up, thus effectively expressing its solidarity with UTNO.[119] The Teamsters, on the other hand, rejected the board's salary offer and joined the teachers on the picket lines—an especially beneficial alliance for UTNO because the Teamsters represented the school bus drivers, who were crucial in bringing students to the classroom.[120] Both groups had a vested interest in the strike because of "me too" clauses in their contracts that guaranteed that their employees would receive whatever raises UTNO secured, further demonstrating UTNO's centrality in the labor movement.[121] Karen Walk Geisert remembers the Teamsters' presence on the picket lines:

> The Teamsters came to help us because the bus drivers would not cross the picket line. . . . But they were also kind of a lot more violent than we would have been. And I was twenty-seven, so I was worried that they wouldn't listen to me if it would get out of control. But they listened and they would say, like, "We're going to climb that telephone pole and turn off the power to the school." And I'd say, "Oh, well let's not do that yet." You know? "Let me get some tacks and they'll blow all the tires of people coming at you." "Oh no, let's not." But it ended up being fine. I mean it was good.[122]

Teachers who reported to work and principals complained about tacks left on the roadway, protesters trying to block food and mail delivery, and general threats and intimidation, but generally the picket lines were confrontational but peaceful.[123]

The union also had significantly more teacher support in 1978, which held through the entire length of the strike (August 30–September 11). Though only about 18 percent of teachers honored picket lines in 1969, nine years later UTNO had more than 70 percent of teachers participating in the strike. Moreover, unlike in 1969, when teachers trickled back into the classroom day by day, in 1978, more teachers called out when they saw the union's strength: "I knew that we were gonna win it because the majority of the teachers, system wide were on strike."[124] In the face of such teacher unity, the board confronted a public relations disaster. LaCour pointed out that administrators had been given large pay raises in 1977 and noted how that was not presented as money "stolen" from students, and he rejected the narrative that teachers were being selfish or uncaring toward their pupils.[125] Moreover, though the board was saving money by not paying striking teachers (substitutes earned much less per day), the board risked losing significant money from the state because of low student attendance, in part because of the bus drivers' solidarity. The board also made several missteps. Assistant Superintendent Jerry Hart fired nine cafeteria workers who refused to cross picket lines, announcing his decision on national television:

> Now if you take any employee group in a system and you say which employee group as a whole was most loyal, the cafeteria people would come to mind. And they did not want to cross the teachers' picket line and they were way underpaid anyway. At one of the schools, they were not crossing the picket line and Jerry Hart goes on national news and says, "In the name of the Orleans Parish School Board, I hereby terminate your employment." . . . That was just a big PR thing. Because here you have this out of state white male administrator over these African American, upper middle-aged ladies who were just good, hard working employees, underpaid. And you're just on national television pointing them out and saying they're fired.[126]

Superintendent Geisert, though likeable, also became a target for the union. He earned a disproportionately high salary and, as part of his contract, had also been given a board-sponsored BMW to drive: "And then we had a couple teachers with children who had to go on food stamps. So here you juxtapose in your picket line and you got one picture of a teacher and her children going to get their food stamps. And then on the other hand you've got a picture of the superintendent in his BMW."[127] Teachers were also supported by the NAACP, the JFT, and the local AFL-CIO, which donated to their strike fund.[128]

Though certainly parents and students held diverse views on the strike, the union received significant support from both groups, indicating its ongoing success in rallying the community behind their efforts. Parents picketed the OPSB offices and joined with faith leaders to voice their support for teachers' demands.[129] Another parent group, led by local civil rights icon Oretha Castle Haley, organized to recall the board and demand Geisert's resignation.[130] Wilson Boveland, then a teacher, said he experienced significant parent support at his school: "We had the support of the police, the other unions in the city and we had the support of the parents. We had parents that would come out and bring stuff to us as well. We had a lot of parents that kept their kids home from school."[131] Geisert saw student absences differently, suggesting that students were kept home not out of solidarity with teachers' demands but because parents "were afraid to send their kids."[132] Like many teachers, Connie Goodly remembered mixed parent reactions at her school: "There were parents who came out there and brought people food and joined them, walked on the lines with them. They had some people who were ugly, they would write ugly things and say ugly things, but for the most part, we had the support of the community. We had the support of the faith-based community. We had parents out there; they were with us. People would pass and honk their horns in support of what we were doing."[133] There was generally less teacher and parent support at magnet schools, which had a higher percentage of white and middle-class students. Diego Gonzalez-Grande taught at Ben Franklin High School, a mostly white magnet school that drew some of the highest achieving students in the district: "[My students] were sharp enough to understand that the strike was not directed at them. I did speak with parents who felt betrayed, who were angry that we had somehow betrayed the mission of the school. There was nothing, really, I could do about that. I just had to move on and continue teaching, once the strike was over."[134] Meanwhile, students at the mostly Black magnet high school McDonogh 35 formed a coalition to boycott classes and join picket lines to demand that teachers and the board resume negotiations.[135]

Principals also had mixed reactions to the strike, but many were supportive, especially those who were former union members themselves:

> Some principals understood because Maxine Copelin was a principal and a former strong union member at Carver, and she would buy refreshments for her teachers and all and say, "You're doing the right thing." When she was a teacher and we had our meetings on Carondelet Street, she was the one, when they had school board meetings, [who] would sit on the floor and block the entrance so the [board] members couldn't come in, and they would have to pick her up and carry her off for them to come in the board meetings . . . [so] she understood.[136]

Brenda Mitchell experienced a similar phenomenon at her school:

> I can remember this one incident when the principal at that time, who was formerly a member of the state federation herself, said, "Good morning everybody. The only person in the building is Ms. Bell and Ms. Bell I need you in the cafeteria." It was just really funny and we were outside on the line. So she was letting us know that everybody was out. It was a wonderful feeling. . . . We were young, very excited about making a difference in our work lives. The parents were coming around, they were supporting us and the kids would come by and wave. Then we had the

tacit support of the administration, so we felt like we were really doing the right thing.[137]

In part, principals anticipated that if teachers won the strike, they too would get pay increases and other job improvements: "[There] was just no animosity between the administration and the teachers. Some were like, they were encouraging us to do it because they knew that, the things that we were asking for, it was going to be better for them as well."[138] At the time, Frank Fudesco had just become principal at Lusher Elementary School, a mostly white magnet school. Though he adamantly opposed the strike, he did not take it personally: "100 percent of my teachers walked out. So, I was in the building alone with a bullhorn. It was kind of fun, actually."[139] A teacher who was hired at Lusher after the strike was told by his coworkers that Fudesco had orchestrated that outcome: "'Look, I don't care what you do,' [Fudesco] said, 'But my recommendation is that you all do the same thing.' And the teachers took that seriously, and they all went on strike except for one person. And supposedly that one person was somebody who they agreed would stay inside the school to kind of make sure that things didn't get so disrupted."[140] Fudesco later wrote his doctoral dissertation on the strike, analyzing why teachers chose to cross picket lines. He found that loyalty to the principal ranked very low in people's calculations.[141]

When Geisert entered the school system, one of his main concerns was that principals aligned themselves with teachers instead of considering themselves management. He recalls a meeting in which he explained to a group of principals, "You're management. You can't join the union. If you don't give me your best deal as a manager, I can't fire you because that was part of the law, but I'll put you down in there as the custodian in charge. . . . But you either decide whether you're management or not because I'm not going to have you up there not understanding what your role is, which is to run the school system."[142] Principals supported the strike by refusing to talk to the press or by not allowing reporters into the schools, and by not disputing Geisert's claim that real education was still occurring. Alan Guma was the principal of McMain, an integrated magnet middle and high school. He said it was "very difficult" inside the school during the strike, despite the board's claims to the contrary: "There were subs. Some parents, a lot of subs. There wasn't a lot of great teaching and learning going on. There couldn't be."[143]

The board continued to erode its support and underestimate the union. Several days into the strike, it performatively lowered its salary offer back to $1 million.[144] Mayor Morial tried to intervene to end the strike and met both with LaCour and OPSB president Mack Spears. He reported that LaCour was willing to return to the bargaining table but that Spears "did not indicate such a willingness."[145] Morial, though ostensibly trying to help resolve the situation, created some controversy through his involvement and seemed to favor the union.[146] Board member Rittiner complained, "The mayor seems to be doing everything in his power to sow discord and to confuse the people of New Orleans."[147] Public fighting between the mayor and the board strengthened UTNO's portrayal of itself as an organization outside the political fray and committed to fair wages and improving education. LaCour took advantage of the board's weakness: "I believe the overwhelming majority of the public believes the school board is wrong. The public now does identify with the plight of the teachers economically. . . . I am convinced there is solid community support behind the teachers, while the image of the school board has been tarnished."[148] One hundred students and parents formed picket lines outside board offices to protest its failure to give teachers raises and its prolonging of the strike.[149]

Though LaCour remained the public face of the union, the strike was organized to maximize teacher participation and worker democracy. Each building had a building rep, who would coordinate that school's picket lines, and then every group of eight to twelve schools was assigned an "area coordinator," who would travel between the schools, bring the protesters anything they needed, and help them increase educator participation. Grace Lomba, who taught at Lawless High, was an area coordinator during the 1978 strike:

> What the union did, they divided the schools into areas based on location of the school and we had people that were in charge—and when I say "in charge"—union members who voluntarily accepted these positions. I was pregnant at that time. I think I might have had ten schools and I would have to go around to all of the schools to check to make sure that the lines were set up and all those things that were involved with the strike, so I coordinated that area for the Lower Nine and Upper Nine and then we had other area coordinators.[150]

For many teachers, this was their first experience with union leadership. Paraprofessionals were also tapped to become area coordinators, as paraprofessional leader Jacqueline Johnson attests: "We would just go around to different schools seeing if everything was okay, if they needed anything, bringing them water, bringing sandwiches and different things like that. Making sure everybody was okay. And if somebody was kind of old and they couldn't do it, we'd take their place for a little while and walk."[151] This leadership development during the strike would inspire activism among the paraprofessionals that continued long past the job action, leading some, such as Geraldine Bell, to take leadership positions in community social justice groups, thus strengthening the connection between UTNO and other fights for justice in the city.[152]

At the end of each day, the union would hold rallies, which were widely attended, and each area coordinator would get up to speak: "They would ask the area coordinators to get up and give a report on the schools, how many people were on strike, how was people's morale."[153] This was an opportunity for teachers to practice public speaking and learn about organizing. Grace Lomba remembers when she gave her first report at an UTNO rally:

> I would get so frustrated because Lawless Elementary School did not have the kind of support I thought we should have had because there weren't enough teachers out on strike. So when I got to the mic to talk about the area I had supervised, I said to them, "You know what people, if y'all know anybody at Lawless Elementary, call them and tell them because they have poor support at that school." I didn't know I wasn't supposed to say that. Nat said, "Grace, no, you don't do that because you're giving information that should not be given as to the strength of the strike."[154]

At the rallies, the participatory and diverse leadership structure of the union was on full display, demonstrating for rank-and-file members new ways they could get involved and build power. It was also an opportunity for member education and development.

Teachers who were used to protesting, especially those who had been involved in civil rights protests, were generally unintimidated by the prospect of striking; both Wilson Boveland and Grace Lomba, for example, remembered the strike as "fun": "Crazy as it may seem, we had a lot of fun and some of us were really just sad that that strike had ended. But we didn't have any money."[155] UTNO offered teachers no-interest strike loans of $300 to help them make ends meet, with the AFL-CIO covering the cost of the interest.[156] These were widely popular and one UTNO staffer suggested that they played a decisive role in changing the tenor of the strike: when the board saw that educators had taken out over $1 million in strike loans, it realized that the teachers were determined to stay out until they won.[157] Boveland also was less stressed about the strike than many educators because he had a second source of income: "I also had a job working for 7/11 so that financially wasn't that big of a problem. We had just gotten married and everything, but we knew that [the strike] was coming down the pipe so we just saved our money."[158] Other teachers, not accustomed protesting and conflict and worried about money had a less enjoyable time on the picket lines. For example, one white teacher remembered:

> We walked the picket line for, it felt like it was weeks. It felt like months, truthfully, it was the scariest thing ever. People that you had worked with and you felt some positivity toward were just so mean to each other. I mean, very few people crossed the picket line there, it was a big time union school at Green. . . . They were so ugly to the people who did, it

was really hard. My roommate and I, when we'd go home, Susan would cry. She was just like, "It's so scary." It was so intense. Plus, you know, money, we were young and we were just scared about how long it would be. I mean, our parents could feed us on the weekends, but . . . But on the other hand, it bonded us with our coworkers in a way that nothing else could have, I'm sure. . . . It was intense, it was really intense, you know and we were young, so it was a big deal.[159]

The strike brought people to the picket lines who had never imagined themselves as protesters, and it demonstrated the power and value of collective action.

To some degree, emotions around striking split along racial lines. Linda Pichon, a Black paraprofessional, said that going on strike never inspired fear in her, partly because of her complete faith in her union rights: "[Fired] from going on strike? Oh no, you weren't supposed to get fired from going on strike. That was your right."[160] Fred Skelton remembers being shocked by the faith that members had in the organization:

It was a Saturday and teachers were coming to the office to sign up for something. And there was a line of teachers out the door and down the street. And we had been in the office preparing for negotiations. This was about three or four days into the strike. Well, we came out of there and the teachers began cheering. I mean, can you imagine how you feel when something like that occurs here? We were scared to death. We had 5,000 people on strike, if we lose, you know . . . ? How long can we do this? Will they stay . . . ? And we walked out of [the building] and teachers in the line began to cheer. And I mean, we were 10 feet tall.[161]

Despite their fears, their money problems, and threats from the board and superintendent, teachers stayed strong in their strike effort.

In the face of growing pressure from teachers, parents, community groups, and the mayor, the board capitulated. Eight school days into the strike, on September 11, the board agreed to 7 percent raises for teachers and a significant increase in its proportion of hospitalization coverage, an offer the union accepted.[162] The strike ended, according to the *Louisiana Weekly*, "with the majority of Black teachers literally getting what they demanded."[163] Geisert blamed Spears, who had rejected his initial 5 percent offer, and Mayor Morial, whom Geisert felt was meddling: "Dutch [Morial] wanted to run the school system. When he got elected, he sat down with my board and told them, basically, 'I'm going to tell you what to do.' And they sat there like Chinese terracotta warriors. They never said a word. I mean, he just ran them down. I couldn't believe it. And he did not like me. We had different approaches about how to run the school system. One time he said, 'Is somebody going to bell that cat?' Meaning me."[164] Following the strike,

UTNO educators and supporters march through the streets in the 1978 strike. Nat LaCour is in the front row, fifth from the left. *Courtesy of United Teachers of New Orleans.*

board member William Reeves published a column in the *Times Picayune* in which he accused the board and Mayor Morial of causing the strike: "The failure of the School Board to follow rational and proper decision-making procedures . . . poor decision-making caused the strike, the board's shortage of money and the disastrous settlement."[165] As the board, the mayor, and the superintendent continued to blame each other for the strike settlement, teachers and organized labor celebrated. Neighboring JFT gained 300 additional dues-paying members over the eight-day conflict, and one month later, nearby Plaquemines Parish chartered an NEA local.[166] Meanwhile, LaCour was greeted by "thunderous applause" whenever he spoke.[167]

However, soon the sobering realities of an underfunded school district began to set in. Though the board had saved some money by not paying striking teachers, it still had to make deep cuts to fund the salary increases. Over much community outcry, the district decided to shutter four elementary schools. Geisert saw the budget cuts as an opportunity: "It also gave me the opportunity then to start slashing the budget through the whole school system and it was important that happen because I had schools that were built back sixty years ago. They were falling apart. . . . They had no air conditioning. The roof leaked. The toilet was in the back yard of the school. They were terrible schools. They wouldn't let me close them. But after the strike was on, they didn't have any money."[168] Although LaCour, again, voiced his opinion that the solution was to find more money for the schools through additional taxes or other means, rather than to close schools and cut programming, the cuts inevitably positioned the union in conflict with the community.[169] Teachers, who also had a stake in supporting the schools, joined a "stormy protest" of more than 700 "angry predominantly Black citizens" at the board meeting discussing the closures.[170] Though this seems hypocritical on the surface, it represented a consistent political thread for the educators, who argued that higher salaries were key to retaining quality educators and improving the school system. The widely attended protest also reflects the educators' faith in collective action and democratic pressure following their experience with the strike. The schools were eventually closed, but no teachers lost their jobs. The board also cut the district's successful remedial reading program and threatened to cut its community advisory group.[171]

The striking teachers now had to return to work and confront their friends and coworkers who had crossed the picket lines. Though the union called for striking educators to return to work without animosity, tensions were high, and rhetoric on the picket lines had occasionally grown mean: "When you're in a public group in a protest, you can't control the behavior of everybody in the group. And there were some people that I like a lot, who let their emotions get the best of them and yelled really ugly stuff at our colleagues who were crossing the picket lines."[172] Even when confrontations had not occurred, there was resentment: "A lot of friendships with teachers broke down because friends went in, and you're on the line trying to get better benefits for everybody, because once you strike you can't just get it for the members, you've got to get it for everybody. I was more compassionate, but I was still a little bit upset."[173] Billie Dolce had just started teaching when UTNO called the strike, and she decided to cross the lines because she wanted to make sure her special education students were safe. She remembers being "taunted" by her friends who went on strike: "I crossed that picket line, but that was the last picket line I crossed. . . . They would tease you: 'You're no good, you're low down, you're a traitor, how can you do. . . . We need you. [If] more of us [stay] out, they will shut the school down.'"[174] Though teachers were not violent on the lines, they did harass their coworkers who were entering the schools. Ken Ducote recalls one particular incident:

> They had one teacher who crossed the picket line, because . . . she was an African American teacher, but she was above the riff raff that was going on strike kind of thing. They had a bunch of teachers that were real angry with her and they were going to pop her tires or something like that. I convinced them instead of doing anything like that, she's above us. So when she came in the next morning, we sprinkled flowers all over the sidewalk on the way to enter the door so she would be able to walk on flowers since she was so special.[175]

With such experiences only a week old, animosity flourished in the schools. Though this created a difficult environment in some buildings, it also reflected teachers' strong belief in the importance of the protest and the value of collective action.

Principals were instructed not to punish teachers who had participated in the strike, but Susie Beard remembers that there was some retribution: "[Some principals] would be angry and try to make things rough for you and give you the worst kids with behavior problems. If you were a fourth grade teacher during the time when they started taking those tests and all, they would give you the low students, so you would have a hard time getting those students to pass those tests to be promoted to the next grade."[176] Guma, the principal at McMain, tried to be fair even though most of his staff had gone on strike:

> There were a few teachers who crossed the line, but we struggled every day just to keep the kids in school. There were one or two teachers, including one counselor, who was very engaged in unions. My problem was he was a terrible counselor. He drew the curtain on his door every day. He hated kids. They hated him. They would frequently come out in tears. So, the fact that he was out on the line asking for more money I found deeply offensive. But that didn't color my feeling about the other good teachers, great teachers, who were on the line struggling for better salaries, and they deserved it. I had to compartmentalize in some way. When the strike was over, we got back to business.[177]

The process of reuniting the staff was easier in schools where everyone had gone on strike, compared to schools like McMain where teachers and staff were divided. Patti Reynolds taught at McMain at the time:

> But from my point of view, I always felt some animosity deep in my heart towards people who would not strike on principle. They wouldn't strike but were perfectly willing to take the benefits of the strike. But in my mind, as the person who had been on strike, it seemed to me that when we went back in the building, that the people who had not been on strike were the ones who were more reticent about just getting back to work with people who had been on strike, or were more defensive about how they were treated.[178]

On the other hand, joint experiences on the picket lines helped with cohesion and bonding at some schools: "At this school, this was [McDonogh] 10, it was an integrated staff. We just got closer and closer because we'd had these similar experiences. So many people may not think of it that way, but [a strike] actually helps to solidify the word union and the collective voice in a building."[179] Experiencing the union-wide democratic organization of the strike allowed teachers to build renewed faith in their own ability to effect change in their buildings, sparking a rise in teacher organizing and participation within their individual schools.

Shortly after the 1978 strike, the board voted to discontinue Dr. Geisert's contract. This was a mixed result for UTNO, as Geisert had always supported collective bargaining and was genuinely creating educational improvement in the district.[180] However, it did allow UTNO to bring another group of workers into its bargaining unit: clerical workers. Geisert had bargained with clerical workers as an independent group but refused to let them affiliate with UTNO because many of them worked closely with principals and other administrators. Nonetheless, Geisert's successor, Dr. Charles Martin, allowed them to join UTNO. Geisert was flabbergasted: "When I left the board, a lot of [the clerical workers] joined the union. They were the secretaries of the administration, and they joined the union. I mean come on, how stupid can you be?"[181] Upon Geisert's departure, UTNO waged a campaign to organize clerical workers, offering prizes such as a "portable color television" to the clerical worker who recruited the most new members.[182] Donisia Wise started as a clerical worker in 1968, and she said the working conditions were horrible: "Oh, it was dreadful. Because first of all, schools were not air conditioned. . . . And we would work so hard until your underwear would be soaked and wet. And . . . in most cases, you worked in the office by yourself. And so many of the principals were so demanding. . . . We did everything. We had to order supplies, in my case, and issue supplies, take care of the children when they are sent to the office when they have vomited on themselves."[183] Wise was part of the group of clerical workers who demanded union recognition in 1981, making them the only school secretaries in the state recognized by a union.[184] LaCour threatened a teacher walkout in solidarity if clerical workers' demands were not met, harnessing the power of the middle-class teachers to support their working-class colleagues. "I believe the board is treating clerical workers differently from the teachers, and unfairly," he told the *Times Picayune*.[185] Though the union was in negotiations for over a year to secure the first clerical contract, it won modest pay raises and, more importantly, it was able to add the 500 clerical employees to the ranks of the Health and Welfare Fund.[186]

Finally, the strike inspired similar militant action among teachers throughout the state. A fifteen-day strike by the NEA for collective bargaining rights "crippled" East Baton Rouge Parish in March 1979, though the strike was ultimately unsuccessful.[187] That fall, JFT called a strike for salary increases and other demands that lasted twenty-seven workdays.[188] Jan Skelton, then president of the JFT, saw UTNO's strike as a model: "The UTNO strike was over in a few days the year before. That's what I had to look at. That was the only thing I knew was, well, we'll go out on strike for a few days and teachers will lose some money and I didn't take a salary. None of the people on my staff took salaries either. We thought, we'll just get the job done. Well, not with that school board. They weren't budging on anything, anything. So it just kept going day after day and I couldn't see an end in sight."[189] Many of the JFT's demands were directly based on what

UTNO had won in 1974, including duty-free lunch, planning time, transfers by seniority, and hospitalization insurance. Unlike the UTNO strike, which had featured organized, militant pickets and traditional protest tactics, the teachers in more conservative Jefferson Parish stood their ground without drawing on histories of radicalism: "It was so different that the American Federation of Teachers sent people here to assist us and they didn't like what they saw on the picket lines because they saw teachers sitting out in chairs and eating doughnuts and the principal in some cases bringing them doughnuts. So it was too nice. The teachers were too nice, and they weren't making it difficult for the people to go in."[190] Still, Skelton was impressed by the teachers' fortitude and opined that the strike led to greater unity and a sense of collective voice: "We had very few people who went back in, very few. It was an enlightening situation as to what people will do when they pulled together for the same cause."[191] Ultimately, the teachers won in Jefferson and built a contract very similar to UTNO's that, while not as strong, still stands today.

INSTITUTION BUILDING AND LOOKING TOWARD THE FUTURE

The 1978 strike demonstrated UTNO's power and allowed the union to make new demands that enhanced its reach and effectiveness. UTNO used this power to create lasting institutions that provided new avenues for member participation, along with enhancing the quality of teaching in the parish and fighting for economic equity. Specifically, the Center for Professional Growth and Development (colloquially, the teacher center) and the Health and Welfare Fund employed educators provided free services to UTNO members, and both were run by a collaborative board, often composed of both union members and management. Both organizations provided opportunities for educators to learn new skills and try on different modes of leadership, thus, supporting UTNO's vision for superior education and economic justice and solidifying structures of participatory democracy within the union.

The teacher center first opened in 1980 inside McDonogh 28 Junior High. Originally a collaboration between UTNO, the school district, and the University of New Orleans (UNO), it featured a team of "master teachers" who would help train less experienced teachers, using recent education research by UNO professors.[192] Brenda Mitchell, who later became union president, was the longtime director of the center: "We always wanted to provide the teachers with professional development. That's where the teacher center came about because the district wasn't doing it. We used to tell them, 'You hire people and then want to fire them when they're not doing a good job. But you haven't provided any kind of development for them.'"[193] Along with providing individual mentoring, the teacher center held workshops for teachers and paraprofessionals that allowed them to earn professional development hours. Mitchell says running the teacher center was "the best time of my life:" "We had a staff, it was like three or four of us, and we would do workshops in the evening and during the day we would go into schools to help support teachers. But we would give them a critique but not to turn into the principal, but just for their own improvement."[194] Through her work at the teacher center, Mitchell also had the opportunity to travel all over the country to attend education conferences and AFT workshops, to learn about the latest innovations in the field and bring this knowledge back to New Orleans educators. Eventually, federal funding for the teacher center ran out, but the union successfully bargained to have the facility funded by its Health and Welfare Fund. Initially UTNO only received ten dollars per member for the teacher center, but over time the funding grew, allowing the union to implement a district-wide program developing teacher leaders and mentoring new and struggling educators.[195]

Katrena Ndang saw the center as a direct response to UTNO's concerns about the quality of teaching in the district: "They started offering their professional development, research based, how do we make this better? How do we train teachers to be better teachers, how do we train teachers to come back and train other teachers? So [I] think that's how they looked at it: How do I help?"[196] Along with providing support to struggling teachers, the center provided new ways for members to take on leadership roles, both as staff members and as master teachers. Often the training the center offered—because it was led by other teachers in the school system—was more effective than other workshops open to teachers looking to improve: "I can list several professional development workshops that I went through in the summertime and the ones that the union sponsored were by far the most effective, most informational. Things that I could actually use in my classroom."[197] In later years, the center staff collaborated with professors at Xavier University to offer courses that teachers could take to earn credits or certificates.[198] It also offered a social space that many members valued because, especially in elementary schools, teachers often had little time to collaborate with each other. The center provided materials to make bulletin boards, stencils, laminating machines, and copy machines, so teachers could come and do their work in community, learning from others' ideas. Finally, the union held parent classes at the center, helping parents prepare their young children for school or demonstrating learning activities that parents could do at home to reinforce skills learned in the classroom.[199] In the words of union staffer Jo Anna Russo, "It was like we were educating our own people and we were fine-tuning our own trade."[200] Through the teacher center, UTNO combined the dual goals of supporting educators and improving conditions for students and families.

The Health and Welfare Fund, though more of a standard union demand, was notable in its scope, especially in conservative Louisiana. The fund was originally created as a result of the union's 1977 contract negotiations to provide dental and vision coverage for employees, and it was lauded by LaCour as the first such fund in the Deep South.[201] In 1980, the board agreed to provide sustaining money for the fund, contributing one hundred dollars per employee, and from there the fund continued to grow.[202] By 1985, the fund was so successful that it was also paying for the teacher center.[203] LaCour describes the fund as one of the union's biggest accomplishments: "The biggest thing was we negotiated what we called a Health and Welfare Fund. . . . But over the years that fund grew, and out of that fund we were able to provide for teachers: free prescriptions, a dental plan where some of the services were free and others might cost as much as 50 percent paid for, to get dentures and stuff like that, and a vision plan where practically they got free glasses."[204] Joel Behrman, a teacher at Franklin High, eventually became a leader of the fund. He saw UTNO's work as trying to replicate some of the social democratic systems in Europe, to provide for members the services that all residents should enjoy: "There were 4,000 [UTNO members]. As a health and welfare person, we knew that was 10,000 lives. We had 10,000 lives to insure for benefits. . . . We struggled for giving teachers health and welfare to make sure they could have their teeth taken care of. We were replicating a little bit, what Europeans do for themselves. We had programs to help people."[205] The power of the fund led adversaries to suggest that UTNO had become too strong. Mike Johnson was a teacher whose wife, Violet Johnson, worked for the district. The Johnsons argued that, particularly by the time of the storm [Katrina], the balance of power had shifted too far in UTNO's favor: "In fact, when I was hired, your medical care was paid for as a perk of the job. And the card they gave you to go to the doctors with was an UTNO card. It didn't mention on the card anywhere anything about the Orleans Parish School Board, which, of course, paid for it."[206] The Health and Welfare Fund eventually allowed UTNO to purchase and renovate a building to use for its office, the teacher center, and an educator credit union.[207] These accomplishments speak to UTNO's strength, its ability to mobilize its members, and the innovation of its leaders.

In these years, UTNO also founded its annual conference—Quality Educational Standards in Teaching (QuEST), coordinated by Brenda Mitchell—which provided workshops and training for teachers and the public. At the conference, UTNO gave out "member of the year" awards to a teacher, paraprofessional, and clerical worker and a "friend of education" award to someone in the community who had supported public education. Several teachers and paraprofessionals remembered these events as particularly meaningful, and some had saved for decades the programs from when they had won a "member of the year" award.[208] Though the *Times Picayune* was initially skeptical about the conferences—"If the conference lives up to its apparent potential, the public might actually get something out of it"—the paper later lauded the union for tackling serious

From left to right: Civil rights activist Rev. A. L. Davis, Cheryl Epling, Rev. Jesse Jackson, and Nat LaCour. Reverend Jackson was the keynote speaker at the union's spring 1977 QuEST conference. *Courtesy of United Teachers of New Orleans.*

educational issues, perhaps because it was the recipient of the "friend of education" award itself.[209] The conference provided another opportunity for teachers to share their expertise, take on leadership roles, and participate in educational debates of the time.

Throughout the 1970s and early 1980s, UTNO continued to prioritize tactics borrowed from the civil rights movement, even as it moved toward more mainstream success. It engaged in frequent disruptive action, including the 1978 strike, which increased members' feelings of power and commitment to the union. It galvanized community support and reaffirmed its connections to the working-class Black parents and children who used the schools by advocating for them in the collective bargaining process, fighting for more education funding, and aligning themselves with working-class support staff such as paraprofessionals, clerical workers, custodians, and cafeteria and maintenance workers, many of whom sent their children to the schools. UTNO developed Black and working-class leadership by including rank-and-file members on the bargaining team, providing opportunities for leadership in the strike action, and creating member-run institutions that offered new avenues for leadership, such as serving on the credit union board or becoming a peer mentor at the teacher center. Finally, UTNO prioritized internal democracy, creating structures to maximize educator voice and participation, and leading members to significant feelings of ownership over the union. This, in turn, increased the democratic possibilities of the school system itself, as management began to solicit educator opinions and create avenues for formal collaboration and participation at school board meetings grew. By advocating for educators, therefore, UTNO also worked to democratize the district.

UTNO's successes, however, did not solve all the school system's problems. In the 1980s and 1990s, the district still faced chronic underfunding, a growing population of students living in poverty and the austerity policies of President Reagan and Louisiana governor Dave Treen—as well as a genuine fiscal crisis in the state. However, the union did work to create a model of economic justice and participatory democracy, through protest and solidarity, that provided an alternative to business-centered, neoliberal ideas of market-based freedoms. Instead of advocating for individual rights and lower taxes, UTNO argued that education was a public good that should be adequately funded by the federal, state, and local government. It argued that Black students deserved excellent schools and that Black educators deserved to be fairly compensated for their labor; and it built a health system that provided quality care while protecting its users from medical debt. The union demonstrated to parents, students, and community members the real power of collective action and developed leaders who were not afraid to speak up in their schools and their communities. Moreover, UTNO proved that all those accomplishments could occur within a Black-led yet completely integrated union, in which white and Black teachers worked side by side, even in a district that had lost most of its white students. As UTNO continued to grow in power, the elite-led resistance to its vision and its organization would continue to expand, while it also dealt with neoliberal shifts in the national education landscape. Internally, the union's growth required some degree of bureaucratization that threatened to foreclose the most radical, redistributive, and participatory aspects of its vision. Nonetheless, UTNO continued to fight for its place in city and state politics, and it continued to push a progressive agenda that centered care and economic justice.

3

There's Nothing Wrong with Acting like a Miner

Disruption and Political Organizing amid the Rise of Neoliberal Policymaking, 1976-1998

> Because the most powerful strikes—those that shut down or cripple production—rely not on staff but on an overwhelming majority of workers to engage in collective action, the use of labor's strongest weapon requires an approach to workers that facilitates majority participation in the union.
>
> **Jane McAlevey, No Shortcuts**

Patti Reynolds started her career teaching high school history at St. Joseph's Academy, an all-girls Catholic school in New Orleans, in 1963. During her tenure, St. Joseph's integrated its student body and became one of the few Catholic schools in the city to demonstrate a deep commitment to integration. Reynolds, who is white, realized that she had never learned any Black history and felt unprepared to teach history to her integrated classes. As a result, she applied for, and received, a National Defense Education Act grant that sent her to Fisk and to Johns Hopkins Universities to participate in a Black history education program for schoolteachers. Upon her return, she implemented a program at St. Joseph's in which all classes ceased for a week and students and parents taught mini courses on subjects that interested them, including Black history and the civil rights movement. Eventually,

Reynolds grew tired of working at an all-girls school and wanted the higher salary and retirement benefits that came with a job in the public school system. In 1976, she got a job at McMain Secondary School and immediately joined UTNO. Though Reynolds was perhaps more racially conscious and politically progressive than many other white teachers in the city, educators hired in Orleans Parish in the mid-1970s were choosing to work in integrated or majority-Black schools. They had likely rejected their white peers' flight to the suburbs and were also living in a city in which Black people were rapidly assuming more political and social power. UTNO's leadership was integrated, and UTNO had significant white membership; but support for the union was always stronger among Black educators: "One thing that I was always conscious of was that basically all Black teachers in the school were union members and many white teachers were union members, but if you were going to have a problem recruiting somebody it was more likely to be a white teacher than a Black teacher."[1] Over time, Reynolds became a building rep, a member of the executive council, and eventually UTNO's executive vice president. She stayed involved because she believed in the union's mission and respected its commitment to integration and collective decision-making. She said she was most proud that UTNO remained "a democratic institution."[2] Her husband, Mike Stone, who was also an executive board member, agreed: "I can't think of any one specific outstanding thing, except that I thought it was a democratic institution . . . as she said. We just worked together and we actually, year to year, improved the schools. Teacher pay went up. Health care went up. Money going into the classroom went up. Textbook committees, whatever. We affected the schools from top to bottom including as we improved the plight of the teachers, I feel like we were improving the plight of the students."[3] Reynolds and Stone experienced UTNO's internal democracy in their work on the executive board but also through witnessing how the union promoted rank-and-file participation in its strikes, rallies, and other disruptive actions. UTNO's commitment to fostering democracy and racial equity, valuing public workers, and promoting quality teaching was especially crucial as Louisiana, and the nation, turned to neoliberal solutions to solve the nation's education "crisis."

In this chapter, I analyze the school reform agenda of the 1980s and 1990s and its connections to neoliberal policymaking at the state and federal level. I examine how business leaders and policymakers attempted to reverse labor gains and push through reforms ostensibly intended to increase accountability, rigor, and efficiency. UTNO confronted the introduction of early neoliberal education reforms, such as heightened pressure around learning standards, the rhetoric of teacher accountability, and market-driven solutions such as vouchers and merit pay. The union waged a political battle with business forces in the state, most notably with the LABI, which successfully passed statewide right-to-work legislation in 1976. In its opposition to these developments, UTNO demonstrated the power of political education and educator voice, two elements missing from the top-down school reform movement. As policymakers at all levels turned toward privatization and austerity measures to solve perceived institutional crises, both within and outside of education, UTNO argued that the solution to struggling schools was, instead, increased funding and resources to meet the needs of the poor student population. Specifically, the union campaigned and lobbied repeatedly for increases in millages and taxes to subsidize educational spending. Even as UTNO leaders adapted to the era of education reform, budget cuts, and "accountability," they fought—often in the streets—to create space for an alternative value system that saw educators as active and knowledgeable participants in the struggle to create successful schools.

The union played an outsized role in city and state politics and built a mighty political machine, contributing to the coalescing of Black political power in the city. In this way, UTNO was one of the most formidable opponents to business interests in the state. Though its racial demands were less radical than they had been in the 1960s, the union continued to prioritize redistributive justice and rejected neoliberal "color-blind" rhetoric.[4] UTNO's members remained mostly Black women, and the union continued to represent its members' interests in the local labor movement, supporting progressive campaigns such as a living wage for all workers. The union also housed and supported two organizations of Black union members: the Coalition of Black Trade Unionists (CBTU), a political group, and the A. Philip Randolph Institute (APRI), the AFL-CIO's Black caucus.[5] Additionally, UTNO members started the first Louisiana branch of the Coalition of Labor Union Women, for which Connie Goodly (an UTNO member) served as president, thus demonstrating the union's commitment to uplifting women leaders.[6] Through its political work and educational advocacy, UTNO maintained its support from public school parents as well as from the larger Black community that had first propelled it into power.

I end this chapter with a discussion of UTNO's 1990 strike, in which educators joined the picket lines to demand raises for their lower-paid paraprofessional colleagues. This strike occurred at a moment when the labor movement was on the defensive and teachers strikes across the country were rare, demonstrating UTNO's ongoing commitment to disruptive activism and solidarity across all levels of the educational workforce. It also radicalized members and helped them participate more actively in UTNO's, and the city's, democratic processes. I argue that despite external factors threatening the union, UTNO remained committed to an agenda that was deeply aligned with the Black community, rejecting discourses of "color-blind neoliberalism," and working to improve both the schools and quality of life in the city.

The Reagan presidency marked the beginning of neoliberal policymaking writ large, especially within the education sector. Neoliberal economists such as Friedrich Hayek and Milton Friedman present the self-regulating market, and the idea that private interests maximize public good, as an alternative to the social welfare state that reduces the responsibility of government to manage and control the economy. Though neoliberalism is often associated with austerity—and Reagan did cut government services and grant regressive tax breaks—it also includes large subsidies to businesses, whose profits theoretically "trickle down" to workers, and it supports government-sponsored privatization. Neoliberal policymakers destroy existing public institutions and create new pro-business organizations in their stead.[7] For example, education reformers shutter existing public schools and replace them with privately-governed charter schools, thus opening new avenues for-profit accumulation.[8] Education scholar Pauline Lipman argues that these reforms include a shift from government to "governance," as control is wrested from democratically elected officials and handed over to business elites and experts who are entrusted to make "business-savvy" and "data-tested" decisions.[9] Within education, Reagan advocated for vouchers for students to attend private schools, school prayer, and abolishing the Department of Education.

Historian Nancy MacLean argues that modern neoliberalism has its origins in the South (and West), where white elites have long sought to maintain their power by limiting the reach and redistributive powers of the federal government, by disciplining labor and dividing workers along racial lines to maintain a subservient underclass, and by extracting enormous financial rewards secured by exploiting workers and the land.[10] Dismantling the public education system and remaking it along business lines fits easily into this ideology: it limits the reach of the federal and local government, it disciplines and divides workers by forcing them to compete with each other for jobs and salaries, and it maintains racial hierarchies that keep Black and brown students in low-performing underfunded schools. Though today these systems are widespread nationwide, Louisiana was at the forefront of neoliberal interventions in public education, particularly in terms of testing, accountability, and choice.

Along with cuts to public funding and the privatization of many formerly public functions, neoliberal policymakers worked throughout the 1980s and 1990s to limit the power of organized labor. Reagan fired striking air traffic controllers in 1981, causing the number of strikes nationwide to sharply decline and effectively neutralizing one of labor's strongest weapons.[11] Strikes, protests, rallies, and other forms of disruption are key to maintaining worker power and often serve to increase union democracy by promoting rank-and-file participation and leadership. The neoliberal agenda, therefore, doubly targeted the AFT and UTNO, as they represented not only unionized workers but also public employees. They faced threats from within educational policy, such as increased reliance on high-stakes standardized testing and nascent moves toward privatization, as well as from labor policy, in the form of renewed attacks on benefits, pensions, and tenure. Throughout the 1980s and 1990s, AFT unions, which tended to dominate in urban areas, also confronted ever more impoverished student populations resulting from policies of urban divestment and cutbacks in social welfare. Under attack, teachers' unions struggled both to protect their members, who saw neoliberal policies chip away at their middle-class stability, and to present themselves as educational advocates whose interests aligned with students and families. Conservative and business groups, meanwhile, waged campaigns to discredit educators and portray their unions as narrowly self-serving, opposed to innovation and change, and committed to protecting ineffective teachers. This rhetoric was part of a larger business backlash against the gains of organized labor, in which business leaders exploited the weakness of US labor laws to reassert corporate power.[12] Such accusations were hard to shake for many unions, especially those who represented predominantly white teachers working in districts composed of students of color, and AFT president Al Shanker reinforced them with his insistence on a color-blind focus on economic issues that typified the AFT's avoidance of race.[13]

UTNO, as a majority-Black union, had more legitimacy in the Black community than many other urban teachers' unions, yet the national and local climate still put the union on the defensive. UTNO treaded a middle ground on issues such as increased teacher and student testing and the introduction of charter schools, while it fought tenaciously to oppose other interventions, like vouchers and merit pay. It made questionable alliances to earn raises for its members, such as connecting teacher pay to increases in state gambling revenues, and its rhetoric became more defensive, often enumerating the obstacles teachers faced in unruly students, negligent parents, neighborhood violence, and subpar supplies and facilities. Moreover, teachers watched many of their hard-won economic gains disappear as healthcare costs and inflation skyrocketed. This led the LFT into a seemingly never-ending battle for higher pay, striving to reach at least the average pay scale for states in the South, which was perpetually several thousand dollars out of reach. The LFT's focus on teacher pay bolstered accusations that the union was single-mindedly fighting only for higher salaries instead of focusing on improving education more broadly, which was an especially poignant critique in New Orleans due to students' consistently poor test results. The union's standard line, that higher salaries would result in hiring and retaining more qualified educators, had grown stale by the early-1990s, when neoliberal rhetoric—and intensive lobbying by business interests—had shifted the terms

LFT march and rally in Baton Rouge for teacher pay raises, 1982.
Courtesy of United Teachers of New Orleans.

of the debate. The public now subscribed to the idea that teachers should prove their worth through their output, as measured by higher test scores, rather than deserving a middle-class salary and pension simply as workers providing an essential service to the community. This shift toward viewing workers through a business ideology was a key aspect of the turn toward neoliberalism and resulted in union losses nationwide.

UTNO's victories in the early 1970s, and the ascent of public sector labor unions, were highly contested. The all-white LTA sued UTNO when it won its collective bargaining election in 1974, appealing the case all the way to the Louisiana Supreme Court; and then the LTA sued again when the first contract was finalized, claiming that collective bargaining was unconstitutional.[14] The following year, the LTA reverted to an older strategy and introduced a bill in the state legislature that applied only to the education sector and was intended to "prohibit forced membership of teachers in private organizations."[15] Characterized as a "right-to-work" bill, this legislation was largely symbolic because neither UTNO nor the JFT, the only two teachers' unions with CBAs in the state, forced educators to join or pay dues. The 1947 Taft-Hartley Act outlawed "closed shops," in which employers can only hire individuals in good standing with the union, and it allowed states to pass right-to-work laws that prohibit mandatory union membership and dues deductions. However, from 1955 to 1976, in part because of the strength of the state AFL-CIO, Louisiana was the only state in the South without right-to-work legislation on the books.[16] The year 1976 was the third consecutive legislative session in which the LTA had introduced such bills, which the *Times Picayune* enthusiastically endorsed; but the lobbying arm of the LFT easily defeated them, especially with the support of the state AFL-CIO. Labor saw these bills as a threat because of their creeping encroachment on union rights, and unions wanted to keep the door open to potentially mandating union membership in the future, thus addressing "free loaders" who benefited from union bargaining without contributing. In the early 1970s, public sector labor leaders attempted to pass a national bill that would allow locals to collect agency fees from all employees, regardless of whether they chose to join the union. This effort was defeated.[17]

However, the right-to-work threat was not an idle one. Though Louisiana did not have comprehensive right-to-work legislation in 1976, agricultural right-to-work legislation had been in effect since 1954, following a planter backlash against mostly Black sugarcane workers attempting to unionize.[18] In the early 1970s, manufacturers, oil field executives, multinational companies, and the state chamber of commerce had formed the LABI. LABI represented more than 30,000 individuals in the business community and had pledged to pass right-to-work legislation no later than 1977.[19] Right-to-work legislation disempowers labor unions by removing the obligation of workers who choose not to join the union to pay dues, even while they continue to receive the benefits of union contracts. UTNO was aware of the threat. LaCour spoke at a forum denouncing right-to-work legislation, which he called "a continuous process to destroy organized labor."[20] Though the proposed legislation would not have directly impacted UTNO, which already collected dues only from members, LaCour understood that UTNO depended on the strength of the Louisiana labor movement to achieve many of its goals, especially at the state level. Following a successful media and political campaign by LABI and a hastily organized countermobilization by state AFL-CIO president Victor Bussie, who mistakenly believed he still had the political clout to defeat the legislation, in 1976 right-to-work legislation was signed into law by Gov. Edwin Edwards. This portended a decline for labor, and, though not entirely attributable to the legislation, the state's union participation rate fell from 19.8 percent in 1975 to 14.9 percent in 1980—and then eventually to 7.6 percent in 2004 and a paltry 5.2 percent in 2014.[21] This statewide anti-labor climate, which mirrors union declines on a national level, would shape what UTNO was able to accomplish.

Though right-to-work threatened organized labor, UTNO also had to address educational policies that targeted teachers and unions, including a growing focus on teacher "accountability," the polemical *A Nation at Risk* (1983) report, and limitations to school funding due to austerity policies and new regulations on taxing business and industry. Though many of these policies had filtered down from the federal level, they also received significant support from LABI, which became a persistent opponent of UTNO as the union grew in power. These nascent neoliberal policies looked to transform education along a business model, cutting costs, adding privatized options such as vouchers, and focusing on easily measurable results, such as standardized test scores. Though portrayed as centering "accountability" and passed in the name of low-income students of color, these measures transformed public schooling into a lucrative business for educational entrepreneurs and did little to improve educational or social outcomes for students living in poverty.[22] The ideology of these reforms centers on state-sanctioned anti-racism that expresses concern about outcomes for children of color but does little to address the material conditions that produce and reify racial inequity.[23]

In 1976, amid the right-to-work furor, OPSB announced that a committee would begin evaluating tenured faculty, rating them as acceptable, marginal, or unacceptable, and then recommending to the board the unacceptable teachers who should be dismissed. Teachers feared that the process would be a "witch hunt," and UTNO sued the board, claiming that the new evaluation procedure violated its contract.[24] The union objected to the composition of the three-person committees—which included the principal who made the original unsatisfactory rating, an administrator, and a teacher representative—that left teachers outnumbered; it suggested instead that administrators should also be subject to such evaluations, and it pledged to develop its own evaluation process that would provide a more "positive approach."[25] In part, UTNO objected because of real fears about misuse of the evaluation system and a return to the era before it had earned collective bargaining, when teachers were fired at will because they voiced an opinion contrary to their principal's, raised questions about unethical policies, or even refused an administrator's romantic advances.[26] However, UTNO was also responding to a nationwide push for teacher "accountability," arising amid the waves of disruptive teacher strikes that had pushed public sentiment in many cities against educators. Though the entire decade was characterized by teacher strikes, they peaked at more than 200 in the 1975–76 school year, many lasting for weeks or months.[27]

UTNO lost its lawsuit over the teacher evaluations, and the issue persisted. In 1978, a school board member suggested competency testing for tenured teachers, a proposal the union vehemently opposed, as teachers had already taken a test to become certified in the first place and then were evaluated every three years per district policy. The evaluation procedure had failed to renew public faith in teacher competence because rather than referring "unacceptable" teachers for public hearings, per the policy, administrators and union officials tended to quietly counsel them out of the profession.[28] These demands for accountability reflected an ideological shift across the decade in which people moved from thinking of themselves not as "citizens" but as "taxpayers," dividing the world into productive and nonproductive workers.[29] For example, the *Times Picayune* article detailing the proposal for competency testing claims, "Public school teachers, like public education, has been under the sharp scrutiny of lawmakers and taxpayers for several years."[30] Taxpayers, like business leaders, wanted clear evidence that what they were funding was "working," and evaluating public employees—teachers more so than garbage collectors—was viewed as part of the arrangement. Later, this would explode into the high-stakes standardized testing movement; but at this early stage, demands for evaluation and accountability started and ended with educators in the classroom. Brenda Mitchell believes teachers were scapegoated for the dysfunction of the larger system: "We weren't saying don't hold our feet to the fire, we all had evaluations. Now, hold our feet to the fire, but you hold your own feet to the fire too. You do what you're supposed to do, fund your schools, build the buildings, give us the security, give us professional development."[31] Teachers working in hot, overcrowded classrooms with no air conditioning, paid less than their peers across the country, and often without enough books or materials for their students felt betrayed and threatened by this rhetoric of accountability.

Though regular competency testing was voted down by the board, state superintendent Kelly Nix proposed eliminating tenure and paying teachers solely based on their scores on the National Teacher Examination (NTE).[32] At the time, the test was required of all teacher applicants, but there was no minimum score, which Nix also wanted to change. The Louisiana Association of Educators (LAE; the newly integrated NEA affiliate) and UTNO strongly opposed the plan, both because of Nix's attack on tenure and because they claimed the NTE was culturally biased and discriminated against Black educators. The LAE further argued that standardized tests generally are racially biased and that more holistic methods of measurement should be used.[33] LaCour pointed out that passing a test does not guarantee that a candidate will become a successful educator and added, "An awful lot of people advocate the NTE because they see it as a way to eliminate blacks."[34] By explicitly discussing racial justice, UTNO broke with the color-blind approach of the national AFT and reaffirmed its commitment to addressing racial and economic concerns simultaneously.

Despite union opposition, the *Times Picayune*, in its periodic articles on teacher incompetence, continued to advocate for minimum NTE scores as a solution.[35] In a reversal that speaks to national pressure on the union to address the issue of accountability, Nix established new passing scores for the NTE in 1983, with LaCour sitting on the panel that approved it.[36] However, LaCour continued to argue that higher salaries were a more effective way to attract qualified educators than additional barriers to entry, and he suggested, later, that Louisiana had set the qualifying score too high, resulting in a disproportionate number of Black applicants failing the exam.[37]

In response to *A Nation at Risk*, Louisiana lawmakers doubled down on their push to increase accountability and standards. As part of what LaCour called "a bigger trend to administer reforms from above," Louisiana passed one of the toughest high school graduation tests in the nation with little input from teachers, parents, or students.[38] Several years later, in 1991, Gov. Buddy Roemer tied his education reform package to the implementation of the new Louisiana Teacher Evaluation Program (LaTEP). According to LFT executive director Bob Crowley, the evaluation plan had some merits: "The way it worked was three separate evaluations unannounced during the two-week period. So, you'd have three different evaluators walk in on you and just start taking notes. And there were ninety-one indicators of effective teaching, which was a really good list. Nat showed it to somebody in Washington who said, 'This is the best list of indicators I've ever seen.'"[39] Nonetheless, the LFT and the LAE lobbied heavily against the program because it violated teacher tenure laws: if teachers earned an unsatisfactory rating, they lost their certification.[40] Teachers lobbied the Board of Elementary and Secondary Education (BESE), marched through the streets of New Orleans, and protested at the state capitol to repeal the new evaluation system, demonstrating UTNO members' ongoing activism and commitment to disruption.[41] Though Crowley thought that the "really good teachers" generally were fine with the new system, he recalls, "I was in a school [in Rapides Parish] where they had just announced who was going to get evaluated, and I saw a look of sheer terror in some of these people."[42] LaCour said the lawmakers were scapegoating teachers, the LFT filed suit, and the state indefinitely suspended the program.[43] Despite the unpopularity of the teachers' position on LaTEP, which was widely supported by both the business community and the wider public, the union defeated the program by prioritizing protest and rallying rank-and-file dissent.

LABI was especially irate at LaTEP's failure. The president of LABI announced he would be in the streets fighting to preserve the program: "I can tell you this: If this effort at accountability goes by the wayside, cows will fly and Elijah will take a chariot to hell before the business community stands by and allows the passage of another teacher pay raise financed with business tax revenues."[44] The *Times Picayune* similarly accused teachers of disingenuously accepting the pay raise that was part of Governor Roemer's education reform and then destroying the evaluation component that brought accountability.[45] Business interests in the state, represented by LABI and the *Times Picayune*, wanted to see education remade under a business model, with unsatisfactory employees dismissed and replaced. By contrast, UTNO and the LFT argued that schools would be improved by drastically increasing funding, both to enhance resources and programs available for students and to raise teacher salaries to recruit and retain quality educators. The opposing groups had fundamentally different ideas about how to create quality schools. While the business groups believed top-down reform and eliminating low-performing teachers would improve education, the union argued for a collaborative approach, directly addressing the issues of poverty, drawing on the expertise of educators, and incorporating mentoring, master teachers, copious resources, and smaller class sizes. As UTNO member Joe DeRose recalls, "[The] business community wanted to run things without really having a real insight of what was going on inside. They didn't have any presence in the schools. They never came to teachers and asked, 'What are the problems inside the school? How could your job be better? What are the challenges you're facing?' Nobody ever wanted to hear about kids that were coming in with poverty."[46] Following the LaTEP suspension, LABI began to push even harder for vouchers as a means of funneling public money into private schools.[47] In 1998, when asked to respond to fears that vouchers would destroy public schools, a LABI lobbyist replied: "I would say to that, perhaps it's about time. Because in my opinion, public education has woefully failed the young people."[48]

EDUCATION REFORM: MERIT PAY, RIGOR, AND BUDGET CUTS

Another component of the business model of education reform was the idea that incentives would help improve school and educator performance, which coalesced into the concept of merit pay. UTNO opposed merit pay because it worried about the impact of having teachers compete against one another; it did not believe a merit pay system would fairly reward teachers with especially difficult student populations, and most importantly, it was focused on across-the-board raises for *all* employees.[49] UTNO lobbyist and executive vice president Cheryl Epling, when asked about merit pay, responded, "Adam and Eve failed the test. Should God be blamed? . . . In Louisiana, before we look at merit pay, we need to look at survival pay."[50] Both teacher evaluations and merit pay were strongly supported by LABI at the state level and by the Business Task Force, a similar business association in New Orleans itself. Both measures were also supported by President Reagan, whose *A Nation at Risk* report had called for increased standards for students and teachers. Reagan's education policies demonstrate geographer David Harvey's concept of "creative destruction."[51] Through austerity budgets, Reagan deprived districts of education funding for the neediest students, while increasing funding for programs geared toward reimagining schools under a business model, emphasizing test scores, accountability, and "choice." Then, pointing to poor outcomes, he posited privatization as the only solution.

Following the release of *A Nation At Risk*, which AFT president Al Shanker publicly supported, the AFT voiced its approval for limited merit pay and increased accountability.[52] Though the report did not include many of the more conservative aspects of Reagan's educational platform, such as school prayer and vouchers for students to attend private school, it did promote the view that the educational system was in acute crisis, and it encouraged collaboration with business, setting the stage for the corporate-led school reform movement in power today. Shanker's support of the report constituted a break from prior AFT policy as well as a divergence from the NEA, which critiqued the report.[53] Though the national AFT thus expressed hesitant support for merit pay, LaCour continued to argue instead for raises across the board, noting that teaching was poorly paid compared to other careers that require a college degree and that Orleans Parish currently had a teacher shortage. However, the president of LABI asserted that taxpayers should not have to subsidize mediocrity by giving salary increases to incompetent teachers.[54] Though UTNO under LaCour's leadership never directly opposed the dictates of the national AFT, UTNO did make space to prioritize the values of its members and remained committed to supporting Black teachers, especially when they were being demonized in the national dialogue. In 1986, UTNO hosted the AFT Black Caucus's annual meeting, which focused on concerns that the education reform movement did not include Black voices and was harming Black teachers and students. The reform movement, said LaCour, "seeks to raise the level of excellence by eliminating those who aren't achieving success."[55] The nationwide percentage of Black educators, which had fallen steadily since *Brown v. Board of Education*, continued to decline with the introduction of competency tests, with the largest losses among new teachers coming from HBCUs.[56]

In 1983, one year after the publication of *A Nation At Risk*, the New Orleans Business Task Force on Education announced it was focusing on improving student test scores.[57] Civic organizations, including the Urban League, the AFL-CIO, and the NAACP, held a series of forums to discuss *A Nation At Risk* and, according to Pres Kabacoff, education chairman of the business-civic group the Metropolitan Area Committee,[58] the goal was to dispel the idea that school problems were due to integration, poverty, or other "sociological factors."[59] Even at this early stage, business leaders saw school success, judged almost entirely by test scores, as a product of teacher quality and school administration rather than a result of the endemic social issues facing the city, such as racism, unemployment, paltry social services, unstable housing, and an economy quickly shifting toward low-paid tourism jobs. The Business Task Force latched onto merit pay, or paying teachers based on their students' test scores, as a solution to the schools' underperformance. UTNO fought back, arguing that merit pay would create teacher morale problems and that the first priority should be giving teachers raises across the board.[60] Thanks to UTNO's contract negotiating, teachers did earn substantial raises, and from 1983 to 1984, their salaries increased $1,000–$2,000 per year. Board members that year also voted "reluctantly" to give themselves the largest pay raise allowable by the legislature, $3,000–$3,600 more annually.[61] Nonetheless, business groups, including the Business Task Force, and the statewide LABI continued to advocate tying teacher pay to student performance.[62] At LABI's insistence, Governor Edwards included merit pay as part of a larger education reform bill that he tried to push through the legislature and that was defeated in part due to lobbying by the LFT.[63] LABI revealed its larger anti-union motives when a panel its members sat on recommended, along with merit pay, abolishing teacher tenure, a fixture of teacher contracts nationwide.[64]

Business groups' focus on merit pay was part of a larger statewide effort to develop higher standards and a tougher curriculum for the state, all tied to massive increases in student testing. In 1983, the BESE proposed raising the standards required to receive a high school diploma by, in part, eliminating electives and adding more stringent math and science requirements.[65] Before the state could approve the plan, OPSB voted to extend the school day and mandate tougher standards in Orleans Parish, going further than BESE had suggested.[66] UTNO again protested the changes, this time because it worried about the loss of teacher jobs, especially for those teaching elective courses. Union leadership also believed the board was making decisions without genuinely soliciting parent and educator input. Parents joined the union in protest, worried that older students would be held accountable to new standards when they had not been effectively prepared at the elementary level.[67] However, because of federal cuts to education and withering local tax support, OPSB cut funding to the schools even as they implemented a more rigorous curriculum. The budget, LaCour said, "comes nowhere close" to providing high-quality programs to boost student achievement, especially as it eliminated 131 teaching positions, thus raising class sizes across the district.[68] Much like public sector social movement unions across the nation, or teachers' unions that "bargain for the common good" today, UTNO looked to connect educators' interests to the needs of the students they served.[69]

Repeatedly, LaCour and other UTNO representatives insisted that the real problem in public education, and the barrier to high achievement, was inadequate school funding. Critics accused the union of being interested in school funding only to improve members' salaries, but the union's actions belie such accusations. For example, in 1975, UTNO sent representatives to Washington to lobby to override President Ford's veto of education funding, and two years later LaCour spoke to President Carter about the fiscal issues facing New Orleans schools, which he said had been mostly abandoned by middle-class Black and white families.[70] The union took out newspaper advertisements arguing for more school funding and it repeatedly pushed OPSB to explore new avenues for finding money.[71] With Reagan's budget cuts,[72] the state's low per pupil funding, a statewide homestead exemption that prohibited taxes on the first $75,000 of owner-occupied property, and industrial tax exemptions that shielded businesses from local property tax millages, the union and the school board were often desperate for money. This lack of funding had a very real impact on school conditions for both teachers and students. Leoance Williams, who had started teaching in 1974 and who returned to the same school after Katrina, noted the differences he saw after the storm: "We had internet in the schools, which we didn't have before, so it was better. We had our computers, which we didn't have before, all of the books and supplies, materials. It was really a whole lot better after the storm. If all of these things had been done prior to the storm, the system would have been better overall."[73] Another teacher, who generally opposed the union and never joined, and who spent his entire career at a high-performing magnet school, shared a similar analysis: "The schools needed more money. There were so many things that were needed that I'm not sure that anybody could find the place to start. Lots more money would've been a good place to start but there was enough venality that you would've been afraid that that money might disappear into the wrong pockets. [The district] had very little money."[74] Even the anti-union *Times Picayune* readily acknowledged the financial issues plaguing the district: "It is too bad that money does not grow on trees, but even if it did, the tree allotted to the Orleans Parish School Board would long ago have been stripped bare by vandals and rising costs and strangled at the root by recalcitrant voters."[75] UTNO used the collective bargaining process to push the school board to hold millages and tax elections, working with the OPSB to provide more money for education and attempting to create a more just school system.

The state of facilities was especially dire. Frank Fudesco, who worked for the district, recalled persistent struggles in funding building maintenance: "The buildings and the upkeep, anything that would fall under capital improvements, were critically underfunded because there is no money, there is no capital improvement budget in New Orleans public schools, because there's no millage, because there's a $75,000 exemption on every home out there."[76] Though voters did, on occasion, pass millages for the schools, declining property values and a shrinking tax base due to white flight and racially biased home appraisals meant that those millages resulted in insufficient funds. LABI lobbied against additional state funding for schools, especially if it wasn't tied to school reform initiatives intended to increase accountability, such as merit pay. For example, LABI helped defeat a proposal that would have appropriated money specifically for local school construction, claiming that Louisiana does "far more now than other states to aid local education."[77] The Business Task Force similarly campaigned against local tax increases to benefit education, often complaining that there was insufficient transparency about how the funds would be spent.[78] Concerns about transparency and corruption are raised much less frequently when districts are led by white officials,[79] yet in the New Orleans context, in the middle of a shift toward greater Black control, such claims carried significant weight with white business leaders. The Business Task Force also objected to the school board repeatedly calling for millages to try to solicit more funds: "The [collective bargaining] agreements . . . represent a cop-out by duly elected members of the School Board. We have to seriously look at developing legislation which prohibits a governing body to enter into a contractual obligation to continue to call a tax election ad infinitum until a tax is crammed down the throats of the tax-payer."[80] The lack of adequate school funding hurt union interests both by resulting in poor working conditions and low salaries and by creating a public image that portrayed the union as greedy teachers trying to steal money away from struggling students. For example, a 1979 *Times Picayune* article suggested that UTNO's pay demands had forced OPSB to direct money away from needed school maintenance, resulting in ceiling tiles falling on students' heads.[81] Nonetheless, at a time when neoliberal policymaking meant austerity, budget cuts, and introducing business models of accountability into education, UTNO stood strong in its opposition, emphasizing instead what its members and the students they taught both needed to be successful and deserved.

In the face of the budget shortfall, the union dropped its demand for teacher pay raises—"The union is certainly convinced that there are no funds available for employees' raises without doing irreparable harm to some other part of the budget," said LaCour—and the board agreed, at UTNO's urging, to hold a property tax election to solicit more funds. The Business Task Force, despite its ostensible support of the schools, opposed the tax election because there wasn't a master plan for the schools, and it accused the board of "put[ting] the political gun to the head of the taxpayer."[82] Against UTNO's wishes, the board repeatedly delayed the tax election, which had originally been scheduled for November 1985, for over a year, ostensibly out of fear that the new taxes would be rejected by voters. The union continued to complain about poor working conditions and low salaries, claiming that some children attended classes "in buildings that are not fit for dogs."[83] The majority of schools had no air conditioning and, in LaCour's words, "We're teaching science without microscopes and working in rundown buildings where the restrooms are without tissue and the stench is down the hall."[84] As the millage delay continued, the schools faced an even more dire fiscal climate, and the board proposed cutting $20.8 million to balance the 1986–87 budget, including eliminating the entire athletics budget. Coaches mobilized and pledged their support for the tax election, and UTNO warned, "This could be one of the worst things that has ever happened to this school system."[85]

In response to the fiscal crisis, which was largely a result of federal cuts and urban divestment, the board proposed hiring outside contractors to provide lower-cost services for the district. They suggested privatizing maintenance, security, payroll, student transportation, janitorial services, and groundskeeping.[86] In 1985, AFSCME and the Teamsters represented many of these workers under CBAs; the privatization would, thus, both eliminate stable blue-collar jobs and bust union contracts. Moreover, many of these education support workers sent their own children to the public schools. Eliminating their jobs and replacing them with lower-paid contract workers would further disrupt families' ability to thrive and provide for their children. Schools exist in larger, community-wide ecosystems where their role transcends simply teaching students academics and, in this case, extends to providing secure, decently paying jobs in working-class neighborhoods. LaCour warned that privatization "is not the panacea some people think it is."[87] The Business Task Force supported the proposal and agreed to gather information on outside contractors.[88] Meanwhile, the board continued to vacillate on sports budgets and laid off several hundred more employees.[89] In these debates, UTNO positioned itself clearly in opposition to the neoliberal business agenda.

The board finally set the tax millage election for September 1986. The Business Task Force officially opposed the tax, claiming that the board had not been clear about how it would spend the money. "That's a smokescreen," said LaCour. "If you exempted business from this tax, it would melt away the opposition."[90] He said that people opposed the millage because they didn't trust the board, but voting it down would hurt teachers and kids. In its campaign for the tax, UTNO earned support from Black civic and community organizations, and LaCour called on the larger Black community to demonstrate its support: "The black community must support it. For a long period, we had the luxury of blaming whites for our educational shortcomings. That situation has changed. A majority of the School Board is black. The superintendent is black. Half the electorate is black. The challenge is to the black community. We're going to ask them, 'Are you willing to spend money for your kids?'"[91] Of course, the now majority-Black city had much less financial power than the majority-white city had held merely ten years prior, due to urban divestment, a declining tax base, and the loss of the oil industry.[92]

The millage referendum failed. The board announced it would drop several athletics programs, close two-thirds of their truancy centers, and ask employees to retire early, among other cost-saving measures. Even with the union and the board collaborating, they could not convince the public to approve higher taxes in a moment of citywide fiscal crisis. That same month, due to lack of funding, the fire department closed one-third of its stations and the police announced they would no longer respond to car wrecks.[93] The city was broke.

Though the union struggled to achieve its goals in the climate of austerity, UTNO and the LFT managed to halt many of the most threatening neoliberal proposals in the 1980s and 1990s: the rollback of union rights and loss of teacher tenure, the privatization and outsourcing of educational support personnel, the introduction of school vouchers, and merit pay. At the same time, the union acquiesced to reforms such as higher standards, increased test scores, and graduation tests. While popular narratives presented Louisiana as backward on education issues, its students scoring low on standardized tests, and its school funding and teacher pay near the bottom of even the low-paid South, the state led the nation in its attempts to push though neoliberal reforms. Louisiana developed standards and testing that were used as models for other states, and its nascent attempts at privatization and vouchers now mirror programs seen nationwide. These programs directly threatened the jobs of school employees, many of whom were Black women, as well as the rights of public sector employees more broadly. As MacLean demonstrates, the South's leadership in neoliberal policymaking was always rooted in attempts to maintain elite white control.[94]

THE UTNO POLITICAL MACHINE: PUSHING PROGRESSIVISM

The fact that UTNO and the LFT were able, at least occasionally, to stymie an antiteacher business agenda in Louisiana speaks to the power the union held and the outsized role it played in the city and the state. Along with lobbying and issuing endorsements, in collaboration with the state AFL-CIO, UTNO developed elaborate political machinery in the city, canvassing on behalf of favored candidates and working to get out the vote through its Committee on Political Education (COPE) and collaborations with APRI. As the largest local in the state, and therefore the largest teachers' union as well, UTNO held outsized influence in the LFT and the state legislature. However, it was in local elections that UTNO wielded the most power. Brenda Mitchell explains: "We had a sophisticated political arm, and anybody who wanted state office, or pretty much a local office, had to talk to us and listen to our concerns. We were the union, the AFL-CIO, and the teachers, we could deliver votes."[95] Mitchell believes that lawmakers targeted and destroyed the union after Hurricane Katrina specifically to neutralize its powerful political voice. "We were a force to be reckoned with," recalls teacher Leoance Williams. "If we backed a candidate, nine times out of ten that candidate was going to win."[96] UTNO collaborated with community groups, especially with powerful organizations that emerged from the Black community, and it used its political work to continue to build leadership and involvement among members.[97] Though it did not take radical positions, UTNO did push the AFL-CIO to the left and argued for legislation and endorsements that would benefit workers, women, and the Black community. Before the storm, critics of the union complained that UTNO had too much influence, particularly in school board elections, and that it was becoming dangerously powerful.[98]

UTNO's political work offered another opportunity for union leaders to encourage member participation and democratic decision-making while also providing political education. The union inspired mass rank-and-file participation in its political work via building reps who recruited their friends and colleagues, who then learned more about the union's political operation, endorsement process, and political philosophy. One teacher said he participated in door-to-door canvasing out of "a sense of duty,"[99] but educators also remembered political activities as social and fun. Moreover, explained Lomba, "We saw the results of our participation," as conditions improved for teachers and pro-education bills passed through the state legislature.[100] The union's retirees' chapter was especially active in running phone banks, helping to bolster UTNO's reach and demonstrating the deep loyalty members felt to the organization, even after they had left the classroom.[101]

Many union members remembered the power of UTNO's endorsement process, in which candidates explained their positions before the executive board and asked for the union's endorsement. UTNO interviewed everyone. "Very few people ran in New Orleans for political office that didn't come to seek our endorsement," explains teacher and UTNO staffer Connie Goodly.[102] Because of AFL-CIO rules, the union officially had to follow the recommendations of that body, but UTNO wielded significant power there as well. Stanley Taylor attended Greater New Orleans AFL-CIO meetings as a member of NALC. He recalls, "UTNO played a very critical role in every election . . . since [Moon Landrieu was the mayor] and UTNO, still to this day, everyone seeks their endorsement."[103] Wade Rathke, founder of the community organization ACORN, went to AFL-CIO meetings when he organized the Local 100 service workers union in New Orleans. He remembered the local AFL-CIO as dominated by mostly white, male craft workers who lacked a larger social justice agenda: "You could have them for one job and a dollar."[104] The building trades, in Rathke's assessment, were preoccupied with endorsing judges who would be willing to give them backdoor favors when a union member was accused of a crime. But that was not true of UTNO: "Nat was always four-square. . . . Nat's local had more women, had more African-Americans and his members and my members lived in New Orleans which gave us a different voice."[105] He saw LaCour and UTNO as his greatest ally in the labor movement, pushing for larger systemic reforms.[106] However,

Rathke also felt like UTNO did not always use its outsized influence: "Nat decided frequently that he'd just go along to get along."[107] Though this strategy frustrated Rathke, and perhaps also the union's more radical supporters, it meant that when UTNO did take a stand on an issue, its voice was even more prominent.

This was clear during the endorsement process. "All the candidates wanted our endorsement," recalls Williams. "That was a prized thing . . . and we not only endorsed the candidates, we gave them workers. We would even have someone in their campaign headquarters help coordinate their activities. And also, we gave them money."[108] The union collected around $200,000 per year in political funds, so it was able to give the maximum amount to every candidate it endorsed.[109] Not only did UTNO represent 5,000 or more educators, it also influenced the votes of their families and friends: "It was the reach of the membership and getting those members to also encourage other people. That was pretty much the political power it had, the reach."[110] UTNO trained members in political campaigning and sent them to volunteer with candidates the union supported, serving both to back up its endorsement and to help develop member-leaders. Then, leading up to Election Day, the union would rent a bus called the "Flying Squad," fill it with UTNO members, and canvass target neighborhoods. Wanda Richard, a former UTNO president, first became politically involved through the Flying Squad: "Yes, I used to get on that bus, the Flying Squad. I remember walking to pass the half-cent millage. I got involved with political stuff with that."[111] On Election Day, the union would rent two buses or more to ensure that members could canvass multiple neighborhoods and encourage people to vote, as Grace Lomba explains: "And on Election Day, we had all our volunteers that would come in and we would go around to the neighborhoods and canvass the neighborhood, knock on doors. We worked for every candidate that we endorsed, anybody who wanted to run for office always came to UTNO for endorsements because they'd know we'd not only have our mouths, we'd put our people out there in the fields to work for you. So, the union, we did great things."[112] Community activist Beth Butler worked with UTNO members at Louisiana ACORN and saw its political work from the outside: "UTNO ran one of the most effective electoral machines that this city's ever seen. Back in the day, there were a few unions that really did put people on the ground, and door knock and canvass and do phone banks. But UTNO persisted with that."[113]

Along with canvassing, the union monitored polls in order to maximize its impact: "We also had poll watchers, people were assigned to that. And they would go into the polls and get the count to see how many people had voted. And then they would radio that back us to central office. And if the count was low, central office would call the bus and we would go in that area and canvass that area to try to get the people to come out to the polls."[114] Many members were involved, including paraprofessionals and secretaries. Donisia Wise, a secretary active

The UTNO "Flying Squad" bus, 1995. UTNO members would ride this bus around the city, encouraging residents to vote and canvassing for UTNO-endorsed candidates. *Courtesy of United Teachers of New Orleans.*

in the UTNO chapter, recalls phone banking as well as monitoring polls.[115] Jo Anna Russo was an UTNO grievance specialist on staff but she, like everybody else, worked on their political campaigns:

> They had a big map [in the office], and they would say which streets we covered and what other streets we needed to go to. And [the poll watcher] would call, and they would write down the precinct, how many votes were here at such and such a time. It was an unbelievable political machine that [Nat] had. And imagine if we had cellphones at that time. I mean, if we had the communication devices that we have now compared to what we had then, we could text you the numbers and stuff. . . . When we gave our endorsement, we worked the neighborhoods for the candidate.[116]

This work politicized UTNO members, developed their leadership skills, and connected democracy within UTNO to larger democratic processes in the city and the state. By prioritizing political education for its members, so that they could participate actively in endorsement and canvassing processes, UTNO increased its members' ability to engage democratically both in the union and as citizens.

Candidates endorsed by UTNO, who received UTNO volunteers in their offices and knocking on doors, knew how indebted they were to the union and voted accordingly once they were in office. "School board elections were [UTNO's] bread and butter,"[117] explains Rathke. However, UTNO's influence was weaker in white uptown neighborhoods, and the union frequently found itself at odds with the board. UTNO also, like all organizations, made mistakes. For example, in the 1992 school board election, it endorsed Leslie Jacobs, who would go on to become one of the architects of the city's privatization plan, effectively destroying the union post-Katrina.[118]

With more than 5,000 members, UTNO's endorsements inevitably disappointed some people. Teacher Laverne Kappel was an UTNO member but not very involved: "I applauded when I thought the union did things that were good for us, and I supported what they did. And I criticized them when I thought they did things that hurt the profession. Supporting candidates who had already been convicted of fraud, [Michael] O'Keefe? He was running for state legislature, and the union backed him, and I'm like, what? . . . You're crazy, the man's a felon."[119]

Teacher Juanita Bailey said there were political divides among the members: "You would have members that were upset if we went with too many Democratic [candidates]. But you know what those people did? They would basically call in to us and say, 'I don't want you taking out political money.' Because you can't mix union dues and political money."[120] Bailey estimates that twenty to thirty people every year wrote the office to say that they didn't want money taken out for COPE—as a form of protest. But the vast majority appreciated and promoted the endorsements. According to Richard, people today still call the UTNO office before elections to get a list of its endorsements: "The community still relies on UTNO for a lot of things because when we do political things, we have people at the office be calling, 'Okay, who y'all voting for? Can y'all send me one of y'all endorsement sheets?' They still call for that. Every time we do it, they usually vote with the teachers and for the teachers."[121]

The union's political work not only enhanced UTNO's power in the city and the state, it also served to deeply connect educators to the communities in which they taught. By knocking on doors and talking to parents and workers, union members gained a better understanding of the challenges many of their students faced. Teacher Gwendolyn Adams remembers people being appreciative when she knocked on their doors: "People were receptive. Because people want to know, who has my child's best interest at heart? Or who doesn't?"[122] The larger Black community saw UTNO as the voice of the teachers and of the schools.

In addition to going door to door for candidates it endorsed, UTNO partnered with APRI to increase voter turnout, especially among Black voters. APRI, as the Black caucus for the AFL-CIO, does not issue endorsements but instead promotes voter education and turnout efforts. Stanley Taylor was the NALC representative to APRI: "The A. Philip Randolph worked in conjunction with UTNO. And UTNO provided the space and the time and the money."[123] UTNO was the center of Black labor organizing within New Orleans and played a vital role in encouraging Black democratic participation, both within its membership and in the community at large. It also partnered with Black political groups, as LaCour describes: "[We worked with] SOUL, BOLD, COUP, Dutch Morial created a group called LIFE, Congressman Jefferson created a group called the Progressive Democrats. So, we worked with all of those groups. When there was an election going on, I would assign one of my members to work with each of those organizations to find out what was their agenda, and we would support them on the things that we could support them on, and we would all get together and endorse the same candidates."[124] This strategy gave members unique opportunities to develop their political acumen and also ensured that UTNO remained at the center of political conversations. These groups saw UTNO as an organization with integrity, and the union avoided many of the intergroup conflicts that split Black political alliances in the city. After he went to work for the national AFT, LaCour realized just how exceptional UTNO's political machinery was: "I think we had more membership involved. I think we were more politically involved than most other unions around the country . . . when it came to politics, I don't think we took second seat to anybody, except for perhaps the UFT. It was hard work."[125] Though individuals sometimes disagreed with positions that UTNO took, the union stands as a remarkable example of labor democracy, largely free from public political rifts or scandals, and trusted by the community.

UTNO's bargaining success in New Orleans influenced and bankrolled the union's expansion statewide and its lobbying work in Baton Rouge. Eventually, the LFT hired two full-time lobbyists who worked closely with the state AFL-CIO. Joy Van Buskirk, one of those lobbyists, says the LFT started as a fledgling organization under the wing of the AFL-CIO, but soon grew in power. "[The AFL-CIO] was the legend when we got to the legislature, they still had a lot of clout there. By about the mid-'90s, they had no clout and we had the clout."[126] While the AFL-CIO's membership dwindled, especially after the passage of right-to-work legislation in 1976, the LFT's membership continued to grow. The LFT also diverged from the AFL-CIO because it had made alliances across the aisle, whereas the AFL-CIO lobbied only Democrats. "I knew that Republicans in general would not be able to support all of our legislation, but I could catch various legislators on different pieces of legislation and get them to vote with us. And the president of the Senate [John Hainkel] funded three of our programs. He was a Republican."[127] The LFT used its lobbying arm to develop programs that would benefit some of the union's most low-paid members, such as the paraprofessional tuition exemption program, sponsored by Hainkel, which allowed paraprofessionals to attend college for free to get their teaching certification. "If we could make [educators'] lives a bit better through legislation, that was our mission."[128]

Though the LFT won collective bargaining in three parishes only—New Orleans in 1974, Jefferson in 1975, and St. Tammany in 1992—it formed locals in all the most populous areas:

We sent Bob [Crowley] to the state to work for the LFT, and to organize. I asked Crowley to identify the largest parishes in Louisiana that
would constitute 50 percent of the state population, and that was eleven
parishes in which more than 50 percent of people live. And I told him to
focus his organizing on those eleven parishes, because if we could organize those eleven, then they could each help elect somebody to represent
them in Baton Rouge. And that way we would have 50 percent of the
legislature, so we could then pass legislation, and that's what we did. But
in doing that, we grew.[129]

When he started working for the LFT, Crowley reached out to the AFT locals at
fourteen colleges across the state:[130] "So I wrote a letter to all the board members of the UFCT, the United Federation of College Teachers, saying, 'Look,
we're trying to organize the state. Would you talk to some teachers that might
be taking classes from you or whatever? Give me some leads.' I mean, the leads
just start rolling in."[131] Crowley estimates that he organized fourteen to fifteen
locals throughout the state from 1975 to 2003.[132] "There were three states in the
nation where the union teachers' organization was the largest, that was New York,
Rhode Island, and Louisiana. In the rest of the states, the NEA was the largest
group."[133] LFT's success throughout the state increased its reach and power but
also resulted in compromises, as it now represented locals with majority rural,
white teachers as well. Fred Skelton, an UTNO staffer who became LFT president in 1985, said he didn't think these differences were as great as the public
imagined; all teachers wanted more education funding, higher salaries, and the
protection of union rights, such as tenure and due process.[134]

The LFT lobbyists worked both the legislature and BESE and were largely
successful in stymieing, or at least delaying, the neoliberal education agenda.
They also could rely on member support when the legislature threatened their
interests. For example, in April 1997, "in an extraordinary concession to union
power," the OPSB canceled school for one day so that UTNO members could
attend a rally in Baton Rouge to demand pay raises and the preservation of teacher
tenure, extended sick pay, and sabbaticals.[135] Approximately 6,000 teachers
attended the rally and Governor Foster promised them pay raises.[136] The *Times
Picayune* was aghast at the school closures, claiming they were anti-child and a
misuse of union power: "Evidently, lots of teachers changed their minds [about
attending the rally] and decided to lollygag around town that day. Hardly surprising, since teachers are great lollygaggers. . . . If they are not lollygagging in
the park, it is fair bet they're hanging around a school corridor whining about
the alleged pressures and privations of a teacher's life."[137]

Despite the newspaper's outrage, many educators reflected positively on
traveling with UTNO to Baton Rouge for one protest or another. Though Leoance

Williams never spoke at rallies or in front of the legislature, he recalled, "It was fun. We'd go to Baton Rouge and sit in the chamber. Listen to the [discussion]. And certain people were designated to speak. Most of the time it was the leader of the group. But we were mostly there for our presence."[138] Larry Samuel, UTNO's longtime lawyer, recalled lobbying in the capitol less fondly: "I still to this day grudgingly go up to Baton Rouge kicking and screaming on stuff. If you've ever done that, don't. It's just awful."[139] However unpleasant, UTNO's lobbying efforts played a large role in sustaining labor power both in the education sector and in state politics writ large. Skelton felt like state legislators saw the union as a tough opponent but also as fair and student-focused. UTNO often collaborated with BESE on textbook selection and UTNO staff would recommend teacher leaders to sit on committees and advise the board: "One of the proudest things that has ever happened to me was that when I retired, BESE gave me a plaque thanking me for leadership. . . . The change from they never had even heard of us to now them saying thank you for leadership, I was very proud of that. I was very proud that they recognized us as saying something that represented what teachers wanted and what was good for education. If I had just been solely partisan, I'm sure that it wouldn't have worked."[140] Though this dynamic shifted in the years immediately preceding the storm, as BESE threatened to take over the Orleans Parish district, the collaborative relationship between the LFT and BESE ultimately helped the union secure more education funding and protect workers' rights even through several conservative administrations.

In part, UTNO's reputation at both the state and local level can be attributed to LaCour's talents. He developed effective leaders and sent knowledgeable people to serve on committees and do political work. "Nat was always issue oriented, problem-solving oriented," remembers teacher Mike Stone. "He was the least personally ambitious person. He was always interested in serving the rank and file, improving education, those kind of things."[141] While maintaining a culture of participatory democracy and incorporating everybody's feedback, LaCour pushed the union toward fair and just education positions. Connie Goodly recalls, "Nat was a person that involved us and made certain that we stayed involved in the political arena, and in the community and all . . . and Nat was very, very well respected in the community. Even though there were people that were not always supportive of us, such as the chamber [of commerce], there were people who were part of the chamber, like the Pres Kabacoffs and all those people who respected him. Who made certain that we were involved in certain things."[142]

For example, LaCour wrote a letter to the editor of the *Times Picayune* in response to the column accusing teachers of being self-serving lollygaggers. He calmly discussed every point raised by the newspaper, reasserted the union's position, and encouraged civil discourse and compassion, all while discussing teachers' integrity and industriousness.[143] Even residents angry about the one-day school closure were likely to exit the exchange believing that LaCour and UTNO had the upper hand.

Along with pushing for educators' rights, UTNO used its political machine to generally support progressive candidates and a Black and working-class agenda. This was especially on display during the 1991 election in which David Duke, former grand wizard of the Ku Klux Klan, ran for governor. "UTNO really worked in that campaign," Stone recalls. "School teachers and others came in from everywhere to oppose the Ku Klux Klan guy."[144] The union endorsed Democrat Edwin Edwards and campaigned tirelessly on his behalf. UTNO sent out a newsletter imploring its members to vote for Edwards: "Louisiana's reputation is at stake. If Duke wins, *every* Louisiana citizen, now and for generations, will suffer the ignominy of being from a state that elected as its chief official ambassador and spokesman a man whose fame and following is a result of racist rhetoric. . . . For a respectable future for Louisiana, for our own dignity and the dignity of every other Louisiana citizen, we must vote Saturday and get others to vote, also."[145] Connie Goodly argues that the anti-Duke sentiment in New Orleans brought together an alliance that might never occur again: "Everybody came together, even the Chamber of Commerce did not want to see him as the governor. Everybody. Labor, business, everybody came together and that was a coalition that we might never see again in the city for a long, long time."[146] Edwards won the election, defeating both Duke and Republican incumbent Buddy Roemer, who had earned teachers' ill-will for his controversial LaTEP evaluation program described above.

UTNO's political work was renowned throughout the state, and it was successful because of the consistent active participation of its members. In part, this energy was a holdover from the original collective bargaining campaign, which had inspired mass participation, but it was also buoyed by UTNO's genuinely democratic structure and ongoing protests and strikes, which created solidarity and loyalty to the union. LaCour and his staff visited schools every morning to talk to teachers, hear their concerns, and get them involved.[147] The educators responded in kind. They worked on campaigns, lobbied in Baton Rouge, held work stoppages, educated voters, and promoted democracy. They phone banked, canvassed, donated money, and solicited their friends and communities. UTNO was able to fight business interests because of its reach, both in New Orleans and throughout the state, and as it did, it built community and member loyalty. "It's a really a tragedy of human nature or something that as good as we feel about UTNO and our involvement with it, most New Orleanians thought we were scum. Protecting bad teachers and a lousy school system," laments Mike Stone. The contribution that UTNO made to participatory democracy, working-class and Black politics, and labor progressivism throughout the state has been largely obscured by post-Katrina debates about the relative merits of charter schools. Yet the loss of UTNO's political machine has altered city and state politics perhaps to an even greater extent than other aspects of school privatization.

LABOR POWER: MILLAGES, THE 1990 STRIKE, AND "ERASE THE BOARD"

UTNO also translated its political power into increased education funding. It was particularly difficult to get millages passed in New Orleans because of the high percentage of families, both white and Black, who sent their children to private and parochial schools. These parents worried about being hit twice by tax increases because they expected that once public school teachers won raises, parochial school teachers would demand increases as well, and tuition would rise.[148] Though voters defeated the 1986 millage by nearly 2–1, in their 1987 contracts both UTNO and the Teamsters (who represented school bus drivers and maintenance workers) agreed to accept no raises and pledged instead to work on a millage campaign.[149] As part of the negotiations, OPSB agreed again to hold a millage election, this time in April 1988. The board structured the millage like a menu, with voters able to say yes or no to five separate millage categories: teacher and administrator raises, purchasing new textbooks and materials, expanding early childhood education, installing air conditioning and removing asbestos, and new schools and renovations.[150] Lee Gary, former head of the Business Task Force, again opposed the millage, calling it "vague" and "crafty," but this time the board and teachers had earned support from other business groups, including the chamber of commerce, as well as from community groups such as the NAACP and the Urban League.[151] Voters approved four of the five allocations, rejecting only the money allocated for new schools and renovations by 151 votes, despite campaigning by opponents who posted "Taxes, Hell No" signs all over the city.[152] This was the first property tax increase in New Orleans in thirty-three years.[153]

Joe DeRose, a teacher and UTNO staffer, spent some of his time photographing schools to document deteriorating and unsafe facilities, overheated classrooms, and mold growing on the walls. He thinks that, particularly after the storm, lawmakers and community members blamed teachers for poor educational outcomes which were really the result of community apathy:

> The general population was responsible for that. And to some extent, I'm going to put some of this on the white community that did not want to support public schools. When we would have an election for a tax referendum for schools, we would analyze the statistics afterwards. And you can look at the statistics and see that the lowest support for school issues was in the [white] university district . . . [In the 1988 tax referendum,] I

think [the university district] was the only district in the whole city where they voted even against the most acceptable thing, providing textbooks for kids.[154]

DeRose estimates it would have taken a billion dollars to transform the school district into the safe and well-resourced system he imagined. "The squeaky wheel gets the oil," explains LaCour. "And parents, poor Black parents, are not as effective, as active, or know what to do as much as middle-class white parents."[155]

LaCour lists increased funding for the schools as one of the union's most significant accomplishments. UTNO used its negotiating process not only to get benefits for teachers but also to pressure the board into asking voters for additional funds and thereby improving education for students.[156] The union and the board ultimately convinced voters to increase educational funding four times: the 1988 property tax millage, sales tax increases in 1980 and 1992, and a bond issue in 1995. These campaigns created a sense of interclass solidarity between the middle-class UTNO teachers and the poor and working-class families who used the schools.

Though the board gave teachers 7 percent raises following the 1988 millage, by 1990 much of that money had been eaten up by health care premiums, which rose 70 percent over those two years, according to LaCour.[157] Thus, the union again sought teacher raises even as the board claimed it was $17 million in the red.[158] The union once more threatened to strike. This was a daring move because of both the exponential decline of strikes nationwide as well as the weakened status of organized labor in the state. The prior year, the vice president of the Greater New Orleans AFL-CIO reported, "Organized labor is at its lowest ebb ever," and cited statistics showing that 28.9 percent of Louisiana's workforce was unionized in 1975 compared with only 13.8 percent in 1982.[159] One teacher critical of the union, who never joined, found UTNO's perennial strike threats unproductive: "[UTNO] didn't have a lot of weapons, and they didn't use the weapons that they had very well. Their tendency was to be pugnacious when the power was obviously on the side of the system. The talk of striking, the threat of striking was less effectual than it should have been."[160] Despite how controversial it was, UTNO's willingness to disrupt the status quo allowed for rank-and-file leadership and democratic decision-making, and it enabled the union to maintain power even as organized labor lost ground statewide. As negotiations between the board and the union continued, teachers reported to school and delayed the strike deadline, indicating that they were unenthusiastic about the prospect of holding a strike.[161]

In 1990, the union specifically demanded modest 4 to 5 percent raises for clerical workers and paraprofessionals, who had been excluded from state raises and who made average annual salaries of $15,860 and $11,040, respectively (approx.

$37,200 and $25,900 in 2023 dollars), at a $2 million price tag. The *Times Pica-yune*, outraged by these demands, published a series of articles justifying the low pay these workers received because they were higher paid than their counterparts in other parishes.[162] The newspaper's callousness toward the support workers' salary needs indicates its inability to see the workers as part of a larger school ecosystem, crucial to students' success not only because of the work they did in the schools, but also because so many of them were the parents and family members of students themselves. Moreover, while teachers often framed their own salary demands as part of a feminist agenda, since traditionally feminized professions such as teaching, nursing, and social work are underpaid compared to other jobs that require a college degree, an even larger percentage of the para-professional and clerical workforce were Black women. UTNO thus aligned its organization with the most marginalized segments of its membership, many of whom had little access to college or other job opportunities. Teachers dropped their own salary demands and pledged to concentrate on getting the board to improve salaries for paraprofessionals and clerical workers.[163] Meanwhile, the board held firm to its line that there simply wasn't any money available. "When a district is prepared to cry broke and poor," said LaCour, "it needs to do some things that are symbolic like cutting comforts of administrators."[164]

As the September 17 strike deadline approached, teachers lowered their salary demands to $1 million, yet again demonstrating their willingness to avoid a strike. Though this was only $400,000 more than the board had offered, the board refused to budge.[165] "We made an offer to settle the contract without a strike if the district would give a raise to the paras and the clericals," recalls DeRose. "And they didn't do that. And of course the stipulation was that if they didn't do that and we went on strike, we were going to be going on strike to get a raise for everybody."[166] Connie Goodly, then a full-time UTNO staffer, was shocked that the strike occurred at all, "because the difference between the union's demands and the school board's demands was so little. . . . People just jumped up and voted to go on strike. It was amazing."[167] Even UTNO staff were surprised by the rank and file's anger at the board and their willingness to engage in labor militancy.

The union met before school on the morning of September 17 to decide how to proceed, as Mike Stone relates:

Nat had explained what the conflicts were and why the negotiating team thought we should go on strike and how important this was da-de-da-de-da. A real good white union member, taught at a school that was overcrowded, so they had two shifts in a day. They went to work earlier than most schools, and then had a second half of the day for different students. Anyway, he got up, after we had been talking, people asking questions, people were nervous. He got up and said,

"According to my watch, I've already been on strike for 15 minutes, and I invite all of you all to join me." And then Mary DeLoch got up and she had been a swimmer and a gymnast in her youth, but she was a heavy woman as she grew older. And she got up and she said, "The last offer we have from the school board comes to a penny a pound for me and I ain't taking it."[168]

This comment brought the more than 3,000 attendees of the rally to their feet with applause. "Mary DeLoch made that strike for us," recalls LaCour.[169] The teachers walked out, reverted to their original $45 million demand, and mounted a recall campaign against all the board members.[170] UTNO members' willingness to strike was in part because of the union's long legacy of disruption and their powerful civil rights history.[171] However, members also had a deep trust in UTNO and, specifically, in LaCour's leadership, which was characterized by transparency and collaboration. Demonstrating their faith in LaCour, picketers chanted: *"I pledge allegiance to the strike of the United Teachers of New Orleans / and to the cause for which we stand / One union, under Nat, indivisible / with dignity and justice for all."*[172]

Teachers remembered the 1990 strike as more contentious than UTNO's prior 1978 strike: fewer teachers participated, and it lasted longer. While more than 70 percent of teachers went on strike in 1978, in 1990, according to the board, 68 percent of teachers were out on the first day, but that number dwindled to 59 percent by the fifteenth and final day of the strike.[173] The climate was also more negative than it had been in 1978. Patti Reynolds remembers that in the late 1970s and early 1980s, school district administrators and UTNO members had played recreational softball together, whereas by 1990, many UTNO members perceived the strike as the board's attempt to break the union.[174] Ken Ducote, a school district employee, affirmed that some administrators saw the strike as an opportunity: "There were some people in the administration who thought it was a chance to break the union by forcing a strike that the teachers were going to lose. And you know, me and a couple other administrators kept saying, 'Nobody's going to win this.'"[175] Whereas the city and the state were in a modest economic boom during the 1978 strike, the 1990 strike came following years of budget cuts to education and other municipal services. From 1980 to 1990, the percentage of families living in poverty in New Orleans rose from 21.9 percent to 27.3 percent.[176] Teacher Diego Gonzalez-Grande argues that these conditions affected community support for the strike:

First of all, in the 1978 strike, it seemed like the city was completely with us. Nobody liked the administrative group and the school board. There was a sense that there would be a fairly fast resolution, and there was. The second time around, for one thing, the city was experiencing, far greater economic difficulties. Oil had left us and, of course, the economy of the state had tanked, in a way, and it was still in the process of transition. There was a greater sense of anger and frustration in the city itself. There was a sense that there was a much greater hostility to the notion of teachers going on strike.[177]

This atmosphere also impacted educators' perceptions of the strike: "The second strike, it wasn't as successful because I think people had gotten into a lull. . . . People were more complacent, and they weren't as gung-ho as they were for that first strike."[178] Cindy Robinson, a white teacher who had participated in the first strike in 1978, crossed picket lines in 1990. She said that at McMain, a magnet school, few of her coworkers went on strike: "By that time, the union was sort of on a negative for me."[179] Though she had vivid memories of the 1978 strike, she had few recollections of 1990, though the latter strike lasted much longer, and she could not remember if there had been a picket line. Patti Reynolds and Mike Stone, both ardent UTNO supporters, also taught at McMain. "I don't know how it was at other schools," says Robinson, "but I don't feel like a lot of people walked out at McMain. . . . I don't know, maybe we weren't unhappy enough."[180] Samantha Turner, a Black teacher at McMain, also crossed the picket lines because she didn't want to let down her Advanced Placement students: "It wasn't that I was anti what the union fought for. Because, at that time, it was a valid strike. But my commitment to these classes was stronger than that."[181] By 1990, UTNO was no longer riding on the energy of the civil rights movement, as they had been in 1978. The strike was seen by the public as well as by some educators as more of a labor dispute than a righteous crusade, and thus it was more contentious. Despite these examples, UTNO maintained high participation throughout the ordeal—it lasted from September 17 to October 7—and the union emerged victorious in the end.

Many teachers remembered this strike as particularly moral because they had walked out in support of the paraprofessional and clerical workers. "That probably is the time we struck because the paras didn't get a raise," explains Brenda Mitchell. "Well, to me, that was all a part of what a union is about. It's the one for all, all for one, and we realized that paraprofessionals are essential to the instructional process. They stood there with us, then we should stand for them."[182] Fred Skelton, then working as LFT president in Baton Rouge, came down to New Orleans to help with the strike: "I thought, in some ways, [the 1990 strike] was even more noble. . . . And I think the teachers felt proud of themselves that they had done that, that they were not just out for themselves, that they did something for the PSRPs [paraprofessionals and school-related personnel] who worked in the schools right beside them."[183] Though business interests often tried to sow conflict between the employee groups by offering raises only to teachers or by trying to outsource and privatize school support workers to save money, the union worked hard to unite the groups. This was prescient in the face of neoliberal policy shifts in which the logic of cost-saving privatization might apply first to custodians and cafeteria workers but would soon extend to support workers and then teachers and entire schools. It also was strategic for the union, as clerical workers and paraprofessionals represented significant membership groups. Moreover, it was part of an educational ideology that sees all workers as crucial to the success of the school:

> We did encounter, from some parents, a greater degree of skepticism, since we were not on strike demanding significant increases for ourselves. There was a sense in some people that if this is not about you, if it's not about things improving for you in a direct way, why are you then out in the street depriving our children of education? Our only answer could be that, in fact, support personnel are as vital for the administration of a school: your clerical personnel, your cafeteria people, the people who clean the bathrooms and toilet. They perform all sorts of tasks without which a school cannot function, and so, yes, providing them with at least an adequate financial compensation, in fact, does benefit your students, your children, in an indirect way.[184]

Though this argument might not have resonated at magnet schools, it certainly resonated with working-class families whose relatives and neighbors held many of those jobs.

Class and race divisions also determined which educators chose to go on strike. Susie Beard, a paraprofessional area coordinator during the strike, was responsible for monitoring the picket lines at ten schools. She says that paraprofessionals were always an extremely loyal segment of the union: "I think all the paras went out. Just a few teachers didn't go out. . . . We were strong. I mean, that's why we were incorporated, because we stood together. We knew we came from a low area and what the union had gained for us, so most of us were out on the line."[185] Just as paraprofessionals were UTNO's most loyal constituency, teachers at magnet schools, especially white teachers, tended to have the least union loyalty. The working conditions at their schools were better, their schools had more funding because of outside (parent and alumni) donations, they had fewer problems with discipline and violence, and if they were white, they were shielded from overt racial discrimination in evaluations and performance reviews.

Louise Mouton Johnson was one of few Black teachers at the selective-admissions NOCCA during the 1990 strike, and she was the only member of the faculty to go on strike: "The first day of the strike I was out there with a sign by myself. What was so great was, after a few minutes Fred Skelton came, Nat LaCour came, so it's like all the big dogs were there walking with me."[186]

UTNO members from Support and Appraisal picket during the 1990 strike.
Support and Appraisal comprised approximately 100 employees who
tested children for special education services. The group, which included
psychologists, speech pathologists, audiologists, and others, joined UTNO's
bargaining unit in 1989. They are standing in the parking lot behind 703
Carondelet, which housed the school board's main offices. The security
guards joined them in their protest. *Photograph by Karen Walk Geisert.*

Johnson went on strike not because she had critiques of the working conditions
at NOCCA, but because she supported the union. "[NOCCA] was such a perfect
situation. It was almost as if there were no reasons to be upset about anything
with the original principal."[187] She attributes her coworkers' decision not to
participate in the strike to their satisfaction with the school. Though the union's
civil rights work was largely in the past, Black teachers still were more likely
than white teachers to see supporting the strike as an important way to show
solidarity with their colleagues across the city.

Of course, there were teachers at nonselective schools who crossed the picket
lines, too. Marta Bivens was an itinerant theater teacher at the time:

> [The strike] was very upsetting to me. I didn't think teachers should go
> on strike, especially at Henderson. [The students] have so much disrup-
> tion in their life to begin with. There were just some horrible situations.
> It was in the Fischer Projects. I had one little kid who was usually very
> enthusiastic about doing drama and music one day just peter out, and
> I was like, "What's with Joseph?" The teacher came and said, "Well, his
> mother was shot in the face by her lover last night. And he was there."
> I'm like, "And then they sent him to school?" There's no place else for

him to go. A lot of kids were in that situation, and they might not get fed if they didn't [come to school]. . . . I thought, how could you walk off the job with these kids in this situation?[188]

However, the union argued that they needed to strike to improve conditions for students in these difficult situations by demanding increased salaries that would help the district retain quality teachers, clericals, and paraprofessionals. The *Times Picayune* featured an article interviewing teachers at Sophie B. Wright and Green Middle Schools. Teachers at Wright reported that they had to purchase soap, hand towels, and toilet paper for the school, in addition to dealing with overcrowded classrooms, no air conditioning, and poor lighting. Teachers at Green asked students to bring their own water because the school had only one functional water fountain for over 700 students.[189] Teacher Susie Beard explained how these conditions put teachers in an untenable situation:

> That perception that you are deserting children, that you are letting them down by not teaching them is an argument, of course, which has been addressed by thousands of teachers in the states that have gone on strike [in spring 2018], which is that you are doing a disservice to students if you don't have adequate facilities, if you don't have adequate resources, and to expect teachers to invariably provide them, in the absence of a community's support, is unrealistic and is, in fact, a formula for defeat, because those teachers eventually may leave for a more sympathetic environment.[190]

Beard believes these other needs eventually won parents over into supporting the strike: "In the beginning, a lot of parents were against [the strike], but then they found out that we were not just fighting for benefits for us but for the students as well, their safety, the curriculum that was being taught and all of that. We just didn't strike just for benefits for us and working conditions that we benefited from, but the student populations and the principals [benefited] too. [We all were working] in buildings that were unsafe."[191] Though the union played a crucial watchdog role, documenting persistent inequalities and unsafe conditions in the schools, critics complained that it too often settled for salary increases alone and let these other issues fall by the wayside.

While such problems were less prevalent at magnet schools, many teachers chose to honor the picket lines at those buildings as well. Diego Gonzalez-Grande taught at elite Ben Franklin High, which at that time had a mostly white teaching force. He estimates that approximately 60 percent of teachers went on strike, a little lower than the average for the city at large.[192] Joel Behrman taught alongside Gonzalez-Grande at Franklin and participated in the strike: "Franklin was very important in that strike, because it was a different kind of school. I think some people didn't give a shit about Black schools on strike. That was someone else's kids. They were kids that weren't going to learn anyway. Franklin teachers going on strike suddenly involved people that were connected with power."[193] Magnet schools such as Franklin, McMain, and NOCCA were therefore central to the public's understanding of the strike, even though these schools had lower teacher participation. A lot of Gonzalez-Grande's work during the strike entailed convincing ambivalent coworkers to continue holding the line:

> Part of my job, then, was to reassure [a colleague] that it would be okay, that she shouldn't have to worry about listening to a hostile media, reading a hostile newspaper, because the *Times Picayune*, on both occasions, described our behavior as basically unprofessional. I told her not to worry. On one occasion, we were described as behaving no better than coal miners and Teamsters, or words to that effect. I told her, "There's nothing wrong with acting like a miner or a Teamster. Those are perfectly respectable professions," because as I said, it was something that ran contrary to the value system that she had been raised with, that strikes are the sort of thing that only working-class people engage in.[194]

The strike provided a unique opportunity for UTNO members to develop their class analysis, show solidarity with their colleagues, learn from each other, and rise to positions of leadership within their schools as well as the union.

The argument that it was "unprofessional" for teachers to belong to a union had been levied against the teachers for years, and it speaks to how radical union participation became during the era of labor's decline. Violet Johnson, who worked for the school district and helped coordinate its strike plan, saw this as a negative outcome of the strike: "It also radicalized so dramatically so many people this strike . . . [One of my kids' teachers] became so radicalized after that, just very angry at the district that they didn't give in to the teachers, and couldn't see the other side at all. [Another friend] never really talked to me again."[195] State business interests, such as LABI, rightly viewed union participation, and especially the labor militancy seen in strikes, as directly threatening its interests, even when those on strike were not factory workers. The act of going on strike inherently fomented a class analysis as well as a sense of racial solidarity that aligned teachers not only with the support workers and other unionized school employees but also with the labor movement writ large.

Donisia Wise was a clerical workers' leader during the strike. Despite the strike ostensibly being over salary increases for paraprofessionals and clerical workers, she notes that clerical workers were more hesitant to strike because many of them worked so closely with principals: "We had a good number of teachers who went out at that particular time and we did have clericals, but not too, too many clericals. A lot of the clericals felt as though they didn't want to leave their jobs. I don't know for what reason, but they had that embedded in their minds."[196] Wise was a single parent who says it was stressful to forgo pay, but she went out anyway because she wanted "to be a part for the betterment."[197] Teachers who chose not to join the union or participate in the strike often justi-fied their decision by bemoaning the high cost. For example, a white teacher at McMain, whose wife was also a teacher, felt that participating in the strike would cause them excessive financial harm: "I thought about going on strike, but an awful lot [of] my position was driven by money. I just didn't see how we could get along monetarily, financially. We had no resources. We didn't have any savings. Having said that, I had a lot of friends who were in that same position and still went out on strike and suffered seriously because of it."[198] Alorea Gilyot, for example, got a loan through the UTNO credit union so she could go on strike and still afford to pay her six-month-old son's daycare costs.[199] Black educators were often more willing to make sacrifices out of loyalty to the teaching corps and the larger Black community—and they had greater faith in union decision-making: "It is true, I think, among African American teachers at Franklin, there was a much greater sense that this was an issue [in] which you had to demonstrate solidarity with the rest of faculty in the city. . . . Certainly today, when we have even less diversity, if we were to go on strike, I have no doubt that my African American colleagues would walk out, because I think they also recognize that if the union here decides on that tactic, it must be for a fairly good reason."[200] Paraprofessional Linda Pichon felt like white educators were more fearful of the potential consequences of going on strike: "You have some [white people] that're so afraid to . . . They'll pay their dues, but they would be afraid to say something. You can't make it like that. You don't have to have an angry voice or something."[201] Cindy Robinson suggests that the racial divide in strike support reflected a larger moment of racial tension in the city: "I don't think it had to do with the strike. I just think that there have been times in my career that I've noticed this more than other times, that Black teachers stay together, and white teachers stay together more than other times, you know?"[202]

Due to these racial and ideological divides among educators, the strike was contentious. Though the administration kept all the schools open, 32 to 40 percent of teachers crossed through picket lines of their striking colleagues to get to work. Grace Lomba says that only four or five teachers crossed the line at Lawless High:

Two of whom were very dear friends of mine. One said to me, "Well you know Grace, my mother is sick and I need, blah blah blah." I say, "All of us have issues." And then there was another one, he was a coach, he was dear friend of mine, he said the same thing. "Make up your mind what you're gonna do." . . . So, I had one teacher [who] used to ride with me to school every day, she crossed the pickets. Her husband would take her to school early in the morning and she'd go through the fence to get into the school. I didn't know that because I wasn't around the schools. So, somebody called to tell me that she crossed the picket lines. I said, "Hmm. Okay." I knew her husband worked at Piccadilly's [restaurant] in Gentilly. So group of us go on [over] there after we get off the line to eat lunch. And I saw him and I say, "Oh Mr. So-and-So," I say, "Why is your wife crossing that picket line at Lawless? She crawled through the fence." Everybody in that restaurant looked. He went to the back and never came back out. And I told her after, I said, "You can't ride with me anymore. You have to get another ride to school, I cannot bring you." And she worked on the same hall with me, she was in my department. I kind of mellowed out a couple of years later.[203]

Many teachers, like Lomba's friend, arrived early in the morning to avoid crossing a picket line of their colleagues: "I always got there very early. It was dark. So, there weren't picket lines when I arrived and I was always parked in the lot, and teachers were not supposed to stand in front of cars or . . . I did have one person who stood in front of my car once. I had the uncharitable thought of hitting the gas, but I didn't."[204] Katrena Ndang was at Kennedy High during the 1990 strike and later transferred to Lawless. Even though she had not been at Lawless during the strike, she still knew who had not participated: "One thing about strikes is that they let you know who is who. . . . It had nothing to do with race. It had to do with the fact that your butt came in this room and walked across that picket line or crawled under a fence to get inside the school, and we're not talking to you."[205] Because the 1990 strike was more contentious and had less member participation, animosities lingered between some coworkers for years. These divisions were exacerbated by the school board briefly paying nonstriking teachers an additional fifty-five dollars per day, though they almost immediately reversed the policy.[206]

The strike also divided the larger community, including parents. Paraprofessional Jacqueline Johnson worked at McDonogh 28 Elementary, which is located on central Esplanade Avenue:

It was fun because it was more of a picnic thing. We had the coffee shop across the street. We had Canseco's [Grocery] down the street, and we could go get food. It was good. We could sit down here at the trees under there. You know how they have the tour buses going down Esplanade, going to visit the cemeteries and all? All the people on the tour buses were waving and yelling at us, "C'mon, keep it going!" So it was fun. What I liked about it too, the old white people in the neighborhod, they were very nice, because we tried to control our kids to not tear up their neighborhood, because that's a historic neighborhood. Those old people were bringing hot foods to us and everything. The ladies would come out and bring chairs and see if you'd need anything. It was a good little strike.[207]

Many teachers remembered parents who supported the strike and who even joined them on the picket lines, sometimes bringing their children along as a makeshift civics lesson.[208] Leoance Williams was friendly with his students' parents, and some of them came into the school during the strike to substitute in his kindergarten classroom: "We were glad they were there, because we didn't want our kids traumatized by the big kids, and things of that nature. So it became like a symbiotic thing. We were glad that they were there. They wanted us back in the classroom, but they understood why we were striking."[209]

By contrast, at another school, teachers were angry that parents crossed the picket lines to hold classes and considered them scabs: "I know there were parents who were teaching our classes at the time. And it really caused a big strain, because our school was really a family."[210] Teachers told the media that unqualified parents were holding classes, which led to the popular principal receiving widespread criticism: "I think [the principal] was hurt, because it made it seem as if he was just letting anybody in the school. Yeah, it was not a good time."[211] Other parents threatened striking educators. Susie Beard recalls:

> Parents were out there angry because we were striking, and a lot of friendships with teachers broke down because friends went in, and you're on the line trying to get better benefits for everybody. . . . Even the schools that were located by the Baptist Seminary on Chef [Highway], the pastors and all that were in those seminaries, they had children in one of my schools that was located on Mirabeau [Avenue]. Those men who were going to be pastors would get out there and try to run over us while we were on the picket line.[212]

Frank Fudesco, lead negotiator for the board, says that parent opinion was mixed: "Some [supported], some did not. I think it was split. [It is] in all strikes. I don't care what they tell you. At least in New Orleans."[213] However, unlike in contentious teacher strikes in the northeast, the strike did not divide educators or the community along lines of race, because UTNO worked hard to maintain the support of the Black community.[214]

However, parents, as well as teachers, were more united in their antipathy toward OPSB, so the strike's slogan, "Erase the Board" had some resonance. As Mike Stone explains, "The management of the strike got out of our hands, our being the executive council and the negotiating team. Rank-and-file members came up with this. . . . It came up in a general membership meeting as we were getting ready to strike and whatnot. Just out of a group of people there, they came up with a slogan, 'Erase the Board.' Before we could figure out what to do or what to say, the rank and file basically demanded that not only were we going to strike, we were going to recall the board."[215] Teacher Gwendolyn Adams put it succinctly: "At that point the school board was not performing to the best interest of either the children or the educators."[216] However, the executive council worried about the politics of both negotiating with a body and advocating for their dismissal:

> Somebody said, "Well, actually, it is not a problem because we can't do it. It is hard to recall people. There is no way we are going to recall most of the people on the school board." Nat said, "Oh, we can recall them if you want to." He said, "There is an election in a week. We put petitions at every voting precinct, 100 yards from . . . whatever the state law is. We'll have union members with petitions at every voting precinct. We'll get all the signatures we want." We all just sat there flabbergasted. We said, "You know, that's right, Nat." For some reason that I don't know or can't remember, we decided, "Well, we are into this. The school board thinks we are trying to recall. Let's just put the pressure on. Let's just go through the process. Let's try to recall."[217]

Educators were angry because the board had refused to compromise even when the teachers had significantly reduced their salary demands. The board added fuel to the fire by refusing to pay its share (80 percent) of striking educators' health insurance premiums, a tactic intended to push educators back into the classrooms: "You force them to come back. And you do that by taking their retirement and taking their health insurance. Those are very near and dear to teachers who don't make a lot of money. And you become the real evil guy when that happens. . . . And those are basically the only threats you have," explains chief board negotiator Fudesco.[218] Susie Beard saw the loss of insurance as a reasonable excuse for crossing the picket lines: "I was more compassionate, but I was still a little bit upset because some people had illnesses, they couldn't afford to strike because they needed insurance, and that was one thing, they said if you struck, they would cancel your insurance. . . . You needed your medication and all of that."[219] Years later, when teachers who had struck in 1990 wanted to retire, many had to work fifteen days of a new school year to recoup the lost time.

Anti–school board sentiment was not confined to educators. Ken Ducote, who worked for the district, remembered: "I was angry at the board too. I was having to keep the lid on the cookie jar all the time because they were trying to steal money."[220] In a letter to the *Times Picayune*, a teacher spoke to larger suspicions of financial mismanagement, both within the schools and the community: "All of us involved in education in this city are at the mercy of the School Board. . . .

This group of people has in its hands the largest budget in this great city, more than $300 million. . . . When School Board members get their priorities mixed up, they sometimes spend our children's money on projects that are beneficial to themselves, their friends and even their relatives."[221] Fudesco suggested that such kickbacks and corruption are endemic to all major cities, and he disputes claims that the OPSB was particularly venal.[222] The board did come off during the strike as unable to successfully collaborate, as the media broadcasted their public infighting. Board member Woody Koppel, one of the union's most ardent OPSB supporters, continuously shared information about the board's closed-door executive sessions with the media and publicly attacked other board members for their unwillingness to compromise with UTNO.[223] The board held a two-minute long meeting in which they voted to spend $75,000 to publicize its side of the story during the strike, which it then both commenced and ended while one board member was taking the elevator up to the meeting room.[224] Such tactics reinforced the sense that the board was acting impulsively and failing to appropriately manage its budget.

OPSB also spent over $200,000 on extra security at schools, ostensibly to protect substitutes and nonstriking teachers from the picketers, which outraged striking educators who claimed they behaved peacefully on the lines.[225] UTNO argued that the board was refusing to negotiate in good faith with the union, citing its refusal to compromise over the $400,000 before the strike began, its reticence to meet at all at the beginning of the strike, and then its refusal to budge on salary demands as the strike continued. The board seemed perpetually surprised by the union's commitment, both to continuing the strike and to the recall campaign: "The administration was so structured and secure, it never occurred to them how much school teachers hated them and that they could get petitions signed to recall the president of the school board."[226] The board also rejected the union's call to bring in a federal mediator to help resolve the strike.[227] As fifty teachers picketed her home, board member Avra O'Dwyer told the Times Picayune, "Mr. LaCour must be feeling insecure in hoping a federal mediator can come in and side with him. The fact remains that there is no money. You can't get blood from a turnip."[228] LaCour was likely thinking about the federal mediator who had worked the 1978 strike, earning praise from all sides and helping the union and the board achieve quick resolution.[229] The Black community, at least, seemed swayed by UTNO's arguments; fifty community leaders met at the Urban League and pledged to join the recall effort if the strike was not resolved quickly.[230]

The union announced that it was going to focus its recall campaign on four school board members, though they eventually hoped to replace all seven.[231] On the Saturday of the local election, while UTNO leadership continued negotiations with the board, members fanned out across the city to voting precincts and collected recall signatures, netting over 10,000 in one day.[232] Presumably, this helped some board members decide to reach a settlement, as Mike Stone recalls:

> We were negotiating in a hotel somewhere, and going back and forth. We took a break. Nat and Fudesco went to the bathroom, or as we used to say, they went in the closet. A few minutes later, Nat came in. Connie Goodly, who was the number two power in the union, she called the room and Nat answered the phone. She said, "How are things going?" He said, "Oh, we are making progress. I think we will come to an agreement soon." Then she said, "Well, don't give up the recall. The union office is full of petitions. We can recall as many as you want to recall." Nat said, "Too late. I just told Fudesco that we would drop the recall if they would agree to something, and we could settle the negotiations."[233]

Though the board had originally rejected the union's $1 million offer, the eventual agreement had a $15.7 million price tag over three years, guaranteeing 3 percent raises for all employees in 1990–91 and 4 percent raises for the 1992–93 school year. The board paid for the raises with money saved from not paying striking teachers' salaries, $3 million in proceeds from refinancing bonds, and $600,000 in personnel and program cuts.[234] Though certainly the board lost out, Fudesco suggests that school boards often rely on the money saved through not paying teachers to finance a strike settlement:

> I would guess we made 14 million on the difference between teacher salaries to be able to pay. It's the only way you would do that. School boards work for the public. Teachers are the public. So, if I can give you an 8 percent raise, fine, I'll give it to you. I don't care. It's not my pocket, I get a vote. But if I don't have it, then I'm in an uncomfortable position. So, I persevere [in] a strike, which is ugly, till I make enough money between the difference of teachers and subs, to be able to give you your raise.[235]

Nonetheless, the board did not emerge unscathed from the strike. When UTNO leadership met with the rank and file to recommend the contract, teachers remained so angry with the board that they didn't want to settle if that meant they had to abandon the recall effort: "We were there for hours, arguing," remembers Mike Stone:

> We had teachers that were willing to keep striking, lose paychecks, never make the money back in subsequent contracts. The most important thing to them was to throw the motherfuckers off the school board. The meeting, when [the negotiating team] made our recommendation and then there were speeches, questions, answers, and we went on for hours, trying to explain to people that we had scared them so bad that they were

not going to agree to anything if we kept on with the recall, and that if we kept on with the recall and settled later, they would have lost so much money, they would never make it back in their lifetime. Whereas if we settled now, you're going to get a pay raise and not lose any money. Finally, we convinced them, mainly because people respected Nat so much . . . I remember that I got up and said, "We don't need the recall. That train is going down the tracks. I guarantee you most of these people will not be reelected," and they weren't.[236]

Though the membership eventually accepted the agreement, more militant educators were frustrated with the settlement and spoke out to the newspaper: "They blackmailed the union. Nat LaCour has sold us out."[237] Many teachers continued to participate in the recall drive as private citizens, and parents joined the campaign, demonstrating how UTNO involvement led to greater political engagement.[238] The recall faded, but before the school board elections of 1992, two members of the board resigned in scandal: Dwight McKenna was indicted for income tax evasion and board president Carl Robinson was indicted for defrauding the state's Medicaid program.[239] UTNO refused to endorse any of the remaining five incumbent board members and, in the end, only two were reelected. The *Times Picayune* attributed this outcome to UTNO: "The surprise factor in the race, and in some districts a decisive one, was the influence of the teachers' union, United Teachers of New Orleans. The teachers did their homework both before the election and on election day. . . . It had an army on the streets before the election. UTNO members, including Nat LaCour, the president, canvased door to door before the election. On election day, the union had more than 90 teachers distributing flyers and monitoring precincts."[240] Though it wasn't a clean sweep, UTNO had helped erase a significant portion of the board.

The 1990 strike demonstrates UTNO's ongoing member participation sixteen years after it won collective bargaining, its commitment to acting in solidarity with lower-paid support workers and the larger working-class community, and its labor militancy despite a growing statewide and national anti-labor climate. Even as OPSB claimed there was simply no money available, pushing the union to accept an austerity-based status quo, UTNO demanded that it find creative ways to obtain funds and solicit more money from the community and the state. The union directly confronted the state's business interests, interrupting education in New Orleans for fifteen school days and demonstrating an alternate ideology in which all workers deserve decent pay and benefits, regardless of their job, their students' test scores, or their direct connection to the classroom. Moreover, because bus drivers and maintenance workers, covered by the Teamsters, as well as custodians and cafeteria workers, covered by AFSCME, had "me too" contracts, these employees also won raises. UTNO wielded significant leadership in the

UTNO members Margel Brooks (*left*) and Cindy Ferrara-Riedl (*right*), both from Support and Appraisal, display their "Bury the Board" cake from the 1990 strike. *Photograph by Karen Walk Geisert.*

local labor movement and proved, yet again, its capacity to win. Though strikes were difficult for many members—they included financial sacrifices, stress, and often conflicted feelings about leaving students in unstaffed classrooms—they also brought educators together and are a poignant example of union democracy: "An UTNO strike, or a King March on Washington, or anything bigger or smaller entails people working together, coming up with strategy, logistics on how to do things. Making group decisions, talking to each other, and going back and forth," Mike Stone explains.[241] Members spoke with pride about their work during the strike, whether it was managing a network of schools, speaking at rallies of over 3,000 people, or even just holding the picket line. Though animosity lingered after the strike, the action also renewed educators' commitment to the union and to participating in union democracy.

CONCLUSION: HOLDING THE LINE

Though UTNO did not directly confront all aspects of the neoliberal education agenda, it did fight to protect its members' interests, successfully fending off austerity budgets and other attempts to undermine union gains. The union resisted the shift toward "neoliberal multiculturalism"[242] and instead fought for a redistributive agenda that would disproportionately benefit UTNO's Black, women, and working-class members. Even as the power of organized labor diminished in the state, UTNO continued to provide strong representation for its majority women and Black membership base, anchoring Black middle-class political power in New Orleans and fighting off the worst of the anti-labor and white supremacist mobilizations. UTNO helped defeat David Duke in his gubernatorial run, held legislators and school board members accountable, and mounted enormous voter turnout initiatives through its collaboration with APRI. It also protected teacher tenure, fended off charter schools and vouchers, and won several key salary increases for educators, both at the city and the state level. At the same time, other initiatives that would later be used to undermine the union snuck through. For example, in 1995, LaCour praised the Teach for America (TFA) program, which brought young, mostly white, highly educated teachers to work in urban schools.[243] Though TFA helped fill gaps when the city could not find enough certified educators, following Katrina, TFA recruits would be used as cheap replacements for veteran educators who had been fired. Marta Bivens, who worked at Henderson School in the Fischer Projects, said the TFA teachers at her school, in 1990, chose not to strike.[244] By contrast, Patti Reynolds, who worked at the magnet school McMain,[245] said all the TFA teachers at her school had joined her on the picket lines: "They were asking us, 'Do you think we should strike?' And we would tell them, 'Oh believe me, you don't want to be in the school. The fun, the laughs, they're going to be out here on the picket line. They are not going to be in that building.'"[246] UTNO's strategy was to try to incorporate TFA recruits into the union; however, because they were such an unstable workforce, as most recruits teach only for two or three years, they were less involved in union activity. Relying on TFA recruits post-Katrina allowed reformers to circumvent UTNO's influence and produce a more tractable workforce.[247]

UTNO opposed neoliberal education reform on various levels, fighting against merit pay, austerity budget cuts, and teacher competency testing as well as against the legislature's attempts to save money by outsourcing the jobs of school support personnel, such as bus drivers and custodians. When Governor Foster's education commission created a blueprint for schools in the twenty-first century, UTNO lambasted its many references to privatization and vouchers and scant mentions of financing to improve conditions in the schools.[248] Over and over again, UTNO argued that the solution to underperforming schools was not a business agenda or new management but the injection of more funding: for updated textbooks and materials, for high-quality facilities, for competitive educator salaries, and for programs and services that targeted students who dealt daily with poverty and trauma. Teacher Joel Behrman says that UTNO did much of its political work in an attempt to secure more funding for the schools: "New Orleans people, they don't want to pay taxes for anything. They had a feeling that New Orleans is a sinkhole. But I should tell you, if you look back at UTNO, I don't think you see scandals. I don't think any UTNO people went to jail or were even indicted for anything. That tells you something is right in New Orleans. I think we were plugging away at a very difficult job."[249] Even teachers at magnet schools remembered decaying facilities and overheated classrooms. If UTNO looked inward and did not always take the lead in pushing groups like the AFL-CIO toward broader social movement work, it was because so much within the school system itself needed improvement.

Moreover, through its political work, UTNO regularly pushed to elect progressive candidates who would support a pro-labor and pro-Black agenda. Beth Butler, a community organizer who worked with several UTNO paraprofessionals, thinks that UTNO presented a real threat to business interests in the city and the state: "Because UTNO had so much power, they not only had the membership who were solid, who had won at least two strikes, big time, and been able to pounce the elites back into their corner. But they had this power in the legislature ongoing, they had it in political races every time there was an election. They were not about the agenda of the elites, ever, they were progressive."[250] Social movement theorists argue that organizations inevitably become oligarchic over time, with unions presented as paradigmatic cases.[251] Yet UTNO demonstrates that progressivism and democracy can exist in a labor union even as it grows more bureaucratic and as leadership becomes entrenched. Though UTNO became less radical over time, it continued to be member-driven, as evidenced by its rank-and-file leadership on the "Erase the Board" campaign. UTNO members revered Nat LaCour, but they also deeply believed the union was their project to run.

By demonstrating an active commitment to Black and women's leadership, and by supporting the larger Black working-class community and fostering a culture of participatory democracy within the union, UTNO was able to play a key role in the community and maintain its clout over several decades. Though their membership was made up mostly of college-educated middle-class teachers, UTNO was seen as an ally to the students they taught and to the families who trusted UTNO to represent their children's interests. The union supplemented its political work with various programs aimed to benefit students and families: giving out annual college scholarships to two graduating seniors, sponsoring an "art on the bus" program where students competed to design artwork for the city's municipal transit system, holding an annual Martin Luther King Jr. Day concert, and staffing an afterschool "homework hotline," among other activities. The union earned the community's trust.

In the years to come, especially immediately following Hurricane Katrina, policymakers and business leaders' neoliberal reforms would be pushed with even greater force, eventually transforming the city's educational and labor landscape. These transformations could only come to fruition in the aftermath of the storm, alongside UTNO's evisceration. However, at this earlier stage of neoliberal policymaking, the union still fought to carve out space for worker rights and union democracy with significant success. Though educators remembered the 1990 strike, their greatest display of union solidarity during this period, as more divisive than the 1978 strike, the union achieved only slightly lower participation numbers. Moreover, the 1990 strike, unlike the prior one, was dictated in a large part by the rank and file who were outraged that the board wouldn't meet their demand for modest raises for support workers. By prioritizing member participation and decision-making, interracial collaboration and integration, and protest and disruptive mass actions, UTNO maintained significant member loyalty and continued to grow, in members and services, even as organized labor nationwide continued its slow decline.

4

Union Bureaucracy, State Takeover, and the Bid to Dismantle a District, 1999-2005

Though UTNO had withstood the anti-labor backlash and early neoliberal policies of the 1980s and 1990s, by the late 1990s and early 2000s, the union was
clearly on the defensive. As the union underwent a major leadership transition,
it was faced with a series of attacks from the state legislature and the business
community as well as from the local and national school reform movements.
In this chapter, I analyze both the external and internal challenges that UTNO
faced. Along with the "hollowing out of government" on national, state, and local
levels and the continuation of austerity budgets,[1] the union had to contend with
the OPSB's ongoing incompetence and occasional corruption. Specifically, it was
forced to cope with a string of short-lived superintendents, apparent financial
mismanagement, and the state's repeated threats to take over the district. All
this came alongside the federal government's growing commitment to neoliberal reforms as codified in the No Child Left Behind (2001) legislation. Prior
to Hurricane Katrina, however, despite very real attempts to dismantle the union
and privatize the district, UTNO's power in conjunction with the Black political
machine in New Orleans held off a drastic overhaul.

This chapter examines UTNO's trajectory from 1999 to 2005, from Brenda
Mitchell's election as union president until Katrina hit the city. Mitchell had a
more authoritarian style than LaCour, which alienated some members, even
as others saw it as "tough love" mentorship that helped them realize their own
power and potential. I analyze Mitchell's leadership that, due to her extensive

experience as an educator, should have worked to neutralize complaints that the union did not care sufficiently about quality education; instead, her lack of political acumen constituted a weakness that the union's opponents exploited. I argue that, during this period, there was a shift in how many UTNO members viewed the union; that is, members turned to it for services, such as for protection against unjust termination, but did not see it as an active, democratic project that they had a crucial role in building. Echoing critiques popularized and funded by the school reform movement, both educators and outsiders accused the union of protecting bad teachers, succumbing to endless bureaucracy, losing its responsiveness to members and the families who used the schools, and stymieing attempts to improve the district. I examine the merits of these critiques while also looking at why educators *did* join UTNO, both in this era and in previous ones.

Ultimately, I argue that in the years leading up to Katrina, the union continued to threaten the state's business interests and remained the bedrock of the local and state labor movement. Despite the serious threats UTNO faced and despite the nationwide cultural tide turning toward school choice, without Katrina flooding the city and shuttering the schools, UTNO would not have been so easily defeated. UTNO's story demonstrates that strong, community-backed unions are a potentially potent force in stymieing neoliberal reforms. Moreover, despite the ways in which UTNO internally inched away from participatory democratic models, it remained one of the only groups providing citizen and stakeholder input on the school system. In the face of attempts at state takeover and charterization of the district, UTNO provided one of the only avenues for educator and parent voices to be heard. In the post-Katrina landscape, however, complete charterization would foreclose any opportunity for democratic governance or oversight of the schools.

BRENDA MITCHELL TAKES THE REINS

Brenda Mitchell's grandparents grew up in Mississippi and Alabama, then got married and moved to New Orleans in 1919. In the late 1940s, her parents migrated to California with other Black Americans seeking better opportunities, and her father became a Pullman Porter on the trains. Mitchell was born in Oakland, California, but was sent to live with her grandparents when she was a young child; she spent the rest of her life in New Orleans. "I remember my grandfather telling me stories about him going to see Booker T. Washington. Between my grandfather and my father, who was a Pullman Porter and knew all about A. Philip Randolph, I guess it was just natural for me [to support the labor movement]."[2] Mitchell started teaching in 1968, immediately joined Local 527, called out sick in solidarity during the 1969 teacher strike, and then was transferred to the formerly all-white Howard #1 Elementary in 1972, during the overnight desegregation transfers. She became the building rep at Howard and, she recalls, "Boy, did I have a lot of work to do. I was trying to recruit everybody."[3] In the early 1970s, she joined UTNO's executive board, and Nat LaCour appointed her head of the union's education committee. She organized UTNO's first QuEST Conference in 1975, which she ran for more than twenty years, and she then became the first director of the teacher center in 1980. Meanwhile, she earned her doctorate in Education and renewed her focus on mentoring young educators and fostering innovative and successful teaching.

While LaCour was first and foremost a politician and tactician, Mitchell was, at heart, an educator whose interests lay closer to the day-to-day operations of the classroom. Thus, when LaCour accepted a position with the national AFT in 1998 and UTNO's membership elected Mitchell as president the following year, it was clear that aspects of the union's leadership would shift. LaCour had been president for twenty-seven years, essentially building both UTNO and the LFT from scratch, and he was well-known and respected in the community. Mitchell, by contrast, was known mostly inside the union, where countless teachers and paraprofessionals had benefited from her expertise and guidance. "Nat came from the labor, from the human rights part of it," explains UTNO staffer Jo Anna Russo, "and Brenda came from the professional development part of it. That's what made their leadership different."[4] Yet Mitchell was also a member of LaCour's executive board and, though not a close confidant, was certainly an ally. "I selected her," LaCour recalls, "met with her, made some suggestions when I called her into my office and told her that I was going to go to Washington, and [said], if she wanted to run for the presidency, I would support her."[5] Mitchell was elected overwhelmingly, beating her opponent 1,326 to 199, though it was a low-turnout election, with less than one-third of UTNO's more than 6,000 members participating.[6]

Mitchell's leadership style was a significant shift for the union. While politicians and members described LaCour as calm and conciliatory, Mitchell was tough. She entered the school district fighting from the outset, when district officials had told her she needed to lose weight before they would hire her, and then got into a highly publicized argument with a principal who tried to take credit for a grant she had written. LFT president Fred Skelton recalls: "Brenda's standing up there and saying, 'That's wrong.'. . . She said, 'Put it in the newspaper what happened to me.' Her life could have been hell at that school. . . . Brenda's got balls. I mean, she just said 'No, what's right is right.' And she took the heat. I remember that, and I suspect that some other people remember it as well. And so I think that made her popular. There was a legacy that she had that you knew that she had the guts to stand up when it counted."[7] Unlike LaCour, Mitchell had the disadvantage of being both Black and a woman, an intersection of identities whose sum was greater than its parts.[8] Of necessity, she was more combative than LaCour so that she would be heard in male-dominated spaces, yet she also risked being dismissed as "angry" or "unprofessional" since she was Black and a woman. She decided to earn her doctoral degree in part because she was tired of being dismissed and not taken seriously as an educational expert by principals and policymakers.[9] Tellingly, her opponents in the 1999 election were all men: "They have not had a woman president since Veronica Hill.[10] So, of course, they know better, right?"[11] Once she was elected, people both within and outside of the labor movement accused her of being only a titular president, implying that LaCour was still telling her what to do: "They wouldn't have said that to a man. But baby, one day in one of the meetings I told them, 'There's a new sheriff in town and her name is Brenda.' I realized that I had the largest union in the state, and then I stepped up and I made them respect me."[12] Larry Carter, who became UTNO president after Mitchell retired in 2008, said she had to demand the recognition she deserved: "That's an aspect that I admired as well, because for an African American woman to be in that role in this city, where most people, even though Nat had been gone, they were still looking at the union as his legacy. For her to have to come from under that, I think she had to really show her true self, and she did that."[13] Mitchell had to fight to prove herself, both because of her identity as a Black woman and to emerge from under the long shadow of LaCour's leadership.

Perhaps because of her combative rise to power, Mitchell was less trusting than LaCour. "[Nat] took his opposition and embraced them and made them part of his executive board. He never surrounded himself with yes people," recalls LFT lobbyist Joy Van Buskirk.[14] By contrast, Mitchell was suspicious of UTNO executive board members and staff whom she perceived as more loyal to LaCour than to her. "Some of our disagreements were probably my fault," reflects executive board member Mike Stone. "I was used to telling Nat what I thought, and it didn't bother him. But I think sometimes Brenda took it as personal criticism, which I didn't mean. So we had some conflicts working together on the negotiating team and whatnot after Nat left."[15] After a long career of being ignored, underestimated, and dismissed, Mitchell sought to surround herself with people whom she could trust. Wilson Boveland—who wanted to be UTNO president himself but was ineligible to run as a staff person—felt micromanaged by Mitchell: "Nat pretty much gave us free rein to do what we needed to do. . . . You report to him and everything else like that, on the cases that you were working on, you say how they're going and what's going on. As long as nobody was complaining or anything else like that, then it was fine. As long as we were doing what we supposed to be doing. Well, when Brenda comes in, she decides that she wants to have more control over us."[16] Boveland said that Mitchell was confrontational and pugnacious as a leader, especially with district employees: "She would always fuss with the people in administration and everything else.

So we could never accomplish anything. And therefore, people in administration never went to talk to her. They'd rather talk to one of the other staff members."[17] Mitchell's leadership was a departure from LaCour's diplomacy, but it was not necessarily out of step with most union members. "Brenda had a pretty good following," recalls UTNO communications director Joe DeRose. "There were a lot of people who liked that kind of outward appearance of outrage or whatever. So we didn't lose members I don't think."[18] Teacher Leoance Williams described Mitchell as "temperamental" but possessing "a brilliant mind."[19] He enjoyed working with her, but "there were a lot of distractions along the way of people who didn't like her style."[20]

However, the educators that Mitchell nurtured and brought into leadership positions were talented teachers and extremely loyal. Juanita Bailey, a young teacher who started her career in 1995, saw Mitchell as a mentor: "Let me put it this way: she basically made me a woman. When I say that, her strength in knowing who she was as a woman, she was tough on me, but then I began to see her as a mother. Because she broke me out of that timid, not standing up for yourself, you know. . . . She's very blunt. . . . If she was tired of a subject, it was like, 'Next.' She was very, very commanding. She didn't have a lot of time for bull, and she would let you know."[21] Several Black women teachers reported that they had originally been afraid to take on leadership roles, but that Mitchell pushed them, and they became building reps in their schools or even UTNO staff. As union president, she remained committed to her passion for educating and developing young educators and leaders. "There are a lot of people out there in the buildings that never get recognized because they're not coming in contact with the leadership," she explained. "But because I had been the one who was going on into the schools, I got to meet a lot more of them. I think that my work at the teacher center gave me a different perspective."[22] Many younger union leaders saw Mitchell as a mentor, bringing them into leadership positions while also holding them to high standards.

Mitchell focused on shoring up her own power and supporting educators at the expense of maintaining the political and social connections that had characterized LaCour's tenure as leader. She rejected his assistance, wanting to establish her own style, and she tried to start anew. Wade Rathke, who served on the Greater New Orleans AFL-CIO council with both LaCour and Mitchell, remembers: "Brenda was a wonderful woman, she just wasn't the same kind of union leader that Nat was. She never was much of a voice or a participant in the Labor Federation. Connie Goodly [an UTNO staff person] was pretty much the only representative for the AFT during Brenda's term. So, she was a sweetheart, I got along with her great. She, once again, never failed to support anything I tried to do, but Nat could actually make stuff happen."[23] Rathke's description of Mitchell as a "sweetheart" highlights the ways in which gender undermined Mitchell's

Brenda Mitchell at the 1977 UTNO Awards Banquet. Mitchell organized the annual QuEST conference and directed the teacher center. She served as UTNO president from 1999 to 2008. *Courtesy of United Teachers of New Orleans.*

power and effectiveness, even unintentionally by her allies in the labor movement. However, Rathke also points out a real shift in UTNO's political strategy.

Similarly, Wilson Boveland felt like Mitchell let UTNO's political connections fall by the wayside:

> When Nat LaCour was the president, we had a very visible presence in the legislature and also in city government. Anybody who's running for office would come through the union and ask the union for support. Because we pretty much controlled the labor market here in terms of the New Orleans AFL-CIO and [we were] very strong at the state level and we had lobbyists that were working at the state level. That began to slowly erode, I'm going to say in about 2002, under Brenda Mitchell. Because when Nat was president, he would meet with superintendents and area superintendents and what have you. All the time! And they respected him, he respected them . . . and we were able to work things out. When Brenda came on, Brenda had this abrasive attitude toward people. And that didn't help us out, not one bit.[24]

She also was less connected to middle-class Black political organizations than LaCour, who had built deep partnerships with groups led by former mayors and congressmen, such as BOLD, COUP, LIFE, and the Progressive Democrats. According to the *Times Picayune*, "The sapping of UTNO's political clout [was] apparent. In 1992, when there was a groundswell of support for reform-minded School Board candidates, five of the seven the union endorsed were elected. In 2004, with a similar reform movement brewing, the union endorsed a majority of the incumbents on the board but only one, Una Anderson, was re-elected."[25]

Longtime union members tended to view LaCour's presidency through rose-tinted glasses, forgetting that Mitchell inherited many of the political problems the union faced during her tenure. The legislature made charter schools legal in 1995, as part of a nationwide trend, and education reformer Leslie Jacobs, who would be a leader in the post-Katrina school privatizations, ascended to power in 1992, when she won a seat on the OPSB with UTNO's endorsement. Moreover, the AFT had moved to the right by the late 1990s. Longtime AFT president Al Shanker embraced President Bush's education policies including increasing standards, accountability, and testing, for which he was rewarded with appointments to several of Bush's educational panels.[26] During the 1994 merger talks with the NEA, the AFT fell to the right on most major education policy issues, rejecting extensive bilingual education and race-based layoffs to preserve the jobs of educators of color and supporting "tough" discipline, closing "failing" schools, and the extensive testing of teachers and students.[27] This national framework helped justify the implementation of high-stakes testing regimes throughout Louisiana, the takeovers of poorly performing schools (that were often replaced by privately run charters), and the color-blind firing of all New Orleans educators following Katrina.

Mitchell allied herself with the Black working-class community and continued UTNO's history of social movement unionism that connected educators' goals to larger community struggles.[28] Jim Randels, another future UTNO president, was known for his work with Community Labor United and the anti-poverty organization ACORN:

> One of the reasons that Brenda asked me to be on the [UTNO executive] council, was that we needed to begin to move toward social justice unionism. . . . [Brenda said,] "And we know you're already doing that because the first time you came to our executive council it was about a living wage campaign. And we know you're connected with these various groups, we know you're involved with the 1811 slave revolt commemoration, we know you're involved with a range of community-based issues. . . ." So I was asked to be on the executive board, along with other people, particularly to push that stuff.[29]

Mitchell saw working with the community as the continuation of UTNO's legacy: "The community has always been important to us. That's why we did those workshops for parents and why we linked up with different organizations to work with them. Because you can't do this in isolation."[30] Mitchell also served for a long time as the chair of the national AFT's Black Caucus, where she pushed the national union to support policies that would benefit Black teachers and families. In the early 1990s, she even wrote a letter to AFT president Al Shanker critiquing an AFT policy document that promoted tracking students by ability, a policy that Mitchell saw as inherently racist.[31] "I think I'm most proud of the fact that I tried to hold myself and the union to a high standard, and that we always kept at the forefront of what we were doing and how we could improve our situations. It wasn't a fight just because we had strength, but what could you do with that strength to improve the work, life, and educational opportunity for children in the city. That's what I'm most proud of—and that I never cussed on TV and I was right there."[32] Though Mitchell cared deeply about the education of the city's schoolchildren, white policymakers and journalists portrayed Mitchell and the union during her tenure as justifying mediocrity and sacrificing learning to fulfill the ambitions of self-serving Black teachers. Unlike LaCour, Mitchell was largely unable to redefine that narrative.

Though no one could foresee the devastation of Hurricane Katrina, Mitchell still had clear challenges ahead in confronting the ongoing neoliberal education reform agenda that looked to remove teacher protections, privatize schools through charter processes, and bypass public education altogether via voucher systems. She also became UTNO president in a strikingly different cultural moment than LaCour, which shaped the options and tools available to her. The Democratic Party, to which most of organized labor was uncritically wedded, was promoting what theorist Nancy Fraser has dubbed "progressive neoliberalism."[33] Though the Democrats' turn toward neoliberalism started with President Carter's deregulation of industry and his losing battle against inflation in the late 1970s, the melding of neoliberal and progressive values coalesced during the Clinton administration in the 1990s.[34] According to Fraser, "In place of the New Deal coalition of unionized manufacturing workers, African Americans, and the urban middle classes, [Clinton] forged a new alliance of entrepreneurs, suburban-ites, new social movements, and youth, all proclaiming their modern, progressive bona fides by embracing diversity, multiculturalism, and women's rights."[35] Despite co-opting progressive language and values—"neoliberal multiculturalism" in the words of theorist Jodi Melamed—Clinton passed policies, such as free trade agreements and the deregulation of the banking industry, that devastated poor and working-class communities.[36] By projecting a type of "New Democrat" that emphasized personal responsibility and eschewed "government handouts," Clinton successfully won the presidency, while effectively severing the Party's connection to New Deal social welfare policies on which labor relied.[37] Moreover, Clinton, as well as all his presidential successors to date, supported the school choice agenda, including the establishment of charter schools and other reforms aimed at eliminating some of the restrictions of teachers' CBAs.[38] By the late 1990s, teachers' unions, like most of organized labor, were on the defensive.

Mitchell also faced obstacles within UTNO in terms of maintaining the high member participation rates that had characterized the union in prior years as well as in addressing the very real issues of students in poverty, school violence, and dismal standardized test scores. With the school reform movement, which championed charters, claiming language of innovation and change, the media began to portray the union as the old guard, bureaucratic and slow-moving, and justifying a subpar status quo.[39] Social movement theorists argue that, over time, radical organizations become more conservative, with entrenched leadership, as they move away from oppositional politics and disruptive protest and begin to focus instead on institution building and servicing their members.[40] Robert Michels's "iron law of oligarchy" states that even the most democratic organization will eventually develop into an oligarchy as the organization increases in size, as paid leaders begin to use their positions to enhance their own power, and as it becomes less likely that membership will vote leaders out.[41] Despite a splattering of cases to the contrary, movement theorists present unions as the paradigmatic case of the iron law; through the 1980s and 1990s, unions' power gradually eroded as organizing drives nearly ceased and labor became "more like an institutionalized interest group than a social movement."[42] Though UTNO resisted many of these trends—it had a confrontational protest in 1990 and maintained high member participation—in other ways it acquiesced. Despite their differences, Mitchell was LaCour's chosen successor, suggesting few opportunities for outsiders to assume leadership positions, and both teachers and district employees would accuse the union of possessing a bloated bureaucracy that led it to enforce arcane contract provisions instead of considering the larger impacts of its actions on students and education.

THE NEOLIBERAL THREAT EXPANDS

Even without the coming storm, Mitchell took over at a difficult moment in the union's history. President Bush signed No Child Left Behind (NCLB) into law in 2002, greatly increasing the impacts of high-stakes testing and school accountability and furthering the neoliberal education agenda. NCLB led to a renewed focus on reading and math education at the expense of other subjects and electives, and it threatened schools with closure if they failed to meet yearly progress goals, thus opening the door to private school voucher programs or new charter schools. The law also prioritized parent "choice" over school equity, promoting a narrative that it is the family's responsibility to choose the right school for their children, rather than the state's responsibility to provide quality education for all children.[43] NCLB standardized at the federal level the push toward treating schools like businesses, in competition with one another for students, and treating families like consumers, responsible for selecting the most appropriate educational package for their children.

However, Louisiana, like many states, had implemented its own high-stakes testing and accountability programs years before NCLB. In September 1999, under an accountability plan designed by Leslie Jacobs, state officials released the rankings of 1,200 public schools, with the bulk of the poorest performers in Orleans Parish.[44] The rankings were the result of a law passed by the legislature the prior year that was intended to reward or assist schools based on their standardized test scores.[45] Jacobs, widely cited as the architect of the accountability plan, was a former OPSB member then appointed by Republican governor Mike Foster first as the head of his education transition team and later, in 1996, to serve on BESE. The union's endorsement of Jacobs in 1992, when she ran for the school board, speaks to the local's delay in recognizing the neoliberal shift in the national Democratic Party that caused the Party to abandon organized labor and adopt rhetoric of responsibility and choice.

Immediately upon her BESE appointment, Jacobs established herself as an anti-union education reformer by refusing to consider any teachers who belonged to unions or union representatives for appointments to the BESE board, thus breaking with the tradition that gave two spots to union-affiliated educators.[46] The *Times Picayune*, in a laudatory profile piece, described Jacobs, a wealthy insurance executive,[47] as "unfailingly poised, prepared and frank" and noted that her favorite book was *Atlas Shrugged*, Ayn Rand's famous novel about how the unintelligent masses survive off the creative and intellectual genius of a select few. Jacobs attended elite Newman private school in New Orleans and sent her children to private schools as well. Jacobs "does not easily fit into stereotypes," the newspaper wrote. "She grew up in New Orleans, but walks and talks more like Manhattan. A Democrat, she has managed to become the education guru for Foster, a Republican. She's rich, but not showy."[48] The community group Parents for Educational Justice, who opposed Jacobs's accountability plan, filed a complaint with the US Department of Education's Office for Civil Rights that read, in part, "There is a good reason that none of the other fifty states has yet implemented such a program because it has proven to be a disaster for children in minority and poor schools."[49] Despite these protests, and widespread opposition from educators, Jacobs's accountability system survived several lawsuits and remained in place.

Jacobs also provided seed money for New Orleans's first charter school, New Orleans Charter Middle, which opened in 1998.[50] The following year, the OPSB approved three more charter school applications and, one year later, BESE added a fourth, bringing the city's total to five by the fall of 2000.[51] Charter schools are publicly funded but privately run institutions that are exempt from many of the laws governing public education. Unlike traditional public schools, which are run by an elected school board, charters have appointed boards, thus limiting the democratic input residents have over school governance. Because they are privately run, charter schools also tend to lack oversight and transparency.[52] The idea is that charter schools, freed from the bureaucratic regulations of districts and unions and run according to a business model, will produce more efficient and higher-quality educational outcomes. Charter schools combine free market ideals with an equity argument, claiming to improve outcomes for low-income students of color, thus appealing to the left.53 UTNO was particularly threatened by charter schools because they did not recognize the union's collective bargaining agreement. The LFT lobbied extensively to prohibit charter schools and then, once legislation permitting them was passed in 1995, to limit their spread. According to the 1995 law, a school could be converted into a charter only if 75 percent of the school's teachers and parents agreed.54 "There were two amendments [to the charter law] that were not accepted," recalls LFT lobbyist Joy Van Buskirk, "which really fried me, and I went to the governor about it."55 First, the LFT wanted oversight teams that would ensure that schools were following their charter. Second, the LFT wanted the schools to be audited every other year. "They didn't want that. Well, it turned out that people were embezzling money, they were misusing MFP [Minimum Foundation Program] money. I mean, nobody knows what goes on in those schools. You don't know."56 Though it lost on those two amendments, the LFT succeeded in raising the bar to create a charter school. "We did everything we could to make [the bill] more palatable. If you're going to compare a traditional public school with a charter public school, you ought to be on the same playing field. We were not, but we were close."57 UTNO and the LFT fought to limit the spread of charters and ensure that the charter schools that were formed held space for teacher agency and were accountable to the same democratic standards that governed the public schools.

UNO expanded the charter threat significantly when it offered, in summer 2001, to take over ten city schools and run them as charters.58 The university's offer came shortly after a publicized visit by President Bush's education secretary, Rod Paige, who spoke at New Orleans Charter Middle, dubbed "the highest performing non-magnet public middle school in the city."59 Paige detailed the president's extensive financing of charter school construction and expansion, and he praised the TFA program, an alternative certification program intended to bring high-performing college students into teaching on short-term contracts. "Every year our best teachers [come] from Teach for America," Paige told the crowd. TFA also undermined teachers' unions by suggesting there was little need for veteran educators and by bringing in non-career teachers who were less likely to join a union. The program also threatened education schools by providing fast-track, low-cost or free pathways to becoming a teacher, skipping the internship aspect of student teaching and, with it, the mentorship and guidance that young teachers otherwise received. Paige's talk demonstrates the ways in which privatization works synchronously across the education sector to recreate schools along a business model, complete with cheaper nonunionized labor that bypasses schools of education. However, UTNO was still a force to be reckoned with in New Orleans. UNO pared down its proposal to five schools and, of those five, teachers voted against the charter proposals at four of them, effectively shutting down the deal between UNO and OPSB.[60]

UTNO as well as the national AFT tried to tread a line in such a way that they did not outwardly oppose charter schools, which school reformers portrayed as the key to innovation and rising test scores, yet also neutralized the threat the schools presented to CBAs and teachers' rights. Repeatedly, educators and union leaders noted that charters had been supported by longtime AFT president Al Shanker, who thought they could be used as incubators for change and reform. In Shanker's vision, the union would agree to waive certain contract provisions, with educators' consent, to experiment with new programs and ideas. Then, if those ideas proved successful, the union would negotiate to change its contract provisions and implement the reforms district-wide. However, by the late 1990s and early 2000s, the idea had been transformed from Shanker's notion of small incubators of innovation to top-down, privately run public school alternatives, many of them for-profit businesses and cookie-cutter replicas of other schools.[61] "[The union] definitely knew charter schools were coming," states teacher Juanita Bailey.[62] Though she was not in a leadership position in the late 1990s, she remembers UTNO staff warning teachers about charters and explaining the danger they posed to union rights. "Nat fought the charter movement way ahead of its starting," says UTNO staffer Jo Anna Russo. "We were tracing it."[63] In the case of the attempted UNO takeovers, UTNO wrote a letter to teachers in all the affected schools urging them to vote against the charters, claiming the charter schools would result in the loss of collective bargaining and "no guarantees to job security, seniority and the grievance process and many other benefits."[64] "They tried to start charter schools," recalls Wilson Boveland, "and we fought them on it. UNO came in . . . they wanted to take over the schools and they wanted to kick the contract out altogether. And we weren't about to let them do that."[65] UNO later canceled its bid to take over the one school that had voted in favor of charterization because it was unable to reach a deal with OPSB about time off for teachers.[66]

However, school reform and charter school advocates continued to point to the dismal test scores in Orleans Parish to justify school takeovers. In 2003, Louisiana ranked sixty-five schools as "academically unacceptable," and fifty of them were in New Orleans. The *Times Picayune* targeted the union in an article about the struggling schools, accusing them of "cling[ing] to the status quo."[67] Mitchell responded with a list of reforms the union had proposed for failing schools—the use of a research-based reform program, professional development, extended school days, staffing the schools with veteran teachers—few of which had been implemented.[68] Moreover, the union had been a local leader in professional development, running workshops and classes through the teacher center, providing mentoring for new teachers, and even creating a labor/management partnership with the district to ensure teachers continued to learn and grow. UTNO brought principals, district superintendents, and teachers to the nationwide AFT education conference every other year so they could learn about current best practices and collaborate with each other.[69] The charter movement was not an attempt to improve teaching and learning in Orleans Parish, union officials argued, but rather a tactic to take over the school district and void the union contract. "I think [the charters] came out of No Child Left Behind," says Russo. "That was a way of being able to test us, to rank us, and to say whether we had quality education going on."[70] Instead of addressing the root causes of poor school performance, including students living in poverty, dealing with violence, and facing few job opportunities once they graduated, school reformers blamed teachers and schools and posited privatization as a solution.

While UTNO was only partially successful in stymieing the growth of charter schools, the union did fend off vouchers, another program that aimed at scaling back public education. In early 2005, the lobbyist for the archdiocese of New Orleans successfully got a voucher bill passed out of committee, only to have it fail on the House floor. The lobbyist said it was the first time he had gotten a voucher bill passed out of the education committee since he first began pushing the issue in 1968.[71] Both private schools and LABI had long advocated for vouchers, using explicitly neoliberal logic. "The business community is generally supportive of choice," explained LABI vice president. "It allows parents to become consumers of education the way they are of other goods and services."[72] LFT lobbyists had stymied earlier voucher bills by mandating that private and parochial schools give voucher students the same tests that public school students receive and then publish the results. The archdiocese rejected this proposal, saying that to give its students the state standardized test "would change the nature of Catholic education."[73] When Louisiana finally implemented a voucher program, which Gov. Bobby Jindal authorized in 2008, several years after the evisceration of UTNO, analyses of the program revealed that students who received the vouchers performed worse than their public school peers.[74] UTNO was skeptical of neoliberal reforms that posited privatization and private schools as the solution for endemic educational inequities and, until Katrina, it was successful in limiting, though not completely preventing, the implementation of vouchers and charter schools.

OTHER EXTERNAL THREATS: THE SCHOOL BOARD AND THE LEGISLATURE

Beyond fighting the neoliberal reforms of charters and vouchers, UTNO also had to contend with school board corruption, mismanagement, and incompetence. Though the corruption charges were surely exaggerated to justify taking power away from the majority-Black board, and while New Orleans has a long history of venality across the color line, the charges were serious enough for the FBI to launch an investigation. Ken Ducote, a former teacher who worked in facilities and planning for the district, was the person who eventually called the FBI:

> The first time I talked to the FBI was probably around '83, '84. I had a board member who caught me on the elevator after a school board meeting, tried to get me to steer the school board's real estate to his campaign manager. He told me he had accessed my medical records at Oschner [Hospital] and he would destroy me publicly if I didn't do what he wanted. I told him I had two things in life I had no problems with. One was my medical record, but that was none of his business, and two, I had no problems putting a school board member in Angola [Prison] for extortion.[75]

Years later, in 1989, Ducote wrote a twelve-page memo to then superintendent Everett Williams accusing the board of illegally issuing $35 million in bonds without public bidding. The board then voted to fire Ducote, but Superintendent Williams protected Ducote's job.[76] Ducote likely witnessed more corruption than other district employees because of his position. Awarding lucrative construction bids to friends and donors seems to have been commonplace.

Though Superintendent Williams had protected Ducote's job in 1989, in 2003, then superintendent Anthony Amato demoted Ducote back to an assistant principal, apparently in response to a civil lawsuit Ducote had filed: "I'd signed a forty-seven-page affidavit charge in a civil lawsuit, [accusing] twenty politically connected individuals or entities of racketeering, a civil suit to get recouped the money they had stolen from racketeering, bid rigging, fraud, bribery, money laundering, insurance fraud, wire fraud. It was pretty wild. But the time the dust settled down, they had twenty-four people in jail, including the mayor's aunt and uncle."[77] Though Mayor Marc Morial's relatives fell to larger insurance fraud charges—including their involvement in "suspicious" school fires that resulted in large insurance payouts—some teachers and secretaries were also indicted, for example, in "Operation White-Out," which involved the modification of teachers' time sheets.[78] Finally, school board member Ellenese Brooks-Simms, who less than two months earlier had joined Superintendent Amato in inviting the FBI to use office space at district headquarters in a display of anticorruption fervor, pled guilty to accepting more than $100,000 in bribes.[79] Frank Fudesco, a former principal and the board's chief negotiator in the 1990s, downplayed the corruption: "To this day, all school boards do that."[80] Fudesco suggested that Ducote's experiences were not indicative of larger system-wide corruption but instead endemic to the departments that Ducote oversaw.

Nonetheless, teachers did see the results of no-bid contracts and wasted money in their classrooms. Teacher Leoance Williams recalls when air conditioning units were installed in his school: "They spent over $1.5 million in repairs and renovation at that school. . . . And they were supposed to put new windows throughout our school, windows that worked, that open and close. There was nobody at the time to supervise what they were doing. And they spent the money, but we didn't get the results. . . . [The windows] were not done well. The air conditioning system wasn't working well. They had put in cheap units. See, that kind of stuff affects us."[81] These issues also impacted students. On a school survey sponsored by UTNO in the early 1990s, 51 percent of teachers reported that their schools had nonfunctioning water fountains, and 27 percent said student toilets were often nonoperational. A further 43 percent of teachers were cooling their classrooms, throughout the hot New Orleans summer, with fans or air conditioners they had personally purchased.[82] However, while school reformers pushed charter schools as a solution to the school district's endemic corruption, the charters have been mired in scandals of their own.[83] Moreover, with schools independently governed, today there is even less transparency around which companies are awarded bids and how well that work is completed.

Though some teachers mentioned board corruption, their greater complaint centered on board incompetence: "If you look back, a lot of things school board did were shaky and shady. We had a lot of people stealing, messed up checks sometimes."[84] The board's apparent inability to issue employees their correct paychecks on time was a persistent problem from 1999 until Katrina. Originally, these errors were blamed on a new computer system.[85] In 2001, two years after the first "glitches," UTNO held a protest when hundreds of teachers received paychecks for two cents.[86] Karen Walk Geisert felt like the persistent check problems were an attempt to undermine the union:

> Every six months there was a new employees' relations person, but then they would lose all of the files and everything so that the grievance procedure would have to start all over again. And then they would mess up the paychecks. They got a new computer system and they didn't pay to have somebody come and help them implement it. . . . I mean, there was one pay period when more than half of the paychecks were wrong. . . . Then you'd have a thousand grievances because you'd have to file separate grievances. . . . So, we didn't have enough staff to represent all those people. And then people were saying, "Why do I join the union if they're not helping me?" I think they didn't remedy it on purpose.[87]

At one point, the district sent thirty school secretaries an extra check in error, and then three months later asked for the money back. This incident caused even the anti-union *Times Picayune* to side with the secretaries, calling the district "inept" and "notorious for its payroll mishaps."[88] District employees also complained about payroll irregularities, nepotism in the department (according to Ducote,

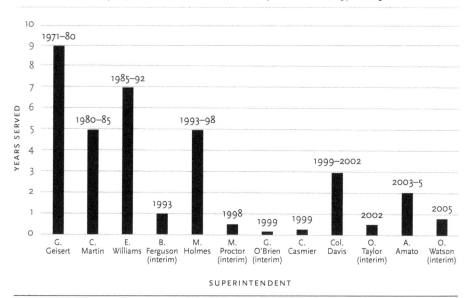

Graph 4.1. Tenure of Orleans Parish superintendents, 1971–2005

"The then COO brought in his girlfriend as payroll director and she gets arrested for pistol whipping her father-in-law"), and general incompetence.[89] Because of an error rate of 20 percent, the district eventually made all employees come to central offices in person to show identification and other documents; and, in 2006, the district abandoned the computer system altogether because "school workers had been entering information into the system incorrectly for about six years prior to Katrina."[90] UTNO attempted to work with the district to solve its payroll issues and provide assistance to educators seeking redress, but the errors continued.[91]

Compounding the payroll issues, the district had a series of superintendents who left after only a few years, followed by years of scrambling and searches for new superintendents, all of which led to a sense of instability among educators (see graph 4.1). All the superintendents in the 1990s and early 2000s (Morris Holmes, Colonel Davis, and Anthony Amato) were pressured into leaving or were fired by the board. "Well, keep in mind that big city school superintendents, their job expectancy is like two and a half years. Smaller districts it's about six years. . . . It's very political. What's the easiest thing for a board member to campaign on? Let's replace management," explains Fudesco.[92] Each superintendent entered the district after an extensive search, bringing with him sweeping changes and reforms, only to see those abandoned a few years later. "The stability of leadership at the top of a school district is in large part determined [by] how things were run, just like the stability of the leadership at a school determines how that school is run, or for that matter the stability of the leadership at a department store or restaurant or any other place," explains teacher and post-Katrina UTNO president Larry Carter. "There were occasions when things were being run so poorly that I think the trickle effect happened to trickle down, and it increased our workload."[93] Mitchell says that she got along with the superintendents during her tenure, Colonel Davis and Amato and, indeed, from 1999 to 2005 UTNO resolved its contract negotiations without even a hint of a strike threat.[94] Though this speaks to some needed sense of stability in the district, it also represents a retreat from UTNO's earlier commitment to disruptive action, which was one key way in which the union maintained high member activism.

Teachers and community members, however, blamed the string of super-intendents, particularly Colonel Davis and Amato, for bringing down the district. "People do not remember that we had five superintendents in five years," argues community activist Beth Butler. "One of them was a military general, which shows just how racist that decision was. He had no background in education."[95] At the time, Butler's perspective was echoed by many in the community who claimed that New Orleans's schoolchildren deserved an educator to lead the district, not a military disciplinarian.[96] Just three years after they appointed him superintendent, the board forced Colonel Davis to retire, citing declining test scores, ongoing payroll problems, and the revelation that his father, a school custodian, had made over $85,000 in overtime during the Colonel's tenure as superintendent.[97] "I think that the business community was involved in getting [Colonel Davis] appointed because their interest was getting somebody from outside the school system to be appointed as superintendent. And they did the same thing with the mayor. They all lined up behind Ray Nagin [a former Cox Cable executive], and you see how successful that was."[98] Shortly before Katrina, Mayor Nagin, against the background of "an acrimonious coup" on the school board that ousted the board president, suggested that the city should take over the struggling district.[99] "Our school system scares the bejesus out of me," Nagin told the *Times Picayune* in his bid for a mayoral takeover.[100] Former mayor Marc Morial had also repeatedly threatened to take over the district. However, prior to Katrina, a plan for mayoral control of the schools garnered little traction. Mayoral control—which exists today in multiple cities including New York, Philadelphia, and Chicago—transfers power from a representatively elected school board to the centralized executive leadership of the mayor, thus reducing the community's input and power over the system.[101] Notably, Randi Weingarten, then president of New York City's UFT but now leader of the national AFT, eventually supported mayoral control when it was implemented in New York in 2002, in part because the deal was tied to a pay raise for educators.[102] Despite the endemic failures of the school board in New Orleans, UTNO offered no such support for the Morial or Nagin takeover plans.

Anthony Amato, the candidate who succeeded Colonel Davis after a string of three interim superintendents, similarly resigned after a public meeting when he was lambasted by the board.[103] Amato had served only two years: "I was at a board meeting when the people that supported [Amato] and gave him that power had to get up in front of the public and basically say, 'We made a mistake doing this.' That was a painful meeting. Just the fact that he had to sit there and listen to that. I felt bad for him. . . . It was embarrassing for him, to hear a state legislator say, 'I've lost confidence in you.' To just go in on him."[104] The turmoil in top leadership, compounded by a board that was inconsistent and micromanaging, led teachers to feel unsupported and criticism of the schools to continue unabated. "I felt like there were still really good things happening in a lot of schools, I mean that nobody ever really noticed because we were so busy concentrating on the negatives, or at least the media was. When Hurricane Katrina happened, they really made it sound like it was a good thing that the school system was blown away," says librarian Cindy Robinson.[105] Luetta Stewart, who taught at the magnet school McMain, summed up the perspective of much of the community, especially the white community, leading up to the storm: "The only schools that really functioned were your magnet schools."[106] Though many educators disagreed with this assessment, it was certainly one shared by the legislature.

In 2003, the state legislature, which had long critiqued the New Orleans schools, developed a pathway to take them over, spearheaded again by Leslie Jacobs.[107] Jacobs proposed the creation of the state-run Recovery School District (RSD), which would allow the state to take control of failing schools from OPSB and run them itself or give a charter to a university or nonprofit to run them.[108] The legislation was explicitly targeted at Orleans, the site of twenty-one of the state's twenty-three schools at the highest level of "corrective action," thus making them eligible for state takeover. The state would not take over any school that was improving, assured Jacobs, nor would it likely take over more than five schools in a single district.[109] The plan was enthusiastically supported by Jim Meza of UNO, who saw the hypothetical RSD takeovers as a way to bypass the union and the board and to develop the UNO-run charter district he had envisioned. In Jacobs's plan, teachers working at the schools taken over by the RSD would have their collective bargaining contracts nullified and would be required to reapply for their jobs.[110] From the outset, the state legislature blamed the mostly Black teaching force and school board for low test scores instead of focusing on anti-poverty programs or other solutions to counteract educational inequity.

Though UTNO and the LFT officially opposed the bill to create the RSD, they presented a tepid resistance, with Fred Skelton, then president of the LFT, saying that state takeover might be the "right solution."[111] The union wanted to be seen as open to change and reform, especially given the low test scores in Orleans Parish; but UTNO and the LFT's acquiescence would prove a costly mistake. The LFT did, however, work to remove from the RSD bill the state's right to privatize support services, much to the *Times Picayune*'s outrage: "If BESE isn't allowed to privatize support services, the union workers who staff cafeterias and mop floors will be able to keep a stranglehold on these jobs. . . . Letting union officials dictate how [a takeover] happens is like letting the fox build the henhouse."[112] Eliminating union jobs that provided a living wage for bus drivers, custodians, cafeteria workers, and maintenance workers would be a key part of the post-Katrina charter landscape. The creation of the RSD was passed via a statewide constitutional amendment and was supported by 60 percent of voters in the state, including 56 percent of voters in Orleans Parish.[113] Though the union and the school board failed to mount a compelling campaign against the amendment, the election results also speak to a significant shift in voter attitudes. New Orleans residents, especially the Black community, had been mostly loyal to the union and the schools through the 1970s, 1980s, and 1990s, even as many middle-class Black families moved their children to private and parochial schools. Yet by the early 2000s, besieged by school reform rhetoric and the promise of highly functioning charter schools, exhausted by years of reports about failing schools and lazy teachers, many voters looked to the state for help. Though the amendment certainly got more support among white voters—its greatest support was from the suburban parishes surrounding Orleans—it is remarkable that it won majority support in Orleans Parish, too, which at the time was less than 23 percent white.[114] School board member Ellenese Brooks-Simms, in a comment that encapsulated the growing divide between the working-class Black families who sent their children to the public schools and the mostly middle-class teachers and board members, said, "It won in New Orleans because our people aren't educated. The people in general did not know what this really means."[115]

The racial implications of the majority-white state legislature targeting majority-Black schools in Orleans Parish and taking control away from the democratically elected school board, bristled some educators. "I think [racism] was an element in this whole fight," argues LFT lobbyist Joy Van Buskirk. "I can't begin to tell you how many times I spoke with legislators, these are off-the-cuff conversations, where they said the kids in Orleans Parish were stupid because they were Black. I just looked at them. I was dumbfounded."[116] Teacher Leoance Williams argues that the district faced significant challenges that were not always acknowledged by state legislators: "Mismanagement. There were a lot of inequities. Supplies, things of that nature. Proper training for the teachers. Proper training for administrators. Truancy was a problem. Discipline was another problem. We were having a lot of problems. And one of the things that contributed, the majority of it, was poverty."[117] Switching the principal, the governing agency, and the teachers would do little to address the deep disparities that characterized the schools. Nonetheless, the state forged ahead, taking over Capdau Junior High and giving UNO a charter to run it for three years. The takeover marked "a historic departure from Louisiana's long-standing tradition of local control over public education," the *Times Picayune* proclaimed.[118]

When the school reopened, in fall 2004, the new leadership fired all the staff except one person and had students apply by lottery. The school also won $1 million in supplementary funding from the federal government and $250,000 from a local bank. "Without some kind of start-up money, I don't know how a non-profit could do this," said Jim Meza, the dean of UNO's School of Education, who helped spearhead the project.[119] Mitchell argued that all the schools in the district deserved such supplementary funding and asked how Capdau could be a model for the other schools when it had received so much more money than the rest of the district.[120] In February 2005, shortly before Hurricane Katrina hit the city, colleges and nonprofits applied to take over seven more failing schools.[121] "There was [a] creeping increase in the number of charters, but it really escalated after the storm. I don't think [the complete charter district] would have happened had there not been the storm," reflects LaCour.[122] The union recognized the neoliberal agenda of charter advocates, and it worked to maintain public schools and solicit the funding it needed to be successful.

However, the charterization of Capdau was only the beginning of the state's attempts to gain more direct power and oversight over the New Orleans schools. Just one month after the RSD announced its first school takeover, Representative Karen Carter, a Democrat from New Orleans serving in the Louisiana House, proposed a bill that would transfer many of the board's powers to Superintendent Amato. The bill, which overwhelmingly passed the House, was in response to several board members attempting to fire Amato after an unscheduled performance review.[123] Foreshadowing what was to come after the storm, Jacobs noted that the state now had the right to take over any failing school and that it could change the definition of "failing" at any time. Thus, she told the *Times Picayune*, the state could take over nearly half of the 120 schools in the city without a public vote.[124] Governor Blanco signed the bill after it passed the state senate as well, transferring "significant" board powers, including district finances and the power to hire and fire employees, to Amato. The new law was constitutional because it did not target New Orleans specifically, which would have violated the Voting Rights Act; instead, it labeled any school district with more than thirty failing schools as "academically in crisis"—and Orleans was the only parish that met that criterion.[125] Notably, in the *Times Picayune*'s extensive news coverage of the legislature transferring board powers to Amato, UTNO is not mentioned once. The union, which formerly was at the center of educational debates in the city, was losing its clout.

Political scientist Domingo Morel conducted a nationwide analysis of state takeovers of school districts. Though Morel does not focus specifically on New Orleans, the Orleans takeover from 2004 to 2005 fits neatly into Morel's paradigm of majority-white legislatures targeting Black city school districts.[126] Morel finds that takeovers do not typically lead to increases in test scores but instead appear to be a power grab by the state legislature. The state's dominant narrative is that the local community has failed and that local officials are no longer responsible leaders for children. For example, the state takeover in Newark, New Jersey, resulted in major layoffs that disproportionately impacted the Black community. The state-controlled district laid off 634 mostly low-wage employees as well as 2,000 part-time employees amid rhetoric that the schools needed to stop being a "local employer" and instead become a student-centered institution.[127] As in New Orleans, accusations of patronage and corruption are often used to justify takeovers, indicting Black leaders only ten to twenty years after they gained power, while white officials had enjoyed control over these districts for centuries and engaged in corruption and patronage with no consequences. New Orleans elected its first majority-Black school board in 1985 and its first Black superintendent the same year; twenty years later, following Katrina, the white-dominated state legislature would take control of nearly all the schools in the district. Though, as described above, the board certainly frustrated educators with its inconsistencies and occasional corruption, the charter networks that have since assumed the board's powers have also been riddled with scandals, economic maleficence, and a troubling lack of transparency. Ultimately, Morel argues, state takeovers promote the view that local Black leaders do not know, or care, what is best for Black children, but white state politicians do.[128]

The march toward complete state takeover continued in early 2005 when state superintendent Cecil Picard announced that unresolved audit problems in the city might lead the federal government to withhold money from the entire state.[129] Two months later, Amato revealed that the district was going broke and might not be able to make payroll by mid-April, and Picard demanded that OPSB voluntarily cede substantial control to an outside vendor.[130] Mitchell, representing the union, said she didn't see any viable alternative: "The district is in financial crisis. The state has offered help."[131] Over the next two months, Amato resigned and BESE voted to let groups take over and run four more New Orleans schools as charters.[132] With, again, only tepid resistance from the union, "in a politically charged and racially divisive move," the OPSB voted 4–3 to give an outside contractor, Alvarez and Marsal, "an unprecedented level of financial control over the school system."[133] At the board meeting when the vote occurred, Mitchell urged the board to table the measure and accused the state of having racist motives; but there was no organized opposition from the union.[134] The three Black board members all voted against the contract, and board president Torin Sanders, one of those dissenting members, refused to sign it.[135] Some post-storm scholars and activists have argued that the alleged financial mismanagement was simply a ploy to allow the state to begin the privatization of the New Orleans schools.[136]

Alvarez and Marsal (A&M), the New York–based "turnaround company," had recently completed a project with the St. Louis schools in which it cut the budget significantly and closed about twenty schools, angering local educators.[137] In the $16.8 million New Orleans deal, A&M gained control of all the district's finances but left academic decisions to the school board and superintendent.[138] Immediately, A&M publicly expressed shock at the state of the finances, setting the stage for layoffs and other severe cuts. Bill Roberti, an A&M employee appointed as the district's chief restructuring officer, described the system as suffering from "political patronage" and "individual fiefdoms."[139] However, educators—even some union members—were open to A&M's reforms because the company provided clarity and promised to fix a system that clearly wasn't working.[140] Teachers were tired of incorrect paychecks, constant budget crises, revelations of corruption, and poorly trained administrative staff who were incapable of helping them when they had an issue. Though many teachers remembered A&M negatively—the company was largely held responsible for the mass dismissal of educators and the failure to reopen the district after the storm—others recalled that in summer 2005, before the specter of Katrina, the company seemed like a potential solution to long-standing issues. "We didn't like [Alvarez and Marsal], but then, the board was almost indefensible," recalls Leoance Williams. "And so we got caught up in that. When I say 'we,' [I mean] the teachers, because it wasn't our fault that a lot of this stuff was going on the way it was. . . . So things had gotten so bad that they had to hire this management firm to kind of get things back together in line."[141] Though the contract was certainly privatizing public services, as A&M was replacing public school district employees, it promised to bring business expertise that would make the district more functional and transparent.

The union was in a strange position in relation to A&M because UTNO's contract was with OPSB, not with the turnaround company. Teacher Bill Scott, who never joined UTNO, said he thought the union became noticeably weaker before Katrina: "The administration that came in from outside made no pretense at dealing with them in a cordial way. They saw them as trifling, and they treated them that way."[142] Though Scott spoke disparagingly of the union, he was even more critical of A&M: "Alvarez and Marsal, those wonderful people. I'm sure worse things could happen to education, but I'm not quite sure how. . . . They cared less than the superintendent that had been there. They managed from spreadsheets. They knew nothing of this city. They knew nothing of our schools. They knew nothing of our history, our traditions."[143] Educators saw A&M as bumbling outsiders, who were unconcerned about the city or its schoolchildren:

"They used to come in monthly, and they'd fly out and they'd come in. It was crazy because they'd just come in and tell you what you have to do, and what not to do. Nothing ever really got done to me. It was a waste of time and money," remembers former UTNO president Wanda Richard.[144] Nonetheless, teacher Diana Brown said UTNO recognized A&M as a "threat."[145] She believes A&M had a plan to privatize the district and eliminate the union from the moment they arrived.[146] Mitchell says she fought with the contractors constantly: "[Their lead person] was very aggressive and assertive and he was like this kind of A-personality man, you listened to him. 'You do what I say' and all that bull. I was not fearful of that, so he and I used to tangle a lot."[147]

Despite Mitchell's personal conflict with the group, A&M met little official opposition from the union or from the board. In early August, A&M announced significant faculty layoffs on the grounds that the student population had declined by approximately 25 percent over the past six years. The board and the union did nothing to try to save the jobs. "I just hope[d] they would do this as painlessly and expeditiously as possible so those individuals can find employment and get on with their lives," Mitchell said.[148] Even OPSB president Sanders, who had mounted significant resistance to A&M's contract, tried only to deflect blame for the layoffs away from himself: "We know that we have inherited tremendous financial problems as relates to overspending over the last several years. The system has put off for a long time doing things that it needed to do."[149] Perhaps because of the union's official acquiescence, teacher Larry Carter saw the two groups as collaborating: "The union actually had great relationships with them and the district. All three groups were involved, because some of the things that they were trying to do impacted our collective bargaining agreement."[150] Carter says that behind the scenes, UTNO halted some of A&M's most significant pre-storm reforms, such as attempts to consolidate schools in ways that infringed on teachers' rights.[151] Despite ostensible collaboration with the union, the solutions that A&M proposed were often about cutting costs at the expense of providing good jobs and were aimed at helping the schools run more efficiently, not increasing learning. In A&M's last significant move before the storm, it asked the state legislature to repeal a law that prohibited the privatization of school cafeteria workers.[152]

In early 2005, a sense of hopelessness pervaded the school system and its educators. The school board had ceded much of its power to an outside entity; the state was trying to dismantle and take over the district both through the issuing of charters and through the RSD; the state superintendent was lambasting the district for misreporting spending; the local superintendent had resigned; and A&M was threatening major layoffs. "Well, the fact that we were being run by an entity as opposed to a board was suggestive of not necessarily privatization, but certainly a point of despair. A point where people had given up on what to do to make things better. There was a sense that the powers that be were flailing around trying to grab anything that might solve their problem. I see it as solve *their* problem. As opposed to necessarily making things successful."[153] Neoliberal reformers often rely on that despair to create change. For example, urban planners and policymakers push through gentrification and privatization in urban neighborhoods that have been devastated by federal and state divestment, declining tax bases, and racist housing policy.[154] As more funding is not presented as a possibility, neoliberal solutions seem like the only choice. Similarly, New Orleans parents, residents, and educators, tired of years of dysfunction and an apparent fiscal crisis, were open to A&M.[155] Neoliberal processes of creative destruction involve the destruction of previous forms of organization, such as a centralized school district staffed by public employees, to open up new spaces of capitalist accumulation.[156] Both processes were happening simultaneously in New Orleans before the storm, as old arrangements were dismantled—district employees fired, the democratically elected school board stripped of its powers—while new ones were built: charter schools opened, private workers hired at all levels. Though UTNO had put up years of resistance to these changes, it was slowly losing ground.

CRITIQUES OF THE UNION

Though many educators and other stakeholders had serious critiques of the school board and the district, some also felt that UTNO had contributed to the situation. Many of these critiques were actively promoted by the school reform movement, whose advocates argued that unions prevented meaningful reform, protected dangerous or incompetent teachers, and advocated for their own interests at the expensive of the students they taught.[157] By far the most common critique of UTNO was that it protected "bad teachers" whom principals or the district wanted to fire. This complaint resonated with paraprofessionals, teachers, principals, and district employees; no one wanted an unqualified educator in front of children. However, the union insisted on due process, presenting the polarizing issue as one of workers' rights. Educators also criticized the union for becoming too bureaucratic and divorced from the needs of its members, too powerful and capable of pushing teachers' needs above the needs of students, and largely unresponsive to serious attempts to improve the schools. Though each of these critiques has some merit, UTNO maintained high member enrollment as well as significant member involvement until Katrina, especially among Black educators—and 72 percent of teachers in the system were Black.[158] Though educators criticized some of the moves that UTNO made, by and large they still supported and worked for the union and reflected positively on its impact on their lives. However, the critiques certainly deterred some educators from joining and also contributed to a post-storm narrative—again, actively promoted by school reformers and charter advocates—that the union was to blame for the district's problems.

Though educators at all levels accused the union of protecting bad teachers, district employees tended to lambaste the union more than others. Violet Johnson told a story of a special education teacher who was given money by the district to take her students with severe special needs on daily field trips but who instead pocketed the money. When Johnson tried to fire her, the union defended her. Johnson also cited examples of the union defending a teacher who was having a mental breakdown and told her students she was an Egyptian princess and another who made racist remarks in class. According to Johnson, instead of getting fired, these teachers would get transferred from school to school, each time jeopardizing the education of yet another class of students.[159] Ken Ducote, who was himself a former union member, lay the blame with both the board and the union: "The school board, in some cases having nothing to do with the union, they would not want to fire a teacher, because they didn't want it to be on their record that they had voted to fire a teacher. So after they had the tenure hearing, they would transfer the teacher, take away their tenure, make them probationary again, and tell the superintendent to transfer them to another school." This could result in an ineffective or even malicious teacher working at several successive schools with few consequences or in teachers being pulled from the classroom and paid to do busy work: "There were several people that were protected by the union that had committed offenses, and the board was afraid to take them on. So, they pulled them out of the classroom and had them on in-house suspension with pay for eight, nine years. One of them was this guy that recently was convicted of child molestation. He was a molester, and they pulled them out of the classroom. He hadn't been convicted or anything yet, but nobody wanted him at any of their schools."[160] Not only does this represent a waste of district money, but it also potentially put children at risk.

Larry Samuel, UTNO's longtime attorney, argues that, just as in the justice system, everyone deserves to tell their side of the story: "So, yeah, we defended everyone. It's not our call to decide who's wrong. If they can't be proven guilty, they shouldn't be disciplined. I'm always reminded, we represented a PE teacher who by all accounts was not a very good PE teacher. But the school board's policy was the principal had to conduct two formal observations of a minimum of thirty minutes. This principal conducted one, and they moved to fire him. Now who's more incompetent?"[161] Many teachers remembered the time before the collective bargaining agreement as one of arbitrary dismissals at the whim of capricious administrators whose actions were often tinged with racism and sexism. Though educators did not want to work alongside ineffective colleagues, they also understood the importance of having checks on administrative power.

Samuel relayed that sometimes other UTNO members would call the union and ask why it was defending an ineffective teacher at their school. Samuel would tell them, "If they are [ineffective], that'll be proven and then the right outcome will be had."[162] Frank Fudesco, who was a principal and an administrator, agreed with Samuel:

> I always told my principals, "If you do it right, tenure does not protect anybody." Makes it uncomfortable. I used to tell them, "Your problem is you don't want to look a teacher in the eye and tell her she's no good. You just want me to make her go away. That's not how it works. You got to be fair. How do I know she's no good if you don't prove your point? You have to document." We used to have workshops after workshops on how to document poor behavior. And Larry [Samuel] was very good on the other side. If they did their work right, and I could show that, Larry would counsel those teachers to leave. And I doubt if he'd tell you that. But I know he did that.[163]

Larry Carter, who was a grievance specialist during Mitchell's tenure as president, affirms that it was Mitchell's policy to counsel educators out of the profession if they were incompetent: "We did that, and it was an unknown secret by some. . . . If it got to a point where I've seen three or four times in one year this particular teacher, whether it was [because they] couldn't get along with their colleagues, didn't know how to treat students, or couldn't get along with their administration, then I needed to have a serious talk about, is this the profession for you? Are you doing more harm to the profession and your own mental health?"[164] Juanita Bailey, another grievance specialist, reported that she counseled out teachers who had no control, were not turning in lesson plans, or were putting kids at risk as well as elderly teachers who needed to retire. "There was not one person we ever counseled that didn't take our advice and leave. It worked, frankly, because they trusted us and they knew that we didn't gain anything at all by lying to them."[165] When asked what he was most proud of, Wilson Boveland, a teacher who became an UTNO staffer, said, "I don't think I ever really fought to keep somebody in a position that never should have been there. . . . I would counsel them out."[166] However, Violet Johnson disagreed: "The union rarely helped us get people out. . . . They helped me with two people. Connie Goodly, one, and Jo Anna Russo. They each helped me with one person. And there's so many that just didn't need to be teaching."[167]

Alan Guma, the principal of McMain, said it was tricky to get rid of incompetent teachers but that he was able to do so by eliminating positions and other creative solutions: "There was a phys ed teacher at McMain who was a big, tall guy, who intimidated the kids and his idea of phys ed was throw a ball and get sweaty. It was no instruction of any kind, it was a disgrace . . . With [him], I was tipped off, we had some vending machines in the phys ed area. I was tipped off that he had a relationship with the vendor and was getting some of the proceeds. We kind of staked it out and got him fired." Guma maintains that both the district and the union contributed to making it difficult to fire bad teachers, so the key as a principal was to hire well in the first place.[168] Diego Gonzalez-Grande reports that his view on the union defending teachers who the district wanted to fire has evolved over time:

> I always argued that I thought there were times that UTNO perhaps was not doing enough to either assist those that needed improvement, or if that did not work, encourage them to seek another line of employment. [My colleague] Joel has always taken the position that, first of all, it was not necessarily the principal task of a union to do so, but he also argued that, in fact, UTNO and the AFT were committed to improving the quality of education and offered opportunities through their professional development and curriculum work and so on. I have to say that making a judgment or evaluation today, I am perhaps prone to be more sympathetic to Joel's point of view than my own. . . . The contract's great virtue is that it provides due process when disputes arise. That perhaps is an issue that I appreciated not enough when I argued with Joel, that in fact, even the "least competent teacher" is entitled to a process to demonstrate that whatever charges are being leveled against him or her are false.[169]

Many educators who started working after UTNO had won collective bargaining had no concept of what it was like to teach without due process protections. For those who returned after Katrina, the post-storm landscape opened their eyes.

Again, the union was caught in a situation in which its belief in worker protections and its commitments to its membership sometimes conflicted with the image it wanted to project as primarily fighting to ensure that children received a good education. The insistence on the part of many UTNO staffers that they counseled people out of the profession attempts to meld these dual goals. However, some leaders such as Nat LaCour and lawyer Larry Samuel argue that there is no conflict; rather, offering teachers protection encourages quality teachers to stay in the district and the onus is on the administration to weed out any bad apples. "I think there's misconceptions about the union, period. I mean, not just UTNO, but people said teachers should not belong to the union because the union tries to keep incompetent teachers in place. That's not true. The union is not involved in the training of teachers. We're not involved with the recruitment of teachers. We're not involved in the assignment of teachers. We're not involved in the evaluation of teachers. And so, to blame ineffective teachers on the union is just outright wrong because we don't assign them."[170] LaCour additionally pointed out that in Toledo, Ohio, the one district nationwide where the AFT is involved in teacher evaluation, the union terminated more teachers for poor performance than management ever did.[171]

Educators and other stakeholders also accused the union of becoming too bureaucratic and divorced from the needs of teachers and students. For example, some educators suggested that the union at its inception played a more nuanced role in defending teachers, looking at both a teacher's rights and their particular situation, whereas by the early 2000s, the much larger union simply followed procedures mandating that it defend people across the board. As the contract grew through successive years of collective bargaining, the rules became more specific and arcane and, some teachers argued, more geared toward protecting the veteran educators who were UTNO's strongest constituency. Cindy Robinson eventually left the union because of her disillusionment with its policies. Robinson had been hired at one school as a librarian, and then a teacher from another school, a person who had one more year of seniority than Robinson, tried to take the job from her: "Someone tried to 'bump' me, is what it was called at the time, where somebody with more seniority wanted my position after I had gotten it."[172] Though Robinson managed to keep her job, she remembered other incidents at her school of teachers being "bumped" and how mean the faculty would be toward the new hire. "It seemed like a lot of negativity to me and like people were hostile."[173] The union was trying to ensure that the person with the most seniority got the job, but Robinson felt that the policy limited a principal's ability to hire the best person, who might have other qualifications aside from simply years in the system. Moreover, not all veteran teachers were necessarily the most competent, as Ducote argues:

> Dr. Proctor, who was our former deputy superintendent and later Dean of Education for SUNO, he used to say that you do want experienced, veteran people, but you don't want people who have one year of experience thirty times over. So they really haven't grown and really haven't learned anything . . . and I said the complete opposite is what happened after Katrina, where you had a few Teach for America schools that every person, including the principals, it's their first year. So that's the other end of the problem. You need some kind of mixture and some kind of freshness. I used to describe it as the reason why the soil around here was so fertile and everything is because the river used to overflow every year and give you a little fresh blood, the new nutrients and everything.[174]

But UTNO refused to let principals fire or transfer veteran educators, even in schools that were academically struggling, preventing, in Ducote's view, meaningful change and improvement. Post Katrina, dismissing the entire faculties of low-performing schools became commonplace, with teachers sometimes being allowed to apply to get their own jobs back and sometimes being automatically replaced.

Violet and Mike Johnson maintain that the union became more powerful over time, eventually tipping the balance toward teachers and away from students. "It became more and more powerful. It was sort of feeling its oats, and it was basically taking over the school system. It was determining who could work where, and seniority was everything. The more years you had, the more choices you had. I think pendulums swing left and right, and this one had swung way over there."[175] Violet Johnson saw the union as holding a broken district hostage and demanding more rights when they couldn't win salary increases: "All the union negotiations, what was negotiated in the contract was not much for students. It was all for teachers: teachers' well-being, teachers not having to teach very long, and moving the locus of control from the principal and the district to UTNO and to the individual teachers."[176] Ducote thinks the union gained excessive power not through negotiations but through its political lobbying: "One of the negative things that happened was UTNO started controlling a majority of the board. An UTNO endorsement was a good way to be on the board. And board members would make concessions so that they would not lose UTNO's endorsement."[177]

It is true that the union contract mostly covered benefits for educators and that the union's political machine played no small role in board elections. However, the union argued that the benefits gained in the contract—including regulating class sizes, providing teachers with a small fund to buy supplies, and guaranteeing a duty-free lunch—also benefited students, just as having a teaching force composed of happy and empowered educators improves learning. Many other issues that the union negotiated around, such as school conditions, equally affected students and teachers, and the union's work in this realm—demanding air conditioning and repairs to leaking ceilings, for example—helped draw public attention to the many inequities of the system. UTNO staffer Joe DeRose explains: "The problems in New Orleans Public Schools were immense. And if it wasn't for the union being like a watchdog, some of it might've not been known. One thing that I was particularly trying to do is to bring attention to the really deplorable conditions inside the schools, the physical conditions. . . . I still have the pictures of some schools with mold all over them."[178] Though the union was sometimes blamed for the problems of the schools, union staffers like DeRose argue that UTNO regularly fought the district and the board for improvements, often using the negotiating process as a means to push through reforms. Mitchell says that the union's goal was not to run the schools, but to create a meaningful forum for teacher voice.[179]

Though claims that UTNO controlled the schools or the school board are likely overblown—after all, the union frequently fought with the board and it was unable to stop the trickle of neoliberal reforms, including the implementation of standardized testing and the loss of schools to charters—there was certainly a shift in the union from when it won collective bargaining in 1974 to the years before the storm. By its involvement in institution-building and by providing for its teachers a professional development center, the Health and Welfare Fund, a credit union, and a large staff of grievance specialists, UTNO became a social safety net for educators unparalleled elsewhere in the South; it helped the system's mostly Black working-class and middle-class educators stay financially solvent and even buy their first homes. At the same time, as UTNO gave up its initial commitment to protest and disruption, especially with younger educators, it lost the sense of participatory democracy that originally pervaded the union. When Mitchell was reelected president in 2004, only around 1,200 union members participated in the vote, less than one-quarter of UTNO's total membership.[180] Though there were ways for union members to get involved, such as in UTNO's political work, fewer teachers saw the union as a central part of their lives and work. "It got to be another hierarchy," explains teacher Laverne Kappel.[181] "There was a sense, perhaps, that it was an organization which had lost a certain degree of energy and vitality," says Gonzalez-Grande, though, he adds, certainly not to such an extent that anyone would have predicted its post-Katrina destruction.[182] Robinson says that the energy behind the union was different: "Like when I started out, people just joined the union, that's what you did, and I didn't feel like that was the case much anymore. People didn't feel as strongly about it."[183] Ironically, the institutionalization of the union's power contributed to its vulnerability when the storm hit; members looked to the union to help and protect them, but they did not necessarily see it as their role to help and protect the union, to be part of the force that allowed it to continue.

While UTNO in the early 2000s relied less on participatory democracy, disruption, and member activism than it had in the 1970s and 1980s, most educators continued to join the union, and for some, it remained a crucial component of their lives. Larry Carter joined the union when he first started teaching because his mother had been a union member in Jefferson Parish. "It was like a family," he recalls.[184] Billie Dolce joined because she wanted protection from a predatory principal.[185] Susie Beard joined in the late 1960s because she saw it as part of the community organizing and civil rights work she was already doing in her neighborhood.[186] Linda Pichon, a paraprofessional, joined because unions were in her family: "My daddy was with the musicians. My stepdaddy was with the longshoremen's. My husband was with the union. It was just union, yes."[187] Joel Behrman joined to be part of the movement: "I come from a left-wing New York Jewish nonpracticing home. So we knew about Pete Seeger and the people's psalms and union songs and Norman Thomas and stuff like that . . . UTNO didn't sing as much as I wanted us to sing."[188] Laverne Kappel joined because her principal was oppressive.[189] Many people joined because union leaders at their schools encouraged them. They paid dues and they also assumed leadership positions, worked on political campaigns, attended professional development seminars, protested for their rights, and, when they retired, joined the retirees' chapter, as Stone describes:

> For twenty to thirty years, I, working in the union, did good work for teachers, made their plight better. I believe [I] made the plight of the students better. There was a lot of people working in a cubicle or somewhere that their job was the least rewarding thing about their life; church, family friends, something else. The union, and my working life, was probably the best thing in my life, except for present company [his partner Patti Reynolds]. Also, it was fun and educational. The way negotiations work, lobbing worked, political campaigns worked, school committees, evaluation and textbooks, and all of this stuff. It just was a better way to spend your time than watching TV or something.[190]

Though Joy Van Buskirk had a very different career trajectory than Stone, starting as a teacher and then becoming the LFT's longtime lobbyist, she expressed a similar sentiment: "When I look at other people doing jobs today, and their mission is not to assist others to the point where they've got to go to the wall to do that assisting, I shake my head, because you glean a lot of satisfaction from helping others and knowing you made a difference."[191] Thus, despite the internal shifts in the union and the institutional exhaustion from being on the defensive for years, for many educators, UTNO retained its vibrancy and meaning. Critiques from the corporate school reform movement had influenced the ways in which people thought and spoke about UTNO, but they were far from controlling the narrative.

CONCLUSION

Sociologists Kim Voss and Rachel Sherman argue that unions can reverse their shift toward oligarchy and institutionalization and become radical, participatory, and democratic once again, particularly when faced with a crisis.[192] They found that unions were able to revitalize when they got new leaders with activist experience from outside of the labor movement, especially when the national union was pushing toward innovation. In the locals Voss and Sherman studied, new leaders were not swept in by democratic movements from below but rather when top-down reforms broke up the unions' "bureaucratic conservatism," which then opened up space for participatory democracy and leadership building once again.[193] The Chicago Teachers Union (CTU) is a clear example of this type of revitalization. In 2010, a progressive caucus won power in CTU internal elections, reinvigorating the local and leading to increased rank-and-file participation and a successful 2012 strike.[194] UTNO was not able to transform the crisis of Katrina into this kind of union revitalization, but the hurricane also presented an existential threat to the city and members' lives far greater than the crises that Voss and Sherman analyzed. Moreover, although the leadership change that brought Mitchell to power represented a shift, and although Mitchell brought in many new, young educators, her leadership style was less democratic than LaCour's, foreclosing significant shifts toward participation and member involvement. Though UTNO won meaningful reforms that improved the lives of the city's educators, the vast majority of whom were Black women who were often left out of economic gains, the union was unable to effect changes that fundamentally improved education in the district, such as procuring the immense amount of funding needed to build state-of-the-art schools, to provide tutoring for struggling students, and to equip schools with the necessary numbers of social workers, nurses, and counselors to truly address the trauma faced by children living in poverty.

In the years leading up to the storm, the district was in disarray. It had unstable top leadership, and the general public, whether rightly or not (and certainly racism played a role) believed that the school board was corrupt and the schools dysfunctional. Test scores were abysmal, though teacher Jim Randels points out that several years after the storm the district started using a "growth metric" to measure schools' success instead of test scores alone, and schools were given extra points for working with students who lived in poverty, had special needs, or were learning English as a second language, which resulted in a more holistic and fair measurement.[195] Discipline and violence were persistent issues, both on school grounds and in students' neighborhoods. The state was slowly taking over schools and turning them into charters using the mechanism of the RSD, and the OPSB had ceded all its financial control, as well as unclear additional powers, to the outside contracting company A&M. The union, though successful in preventing total takeover by private interests, was clearly on the defensive, had historically low member participation, and had forged a relationship with the board and A&M that was alternately ineffectively combative and acquiescent. UTNO also operated in a national climate that undermined progressive education organizing. Both the Democratic and Republican Parties were pushing for the expansion of charter schools, and the national AFT supported standardized testing and the closure of "failing" schools.

However, there were some positive signs as well. In May 2005, test scores in the district showed signs of improving.[196] Most teachers continued to join the union, and they had won a strike only fifteen years before. By and large, educators saw the district's problems as caused by incompetent leadership from the school board and superintendent, as exemplified by the district's financial mismanagement and its inability to properly complete payroll, rather than as the consequence of subpar teaching; and they assumed that parents and the public saw that as well. Though teachers agreed that some of the schools were struggling, they attributed that to chronic underfunding, not to uncaring teachers or a union that was afraid of change and innovation: "Schools are only as functional as you allow them to be. We had classrooms with thirty and thirty-five kids in a classroom, we didn't have enough materials. So you were either making or buying things that the children needed. And you didn't make a lot of money."[197] Teachers in both selective-admissions schools and regular public schools spoke about the work they did with pride and remembered many of the students they taught as successful. "Those kids, even before the storm, I taught special ed hearing impaired, those kids were still successful. They went on, got their high school diplomas, they took the LEAP test, they did well on the LEAP test, went on to college. And they were all products of Orleans Parish public school system," recalls Shelly McAlister.[198] When she was bumped from her magnet school job, Samantha Turner taught briefly at Carver Middle School, one of the lowest performing schools in the district: "Horrible. It was horrible. It was dark. The halls were dark. It was a cinder block. The walls were like gray and navy blue. And poor windows. And it just wasn't pleasant." The first thing Turner did when she arrived was paint her room bright pink and lavender. "And then we set up aquariums. And the students were not used to seeing any of that. We did a family night. People came. We did what we had done at our former schools. And so, I enjoyed the students and they enjoyed me."[199] Even within the district's most difficult schools, teachers worked to connect to students and provide quality education, and many of them were supported by UTNO.

Though policymakers at the local and state levels continued to push neoliberal policies and the city saw a creeping increase in privatization through TFA recruits and charter schools, by and large, UTNO held the neoliberal agenda at bay. Its work obviously benefited its membership, particularly its Black and working-class members, but it also resulted in more redistributive policies across the city. Working-class school support employees benefited from UTNO's organizing because of their "me too" contracts that guaranteed them salary increases whenever the teachers won raises. UTNO anchored the local labor movement and continued to play a significant role in the Black political machine in the city, particularly through its voter registration and turnout efforts. UTNO members like Jim Randels supported citywide initiatives such as the Living Wage Campaign of the early 2000s. UTNO provided a strong, respected, well-organized alternative to the neoliberal privatization agenda, and despite the power and wealth of its opponents, the union was often successful.

Despite the challenges the district faced and the state's forays into seizing control, in early 2005 the district looked to be on a path of gradual reform with slowly increasing privatization. UTNO remained the largest local in the state, and it continued to play a significant, if diminished, role in both the Louisiana AFL-CIO and the state legislature. Mitchell, though more combative and less trusting as a leader than LaCour, genuinely sought educational improvements in the district, making her a potentially advantageous partner for education reformers. Moreover, though Mitchell herself did not foster participatory democracy, she was likely to retire soon, having worked in the system for more than thirty-five years, thus opening the door for new and potentially transformational leadership from among the young educators she had mentored. Yet when Hurricane Katrina hit in August 2005, policymakers and education reformers would use the storm to push through their neoliberal education agenda in its entirety, fire the unionized educators, and almost destroy the union. The post-storm targeting of educators and the union demonstrates the power that UTNO continued to hold and the real obstacle it posed to the privatization of the schools and the city—as well as the power it helped mobilize via the Black middle-class voting bloc that generally continued to support both public sector workers and the public schools. Despite UTNO's flaws, the diminishment of the union's power would be yet one more blow against the beleaguered city and its teachers, as the member-built and member-led organization that fought tenaciously for the rights of mostly Black women educators and helped to cement the local labor movement faded into the background.

5

Color-Blind Neoliberalism

Hurricane Katrina, Mass Dismissals, and the Privatization Agenda, 2005–2008

The systematic political disempowerment of black communities
through the state takeover of local school districts shows how education
has been central to the project of state-sanctioned political inequality.

Domingo Morel, *Takeover*

Everyone recognizes that the storm provided an
opportunity for all this privatization bullshit.

Stanley Taylor, National Association of Letter Carriers

When Hurricane Katrina hit New Orleans in August 2005 and the levees gave way, flooding the majority of the city, McMain Secondary School remained mostly unscathed. Located Uptown, at the busy intersection of Nashville and S. Claiborne Avenue, McMain was, in many residents' eyes, a jewel in the mostly dysfunctional New Orleans public school system. In 1974, as white people fled the district, Superintendent Geisert transformed McMain into a magnet school with a racial quota system: the school was required to enroll close to a 50 percent Black and 50 percent white student body.[1] "There was a deep concern that things were re-segregating," explains longtime McMain principal Alan Guma. "The mission of the school, as I articulated it, was we were going to show a city that disbelieves in public education that there could be quality, integrated, public education."[2] Though critics complained about McMain's selectivity and the way in which the racial quota system disproportionately benefited white students who made up a small minority of the public school population, students and teachers fell in love with the school. "It was a very, very, very special place," recalls Maude Harris.[3] Luetta Stewart student-taught at McMain and then was hired on as faculty: "Nobody left McMain. Everybody was highly experienced. Some of them had come to education as a second career, so you have former lawyers and just these profoundly intelligent people, and that was my mentoring into education. So, I got a phenomenal foundation as an educator."[4] Teachers loved teaching diverse students and, by virtue of the admissions requirements, they had little trouble with standardized tests and the discipline issues that riddled other schools in the city. Many sent their own children to the school.[5] Laverne Kappel taught at McMain for decades: "And I knew that McMain was part of the problem. . . . I worked for Orleans Parish School Board. My kids went to elementary schools that worked, I taught at a school that worked, but in the big scheme of things, I was part of a failing system. And I think if you don't accept that, not that the magnet school was sucking kids, no. But we were on the top deck and all hell was breaking loose down below. And all on the same ship."[6]

Shortly before the storm, McMain removed the racial quota system, acquiescing to arguments that it discriminated against Black students. The school's demographics changed dramatically—according to Harris, it became about 80 percent Black, 10 percent white, and 10 percent Asian[7]—but it maintained its admissions requirements, so the school continued to score highly on standardized tests and draw talented teachers and students.

The impetus for McMain, like UTNO, emerged from the civil rights movement. Both institutions explicitly discussed race and worked to create meaningful racial balance and integration. But by the late 1990s, the climate had shifted politically and economically, and the civil rights ethos of acknowledging and accounting for the legacies of racism had been replaced by color-blind neoliberalism. Theorist Jodi Melamed argues that state-sanctioned anti-racist discourse, such as rhetoric about color blindness or diversity, serves to support US imperialism and neoliberal values, such as the free market and the preeminent importance of property rights.[8] Economically, this shift meant the destruction of public services and their replacement with private, market-driven alternatives, the erosion of stable working-class jobs and the emergence of temporary jobs and the gig economy, the massive disciplining of organized labor, and a taxation system that grossly exacerbated wealth inequality, producing staggering gains for those at the very top.[9] Rhetorically, it meant a shift in discourse away from explicit conversations about race and toward a belief that acknowledging race at all was racist, that our goal should be to promote a race-blind meritocracy in which everyone is judged by their individual achievement.[10] Even as reformers shuttered public housing projects and public schools in the name of people of color, affirmative action laws were ruled "reverse racism" and repealed as policymakers pushed for a system that would rely on individual merit alone.[11] UTNO and McMain, in their commitment to integration and racial quotas, appeared almost anachronistic.

Though McMain was spared the worst of the flooding, post-Katrina policymakers dismantled its program just as they dismantled UTNO. Following Hurricane Katrina, policymakers fired approximately 7,500 school employees, including 4,000 teachers, and began the process of transforming New Orleans into the nation's first-ever all-charter school district. In this chapter, I focus on the impact the storm and the subsequent mass dismissals had on educators; and I analyze how policymakers' choices shortened teachers' careers, contributed to their financial instability, and influenced their decisions about whether to return to New Orleans to rebuild. UTNO was ineffective at protecting its members during this time, and it failed to mount a significant fight against the coming privatization. I argue that this was because of both the scale of the disaster and the union's move away from participatory democracy in the years leading up to the storm. At the same time, the union did recoup some members, enough to mount a spirited campaign to demand that the city reopen schools to allow residents to return—a move that harkened back to the community activism of UTNO's heyday. Yet despite an influx of money, resources, and personnel from the AFT and the AFL-CIO as well as meaningful community support, UTNO organizers were unable to successfully counter the powerful school reform agenda or secure a place for the union in the new charterized system. In the post-Katrina landscape, as the national guard patrolled the streets and residents struggled to return and rebuild, opportunities for democratic participation suffered. With most of its members displaced, the school board essentially defunct, and educational decisions made largely by business elites in private—or faux-public—meetings, UTNO did not stand a chance.

In the months that followed the devastating storm, policymakers at the local, state, and national levels used the absence of residents able to organize resistance to force through neoliberal reforms in their entirety—reforms that they had been able to pass only piecemeal before the disaster. Reformers presented mostly white educational entrepreneurs as the saviors of the district and focused their rhetoric on bureaucratic issues, such as school board corruption and financial mismanagement, instead of the legacy of neglect and racist public policy that had marred education in the city. City officials and private sector educational entrepreneurs worked tirelessly to convince the public that "we must not alleviate poverty to work toward equity."[12] Ultimately, I argue that policymakers' targeting of UTNO, as well as the anti-UTNO rhetoric that coalesced after the storm, was an intentionally anti-Black, anti-labor neoliberal project. The charter school system, which the state established at the expense of Black educators' careers, is characterized today by its community disempowerment, its few avenues for democratic participation, its ongoing issues with transparency and corruption, its lack of teacher voice, and its dearth of Black, local, and experienced educators.[13] Moreover, revisionist portraits of the union that paint it as opposed to change and reform, or simply as protecting bad educators, contribute to a racist caricature of an organization that for more than thirty years fought for the rights of mostly Black women educators, demanded more money for a severely underfunded school system, and helped coalesce Black political power in the city and the state. Like any organization, UTNO had its flaws, and those flaws were on full display after Hurricane Katrina. However, despite these shortcomings, the union also presents a model of how to fight against anti-worker and anti-Black processes of neoliberal privatization in the Deep South.

THE STORM AND ITS AFTERMATH

The trauma of living through Hurricane Katrina still sits with educators today. Educators' stories reveal the horror and destruction of the storm and the levee breach, the ways in which educators were dispersed, sometimes haphazardly, throughout the country, and why it was so challenging for UTNO to drum up organized resistance to the school reforms implemented in the fall of 2005. The disaster was an incalculable loss for many families and, because of the ways in which segregation, redlining, and racial covenants had structured housing patterns in the city, Black families tended to live in lower lying areas and bore a disproportionate share of the destruction.[14] The disaster lasted, for most people, long after the flood waters finally drained. Teacher Billie Dolce described how the aide who worked in her classroom perished in the floodwaters, and how the woman's funeral was only the first of many she attended after the storm.[15] Susie Beard, a paraprofessional, was helicoptered from the roof of her house to the superdome, where she stayed until the AFT sent buses to evacuate union members: "[We] got on Greyhound and they carried us to Baton Rouge. They weren't accepting any more. We then went to Houston. They weren't accepting any more, and from there, they fed us and they took us to a military base that had been closed down in Oklahoma."[16] Eventually she made it to her daughter's house in Maryland. After staying in Baton Rouge for six months, Leoance Williams, a teacher and member of the UTNO executive board, lived in a FEMA (Federal Emergency Management Agency) trailer for a year and a half while he worked to rebuild his house.[17] Many educators enrolled their children in other

Table 5.1. Timeline of events, August 2005–January 2006

August 29, 2005	Hurricane Katrina hits New Orleans.
October 3	Jefferson and St. Tammany parishes reopen schools.
October 8	Federal government offers state $20.9 million in educational disaster aid, but only for charters.
October 20	Catholic Archdiocese identifies fourteen Catholic schools in Orleans Parish that can reopen.
October 29	OPSB approves chartering of twenty schools, including all thirteen Algiers schools unaffected by the storm.
November 14	St. Bernard Parish reopens first schools.
November 15	State legislature passes Act 35 and takes over 102 of New Orleans's 117 schools.
November 28	Ben Franklin Charter High reopens, the first public school in Orleans to do so.
November 30	7,500 New Orleans educators informed they will be fired and lose health insurance effective Jan. 31, 2006.
December 14	Algiers Charter Association opens its first five campuses on the West Bank.
January 9, 2006	OPSB opens its first school, McMain Secondary School.

districts and got jobs in other school systems, in part because the New Orleans schools were so slow to reopen, thus further delaying their return to the city. "Had we been able to go back to our schools, let's say Katrina happened, August 29 is when it really hit the city, if they had gotten things together, September 20th, we would have all gone back to our jobs. We would have lived together. Then they started offering pods and doing all kinds of things. But at that point we were just wholly disgusted."[18] These stories are not anomalies. It took many residents months, or even years, to return to the city, if they made it back at all. Amid this trauma and displacement, all the major post-storm decisions were made (see table 5.1).

Naomi Klein argues that governments use both natural disasters and human-orchestrated disasters to push through economic policies that never would have been accepted by residents under normal circumstances, a phenomenon which she calls "disaster capitalism."[19] For example, in the words of the BESE board president, "The painful devastation of this national catastrophe became the opportunity, the catalyst, for change."[20] Though New Orleans, like many major cities, was slowly acquiescing to the erosion of formerly public institutions and growing privatization, Katrina allowed policymakers to destroy existing institutions outright and erect new, profit-driven ones in their place. This elite-led "creative destruction"[21] transformed the city, leading to the complete elimination of public housing complexes, a process that had begun before the storm, all of which were replaced by lower-density "mixed-income" developments; the contracting out of public bus services to the French company Veolia; the shuttering of public Charity Hospital, which was replaced by University Medical Center and run as a private/public partnership; and, of course, the destruction of the public education system, with all schools, as of 2019, operating as publicly funded and privately-governed charter schools.[22]

These policies, though primarily motivated by a desire for profit and the belief that private management and businesslike organizations are inherently more efficient, explicitly targeted New Orleans's Black residents. While the Bring New Orleans Back commission's plan to turn several prominent Black neighborhoods into green space was abandoned due to widespread outrage, the intentional elimination of Black housing and jobs served a similar purpose.[23] None of the public housing projects reopened following the storm, leaving many former residents with nowhere to live if they returned to the city, and FEMA's response woefully underserved Black residents, leading one researcher to label the Katrina recovery a "privately organized, publicly funded bureaucratic failure."[24] Meanwhile, policymakers eliminated thousands of working- and middle-class Black jobs by closing Charity Hospital and by firing approximately 7,500 educators. One month after the storm, President Bush's secretary of Housing and Urban Development said, "New Orleans is not going to be as black as it was for a long time, if ever again."[25] Ten years after Hurricane Katrina, that prediction had been actualized: the city had 100,000 fewer Black residents than when the storm hit.[26]

The elimination of UTNO was not an unintended consequence of the move toward privatized education but rather a key ideological aspect of the new system. By design, charter schools are run by a central leader, typically a CEO or principal, who has absolute control over every aspect of school management including hiring and firing, work hours, pay, and the curriculum. The CEO reports to an appointed board, whose main job, like any nonprofit board, is fundraising. If the school performs poorly, the board holds the principal accountable and potentially replaces the person; and if the school fails to improve, eventually the authorizing agency (typically the school district) revokes the charter and gives it to another agency to run, often replacing all administrators and staff. A union interrupts this system by introducing teacher voice and teacher demands, thus limiting the CEO's absolute power and, perhaps, the degree to which the board can hold the CEO accountable for the school's troubles. Moreover, a union is centrally concerned with workers' rights, preventing, in theory, the nimble management the CEO needs to effectively run the school. By regulating work hours, lunch breaks, pay, and disciplinary procedures, the union gives some agency to educators while undercutting the CEO's ability to make quick decisions that might improve educational outcomes (for example, mandating that teachers tutor struggling students on Saturdays).[27] As policymakers moved

New Orleans toward an all-charter system, neutralizing UTNO was a necessary step. Moreover, minimizing UTNO's influence furthered the larger neoliberal goal of reducing the power of organized labor, because labor promotes higher salaries, job security, and workers' rights regulations that tend to limit profit accumulation. These economic motivations are also deeply connected to race; policymakers used tropes of lazy Black teachers and violent and unruly Black students to justify the wholesale dismantling of the pre-Katrina school system.[28] Narratives today that paint the city as a "lab" to study the effects of charter schools, further serve to dehumanize and devalue the mostly Black students and families who use the schools, who have effectively become the nonconsensual subjects of a citywide experiment.[29]

The push to make New Orleans an all-charter district, to fire the displaced educators, and to remove local control over the schools occurred at the local, state, and national levels and in both the public and the private sectors. The federal government offered the state $20.9 million in educational disaster aid—but only to open charter schools.[30] At the same time, education reformers urged the board, the state legislature, and A&M, the turnaround company managing the schools, to completely eliminate the old system. The chief operating officer from the Broad Foundation, a philanthropy funded by insurance tycoons, offered money and resources to the city under the condition that the city adopt market-based reforms: "This is a real historic opportunity to take what has obviously been just a terrible thing and create something good out of it. . . . People around the nation who are poised to help bring resources to the table might turn their attention to other places."[31] The *Times Picayune* noted that the Broad Foundation was "one of several education organizations" offering resources to pressure the city to adopt charter reforms.[32] At the state level, Gov. Kathleen Blanco, a Democrat, developed Act 35, a plan for the state to take over 102 of the city's 117 schools and place them in the state-controlled RSD, effectively removing them from local jurisdiction and allowing the state to reopen them as charters.[33] The RSD, as described in chapter 4, had originally been set up to target a few of the worst-performing schools in each district, not to completely usurp local school board control. Nonetheless, Act 35 was fast-tracked through the legislature and passed in November 2005, less than three months after Hurricane Katrina hit the city.[34]

Meanwhile, at the local level, the OPSB decided to open all thirteen schools on the city's mostly undamaged West Bank as charter schools.[35] Though BESE had already been pushing to open additional charter schools in the state, it painted the charterization of the Algiers schools as a fiscal necessity: "These charter schools will be eligible for the $2,000 per pupil allocation from the federally award[ed] charter school grant. . . . Schools that reopen in the Orleans Parish School System that are not chartered will be ineligible for this additional funding source and will have no funding source to replace the local funding that has been lost due to the hurricanes' economic impact on the area."[36] This move foreshadowed the path to privatization ahead.

Displaced teachers would have to reapply for their jobs to work in the Algiers Charter Network. Meanwhile, two weeks after the storm, A&M, which became the public face of the district, told displaced teachers to look for jobs elsewhere.[37] Suddenly, it seemed like the powerful teachers' union had no allies, as Mike Stone recounts: "As much as we had done for teachers and as many politicians and business people and whatnot that over the years we had dealings with, the supporters that the union and teachers had after Katrina, there were very few. Unfortunately, probably our most loyal friend was Bill Jefferson, who of course ended up in prison for taking a bribe. As far as I'm concerned, Bill Jefferson, crook or not, is morally superior to the others I just mentioned."[38] As politicians and policymakers mobilized against the union, teachers were stunned: "I think in their mind, [politicians] thought they were doing the right thing, and wouldn't listen to us. . . . It's like they make deals with devils," reflects former UTNO president Wanda Richard.[39]

Both the state takeover and the outsized role of A&M threatened local democracy. Whereas the OPSB had voluntarily ceded its power to A&M in a racially divided 4–3 vote in May 2005,[40] the state seized the majority of the district without consulting New Orleans's residents. Though voters had approved the original takeover legislation, it had been targeted at only a few schools in the district, all of them severe underperformers. Act 35 allowed the state to take over any school scoring below the state average, which drastically modified the state's scope and power. "We learned that there was a plot in Baton Rouge, among some of the legislators, to kind of take control of the schools, period. Even before Katrina, they were trying to pass different legislations that would disenfranchise us, as citizens, and in turn by putting Alvarez [and Marsal] in charge, they were doing that because we did not elect them to be in charge of our schools."[41] UTNO struggled to counter the market-based reform agenda of organizations like A&M and the Broad Foundation because it simply did not have the money and resources, especially not after the storm, with educators unemployed and no dues coming in. UTNO staffer Wilson Boveland explains, "You had these people like Alvarez & Marsal who were throwing money into this because they were getting million-dollar contracts and what have you, and that's what it was all about. And they were throwing money behind it and everything else like that. We had no money to throw behind it."[42] Organizations that influenced the New Orleans reforms, such as private philanthropies, A&M, and the myriad education entrepreneurs and charter management operators that entered the city, operated essentially without public oversight or transparency and presented residents with few pathways to democratically influence their education landscape. Moreover, this disenfranchisement was largely racial, with the majority-white state government, A&M, and venture philanthropists stripping power from majority-Black city residents and public school stakeholders.[43]

Though the New Orleans charter transformation is notable because it happened so quickly in the wake of a disaster that upended the city, similar moves toward educational privatization and union busting were happening (and are ongoing) in urban areas nationwide. For example, neoliberal education policies in Chicago resulted in the creation of hundreds of charter schools and union losses as well as in new mobilizations by the CTU against corporate school reform.[44] Nearly 40 percent of the schools in Detroit are now charter schools, which are characterized by instability from teacher and student turnover as well as from the frequent shuttering of entire campuses.[45] The Los Angeles teacher strike of 2019, held up as an example of educators striking to support reforms that would directly benefit students, was called in part to demand a cap on charter schools.[46] Today, there is more resistance to charter schools, especially among the Democratic Party, than there was in 2005. President Barack Obama, for example, in a ringing endorsement of charters, appointed former Chicago Public Schools CEO Arne Duncan, who had presided over the majority of that district's privatization, as his Secretary of Education in 2009. Yet, despite growing resistance, the charter sector continues to grow, albeit at a slower pace.[47] And there have also been attempts to organize charter schools, some of them successful, across the nation.[48]

UTNO's story adds substance to the many critiques of charter schools, demonstrating the impacts of school privatization when implemented at full scale. There are many studies analyzing whether charter schools increase student test scores, with generally mixed results, though post-storm results from New Orleans have been more positive.[49] Researchers have also compared educators' experiences in charter schools and in traditional public schools, finding that charter school teachers tend to have longer work hours, less job satisfaction, higher turnover rates, and less experience than their public school counterparts.[50] Yet the experiences of the UTNO educators are unique, capturing the effects on educators, and a city, of total privatization, union loss, and school transformation all at once. The New Orleans schools today present an atomized picture of a system of schools competing with one another for students, with a whiter, less experienced teaching force, and completely privatized support workers.[51] Educators nationwide can look at the city to understand the goals of the charter movement and the pain, loss, and "dispossession" that accompanied the New Orleans transformation.[52] Moreover, by focusing on the experiences of educators, UTNO's story allows us to see schools as part of larger citywide ecosystems, where seemingly disparate issues such as employment, civic participation, social justice, and education are all interconnected. Firing New Orleans's educators transformed not only its schools but the city as well.

Soon after Katrina hit, while most New Orleanians remained scattered across the country, policymakers began implementing reforms that would lead to the total privatization of the school district.[53] By early September, the Louisiana Department of Education (LDOE) announced that New Orleans schools would be closed for the year and encouraged educators to seek other jobs. LDOE made this announcement even as other districts prepared to reopen; the schools in neighboring Jefferson and St. Tammany Parishes, which were hit by the storm but not as devastated as Orleans, reopened their schools in early October. St. Bernard Parish, downriver from New Orleans and equally flooded, reopened its first schools on November 14.[54] The Catholic Archdiocese reopened fourteen of its parochial schools in Orleans Parish and offered 3,000 seats to public school students in mid-October, months before any public school reopened.[55] UTNO argued that this delay in reopening schools prevented families and teachers from returning to the city, and it filed a mandamus writ to force the board to open schools more quickly, especially in buildings that had sustained minimal damage.[56] Educators wanted to return to the city and start rebuilding their homes and their lives, but first they needed to know that they would have jobs and could enroll their children in schools. "That right there tells you what their mentality was," says UTNO president Brenda Mitchell. "Don't educate the children. Even the people in St. Bernard, who had as bad or worse time than us, opened their schools back up. We had to sue them. . . . I don't think they wanted poor Black people to return to New Orleans."[57] UTNO members like Leoance Williams also felt that the delay in reopening schools was intended to marginalize dissent from educators and undermine the union: "The state did not want Orleans Parish to open the schools because they didn't want us back as teachers. They wanted a whole new system. They wanted a whole new setup. It was by design. They didn't want us back, and it's because they didn't want the political clout that we had back in the system."[58]

Some school employees felt that the delay in reopening schools and repairing buildings was always part of the plan and key to remaking the city and its schools in a whiter, more middle-class mold. They believed the buildings were left to rot in floodwaters in order to ensure that they could not be put quickly back into use by returning teachers and families, as Grace Lomba explains:

> Douglass [High School] didn't have water. The only water in Douglass
> was in the band room, because the band room was in the basement.
> Because my husband said to me, the Coast Guard and all of the people
> were stationed at Douglass because there was no water. But we couldn't
> come back because the schools weren't open. Now I understand that our
> custodian said, he told the district that, "I could get my team together

and get this school together. You could reopen this school." They told him leave it alone, leave the windows open and [let] mold built up.[59]

The schools were not the only institutions neoliberal reformers hoped to remake in the wake of Katrina. Healthcare workers and activists also accused policy-makers of purposely flooding the mostly undamaged public Charity Hospital, in order to justify closing the facility, razing several city blocks, and using disaster aid to fund the new University Medical Center as a public-private partnership.[60] As medical workers and community members protested to demand the opening of Charity, families and educators organized to demand that Douglass reopen. Charity remained shuttered. Though the RSD opened Douglass in fall 2007, it closed the school three years later and gave the building to the charter management company KIPP, an international organization specializing in "no excuses" schools.[61]

That delay in reopening schools was exacerbated on the local level by A&M, the consulting firm running the schools. Post Katrina, A&M assumed unprecedented control, announcing, "We have gone from turning around a broken school system to creating one from scratch."[62] A&M made decisions about personnel, such as putting nearly all employees on unpaid disaster leave, which exacerbated the post-storm breakdown in communication and the inability of the district to quickly reopen schools.[63] "[Alvarez and Marsal] was like a wholesale cleaning out, not only of [school] employees but district employees also. Anybody with historical knowledge, it's like, 'bye bye.' Those people had no loyalty," recalls UTNO staffer Juanita Bailey.[64] Ken Ducote, who worked for the district, concurred:

> They had to bring me back on contract by the state department to help them because they'd lost everybody with institutional memory. In fact, when the storm hit, because Alvarez and Marsal wanted a ton of money as a consultant, Alvarez and Marsal laid off the facilities department. All your facilities are destroyed. They kept the staff architect, the data manager, one maintenance guy, and one inspector. . . . And they canceled all the contracts. We had service contracts with roofers. The five best roofers in the area, best commercial roofers. Four of the five were small, disadvantaged businesses, and out of those, three were minorities. They were under contract on an hourly basis and an as-needed basis when the storm hit. . . . Alvarez and Marsal canceled all of their contracts.[65]

Another district employee, who was vehemently anti-union, confirmed Ducote's critique: "[A&M] were there from Monday through Thursday. They all lived in Houston. They left on Friday, and that's when Katrina hit. So there's nobody to implement the emergency preparedness plan. And then afterwards, they chose not to implement the emergency preparedness plan. We had a pretty good emergency preparedness plan. But there was nobody that Friday to trigger it, to get those bus drivers moving those buses to their designated areas around the city. And the buses drowned."[66] Whether or not A&M's negligence around the storm was intentional, the result was an enormous delay in reopening schools that prevented teachers and parents from returning and allowed the legislature sufficient time to push through its takeover and charter plan. A&M's actions also exacerbated the disaster, allowing flooded buildings to sit and rot while minimally damaged roofs let in rainwater for months on end.

While UTNO sued the city to reopen the schools, it also scrambled to connect to its members who were scattered across the country. At the beginning, it worked to provide assistance and aid, not to mobilize members for a political fight. Juanita Bailey, an UTNO staffer when the hurricane hit, evacuated to Houston. "That was my job basically to reach out to membership, find out where they were, what they were doing, and tell them how to get to the AFL-CIO office because there was a disaster center and so the people there were helping us . . . I recognized a lot of members and they were grateful. Some people were trying to get back and some just didn't know what to do."[67] UTNO set up a command center in Baton Rouge where members answered the phones, while Brenda Mitchell and other union staffers traveled around to major cities trying to find members. Much of UTNO's infrastructure had literally washed away, Mitchell recalls: "We didn't have a centralized phone system where the people could just call back because everything in town was gone. Not everyone had cell phones. Even if they did, we didn't have access to that information. It was in the buildings and all of that was gone."[68] Even members UTNO communicated with were rarely thinking about the future of the union. UTNO staffer Jo Anna Russo explains, "We had problems contacting even our own families. We were months away from home. . . . It's like a disaster. And then people were struggling just with their own survival, much less thinking about pulling together as a union."[69] Russo described how the union had relied for years on connecting to educators through a well-developed network of neighborhoods and schools, but that all fell apart after Katrina: "And before, you used to have all your teachers' names. You knew the union person there. You would get in contact with them. They would feed the information to the people. And you would work that way. We couldn't even get a group of people to go on a bus to do anything, to go and work politically . . . you had all these missing components."[70] On the whole, Black working- and middle-class neighborhoods were hardest hit by the flooding, in effect devastating UTNO's membership.

Union leadership did not immediately realize the threat the post-Katrina redevelopment movement posed to its power. Policymakers and reformers included UTNO in discussions, even as they lay the groundwork for the union's evisceration. "The day after the storm hit, I called the state superintendent [Cecil Picard] at his home. I had his number. He and I got along," recalls Mitchell. "I sat at the tables with the state superintendent and the leadership from the school system, including [Senator] Mary Landrieu and a whole bunch of other bigwigs. I think they made this decision that they were going to change New Orleans and we were in the way."[71] Similarly, union staffer Larry Carter participated in conversations about the future of the school system with Mayor Ray Nagin and other stakeholders: "At the same time, Dr. Brenda Mitchell was talking to Governor Blanco at the time, talking about what they would look like in the school district. I was here on the ground, as eyes and ears, to really understand the conversation from the community, from the mayor, from the city, about, what would New Orleans look like post-Katrina?"[72] Despite the union's participation in these discussions, it was unable to predict, or effectively mobilize against, the total privatization and takeover of the district. Community activist Beth Butler recalls:

> UTNO had been so strong and had been the number one union in the state, probably, that none of us foresaw this absolute power play to break them. I certainly didn't see it. We actually were talking to the president, Brenda Mitchell, at the state legislature, the state capitol, right before she went into the vote [on Act 35]. We were standing there with Ann Duplessis, who was the state senator. Before she left to go in, I said, "Brenda do you need us to come in and do anything?" And she was like, "No, I got this." And she went in, and they just back stabbed her and lost the vote. She had been lied to straight up to that moment, and why wouldn't you believe that you would have your people who you have always had?[73]

UTNO's longtime opponents, such as Leslie Jacobs and LABI, who had repeatedly pushed for state takeover and privatization, joined with UTNO's historical allies—Governor Blanco, state senator Ann Duplessis—to push through Act 35, effectively voiding the union contract in 102 of the city's 117 schools.[74] Economist Doug Harris argues that unions offered only "soft opposition" to the reforms, tacitly allowing Governor Blanco and other historic labor allies to support legislation intended to destroy UTNO.[75] Perhaps the LAE, the LFT's rival in the state, saw an opportunity in UTNO's evisceration, but the LFT's and UTNO's weakness in opposing the legislation speaks more to their inability to mobilize in the wake of the disaster than to their leaders' belief that state takeover was an appropriate course of action.

Researcher Brian Beabout argues that, "UTNO sought a reopen-first, reform-second strategy that ignored the desire of the public to overhaul the New Orleans Public Schools in the wake of Katrina," and he concludes that UTNO was too bureaucratic and slow-moving to be a leader in the district after the storm.[76] Though there is some truth in this statement—UTNO certainly had adopted a more bureaucratic structure over time, and it relied on slow-moving lawsuits to try to stymie the privatization reforms; however, it was not ultimately the union's bureaucracy that prevented its success but its internal democracy. Teacher Gwendolyn Adams argues that with its members displaced, the union was just a shell of its former self.[77] For an organization that represented 7,500 educators, the union had a relatively small paid staff of around ten. By contrast, the CTU, which serves about four times as many educators as UTNO, has sixty-five paid staff.[78] The rest of UTNO's leadership, including the vice president, the executive council members, the credit union board members, the area coordinators, and the building reps were all volunteers who worked as full-time educators. These members were scattered, many of them dealing with their own personal crises. The union, in fact, did not have *sufficient* bureaucratic structures in place to mount resistance to the reform agenda without its members present. Therefore, its focus on reopening the schools was both a moral and a strategic issue for the union. It needed the schools to reopen so that its members could return, and only then would UTNO have the power to influence the reform conversation. Finally, Beabout suggests that it was the "desire of the public" to overhaul the schools; however, the majority of the public—especially the working-class Black people whose children attended the schools—had not returned to the city in the fall of 2005 when these decisions were made. Even Harris, who mostly lauds the reforms, critiques the lack of community engagement in the reform process.[79] Though certainly working-class Black residents and other public school parents were dissatisfied with the schools before the storm, policymakers excluded them from discussions about reform, which had always been an elite-driven project. According to Harris, "Within days of the hurricane, and probably even before the last person evacuated, [Leslie Jacobs] was leading private discussions about a major overhaul of the school system."[80]

Maude Harris, a white teacher who lived uptown, returned to the city in early October because her house was largely spared from the flooding. Out of work, she attended all the city meetings that related to education: school board meetings, meetings of the Bring New Orleans Back commission, city council meetings. She remembered one, in particular, an educational summit held at the Audubon Zoo on November 19, 2005, just after Act 35 was passed. Though both Willie Zanders, a perennial school board candidate and education advocate, and Brenda Mitchell were at the meeting, it was dominated by white elites who had little stake in the public schools: Ron Forman, head of the Audubon Nature Institute and a 2006 mayoral candidate; Scott Cowen, the president of Tulane University; Bill Roberti from A&M; Don Marshall, the executive director of Jazz Fest; and three non-Black school board members. They were joined by representatives from several school districts around the globe as well as from the Gates Foundation, who presented on the advantages of charters and how competition improves school districts. Maude Harris recalls that Mitchell and

Zanders were seated at chairs away from the tables, spatially sidelined from the discussion. Though this meeting was ostensibly open to the public, it was held in a wealthy, mostly white uptown neighborhood, was little advertised, and few community members attended.[81]

Cowen, who chaired Mayor Nagin's recovery education committee, later wrote a book about his experiences. In it, he writes, "The civil rights movement stopped short of New Orleans, at least in the sense of open hostilities."[82] Cowen's rosy-eyed view of the city's race relations reveals how deeply unqualified he was to lead a commission deciding the fate of New Orleans's mostly Black educators and schoolchildren. Walter Isaacson, president of the Aspen Institute, wrote the foreword for Cowen's book: "The goal was not just to restore what had existed before the storm but to build something better. . . . Some feckless folks flinched, even left their jobs at schools and hospitals and opted for a less challenging life elsewhere," he writes, implying that the fired schoolteachers left their jobs voluntarily to seek more pleasurable work. Isaacson then goes on to laud the TFA corps that arrived to take on the challenge; he never once acknowledges the mass dismissals.[83] From leaders and planning conversations such as these—and Doug Harris describes Cowen's process as *more* community engaged than Jacobs's[84]—it is clear that the decision to adopt the particular methods of reform that Orleans chose (the district-wide privatization and the mass firing of educators) was top-down and made without significant community or educator input.

Still, some educators, including UTNO members, believed the union could have done more. Mitchell had a seat at those planning meetings, even if it was a chair against the wall, and she had relationships with the school board members and legislators. Samantha Turner attended a union meeting in Baton Rouge shortly after the storm and says that the union attorney told the group they should just retire. "I thought, if there was a time that they should have fought hardest, that would have been the time. . . . But I didn't feel, personally, that I was a priority at all."[85] Similarly, Luetta Stewart felt that UTNO just "vanished" after the storm.[86] Joy Van Buskirk, a former UTNO and LFT lobbyist who had retired before the storm, criticized Mitchell and union leadership for their response:

> I looked at the way that current leadership then handled what happened in New Orleans, and I disagreed with them vehemently. I think that the president should have come down to Orleans Parish, she was in Baton Rouge, and should have said to the school board, "Let's suspend everything in the contract except these few things like salary, maybe healthcare benefits, a few other things, until we get our school system up and operating." They did not do that, and then the legislature went ahead and created the Recovery School District and took away all the schools from Orleans Parish, pretty much.[87]

Others expressed the belief that Nat LaCour, who was then with the national AFT, could have saved the union: "[Nat] never let anybody get over on us. He really didn't," explains paraprofessional Jacqueline Johnson, "So, I don't know what happened down the line, but it just kind of went to Hell in a handbasket, because look where we are now."[88]

Though LaCour is almost a mythical figure in the union, it is unclear if he, or anyone else, could have mobilized union power post-Katrina to stop the privatizations. Certainly, Mitchell struggled. Her house in New Orleans was completely destroyed, so she moved to Baton Rouge to be closer to the legislative proceedings. She felt responsible for all the displaced and grieving UTNO members and could not sleep due to worry:

> My husband died in 2004, and I'll never forget, one day in November
> I was at the legislature, I was there talking and trying to do something
> for UTNO teachers. I realized it was the day that my husband died, and
> I had to go out on the steps of the Capitol to cry. It was like I didn't even
> have time to mourn. But it was a lot coming at us, we were everywhere,
> we had an 800 number we got for members to call us from all over the
> country, and they were calling from even as far as way as New York. It
> just was the most upsetting time in my life.[89]

Many union members empathized with Mitchell and appreciated her advocacy. "After [the storm] we were wondering where was the voice for the union. But again, now in retrospect I can see, if I couldn't speak for myself against the one academy leader, I could imagine how one union rep or one union president trying to speak on behalf of all the teachers, against the state. Who do you go to?"[90] The deck was stacked against UTNO: federal, state, and local elected officials and reform advocates were all pushing to make Orleans an all-charter district, to force through a transformative school experiment. And, contrary to Van Buskirk's speculation, those policymakers were not looking for a more flexible union; eliminating UTNO was key to the whole project. The autonomous charter schools and the powerful union could not coexist.

To justify the school takeovers, education reformers waged a publicity campaign to paint the pre-Katrina schools as uniformly terrible, the teachers as lazy and incompetent, and the elected school board as corrupt and bumbling. In a typical example, *Business Week* wrote, "Even before Katrina . . . the New Orleans public school system was the worst of all major U.S. cities and faced intractable corruption, infighting, and racial tension."[91] Harris contributes, "[New Orleans] was a backwater—the last place we would expect anything innovative."[92] Though these narratives dominated after the storm, few teachers, principals, and district employees who worked in the system related similar condemnations. According to Morel's national study of state takeovers, such tactics are commonplace, especially when a white state legislature moves to take control of a majority-Black district.[93] The school board did its part in obviating its own power when it had voted, in May 2005, to cede much of its control to A&M.[94] Though the *Times Picayune* reserved its strongest vitriol for the OPSB, columnist James Gill was also unsympathetic to the dismissed teachers: "We are supposed to be alarmed by the prospect that teachers will decamp to school districts that will continue to protect their rights. But the public can take that threat in stride, suspecting that bad teachers calling U-Haul will comfortably outnumber the good ones. Besides, the prevailing view is that almost any price is worth paying to loosen the baleful grip of the Orleans Parish School Board. . . . Indeed, there is so little sympathy for teachers who feel hard done by that they might be well advised to pipe down."[95] Similarly, pro-reform researchers presented the schools as abysmal and the teachers as maintaining the status quo: "Many teachers were routinely absent; others simply quit midway through the year. . . . Only three in five high school students graduated. . . . The 2003 valedictorian at Alcee Fortier High School flunked the graduation exam five times and could not graduate."[96] Narratives about the horrors of the pre-Katrina system were used to bolster support for the neoliberal reforms: "The depth of dysfunction and corruption in the district was simply overwhelming. It was hard to conceive of a way the city's schools could ever turn themselves around. Ten years later, I am more than happy to admit I was wrong."[97] Scott Cowen also referenced the Fortier valedictorian story in his book about post-Katrina recovery, but in his narrative, the anecdote justifies Tulane and Lusher's takeover of the struggling, all-Black Fortier High to transform it into an extension of the selective-admission Lusher charter, which gave priority admission to mostly white children of Tulane faculty.[98] Instead of targeting the endemic poverty in the district and the city, or the years of institutional racism and neglect that had left schools underfunded and buildings in disrepair, reformers blamed the mostly Black teachers, principals, and district employees for the system's failures. The only solution to save New Orleans's Black schoolchildren was market-driven reform directed and implemented by white experts and entrepreneurs. These narratives set the stage for the mass dismissal of approximately 7,500 New Orleans educators.

THE "REDUCTION IN FORCE" THROUGH TEACHERS' EYES: TO RETIRE, RETURN, OR MOVE ELSEWHERE

Researcher Kristen Buras argues that the post-Katrina school privatizations and other market-based reforms were "premised on the criminal dispossession of Black working-class communities and the teachers and students who . . . contributed to the city's culture and history."[99] This dynamic is most evident in the mass dismissal of educators as well as in the capricious hiring practices, contracts with alternative certification programs such as TFA, and barriers to reentry into the district that were implemented after the dismissals. In late November 2005, shortly after the legislature passed Act 35, A&M announced that all the furloughed public school employees would be fired and lose their health insurance effective January 31, 2006.[100] Nobody notified employees beforehand, Juanita Bailey clarifies: "I thought [that] was the most disrespectful thing you can do to your employee is to let them hear about their job on the news."[101] Because of the delay in reopening schools and the lack of habitable housing in the area, few teachers could quickly return to teach in the parish, and many chose early retirement in order to maintain their health insurance. This, then, created a financial crisis for retirees as premiums skyrocketed because there were no active teachers paying into the pool and swelling ranks of retirees claiming insurance benefits.[102] Teachers felt betrayed by the district to which many had devoted decades of their lives—collateral damage in school reformers' quest to begin anew. Firing entire faculties has long been part of attempts to "turn around" struggling schools and reopen them as charters,[103] but the New Orleans case offers the opportunity to see the impacts of such policies at scale.

Teachers were shocked when they heard about the mass dismissals. After all, none of the surrounding parishes, which were also dealing with significant storm damage, had fired its educators. Teacher Bill Scott recalls, "Getting fired has a really vivid impression. . . . It's really vivid when you're just trying to get over the shock of the hurricane itself. You haven't seen your home. My home is gone. My friends lost theirs. Plus, it made people quit."[104] When they heard about the dismissals, some teachers who had been planning to return and help rebuild the district decided to retire or teach in a neighboring parish instead. "Personally, I did not feel wanted," explains Samantha Turner. "And I felt that so many of us had devoted so much energy to our own personal schools, to training other teachers, to caring about seeing the district as a whole move forward. And to just, I don't know, feel like you were a nonentity. You know, 'We have replacements coming in. Y'all can go out to pasture,' type thing. That was the feeling."[105] Turner took a job at a local university instead of returning to the district. Teacher Gwendolyn Adams retired with a reduction in benefits because she had not yet reached the milestones for full benefits. "I was angry and disgruntled. And I refused to go back into a system that utilized a situation in order to get rid of me. I couldn't do that. . . . A lot of people had been in the system, and they had the years or the age whereby they could retire. And then a lot of people went into the Catholic school system or in Jefferson Parish."[106] Frank Fudesco, a former principal and school board negotiator, suggested that the dismissals were a well-intentioned move with negative consequences:

I think they actually [fired everyone] thinking it was a benefit because then they could apply for unemployment . . . but that was shortsighted. You could have laid them off, they still could've got unemployment. And if they went to work for another parish, they could come back to you. Instead, now you fired them. The only way they're going to come back is they reapply for their job, and now you've made them so angry, they don't want to come back. Now, maybe they wanted to do it to get rid of the union. I wasn't privy to that. It worked . . . and they alienated every damn teacher in 200 miles. Not only just in New Orleans, any teacher from anywhere. They'd say, "I'm not going to Orleans. They fire people there in crisis."[107]

The impact on teachers was deep: "I mean it doubled down on the trauma they were experiencing—that we all in the city experienced," explains teacher Jim Randels, "It exacerbated the trauma exponentially. It pushed people to an even more bitter place, like, really?"[108]

Some teachers who retired felt like it was their only option: "I had to [for] insurance as well as income," explains Leoance Williams.[109] Others, facing the uncertainty of the post-Katrina schools landscape, just decided it was time: "I thought the universe was giving me a signal, and [my partner] just felt, financially, that was just probably the smartest thing for us to do," describes Cindy Robinson.[110] The union, concerned that there would be no jobs for its members, encouraged educators with enough years to receive full benefits to retire. Katrena Ndang says she never would have retired if the mass dismissals had not occurred: "Think of it, I was ready to stay for about five or six more years. And I was healthy, I had gone through my breast cancer and everything like that and was still strong. Many people were."[111] Jennifer Tiller chose not to retire, but many of her colleagues did: "A lot of my friends retired, and it's really a shame, because they retired earlier than they would have . . . because they just said, 'We don't know what's going to happen. We're going to retire and know that we're going to have money coming in.'"[112] That uncertainty was exacerbated by A&M, who were notoriously difficult to communicate with. Louise Mouton Johnson explains: "Alvarez and Marsal made it really, really difficult to get in touch with anybody to find out what was going on. I really feel that they may have had something to do with discouraging people from coming back to the city, teachers and students and everything."[113] Wilson Boveland says that the union offered to help A&M with their communication troubles but were turned down: "They couldn't get in touch with teachers or anything. We set up a portal with our state affiliate in Baton Rouge, and we had the names and addresses of a good 60 to 70 percent of all of the teachers. And we offered to give that to them. But their thing was, at that point, they didn't want to bring those teachers back. So they claimed 'We don't have that information.'"[114]

The health insurance debacle was especially damaging to both educators and retirees, sometimes forcing them into retirement, wiping away their savings, and leaving them delaying crucial procedures. On October 15, OPSB shifted the displaced educators onto a catastrophic plan with deductibles of $5,000 to $10,000 before anything would be paid out.[115] Art teacher Louise Mouton Johnson clarifies the impact: "So you're up late at night worried about how you're going to pay medical bills. And things like, [my colleague] got her cancer like that. And you were saying I have to pay a $5,000 deductible. It doesn't take a lot to know how that person felt, and that was happening to a lot of people."[116] New Orleans educators were not part of the state's hospitalization group but were in a self-insured program, so when the storm hit there were no active members paying premiums.[117] As the ranks of retirees swelled in early 2006, premiums nearly tripled, skyrocketing from $224 to $611 per month.[118] "Premiums went up exorbitantly," explains Joe DeRose. "So a lot of teachers were stuck between not being able to have insurance or having to pay most of their check, and for non-teachers, it's even worse because their salaries are so much lower than teachers. But their premiums of course are the same because it's for the same insurance."[119] Donisia Wise, a member of UTNO's clerical union, was hit hard by the new premiums. "I paid them for a while. And after some time, I realized I could not continue. So I just stayed without any insurance until I reached 65 [and qualified for spouse's Medicare]."[120] The decision to fire the educators and slowly reopen schools had a devastating impact on the health and well-being of educators as well as on their financial futures.

The high insurance costs also pushed retirees back into the classroom. Leoance Williams had been teaching for thirty years when Katrina hit; he initially decided to retire but then had to return to work. "We were able to live on our retirement, but the insurance was killing us. So that's one of the reasons why I went back to work."[121] Years later, policymakers portrayed educators who had retired and then returned to the classroom as gaming the system to collect both retirement and a salary rather than as victims of the state's school reform agenda. In 2010, the state legislature passed a bill to restrict retired teachers from returning to the classroom.[122] Joel Behrman evacuated to Shreveport and finished the 2005–6 school year there, but then he couldn't find a job after he returned to Orleans and retired. Eventually, he was hired in Jefferson Parish and taught there for six years. "One of the reasons I do not feel too personally injured compared to some people is for those years . . . I was getting retirement and a full salary . . . but they closed that door after people like me."[123] Though many states have laws restricting people receiving public pensions from returning to public employment, the New Orleans law was targeted specifically at teachers and furthered the narrative that they were self-interested, unethical, and trying to game the system.

Some educators who wanted to return found the process of securing a job in Orleans Parish arbitrary and insulting. Joe DeRose explains, "I think the process was very unfair and demeaning. Every teacher that was going to be rehired by at least Algiers Charter School [Association] they were required to take a basic skills test, which just on its face is demeaning and insulting. And then on top of that, some teachers who went there and they saw the test, they just tore it up afterwards and just wouldn't even submit it because they felt insulted. . . . Other teachers of course are going to do anything they needed to try to get a job."[124] When Diana Brown heard there was going to be a test required, she decided not to return and instead took a job in another parish: "Maybe I was being selfish, but I felt that I did not have to take a test to teach. I was certified. I was degreed, so that was an insult to me. And then we had options, we didn't have a home to rebuild, or children that we needed to get in school. So, I had the option to wait a little while."[125] However, according to leaders at the Algiers Charter Schools Association (ACSA), 50 of the 250 teachers who acquiesced to the "short math and grammar test" failed.[126] Though this statistic was used to further the narrative blaming the teachers for the state of the pre-storm schools, Fudesco vehemently disagrees:

> Yes, there were some damn terrible teachers in Orleans, like everywhere else, like every other business. But there were some excellent teachers . . . and those teachers put in their blood, sweat, and tears. Again, there were some rotten, dumb teachers. And when you're hiring more than anybody around, and you're paying less, you're not getting the cream of the crop. I get all of that. All the demographics I get. But to just say, all your teachers around here are incompetent, let's fire you all. If they did that, that's terrible. In my opinion, that's just wrong.[127]

The ACSA also started all educators, even those with thirty years of experience, at a salary level commensurate with no more than fourteen years experience, "to give educators an ongoing fiscal incentive to achieve."[128] With the skills test and the salary cap, ACSA explicitly discouraged veteran teachers from applying for jobs, even while they ran the only open schools in the city and actively recruited young, alternatively certified teachers from out of state.[129] "So many people were dispersed," librarian Jennifer Tiller describes, "and when they started opening those charter schools there were some complaints that they weren't hiring people who had taught in Orleans. They didn't look at them first. They went and got Teach for America, people from outside the state . . . they weren't trying to hire the people back, and that was a big stink."[130] Charter leaders wanted young, TFA teachers with little education experience because they would follow administrators' directions and were willing to work long hours, as most of them did not have children or other relatives to care for.[131]

The role of TFA in the post-Katrina landscape is notable. Shortly after the storm, TFA signed a contract with BESE to supply new teachers to the greater New Orleans area.[132] Sarah Usdin, the founder of New Schools for New Orleans as well as a TFA alum and former TFA regional executive director, was tasked with finding educators to replace the fired teachers. Quickly, the size of the corps tripled in the area. By 2014, the greater New Orleans area had the highest concentration of TFA corps members and alumni in the country, and TFA teachers made up approximately 30 percent of the New Orleans teaching force.[133] Former UTNO president Jim Randels claimed that before the storm TFA had a much more collaborative relationship with the union and veteran educators, who often mentored TFA teachers. However, "TFA has in many ways become much more independent and separate from veteran teachers and much more exclusively aligned with schools run by organizations and school leaders concerned with replacing rather than working with those of us who have taught for years in the challenging and invigorating conditions of public education in New Orleans."[134] TFA also receives extensive funding from the Walton, Gates, and Broad Foundations, all of which have been major promoters of privatization and charter schools.[135]

The TFA workforce is typically composed of young, white, recent college graduates from elite universities and without backgrounds in teaching or education. Through their recruitment practices and policy, TFA has contributed to the displacement of Black teachers in urban areas throughout the nation.[136] "I didn't realize that Black teachers could join TFA," reflects Leoance Williams.[137] After Katrina, TFA teachers provided cheap and malleable labor but often lacked the cultural competency to understand New Orleans students and typically stayed only two to three years in the district, thus undermining union drives. In the years following the storm, the school system was bifurcated between charter schools—which mostly hired novice teachers from TFA or TeachNOLA, a local recruitment program based on TFA—and direct-run RSD schools that often hired returning veteran educators and were slowly being phased out. Because many TFA teachers worked in schools whose staffs were composed almost entirely of other TFA teachers and alums, they often did not benefit from the mentoring and cultural exchange that teaching alongside veteran educators could have provided. TFA educators learned little about the history of the school district or the union beyond stereotypes about how awful they had been, further reducing the possibility of their engaging in union drives. Hannah Sadlter taught for two years as a TFA corps member in New Orleans and was "shocked" to later learn about the mass dismissal of educators: "I believed what [TFA] told me at the time—that there was a shortage of qualified and dedicated teachers, and that TFA was a response to that shortage." Sadtler went on to form a group called the New Teachers Roundtable that worked to support new teachers and inform them about the district's rich history.[138] The influx of TFA teachers reflects the ways in which the post-Katrina reformers relied on elite, corporately funded networks at the national, state, and local levels to undermine UTNO and bypass local communities. Alternative certification programs such as TFA further undercut teacher power by bypassing licensing requirements that otherwise limit whom schools can hire, thus giving teachers more power.[139] TFA also employed a rhetoric of social justice and civil rights to recruit applicants, even as it played a key role in cementing the displacement of Black veteran teachers, yet again demonstrating how "neoliberal multiculturalism" is used to mask the anti-Black, antidemocratic, and anti-worker agenda of the neoliberal project.[140]

The mass dismissals, the crisis in health insurance, the demeaning basic skills test, the paucity of open schools, the difficulty communicating with A&M, the contract with TFA, and the lack of union representation all contributed to pushing veteran teachers out of the system and ushering in an enormous demographic shift among teachers, administrators, and school employees. "They were intentionally trying to discredit the union and restructure the schools, whereby administration had more power, because they knew they could do that if the union was not mobilized," explains Gwendolyn Adams.[141] And UTNO could not muster much strength when the majority of its members remained scattered across the country, unable or unwilling to return without a job waiting. Beyond changing the educational landscape, Grace Lomba argues that the mass dismissals also had a large effect on the city: "Especially financially it impacted the city because you destroyed the middle class. So, you destroyed people who had jobs, who were paying taxes, who were helping to build the city, who were spending money and what have you. It affected the schools because you destroyed a whole class of certified instructors. And you brought in people who were not certified, who did not have degrees in education."[142] When they were not explicitly blaming them for the schools' poor performance, school reformers presented these veteran educators as collateral damage in the larger mission to create a new, functional school system. The only way forward, according to these reformers, was a privatized neoliberal model that required fresh, young, and often white administrators and educators; cheaper support staff; and freedom from union regulations. Yet the toll on the 7,500 educators was enormous, as Brenda Mitchell describes: "Maybe if you were having a clothing store and you have a flood, you'd just throw all the clothes out and get some new ones. But you can't do that with children, and you can't do that with adults who work in those buildings."[143]

THE POST-KATRINA LANDSCAPE: UTNO ATTEMPTS A COMEBACK

By early 2006, as pink slips went out to the district's 7,500 employees, UTNO leaders fully realized that school reformers' post-Katrina plans did not involve a union presence. The union used various strategies to attempt to maintain its power, many of which harkened back to its original collective bargaining campaign, but it met with little success. The strategies can be organized into three categories: legal, political, and organizational. Though in each category UTNO did win some victories, the tide continued to roll forward on school reform and privatization. Social movement scholars Frances Fox Piven and Richard Cloward argue that the strength of community organizations is their capacity for disruption, yet both national and local forces made this a challenge for the union post Katrina.[144] Unions nationwide were on the defensive, and strikes and other forms of disruption had become rare. More crucially, the majority of UTNO's membership, as well as most of the city's residents, were still displaced, and those who had returned were preoccupied with managing their own traumas and rebuilding efforts. With most of its executive board and members still evacuated, UTNO's decision-making structure became less democratic and more top-down, with added influence from the national AFT and the AFL-CIO, who sent both money and personnel to help. Though leaders tried to reconnect with educators who had returned to the city, they had no way to get in touch with most members and thus there was little opportunity for consensus-building or collective decision-making. UTNO organizers were at a clear disadvantage. In the words of a May 2006 UTNO report, "Efforts to date have yielded some success, but the challenges have been nearly overwhelming. Never before have we seen such direct and blatant attacks on the rights of workers and on the fundamental principle that government has a responsibility to provide a free quality public education to all children in our nation."[145] Education would be privatized in New Orleans and policymakers and school leaders would not allow the union to stand in the way.

The union's legal challenges to the post-Katrina reforms were robust, yet the courts moved too slowly to halt reforms that were already rolling forward, and UTNO did not receive significant public recognition for its work in this arena. For example, UTNO filed a lawsuit demanding that the district reopen schools in late 2005 and then dropped the lawsuit when the district agreed to do so; yet much of the public was unaware of the union's efforts to force the district's hand.[146] UTNO also filed ethics violations when OPSB members attempted to become charter board members in schools the OPSB had authorized—a conflict of interest—and those were resolved without significant fanfare.[147] The union also filed suit claiming that Act 35 was unconstitutional, thus trying to reverse the state takeover; but the courts sided with the state.[148] The most significant lawsuit UTNO filed, as co-counsels with lawyer Willie Zanders, *Eddy Oliver et al. v Orleans Parish School Board*, was a class-action suit that argued that the OPSB violated tenure laws by terminating tenured employees in the mass dismissals.[149] Though the educators won the suit at the local and appellate levels, the Louisiana Supreme Court overturned the decision in late 2014. The length of the court proceedings ensured that most educators had already found other jobs or had retired by the time of the decision; the loss meant that they would not receive backpay or legal acknowledgment that they had been treated unfairly.

Katrena Ndang, a teacher who became a community organizer for UTNO after the storm, does not think the length of the lawsuit mattered: "There are a lot of lawsuits that've been longer than that. I mean, they were working on the 1954 decision a long time. They were working on the civil rights thing a long time. They were working on the voting rights forever . . . so I don't think time has anything to do with it. It's about justice."[150] Ndang, nearly forty years after the union's first strike, still saw UTNO as a civil rights union, fighting for justice. The educators who were involved with the class-action suit, such as Billie Dolce, talked about their work with pride:

> I knew we weren't going to win a lawsuit. I figured that from the very jump and it wasn't about the money for me. It was about my reputation because they [hired] uncertified teachers. I was a master's degree teacher. And I hated how they talked about us because I taught for years in a school where I didn't have anything. I was spending $500 to $600 every year out of my pocket for children to have supplies. . . . I loved what I did and I loved my children and I always taught my children.[151]

Many educators felt that the lawsuit vindicated their struggle and connected it to larger Black struggles for equality and justice, even though it was later overturned. Though, overall, the lawsuits helped demonstrate UTNO's commitment to fighting for educators and students, they did not successfully showcase the union's power or result in the reversal of anti-labor reforms.

UTNO's political work faced an even more dismal landscape. Its closest allies had betrayed the union shortly after the storm, with Ann Duplessis, a Democratic state senator, leading the charge toward state takeover and privatization.[152] UTNO was outnumbered at the school board, with only three of seven members supporting the union, and it had an antagonistic relationship with Governor Blanco and little support from the BESE board. It attempted to revitalize its political machine, but its office was flooded and destroyed, and the volunteers the union relied on to canvass and monitor polls were scattered throughout the country or busy rebuilding their own homes. Former teacher Maude Harris explains, "They worked . . . trying to get people that were sort of pro-union to be [elected to] different positions in politics, not just the school board. [But] UTNO was just this little shell that had no money, and they had flooded, so it was just miserable."[153] Nonetheless, UTNO launched its "Refuse to Lose" campaign with the help of an outside brand consultant.[154] The campaign attempted to portray UTNO as the voice of the community, channeling widespread disgust with the recovery efforts into support for the dismissed educators. The campaign originally focused on UTNO's demand that the district reopen more schools, which successfully merged community and teacher interests: "We cannot truly bring New Orleans back to life until we bring her schools back to life. My colleagues and I desperately want to help in this effort but cannot do so under the current circumstances," explained teacher Gwendolyn Adams for a 2006 article in *American Teacher*.[155] The union produced pamphlets and TV and radio announcements in support of the "Refuse to Lose" campaign, and they also used it to mobilize members and plug returning teachers back into UTNO's efforts. The campaign attempted to dispel the negative feelings educators and community members might have had following the union's inability to protect their jobs. An UTNO organizing plan from early 2007 reported, "Much of the frustration felt by members at UTNO's inability to save them from the actions of the OPSB is directed at the elected leadership."[156] The language of this document reflects a significant shift in UTNO members' perception of the union and, perhaps, a failure in organizing during Mitchell's tenure. Members did not see it as their responsibility to work with the union and their colleagues to fight for the schools and their jobs; rather, members believed it was the union leadership's responsibility to protect them from the board and from the reformers. Yet the union had little power beyond the strength, loyalty, and activism of its members, whose energy was still being spent mostly on their own recovery processes, especially if they had not yet returned to the district or found new jobs.

UTNO's greatest political struggle was its summer 2006 push to convince OPSB to renegotiate the pre-storm collective bargaining contract that was set to expire. By this time, the contract covered only the four schools that the board ran directly (not the charters they had authorized), so even had UTNO won a new contract, it would have covered relatively few employees in the district.[157] Nonetheless, the collective bargaining agreement with OPSB represented one of the last formal footholds the union had in the district and was one of the reasons it retained any voice at all. UTNO proposed a more flexible and slimmed-down contract to reflect the very different teaching circumstances across the district, which by this time was composed of a patchwork of state-authorized and OPSB-authorized charters and directly run schools.[158] The union, which in its heyday held rallies of 3,000 members, gathered 100 members in "Refuse to Lose" T-shirts to attend the board meeting; they left singing "Solidarity Forever" following the board's vote not to extend the contract.[159] Abdicating responsibility, or perhaps speaking to the sense that the reforms had been handed down from the state and were out of OPSB's control, OPSB member Una Anderson said she did not support collective bargaining: "I think we all realize the world has changed around us."[160] On July 1, the contract expired. The *Times Picayune* almost eulogized its weakened adversary: "Thirty-two years after thousands of

New Orleans public school teachers used strikes and walkouts to win the first collective bargaining agreement of its kind in the Deep South, the school board quietly let the union's contract expire Friday, marking the end of an era for what had long been one of the most powerful labor organizations in the city."[161] The newspaper also noted that the only attendees at the board meeting had been two security guards, their reporter, and "a lone man reading a magazine."[162] The diminishment of the union, combined with the reduction of OPSB's power and significance, meant that two avenues for democratic participation in the public school system were lost for both educators and the public. Doug Harris, and other pro-charter advocates, argue that market-based school systems actually enhance parent agency by transforming them into consumers, who can leave a school if they are displeased.[163] However, this power is limited by many factors—the choices of schools available, a parent's capacity to deeply investigate the system, the effect of school disruption on the child—and forecloses the possibilities of neighborhood-based advocacy, educator voice, open school board meetings with community input, and the ability to elect leaders at the polls.

UTNO's organizing work, boosted by significant financial and personnel support from the AFT and the AFL-CIO, was perhaps the strongest arm of its rebuilding campaign, though it was ultimately undermined by a failure of long-term vision. The union still believed it could operate according to its old model, and bring the schools back under local board control, long after policymakers had foreclosed that option. However, UTNO offered financial assistance to members, built meaningful collaborations with community groups, and rebuilt its membership. Immediately after the storm, the union worked to establish contact with as many members as possible, both on the ground in neighboring cities and via phone. Larry Carter, for example, tracked down public school educators and students for UTNO first in Texas and then later in Atlanta. "[I was] organizing and also connecting with former either students or teachers from New Orleans, to see about having conversations about when they wanted to return."[164] He said that in both Texas and Atlanta parents and educators found the schools much better resourced than in New Orleans, and many decided to stay. "Those high schools looked like college campuses. . . . In Houston, I went in a classroom that had a closed circuit TV, that worked!"[165] Meanwhile, to help its members recover, the national AFT raised $2 million and sent every affected member in the Gulf Coast region a check for $500.[166] These efforts were followed by a four-day AFT "blitz" in late August 2006, in which UTNO employees and AFT volunteers from around the country made 3,000 house calls to UTNO members.[167] "We went door to door talking to people and it was storming like crazy," recalls teacher Grace Lomba. "We worked twelve hours a day, from nine in the morning til nine at night, going knocking on doors. And we might have signed up in that time period, maybe 1,200 to 1,500 people."[168] Much of this was financed by the national AFT. "The union invested a fortune trying to bring us back."[169] Though UTNO needed the assistance, there were also conflicts between local educators and organizers sent by the national AFT:

> There was some resentment about that. Some of us locals, they got paid much higher salaries than we did. And they were going around, telling us what to do, and sometimes they didn't know the community. I got in very big tussles with national reps who would come in and yell at local members and tell them to leave the meeting. And they were saying, "We never told anyone to leave the meeting. How can you do this? You're not from this town, you're telling people what to do. You don't know how things work here."[170]

The union still had a strong culture of democracy in which a core value was everyone being heard; this was not always respected by the national AFT representatives.

Door-to-door canvassing was a new type of organizing for UTNO members who had always been able to rely on networks of building reps and area coordinators to recruit new members. It was also hard work, as Juanita Bailey explains: "I think at that point, what kept me on was loyalty. Because I honestly was not doing something I wanted to do, but I felt it was necessary. . . . Just having to, day after day, go door to door to see who was living where, meeting with people in trailers, and having to listen to story after story after story. It was mentally exhausting."[171] The strategy was more successful with some members than with others. Cindy Robinson recalls, "One night, I was cooking dinner when [my partner] came in, she said, 'There's a car in front of the house, I think it's UTNO. And they want to talk to you.' I said, 'I don't want to talk.' And she just went out and said, 'You know, she's at the end of her career, she's not interested.'"[172] Despite some educators who shut the door on UTNO, the union succeeded in recruiting significant numbers of returning members to rejoin, yet it never developed into a movement. "I want to say we got maybe a fourth of what we had [pre-Katrina]," Juanita Bailey explains, "which is pretty good considering what was going on . . . but then numbers started to dwindle as schools started to turn over."[173] UTNO leaders felt loyalty to the fired and displaced educators and wanted to prioritize them even if they had retired and were not planning to return to the classroom, but this work took away from the union's ability to focus on organizing teachers who were working in charter schools and who could actively have benefited from union representation. Without school-based organizing and a push for collective bargaining, the union could recruit returning members who were loyal and a few new members who wanted legal protection or access to the union's professional development, but it was not able to build meaningful power.

UTNO was most successful in organizing teachers who had been displaced and then returned rather than the young out-of-town teachers who mostly staffed the charter schools. These veteran teachers tended to be clustered at the few high-performing OPSB-run schools as well as at schools directly run by the RSD. The RSD was moderately open to working with the union: "The RSD adopted a memorandum of understanding where they kind of followed most of the things [in the old contract]. We hardly had any problems with not having the union."[174] Marta Bivens taught at McMain, a school that was directly run by the OPSB. "I don't remember [the principal] ever interfering with [union organizing] but I don't remember her being a participant either. We had a couple meetings," she recalls, but the school never recognized the union.[175] However, all these schools were gradually phased out and replaced with charters, where the union typically had zero traction, so the gains were short lived. "Some of the schools we could get into and others we couldn't," recalls Joe DeRose. He says the union did make some inroads with charter schools in Algiers, which hired back more veteran teachers than other charters because they opened in fall 2005. "We were able to meet in some of those schools. . . . We had to talk to the teachers about restarting the union just like you were starting from scratch to develop an organizing committee at their school, to talk about issues, and to take on the issues at their school and see if they could have some empowerment that way."[176] The challenge was perhaps greater than what the union had faced in the late 1960s, when it had fought for the first teacher collective bargaining agreement in the Deep South, because the system was so fractured and unstable. Moreover, many charters were explicitly anti-union. "The contract that I signed when I was at Audubon [Charter School] said that they would not recognize the union. It was almost like saying in their contract that you can't be a member and that scared a lot of people," Louise Mouton Johnson recalls.[177] As the directly run schools closed and the state created more charters, veteran teachers continued to retire and leave the district, and UTNO's numbers dwindled once again. UTNO's strategy, to focus on returning educators and RSD schools, where it faced less opposition from administrators, was ultimately an error, as charters were the future of the city. At the same time, it is hard to know if UTNO would have had any more success if it had dedicated all its resources to organizing the charter schools, which present a notoriously difficult organizing environment and small gains even when the union wins, since each collective bargaining agreement typically covers only a single school or small network of schools.

UTNO's community work during this period also harkened back to its early organizing days. It forged alliances with numerous community groups, including the principals' professional organization, PANOPSI, other unions such as the Service Employees International Union (SEIU) and NALC, and leaders in the Black community: the NAACP, the African Methodist Episcopal (AME) Church, the Douglass Community Coalition, and the National Coalition for Black Civic Participation, among others.[178] "What the teachers' union provided was not just the economic stability of being a teacher, but they also had healthcare, and they were supportive of just about every major activity that was going on in the Black community, particularly in the post-Katrina era," explains community activist Kalamu ya Salaam.[179] Katrena Ndang worked full time for UTNO on its community work after the storm. "My role was not just education, it was anything and everything that needed to be reorganized. . . . If it was housing, I was there. If it was transportation, I was there . . . My job was to get any help that we could get in the community."[180] Ndang worked with churches, organized anti-violence marches, and coalesced community support for the union. She helped bring people to the city council chambers, for example, when the school board voted on whether to extend UTNO's contract. But in the end, it was not enough:

> I've said to people, "Did you come back from where you were and live in a trailer or live in somebody's living room?" I did. And I was at all the meetings. Even when I was in Texas I was out there fighting. But you can't stand back and say "UTNO needs to do this," and you're part of UTNO, and you didn't step up and do anything, you were somewhere else complaining. That's how I feel about it. And we didn't have that. If we'd had more of that, we probably could've gone a little farther, but we did not have that, because people were somewhere else and not willing.[181]

Though Brenda Mitchell continued to lead UTNO during this period, her power was somewhat usurped by the national AFT. She also struggled with her own trauma and stress: "One of the things that led me to retire [in 2008] was that it was so stressful. I was beginning to lose myself and I didn't want to embarrass me on TV because, girl, my temper was getting so short. People didn't give me a break. Not only the teachers, anybody in the community, when we first got back from Katrina, they didn't care where they were. They felt like I had the answer no matter what it was. Wherever I went, they were talking to me, and it was driving me nuts."[182]

Yet it is hard to imagine how any leader could have saved the union in the face of the neoliberal coalition pushing for its demise. "I've wondered many times if anybody could have saved us, even Nat himself," muses DeRose.[183] In desperation, the union proposed that it fill "nontraditional" roles in the district, operating a hiring hall to help address the teacher shortage and running professional development seminars.[184] It was turned down. Joel Behrman explains, "[UTNO and the AFT] did a lot. Look. There's a failure involved here, I can't deny that. But I don't know what they were going to do. In those crucial months, we didn't know how much of the city would be alive, no schools were open, people hadn't moved back in. Remember that the governor had taken over the schools

UTNO members march across the Crescent City Connection as part of a voting rights rally with Rev. Jesse Jackson, April 1, 2006. Brenda Mitchell is on the right, holding a "Refuse to Lose" sign. *Photograph by Nijme Rinaldi Nun.*

and closed everything down. We felt there was a knife in our back. I don't know what we could have done. I don't know what people expected."[185] Eventually, in 2009, the national AFT withdrew much of its funding and personnel from the city. UTNO fought on, but in a hostile charter school landscape and with only a tiny fraction of its former membership and power.

CONCLUSION

Educators speak with bitterness about the storm and its aftermath, as well as about the system that replaced them and the assumption that the new young, white educators were more caring, intelligent, or successful than they had been. Juanita Bailey elaborates: "It was almost like if you were a veteran teacher, you were seen as the person that caused the problem before of why the schools were failing. It was like, okay, you're not going to consider other factors that caused the failure? It's like, why are they failing now? You haven't had a teachers' contract since 2006, so what's been happening?"[186] The ideology behind the school reform agenda assumed that the schools were performing poorly because of bloated district bureaucracy, lackluster leadership, and unmotivated teachers; it posited privatization and business-inspired nimble leadership as the solution. Often, this meant replacing Black district employees, school board members, principals, and educators with white ones. The conceptual severing of the interests of Black middle-class teachers and working-class support workers from the interests of the children who attended the schools, as if the children could exist apart from their families and communities, is one of the fundamental fallacies of school reform. It also reflects a misunderstanding of Black social mobility in assuming that the fired workers would simply find jobs elsewhere. That was true for some people, yet many with little wealth to fall back on struggled in the short and long term. As sociologist Mary Pattillo demonstrates, many members of the Black middle class, who benefit from little inherited wealth, are only a small crisis away from falling into poverty.[187]

Although the post-Katrina reforms involved injecting a significant amount of money into the system, particularly to update and renovate buildings and supplies, little was done to address the underlying issues of poverty, racism, and joblessness in the city. "We also had a very poor community. And when you deal with poverty, you deal with another whole issue. When you deal with families that can't pay their rent here and moved to another place, you're dealing with a lot of mobility of people. You're dealing with other factors," explains Russo.[188] The neoliberal school reform agenda creates lean management and competition between schools, putting pressure on teachers to push their students to succeed on standardized tests. In theory, it saves money, though spending in the district had increased 14 percent by 2017 relative to other Louisiana districts since the storm.[189] But educators doubted it was a panacea to improve education and help poor, mostly Black children achieve their goals and become informed, self-sufficient citizens. Moreover, the shuttering of the schools and their post-storm rebranding under various charter management organizations served both to obscure the long histories of the institutions and to present a model of education that is detached from an understanding of the larger role that schools play in communities. "In many communities, schools are at the very center of civic life. They function as gathering places, repositories of neighborhood tradition and identity, and an engine of local employment," authors Jack Schneider and Jennifer Berkshire explain.[190] Because of privatized management, open-enrollment policies, and the elimination of catchment zones, that function of schools has been largely foreclosed in New Orleans today.

Billie Dolce went back to visit her old school, Colton Elementary, a little while after the storm hit. "I had to get permission. Somebody had to meet me there at the school and walk me around. . . . When I walked into my classroom, I saw, oh my God, a promethean board. I didn't have that. I had an overhead projector." The whole building had been renovated: "The cafeteria, beautiful . . . the yard was beautiful. And I came back, I said, 'What I could have done with all of this!' Books, I saw books. . . . But the worth, the family, the belonging, the interpersonal relationship between not just the staff because the staff, they're not close like they used to be. And in order for a school to function, you've got to be close from the top all the way down."[191] Dolce taught for nearly forty years. She watched her students grow up and then she taught their children. She built lifelong relationships and friendships with her colleagues, students' parents, and fellow union members. The Colton she visited post-Katrina looked beautiful, but it lacked the warmth and connection she believes are key to quality education. A study analyzing teacher turnover in Orleans Parish found that, in a sample from 2009 to 2014, nearly 40 percent of teachers left their schools at the end of the year, and 21 percent left the parish entirely.[192] UTNO had a much broader definition of school success than the reformers; instead of looking solely at test scores, they considered the atmosphere of the school, teachers' experiences and retention, and students as citizens.[193] Though the union and the OPSB struggled to create successful schools before the storm, by any definition, they repeatedly advocated for the money and resources they believed they needed to create meaningful change.

The reformers won in New Orleans, and UTNO, organized labor, and the veteran educators lost. They lost their schools, which were privatized, their jobs, their houses, their contract, and their clout. Jim Randels, a teacher and post-storm UTNO president, was dismayed by the outcome, but he wasn't surprised: "It was clear that there were four members of the school board and a white business community that wanted the change. And the way they could get rid of, or greatly diminish, Black power in the city, the number one target for that would be public education and the teachers' union. And so, no. I'm a little surprised by how brazen they were."[194] At every level, federal, state, and local, forces united against the educators, providing funding, personnel, and political will for charter schools and privatization. In the process, they fired 7,500 educators, many of whom had devoted decades of their lives to working in challenging conditions in New Orleans schools. Randels continues, "This was about, get rid of the power. Because every place else on the Gulf Coast got money from the federal government to keep their teachers employed. This city, this community, could have done that and didn't have the political will—the racism was too great to overcome that to provide the political will for that."[195] Today, New Orleans is the only major city in the nation with a 100 percent charter school district.

UTNO, even with the support of the AFT and AFL-CIO, was unable to halt the school privatization agenda or save public education in New Orleans. Powerful pro-charter advocates, foundations, and policymakers saw an opportunity with the storm and united to transform the city into a laboratory to explore the effects of privatization, trampling over the union in the process. Weakened, with its members dispersed throughout the country and coping with their own traumas, the union initially struggled to get back on its feet. "We had a thirty-three-member executive board of UTNO when the hurricane hit. And there were very few of us who were back in the classroom teaching in Orleans Parish. I think at one point it might have been only three of us, in like the fall of 2006," Randels explains.[196] By the time UTNO recouped some energy and staff, policymakers had already pushed through the reforms crucial to remaking the system. By November 2005, reformers had converted all the undamaged schools in Algiers into charters and the state had used the RSD to assume control over the majority of the schools in the district. UTNO was left to negotiate with a weakened school board, which had vastly reduced power and had already acquiesced to—and in some moments even led—the privatization agenda. Though the union mounted a three-pronged campaign, filing lawsuits, organizing educators and the community, and trying to regain its political clout, it was marginalized by lawmakers and school administrators. These processes foreclosed avenues for democratic participation or dissent. OPSB had ceded many of its powers to A&M, the for-profit turnaround company with little public accountability. The Algiers charterizations and state takeover occurred long before most residents had returned to the city. White business leaders, such as Scott Cowen of Tulane, insurance executive Leslie Jacobs, and Don Marshall of Jazz Fest, held meetings to plan the school reforms that while ostensibly open to the public were, in fact, little advertised and elite driven. UTNO's traditional allies either abandoned the union or were also reeling from the storm's aftermath.

The New Orleans story demonstrates that the real aim of charter advocates is not to create a few successful schools in struggling districts, but rather to fully privatize education services. In the absence of meaningful resistance, in the vacuum that the storm created, reformers used "disaster capitalism" to eliminate New Orleans's public schools altogether.[197] Neoliberal theorist Milton Friedman argued in 1962 that the government should get out of the business of education, allowing private groups to run schools as businesses.[198] That vision has become the landscape in New Orleans; however, counter to Friedman's proposal, the schools remain publicly funded. Although Mayor Nagin's "green dot plan" to rebuild the city, which proposed turning several low-lying Black neighborhoods into greenspace, did not come to fruition, the firing of the teachers, privatization of the schools and Charity Hospital, and shuttering of the public housing projects had a similar impact. There are 100,000 fewer Black residents in the city today, and working-class and Black political power and clout are significantly reduced statewide.

The achievements of the union were also washed away with the storm. Its civil rights history forgotten, policymakers today portray pre-Katrina UTNO as protecting bad educators and justifying an unacceptable status quo. Yet it stands as a powerful example of Black-led organizing, union-building in the hostile Deep South, genuine interracial collaboration, and meaningful democratic participation. Diana Brown, a teacher and librarian, had been working in Orleans Parish for more than twenty years when the storm hit. She took a job across the lake, in mostly white Tangipahoa Parish. Four years later, in 2010, a district court overseeing a long-standing desegregation order in the parish ordered teacher transfers to create more equity across the parish.[199] Brown was transferred "because there were too many Black teachers at the school." At the school she was transferred to, "the principal said to me that she didn't want a librarian. . . . That was the very first time, even after Katrina, that I actually cried."[200] Brown resigned, feeling like she didn't have any other options, though she later got hired at a different school that was outside of the desegregation order. She had previously been vice president of the teachers local in the parish, but she quit after the transfer, upset that the other, mostly white union members had not stood up for her rights. UTNO had successfully protected its Black members in New Orleans from the demotions and dismissals that plagued Black teachers in the rest of the state during school desegregation in the 1960s and 1970s. Without a strong union, Black teachers were vulnerable yet again to the whimsy of white administrators, reflecting the limitation of color-blind strategies to deal with racism.

"Any plan to rebuild New Orleans that does not include rebuilding a viable system of public education is a hoax," proclaimed Nat LaCour at an October 2005 rally attended by Governor Blanco and Jesse Jackson, among others. "Education has its own chorus of ideologues who are looking to use our city's tragedy to make a point."[201] Yet the system today is public in funding only. The union that LaCour and his colleagues spent so many years of their lives building, the union that inspired so many loyal members and allies, was targeted, marginalized, and sidelined by the ideologues he critiqued. Organized labor, and a meaningful, powerful voice for teachers and other workers, is incompatible with the top-down business model of charter schools. And the incentive to privatize schools is clear: in many cities, schools' budgets are the single greatest expense.

Mitchell argues that part of why reformers targeted the union was that they had successfully played a watchdog role, limiting corruption and graft:

> It was them wanting to control more of the money. I think at the time, the school district might have been the largest employer. All of this money and all of these people that were around who were saying to themselves, "I need to get a piece of that." It wasn't about educating the children because they could have done that by making our schools better. . . . Fund your schools, build the buildings, give us the security, give us professional development. But they didn't want to do that, it was about controlling the money and I believe to a large degree, that's why the charter schools came about because then there was individual governance of the budget.[202]

The national landscape had also shifted dramatically. From 1980 to 2005, private sector unions lost over half their members, and income inequality nearly doubled.[203] President Reagan's ushering in of neoliberal economic policies was always accompanied by the disciplining of organized labor, which was most apparent in his firing of striking air traffic controllers in 1981.[204] Charter schools and vouchers, the educational arm of the neoliberal agenda, progressed more slowly, in part because of the strength of public sector unions. But by 2005, these policies—especially the introduction of charters—had mainstream acceptance among both major political parties. The public saw unions as anachronistic, a relic of a slower and less efficient economic moment. "I don't think there was very much good will to save us," reflects Joel Behrman. "People hate unions. I'm always amazed how even left-wing Democrats hate unions."[205] By the time that the class-action lawsuit was overturned by the Louisiana Supreme Court, in 2014, many New Orleans residents had stopped following the story of the wronged teachers, the enormous demographic shift among educators, and the tenacious union which had once been the largest in the state. "It's like everything else," explains Larry Carter. "It's the story of a day and then it's forgotten. These were people that were stalwarts in the community, entrenched here, who wanted to spend their last years with their neighbors and their families in Gentilly or Mid-City, wherever, and they were completely uprooted in every sense of the word, and many haven't returned to this day. But I think right now it's long forgotten."[206]

Choice versus Democracy in the Charter School City

As a nation, we have been counting on education to solve the
problems of unemployment, joblessness, and poverty for many
years. But education did not cause these problems, and education
cannot solve them. An economic system that chases profits and
casts people aside (especially people of color) is culpable.

Jean Anyon, *Radical Possibilities*

One of my big criticisms in life, people say, 'What's the problem
with education?' Well, there is no single problem with education
any more than there's a single problem with crime. You could
make a list of a hundred things. The teachers are the easy target.

Larry Carter, LFT president

TEACHING IN NEW ORLEANS TODAY

Longtime UTNO member Katrena Ndang, who worked as the union's community
organizer after the storm, eventually decided to return to the classroom. She
took a job at Miller-McCoy Academy in New Orleans East, an all-boys charter
school founded in 2008. "For a hot minute, I did work in a charter school," she
recalls. "And I don't think I lasted for a week. I could not take the disrespect that

[school leaders] had for the students, that's the first thing. It hurt my heart every day when I saw how they did not respect the students." When Ndang took over a civics course there, she was the fifth teacher who had cycled through the class that year. "One of the days they just walked in the classroom and started searching people. I was like, 'What's going on here?' And the students were so used to that being done, they jumped up and put their hands behind them. All I could see was, here are my grandchildren." Ndang raised concerns about the treatment of students and felt like school leaders failed to take her seriously: "I was always the bad person because I questioned." She explained one instance when administrators asked her to put together curriculum for an advanced business and entrepreneurship course and then failed to use it in class. Furthermore, the school had advertised an innovative program of internships and hands-on learning, but according to Ndang, none of it ever happened. Ndang quit. "I just walked away. They always tease me about it, and I said, 'I wasn't sleeping at night.' My whole teaching career, I always said when I taught, that I would teach the way I would want my daughter to be taught or my grandchildren to be taught, and if I can't do it, I shouldn't be there."[1] The cofounders of Miller-McCoy left in 2012 "under a cloud of cheating and ethics scandals."[2] Following their departure, the school cycled through several interim principals until the board of directors decided to permanently close it in late 2014.[3] The trajectory of Miller-McCoy is now common in the post-Katrina landscape of schools in New Orleans. The charterized school system has been characterized by a chaotic cycle of school openings and closures, leadership changes, and the shuttering and reopening of facilities across the city.

In the years immediately following Hurricane Katrina, both traditional public schools and charters were reopened by the state-controlled RSD as well as by the OPSB. During this time, most neighborhood catchment zones were eliminated, allowing students to attend any school in the city. The move essentially eradicated neighborhood schools. By 2019, the authorizing authorities had phased out all traditional public schools, and the charters that remained were transitioned back to local control under the OPSB.[4] However, OPSB's power has remained limited because charters maintain autonomy over most aspects of their schools. This includes not only finances and the school calendar but also all personnel decisions. The city currently has around eighty public charter schools. Between 2006 and 2016, policymakers closed, chartered, or rechartered fifty of them.[5] Pro-charter scholars, such as Doug Harris of the Education Research Alliance, argue that it is this very factor, the ability of policymakers to close schools, that accounts for the recent gains in test scores in the district.[6] Despite the reports of rising test scores, in 2019 nearly half of New Orleans's charter schools received D or F grades from the state Department of Education.[7]

Harris argues that the New Orleans school transformation has been a success, although he laments the top-down approach that resulted in an absence of community input throughout the process.[8] According to the numbers, student test scores, high school graduation rates, and college enrollment rates went up.[9] Total spending in the district also rose by 14 percent compared to other districts in the state;[10] constituting the much-needed funds that both UTNO and the OPSB had long called for. "With everything the city's children went through—the deaths of friends and loved ones, dispossession of homes and property, and massive disruption of daily life—they deserved a quality school system to help them put their lives back together," Harris writes.[11] However, Harris's analysis fails to consider children, their families, and the larger community as deeply interconnected. The children also need their parents to have stable jobs and incomes, to see role models who look like them in their schools, and to learn from educators with whom they can form lasting relationships.[12] The narrative of school success omits the parallel story of teacher disempowerment as well as the total elimination of opportunities for civic action and democratic participation in the education realm.

In short, school reformers almost destroyed UTNO in order to create the all-charter district; they fired qualified, veteran educators in order to rebuild the schools from the ground up, run and staffed primarily by outsiders. This "creative destruction" is a hallmark of neoliberal revitalization: a process that creates privatized entities with limited governmental or democratic oversight.[13] In the context of the education sector, these policies reduce parents to consumers and reframe schools as marketable products. In this model, school leaders must sell their particular brand to attract students and remain viable.[14]

In addition to the detrimental effect of these neoliberal policies on students and families in New Orleans, the dismissal of thousands of New Orleans educators after the storm had a devastating impact on educators themselves, many of whom never returned to the city. By fall 2007, only 32 percent of the dismissed teachers had returned to work in New Orleans schools, and by 2013, less than one-quarter (22 percent) of them remained.[15] The demographic shifts in the schools as well as in the city at large were also striking. From 2004 to 2013, the teaching force went from 71 percent Black to 49 percent Black, as charter schools sought younger, cheaper, and whiter educators. Furthermore, the percentage of teachers with 0–5 years of experience grew from 33 percent to 54 percent in that same period.[16] Programs such as TFA and TeachNOLA framed teaching as a low-skill job that can be performed by anyone with a college degree. UTNO, which had been a pillar of civil rights, equity, and democracy in the New Orleans community, was a shell of its former self.

In the post-Katrina school landscape, educational entrepreneurs and conservative leaders demonized UTNO, blaming the union for the district's deficiencies before Katrina, and downplaying its legacy of organizing and activism. Joel Behrman argues that the union was unfairly scapegoated after the storm: "People thought the union had Black teachers with fat asses who spoke ungrammatically, and had picket signs that were misspelled and were eating in class and not teaching. And that was a stereotype that was used and it was vicious, and there was a racism in that image."[17] One teacher attempting to organize a union at a local charter school recalled, "[The opposition dragged] up the old UTNO history and that hurt us a lot, because they talked about how UTNO did not get any of the teachers back after Katrina. . . . [I heard UTNO] was relatively ineffectual, that they were fairly corrupt. I heard stories of them having people on payroll that didn't exist just so they can pull in dues from them."[18] As charter school advocates rewrote UTNO's history, the powerful legacy of the union was reduced in the public imagination to tropes of Black corruption and mismanagement. The diatribe was even more ironic considering UTNO's historic role as a watchdog on corruption in the schools, decrying wasted money and buildings in dire need of repair. Corruption charges, as Domingo Morel points out, stick much more easily to Black organizations and individuals, even to organizations such as UTNO that appear to have operated honestly and transparently.[19] Nearly every article published about the New Orleans school takeover uses the school board's corruption to justify the state's actions, yet similar instances of corruption among the mostly white-run charter networks have failed to spark widespread calls to scrap the new system. "I do not feel that the schools became charter schools because of any kind of corruption and theft and stuff like that. I believe that they just wanted to have profit making schools," argues UTNO staffer Connie Goodly.[20]

ORGANIZING CHARTER UNIONS

UTNO did attempt to organize unions at several charter schools, and it successfully obtained contracts at six (table 6.1). It won an election at one more, but it never reached a contract due to teacher attrition, delays, and questionable labor practices within the charter management organization. Teachers report being bullied, bribed, and even illegally fired by school leaders attempting to avoid unionization. Because of the quasi-public realm in which charter schools exist, educators working at charter schools are considered private sector employees, whose labor practices are regulated by the National Labor Relations Board (NLRB). The weakness of US labor laws, combined with the NLRB's mild enforcement mechanisms, give employers a significant advantage in union elections.[21] For example, it is legal for school administrators to hold "captive audience" meetings with educators to convince them to vote against a union. Moreover, since the business counteroffensive of the early 1980s, private sector workers have filed for fewer union elections and have won a smaller percentage of the elections held. Growth of tactics such as the "captive audience" meetings described above, management threatening to close the school or business, and contesting elections have contributed to this anti-union landscape.[22]

Table 6.1. Post-Katrina charter school union drives

SCHOOL	YEAR OF FORMATION OR VOTE	RESULT
Morris Jeff Community School	2013	Successful contract
Ben Franklin High School	2014	Successful contract
International High School	2016	Educators voted in favor; no negotiated contract to date
The Willow School (formerly Lusher Charter School)	2016	Teachers lost union election; paraprofessionals won
Coghill Charter School	2017	Teachers voted in favor and negotiated a contract; school lost its charter and shut down
Bricolage Academy	2021	Successful contract
The Living School	2022	Successful contract
Rooted School	2023	Successful contract

Following contentious elections at two charter schools—Lusher, which the union lost, and the International High School, where the union won on paper but never secured a contract—UTNO filed various complaints of unfair labor practices against the charter management organizations. The complaints alleged that employees had been threatened and coerced as well as discriminated against and even terminated because of their participation in union organizing drives.[23] "They fired me," one teacher recalled. "I was the first one to go after we lost the vote. . . . I was blindsided. . . . They canned two other people later that summer."[24] Teachers in New Orleans charters also reported that they had been promised benefits or raises if they would speak publicly against the union.[25] For example, teacher Bill Scott said his school's CEO confronted him in a private meeting: "[She] called me in to urge me to not vote for the union. Pointed out that she had hired me in spite of the fact that at my age, and level of experience, that I earned at the top of the salary chart. . . . I was appreciative. I thought she got value for money." Scott voted for the union though he had never been an UTNO member before the storm.[26] Though Scott was off-put by his school's tactics and voted for the union, other teachers—especially those who are younger and less experienced—often genuinely fear for their careers, are convinced by the anti-union arguments, or simply decide supporting the union requires too much effort and vote against unionization. Given the few successful contracts UTNO has won in post-Katrina New Orleans, school administrators' tactics and rhetoric appear to have been effective.

UTNO organizers and educators were surprised by the anti-union fervor they garnered from administrators. They were not used to retaliation or the need for secretive meetings. Joel Behrman remembered a post-storm effort to unionize the Lycée Français, a French-immersion charter school:

> [The] thinking being French people don't have an antipathy to the union. . . . There was a meeting of the Lycée Français that was paid by UTNO unionists, paid by the AFT, to come in somebody's house and talk to people. They invited a lot of people, including people from the school board, including hostile people. To organize a charter, it's like organizing a communist cell in Nazi Germany. You have to do it under the radar, you have to be very careful about who you talk to. You know you can't talk about union in front of hostile people who don't want a union. We didn't know what to do. It's going to require extreme professionalism, and you have to be under the table, and be far more discreet than I've been my whole life.[27]

But the potential gains of organizing efforts are small, since a contract would cover only one building. "How much money is AFT going to spend to try to do that, when you have teachers who are coming here and they don't stay?"[28]

Alorea Gilyot was working at Coghill Charter School when she was asked to join the UTNO organizing committee there. Having watched the administrative backlash at other schools that had tried to form unions, the committee members were secretive about their efforts. However, they still experienced retribution. "All of us [on the organizing committee] were reassigned positions. None of us who were on the organizing team had the same position that we had the year before. . . . Of those of us who were on that team and part of the negotiating team, only one person is [still] at the school."[29] Gilyot watched as her colleagues left the school in search of better working conditions or else received "letters of separation" from school administrators that terminated their employment. Though the Coghill organizers convinced 93 percent of the staff to sign the petition for union recognition voluntarily, the administration claimed people had been coerced and demanded an NLRB election.[30] The union won the election, but few of the original staff remained at the school; in addition, the school itself was cycling through its fourth principal in three years. The district revoked Coghill's charter in 2019, following years of failing test scores, thus voiding the union contract.[31] Charter management organizations understand that unions threaten their control over school operations, particularly budgeting and personnel decisions. As a result, they act forcefully to stamp out organizing efforts.[32] Grace Lomba, who worked as an organizer in charter schools after the storm, explains: "They know that with the union, they would have to be transparent, they would have to surrender some of the power that they have, and share that with the teachers and the union that represents them."[33]

Even after winning a contract, it is unclear how much power educators gain since each contract only covers one school. "It's better than nothing," speculates Nat LaCour.[34] Lomba agrees that the successful UTNO contracts have been helpful: "They got the support in the schools, things have changed, things they have asked for they have been able to get. An atmosphere at the school has changed, and people see the benefit of it."[35] Though today teachers at unionized schools may reap modest benefits, the fragmented nature of the post-Katrina charter school system limits teachers' potential to organize system wide. As such, UTNO's victories have not inspired widespread union organizing across the district. Moreover, out of necessity, union organizers have adopted pro-charter stances, arguing that they want a contract tailored to their individual schools rather than one that can help consolidate district-wide power.[36] Arguing that a union contract would actually make the charter school stronger preempts claims that the organizers do not care about the school community or that they are fighting for their own interests at the expense of their students. At the same time, it severely limits the power the union wields if it wins. Despite the dearth of successful contracts, complaints about working conditions and teacher turnover are rampant: "You have something now that people privately gripe about, but they don't know what to do about it," says Juanita Bailey.[37] Though studies show mixed results, teachers at charter schools nationwide generally experience more challenging working conditions, longer hours, and lower retention rates.[38]

Many teachers who returned to New Orleans after the storm faced conditions that shocked them, harkening back to issues educators had raised in the 1960s before UTNO first won a contract. They watched coworkers lose their jobs, seemingly without just cause, and they learned of pay disparities along lines of race and gender.[39] Jennifer Tiller was a tepid UTNO supporter before the storm, but the charter landscape changed her mind:

> Now that I'm older and I've seen what the union can do, I think it's really sad we have to have a union, but I think it's the only thing that protects teachers. Teachers are dumped on right and left, and some of those schools, their school day is seven to five or something ridiculous. I mean, you can't teach like that, and then how are you going to then do your grading? How are you going to prepare for the next day? It's just crazy. The union protected teachers' time and that's not a little thing.[40]

Diego Gonzalez-Grande voted for the union at Ben Franklin High School, one of the schools where UTNO was able to secure a contract: "The school without the union here meant, to a large extent, you were at the whim of those who were serving in administration."[41] Franklin is one of the highest performing schools in the state, and teachers there received little pushback during their unionization drive. Gonzalez-Grande says Franklin's success belies the common argument that unions cause schools to suffer academically:

> The school had a union for thirty years, and it did not suffer academically, so the notion, that by installing a union, academic standards will suffer, is simply a fallacious association. Not everybody was a member of UTNO when I started at Franklin, and you had great teachers who were members and great teachers who were not. Membership in a union or nonmembership had nothing to do with whether you were a committed faculty member, whether you wrote recommendations, whether you went above and beyond what was required in your contract, on behalf of your school and your students.[42]

Veteran teachers who returned after the storm, even those who continued teaching for years in the new system, report negative changes in their work environments and less job satisfaction.[43]

Despite the small number of contracts secured by UTNO, it is unclear what will be possible for the union in the future. "Pre-Katrina, we had one collective bargaining for 120 schools. Post-Katrina, we thought about it one school at a time, to organize for collective bargaining. That means now, we need about sixty-two collective bargaining agreements in one school district. That's some of the hardest work around that I think unions can do in the country right now," says LFT president Larry Carter.[44] Joel Behrman is more pessimistic: "I wish them luck. The problem is, I think the AFT is giving up. Because look at what it takes. It's so hard to do."[45] Lomba argues that UTNO needs a different approach, something more radical harkening back to UTNO's early campaign for collective bargaining in the late 1960s and early 1970s: "It's going to take a lot. It's going to take more than teachers, it's going to have to take outreach to the community, I think it's going to take outreach to politicians to say that this all-charter district in New Orleans is not the panacea for education."[46] Lomba suggests that the piecemeal, school-by-school approach will be insufficient to bring back UTNO and coalesce teacher power in the schools. Moreover, she points to a larger argument: despite the rising test scores, the "charter school city" is not the success that reformers claim.

VETERAN EDUCATORS' OPINIONS ON THE NEW ORLEANS SCHOOL REFORMS

Veteran educators in New Orleans are well-positioned to recognize many of the shortcomings of the charter school system. Some teachers dispute the data on test scores, arguing that the student population today is smaller and has faced with fewer challenges than the population before the storm, or that the tests and scoring have changed in a way that makes post-Katrina scores incomparable with pre-Katrina scores. However, most teachers instead present a very different vision of what a successful school system should look like. They dispute the hegemonic narrative that the schools before the storm were wholly dysfunctional or that Black teachers were to blame for the schools' struggles.[47] They critique the lack of transparency and lack of teacher, family, and community voice in the charter schools, suggesting instead that the charter system excludes the community, encourages top-down leadership, and stifles opportunities for democratic participation. They also bemoan the loss of neighborhood schools and argue that the idea of "choice" promised by the charter model falls far short of its proponents' claims. Finally, veteran teachers claim that these shifts shortchange both educators and students, creating an unstable district with little teacher, student, or parent input. Their claims resonate with a 2019 survey by the Cowen Institute that found that only 30 percent of parents feel "positive" about the charter schools and a scant 14 percent of parents would give the New Orleans public education system an A or B rating.[48] Educators, like parents, argue that despite gains in test scores, the charter system continues to underserve New Orleans's public school children: "We see that it is not working in the best interests of our kids. We have seen many [charters] close because there was financial mismanagement, services weren't provided to kids, especially special ed kids, and they just aren't doing what they said they were going to do."[49]

Despite the OPSB's flaws before Katrina, the school board provided a forum for educator and community voices in the school system to be heard. Today, each school or network of schools has its own privately appointed governing board, fragmenting decision-making throughout the system. "What you've done is you've diluted the problem now," explains Joe DeRose. "Instead of having one school board where everything is focused, now, every [school] has its own board. . . . I think a lot of stuff is going to be hidden in this dilution of power."[50] Joel Behrman says that the school board meetings were sometimes unruly, full of people yelling at one another from across the room, but at least they provided some transparency: "What they have now is they have eighty separate boards meeting secretly, and there's no screaming. There's no accountability, nobody sees them, they're not reported on."[51] Charter board meetings are generally little advertised and poorly attended. An investigation by a local media outlet, *The Lens*, found that the majority of charter boards were not aware of, or complying with, open-meetings laws, thus exacerbating the public's ability to get information about the schools: "Few news media outlets are able or willing to commit the resources necessary to cover the meetings of these publicly funded boards, which collectively manage hundreds of millions of taxpayer dollars. Few parents attend these meetings."[52] This lack of transparency, and the struggle to obtain information, neutralizes community dissent. "In the past, if something came on the news about schools, it was like wholesale Orleans Parish. It was all together. We started school the same time, we ended school the same time. There was a connection, and you don't have that [today]. The bus system, all of it worked together. Now, it's none of that. You don't know what's going on from school to school," complains Juanita Bailey.[53] Though the charter schools are heralded as beacons of "choice," there is little opportunity for parents or community members to influence school policy or participate in district decision-making. Instead, with little information, they are given the opportunity to "choose" a school through a lottery system in which they rank their top twelve choices. Due to lack of transparency about what's happening at the various charter networks, parents find it challenging to rank schools in an informed manner.

Similarly, educators dislike the top-down model of running schools, claiming it limits their ability to participate in decision-making at the school and district levels. The success of a school now, teachers observe, depends almost entirely on administrators, as power is rarely shared. "I'm concerned because I fear that we may have in the making a bigger mess than we had before the storm," says Bill Scott. "You have a lousy leader you're going to end up in a lousy school. Good leaders will hire good teachers, and not so good leaders won't. It's carried down."[54] With union power diminished, the one check on administrators is the authorizer's (currently the OPSB for most schools and BESE for a few state-authorized charters) ability to revoke charters; but that consequence is immensely disruptive for students, parents, and educators. When charters are revoked and schools close, teachers' careers are interrupted, and parents and children scatter across the district looking for a new educational home. Though charter advocates argue that closing poorly performing schools helps students obtain a better education, studies find that most displaced students enroll in other poorly performing schools, and thus experience the disruption of the switch but no rise in test scores or achievement.[55]

Connected to lack of transparency and top-down leadership, educators identify ongoing corruption scandals among charter networks as one of the flaws of the fragmented system. "All you've done is create new opportunities for corruption. Paying off vendors, contractors, construction people, etc., that wouldn't exist if you were in the traditional school situation."[56] By far the most common complaint from veteran educators is the schools' failure to serve students with special needs. This concern was demonstrated to be well-grounded when parents sued the district in 2010 and won a landmark settlement four years later. Yet since then, problems surrounding special needs students have persisted; in 2018, the state placed eight New Orleans schools under corrective action plans for failing to meet Individuals with Disabilities Education Act requirements.[57] "So if you are a parent and you have a child that you want to get into a school, you have to get them into a charter school. If they have a problem like maybe mentally challenged or physically challenged, they won't take them. So those parents have no place to send their children."[58]

Educators were also horrified by the discipline techniques used in the charter schools, which they claimed treated students as if they were in prison.

> You teach the children walk to the right, with a finger over their mouths, and they'd walk on that line. [My friend] said it was almost like they were robots. . . . I went to this one school and the kids were in the cafeteria, they couldn't talk. The teachers were standing around the walls with a book in their hands, reading a book, and when the children would finish, they had to sit there and read a book but they couldn't even teach the children how to have a social conversation in the cafeteria. . . . They couldn't talk. And a lot of the kids were expelled for simple things whereas we had to put up with the kids all but killing you.[59]

Louise Mouton Johnson got a job at the charter network KIPP, but like Katrena Ndang, quit when she saw how the children were treated:

> Kids had to track the teacher. They had had this little chant that they had to practice . . . and you couldn't talk to the person walking on the other side of the hall when you were changing your classes or whatever. That really didn't sit right with me. I came from art school with music playing in the halls, kids with the little drumsticks tapping on a rail as they walked to class, but once you got into class it was strictly business. . . . The thing is, [KIPP] was like military training.[60]

Harsh discipline requirements are sometimes leveraged as a strategy to push out students with special needs as well. For example, students and parents filed a complaint against a charter network in 2014 alleging various discriminatory civil rights complaints, such as punishing a child with cerebral palsy with in-school suspension for failing to walk on the line when changing classes.[61]

Veteran educators also argue that even though test scores have gone up, the gains have not benefited all students equally. "The schools that are excelling and doing well are the ones that were doing well pre-Katrina. The same ones. The Hynes, the Lushers, because they were magnet schools, and they just stayed the same. For the most part, the schools that were good prior to chartering are still good, and the schools that were bad prior to chartering are still bad," claims LaCour.[62] In 2019, the state Department of Education gave eight New Orleans schools an A-ranking, but few of them reflect the demographics of the public school system. Overall, the school system is 93 percent students of color, and 83 percent of students receive free or reduced-price lunch, the federal marker of student poverty.[63] Yet the city's A-ranking schools represent a population

Table 6.2. New Orleans school rankings and demographics, 2019

SCHOOL	STUDENTS RECEIVING FRPL* (%)	STUDENTS OF COLOR (%)	STATE RANKING (A- AND F-RATED SCHOOLS ONLY)
Ben Franklin High	39	64	A
Edna Karr High	80	100	A
Hynes Charter School	34	48	A
Lake Forest Elementary	79	99	A
Lusher Charter School	24	42	A
New Orleans Center for Creative Arts**	48	51	A
New Orleans Military & Maritime Academy**	77	68	A
Warren Easton High	79	100	A
Arise Academy	96	100	F
Craig Charter School	96	100	F
Lafayette Academy	97	99	F
Crocker College Prep	96	100	F
Coghill Charter School	96	99	F
ReNew Schaumburg Elementary	94	99	F
Cohen College Prep	92	100	F
All New Orleans	**83**	**93**	

Sources: Louisiana Department of Education, "Multiple Statistics by School System for Total Public Students," www.louisianabelieves.com/resources/library/school-system-attributes; Marta Jewson, "Compare 2019 New Orleans School Ratings," *The Lens*, November 6, 2019. *Note:* This list does not include three schools that received an "F" grade and were subsequently closed by the state, as their 2019 demographic data is not available.
* FRPL = free or reduced-price lunch.
** Indicates the school is authorized by the state board of education.

that is significantly whiter and wealthier than the overall student population. By contrast, the ten schools to which the state gave failing grades are composed almost entirely of students of color living in poverty (table 6.2). "Everybody can't go to Warren Easton," explains paraprofessional Jacqueline Johnson, referring to one of the city's top-ranked high schools.[64] LaCour argues that the gains of the charter transformation have been inequitably distributed: "The charterization, as I see it has been effective in white neighborhoods and less effective in Black neighborhoods. . . . I'm just waiting to see when the Black community is going to recognize what's really happening and mount a campaign to go back to neighborhood schools at the elementary level. Every school should be a good school, and that's what I'm saying the union has to spend more energy on. Negotiating, meeting with parents, talking about what's needed to make their schools effective in the inner city."[65]

Educators repeatedly lament the loss of neighborhood schools. Beyond being sites for education, schools have the potential to bring neighborhoods together as community hubs, creating opportunities for organizing and collaboration. "I don't think there's such a thing as a neighborhood school anymore. [We lost] a commitment from the community, a buy-in from the community, a support from the community," explains Jo Anna Russo.[66] With the new open-enrollment system, students enter a lottery to attend any school throughout the city. "So the very concept of a neighborhood school is gone. You're spending a fortune getting people in buses to go all around town. What that means is for working mothers, working fathers, anybody, to try to pick up their kids . . . they're lost in this maze of traffic."[67] Several teachers complained about the inefficiency and wasted time of busing students long distances. According to a report from the Urban Institute, a typical child in New Orleans who relies on bus transport spends six hours per week commuting to and from school, and 25 percent of children spend over eight hours on the bus each week. Moreover, some bus pickups begin as early as 5:00 a.m., nearly two hours before sunrise in the winter.[68] Wanda Richard observes:

> Then you're busing kids from one end of the city to the other. I know a teacher that was telling me that one of the kids got sick, and mom works, and they called grandma. By the time grandma got to the school, the regular bus was there to pick up the kid. She had to come from across town. The next time the kid got sick, they called grandma again, grandma said, "You get me an Uber, I'll come get her." If this child was in a neighborhood school, grandma was around the corner, she could have walked there and picked up a sick child.[69]

Long hours spent commuting also make it more difficult for students to participate in extracurricular activities or receive afterschool enrichment tutoring. Connie Goodly says that her brother moved away from New Orleans because he had four kids in four different schools and couldn't manage the scheduling and commuting: "It's horrible when you can't get your kids all in the same school and one is here and one is there. It's ridiculous."[70]

The lottery system, through which students are matched to a school using a computerized algorithm, is the backbone of New Orleans's school choice system, and it similarly inspires despair. "I don't like where parents have to participate in a lottery to get their kids into a decent school," explains Gwendolyn Adams. "Children are not allowed to go into schools that are in their community."[71] Luetta Stewart now lives on the north shore, partly for the sake of her daughter's education:

> I would not live [in New Orleans] because I don't have access to quality public education for my child. And I can't afford, on a teacher's salary, to

send her to private school. So I think New Orleans has shifted to become a haven for twenty-somethings with more of a disposable income, who want a unique cultural experience. It's not really where you raise a family anymore. . . . The Lushers and the Ben Franklins, would I send my child there? Absolutely. But could she get in? I don't know. You can't gamble on that.[72]

Some argue that the lottery system is an effective strategy to equalize public education, rather than allowing parents living in more expensive zip codes to send their children to well-funded public schools while parents in poorer neighbors are left with no choice but to send their children to the underfunded neighborhood school. However, loopholes and admissions requirements allow wealthy and white parents to circumvent the lottery system. For example, parents with means hire private psychologists to assess their children as "gifted" in order to get priority admission for pre-K 4 at sought-after Hynes Lakeview. Similarly, Lusher partners with Tulane University to offer priority admission to the children of Tulane faculty members, who are overwhelmingly white, middle- or upper-class, and highly educated. Though location requirements have mostly been eliminated district wide, some schools in wealthy, white neighborhoods have kept their catchment zones in order to keep their schools elite. For example, Hynes Lakeview, located in a mostly white neighborhood, reserves 66 percent of its spots for children in the surrounding zip code.[73] While wealthy and white parents circumvent the system or enroll their children in private or parochial schools, poor parents and parents of color are left with few options. Wanda Richard points out the absurdity: "This OneApp system, there's no choice. When you have to give a parent an app and say, 'You have a choice, put your choices down,' and you have to put 13 or 12 choices down, that's not no doggone choice."[74] Though the hallmark of the system is supposed to be parental choice, in the end the final placement decision is left to a computer. According to data from the district, 68 percent of children are matched to one of their top three choices on the OneApp.[75] Though this indicates some success in matching students to schools, it certainly is not "choosing" a school in the traditional sense. As a result, poor parents have much less power and agency in the system than parents with money, who can select a private or parochial school for their child if they don't get one of their top choices using the OneApp.

Moreover, though overall spending in the schools has increased 14 percent since Hurricane Katrina, per pupil instructional spending is down. "A lot of money that was once spent on classrooms is spent for people, the CEOs. . . . How much money is there to replicate and have redundant, high-paid administrative staff in the schools? We used to complain that the superintendent got $160,000 when teachers only got $60[000], or $50[000]. And how many CEOs get that amount of money?"[76] Schools now pay less for inexperienced teachers and typically no longer offer pensions or the other benefits that UTNO fought for, such as the Health and Welfare Fund, the teacher center, peer mentoring, and quality professional development. Instead, the increased funding has been allocated to more and higher administrator salaries, as the administrator-to-pupil ratio has increased significantly. Administration funding in the district has increased 66 percent since the storm.[77] Jennifer Tiller, a librarian, says that the decrease in per pupil instructional spending has a clear impact on students: "It upsets me that it's public money and it's being used sort of privately. Each school has to have all these people at the top and so much money spent at the top. Do they have enough teachers? There aren't many librarians in the charter schools in Orleans. I think that's criminal."[78] The new model has also created a disincentive to hire veteran educators: "I was forced out, in a sense," explains Leoance Williams. "They had to pay us according to the years of experience. It was cheaper for them to get a new person in, as opposed to paying me salary up there like that."[79] Principals and CEOs, who no longer have to contend with union seniority regulations, often hire the cheapest and thus least experienced labor they can find.

Despite their complaints about charter schools, teachers feel that they lack the proper channels to voice their concerns. "Teachers can secretly gripe about stuff, but if you want to stay employed, you better tread lightly," Bailey warns.[80] LaCour says that teachers in the charter schools are bullied by administrators: "If you work at a charter school, you can be fired just for asking other teachers how much they make."[81] In many schools, the only way educators can express their concern about certain aspects of the school is by leaving. This has led to rampant turnover in the schools and a continuous teacher shortage.[82] Bailey says, "I really feel for this new generation of teachers coming in, because I don't understand how they are going to strengthen this profession, and get people to invest in it, if you are in a situation where you are treating them at-will, not investing in their professional development, not investing in having them at the table when you are making curriculum, deciding on schedules. I don't understand how you keep people in it."[83] With a few exceptions, the school reforms have created an inhospitable environment for educators in New Orleans. Although school reformers claim that administrators' absolute control over personnel decisions is key to improving schools, the high turnover in New Orleans has not resulted in improved teacher performance. Though lower-performing teachers are more likely to leave than high-performing teachers, value-added metrics show that high-performing teachers tend to be replaced by lower-performing teachers, resulting in no net gain for students.[84] Union leaders would argue that investing in training and professional development for those teachers would be a better strategy than pushing them out of the profession.

Despite the aforementioned critiques of the new charter system, not all veteran educators oppose the charter transformation. "They've shown growth," admits former UTNO and current LFT president Larry Carter. "They've shown a way to meet the needs of the community that they didn't probably over the first ten years [after Katrina]."[85] Violet Johnson, a former district employee who then went on to work for the East Bank Collaborative of Charter Schools, supports the reforms wholeheartedly: "I think the schools are better. I think there's more options for kids and for parents."[86] Joy Van Buskirk, UTNO's former lobbyist, helped write the charter for Audubon Montessori School immediately after Hurricane Katrina: "A school board member called [Audubon's principal] and said, 'We have a handful of schools that are high and dry in Orleans Parish and if you guys don't write a charter, you're going to lose the Montessori school.' . . . I never thought that that would then lead to a school system filled with charters."[87] Though Van Buskirk laments the union's downfall, she's glad Audubon was preserved and was not particularly surprised by the state takeover: "They had been after our school district for years. They had done everything they could to make the mission of Orleans Parish school system difficult. They saw their opportunity. I wish that we would have had a stronger opposition and been able to thwart that happening during that legislative session."[88] Cindy Robinson has worked in a charter school since Katrina and has mixed feelings:

[The charters] are just trying lots of different things, and they think that the solution is to try something new. We don't really try anything long enough to make sure it works, or to find out if it works, so we just have to keep trying new things. Some of them I think are working. . . . I feel like we're doing a good job here. We're a B school, we take any child, total open enrollment, and I think we work really, really hard. But that's probably the reason people don't stay, is because you work them to death, and that's kind of the model. I do think that it's a challenge to get teachers who are career teachers, and to get a diverse group.[89]

Even teachers who support the transformation tend to lament the loss of some union benefits, such as limits on working hours and incentives to recruit career teachers.

Fifty Years of UTNO

Today, more than fifteen years since Hurricane Katrina, many younger educators and community members have no memory of the school district before the storm. As a result, policymakers look narrowly at student outcomes and say that the school reform was a success. However, retelling UTNO's history reveals how much was lost and continues to be sacrificed to enable those gains. "This is a totally different population from what we had," points out former UTNO president Brenda Mitchell. "We had 120-something schools before the storm. We had about 7,000 school employees. There's no comparison at all."[1] What happened to those school employees and students who never returned? Where are the 100,000 Black residents who never moved back to the city? When educators and policymakers think about schools not only as places to educate children but also as employers, centers of community, and loci of democratic participation, the school reform story starts to look more complex. Historian Walter Stern demonstrates how school construction and school politics entrenched patterns of housing segregation in Jim Crow–era New Orleans.[2] His analysis suggests that schools can also be used to promote integration, community collaboration, and neighborhood support. From the mid-1960s to the mid-2000s, UTNO fought for the schools, centering Black, working-class, and women educators. The union's organizational model and agenda promoted democracy both internally, with union members, and externally, in the school board and the city.

I argue that examining the history of UTNO leads to four core conclusions:

1. There is a need to further study the role of Black educators and multiracial and Black teachers' unions and their influence on labor and education policies in the South.

2. The use of strategies from the civil rights movement led to UTNO's early success, and echoes of these same strategies continue

to be effective today in both social movement unionism and teachers' attempts to "bargain for the common good."

3. These strategies, which aim address both economic and racial justice simultaneously, as well as both workers' needs and the community's needs, open up new opportunities for democratic participation and engagement.

4. The neoliberal education reform movement is explicitly anti-union and antidemocratic and, particularly when implemented district wide as it was in New Orleans, has devastating and disproportionate impacts on Black workers and the Black community. These takeaways suggest the importance of bringing labor history into discussions of school reform and the limitations of educational analyses that rely only on student outcomes to determine the success of educational policies.

UTNO'S RISE AND FALL: 1965–2005

In its early years, from the late 1930s to the mid-1960s, Local 527 fought for the rights of Black teachers and students, advocating for salary equalization, adequate schools for Black children, and school integration. It rose to power in the late 1960s and early 1970s as a civil rights union, modeling its actions after powerful public sector unions such as the Memphis sanitation workers as well as the mighty ILA in New Orleans. Along with demanding collective bargaining, it advocated for equity in hiring across the district, justice for Black students, and meaningful student integration.

Local 527 held the first teachers' strike in the South, in 1966, and orchestrated a historic merger of majority-white and majority-Black locals in 1972, forming UTNO, and setting the stage for its future success. In 1974, when the union won its collective bargaining agreement—one of the first in the region—it did so with the overwhelming support of the city's Black community and the backing of both the AFT and the NEA. UTNO represented a hopeful future for working-class and Black New Orleans residents and demonstrated that protest and disruptive action produces positive results. The union's commitment to uniting educator and community struggles resonates with the strategy of "bargaining for the common good" employed by teachers' unions in Chicago and Los Angeles today. In this, UTNO helped bridge the civil rights unionism of the 1940s through 1960s and social movement unionism, which emerged in the 1990s, demonstrating how both movements sought to unite the struggles of workers with the challenges faced by the larger community. Though the South is largely ignored in histories of teacher unionism, some of the most successful strategies that we see today were used nearly fifty years ago by educators in New Orleans.

UTNO won collective bargaining by relying on a massive network of members, who reached out to their families, friends, and communities to garner support for the union. UTNO's leadership galvanized its members in part through the democratic potential of the union and the open and democratic leadership of longtime president Nat LaCour. Drawing on strategies from civil rights activists such as Ella Baker and Septima Clark, UTNO built a structure that privileged collective decision-making and active member participation. These approaches in turn, inspired great member loyalty to the union.

As the city's demographics shifted, following faculty and student integration and white flight to the suburbs, UTNO coalesced its power and began the project of institution building. It held a popular and successful strike in 1978, winning significant pay raises, and over the subsequent decade built a Health and Welfare Fund, a teacher center that promoted professional development, and a credit union. It also developed an effective political machine that gave significant weight to the union's endorsement and bolstered the voice of the weakening Louisiana AFL-CIO. UTNO's work inspired union organizing across the sector as teachers won collective bargaining in neighboring parishes, clerical workers and paraprofessionals joined UTNO's ranks, and cafeteria workers, janitors, maintenance workers, and bus drivers all organized noteworthy contracts.

The state's business interests, particularly the industry lobby (LABI), long opposed UTNO and unions more broadly. LABI won right-to-work legislation in 1976, undermining the reach of private sector unions, and continued a relentless battle to chip away at union rights. However, UTNO remained mostly untouchable. It held another successful strike in 1990, in large part to demand raises for low-paid paraprofessionals, and it developed a strong lobbying arm that fought tenaciously in the state legislature.

Even as neoliberal policymaking began to impact the city in the 1980s and 1990s, through austerity measures and early attempts at privatization, UTNO held strong, defeating proposals to privatize education through the implementation of a school voucher system and the introduction of for-profit charter schools. UTNO maintained its position that education was a public good that should be publicly funded. The union successfully convinced voters to increase educational funding four times, generating much needed money for the struggling school system. UTNO also played an invaluable role as the district watchdog, documenting poor building conditions, lack of materials, and other endemic issues. Union educators worked closely with BESE and the OPSB, collaborating on professional development, helping to select textbooks, and refining evaluation procedures. Through the 1990s, the union continued to garner widespread educator and community support, particularly from the Black families whose children attended the schools.

In the late 1990s and early 2000s, neoliberal inroads in education policy increased. The state passed a law permitting charter schools in 1995, and the first charter school opened in New Orleans in 1998. However, strong opposition from UTNO greatly limited the spread of charters, particularly a regulation stipulating that a school could be converted into a charter only if 75 percent of the school's teachers and parents agreed with the decision. UTNO's resistance during this period demonstrates how powerful unions serve as one of the last bulwarks against neoliberal privatization. Nonetheless, a greater focus on accountability and test scores, implemented after the 2001 NCLB legislation, put additional scrutiny on the New Orleans schools, which struggled academically. In 2003, the state legislature created the RSD, a mechanism through which the state could seize control of failing schools. Desperate to appear open to positive change and reform, UTNO and the LFT offered only tepid resistance. As neoliberal policy-making increased, teachers' unions were put increasingly on the defensive, and UTNO began retreating from its earlier commitment to strikes and disruptive action, its leaders a little less trusting and its membership more complacent. Still—despite repeated school board scandals and a string of short-lived super-intendents—the state was unable to remake the school district until UTNO's members were, quite literally, washed away.

When Hurricane Katrina hit in 2005, educators scattered across the country, their schools were closed and their homes were destroyed. Policymakers took advantage of the absence of opposition to push through a top-down transforma-tion of the school system, assuming control of the vast majority of schools in the system through the RSD. Reformers fired 7,500 educators and, with significant federal and grant funding, began to open schools as charters. By the 2019–20 school year, New Orleans became the first major US city to operate all its schools as privately run publicly funded charter schools. "Part of the post-Katrina era that happened was the intention by the economic and political leaders of New Orleans to destroy the teachers union, and it was done under the guise of the charter school movement," argues community activist Kalamu ya Salaam.[3]

After the storm, UTNO struggled to regain its footing. The union made some headway recruiting veteran teachers who returned to the city, but it then lost those members again as the RSD schools were phased out and replaced by charters. The school board declined to renew UTNO's contract in 2006, and the union has had only limited success in organizing charter schools. The local that was once the largest in the state, one of the political and social anchors of the local Black community and a powerful voice for working people in the region, now rents a small office in a church off Canal Street. Their largest meetings are for the retirees' chapter.

Post-Katrina privatizations did not only impact the schools; policymakers also privatized the disaster recovery efforts, the public housing projects, the public hospital, and the public transportation system. These reforms disproportionately harmed Black, poor, and working-class residents. For example, from 1999 to 2016, the white median income held steady while the median income for Black households fell by 14 percent. Black families in New Orleans today earn less than half of what white families earn.[4] Though this is not entirely attributable to the neoliberal reforms, the numbers speak to the failures of these reforms to improve outcomes for the city's Black residents. While the reforms were implemented alongside promises to significantly improve conditions for the Black poor, it is clear they have failed to deliver. "People who struggled before struggle more now," reflects teacher Patti Reynolds.[5] Political scientist Adolph Reed situates the educator dismissals and the gutting of UTNO at the center of this post-Katrina neoliberal policymaking: "The imbalance of power was exacerbated almost immediately after the city's devastation by the swift, peremptory and unilateral firing of 7,500 school employees, including 4,000 teachers, in Orleans Parish schools and the consequent debilitation of the local teachers union, the United Teachers of New Orleans (UTNO)/American Federation of Teachers, the main institutional force capable of mobilizing and sustaining opposition to marketization."[6] Union busting is central to neoliberal reform in education as well as in other sectors. This is both because unions are incompatible with the neoliberal agenda and because they can rally significant resistance. While unions, when they are working well, fight for collectivization and democracy, neoliberal reforms seek to divide and create profit. Despite UTNO's shifts in the years leading up to the storm, it remained a powerful force that fought for working-class people and Black residents in New Orleans and throughout Louisiana, and it was still capable of standing up to the legislature and the school board and winning.

UTNO's decline also resulted in the loss of Black educators from the school system. The district today, from teachers to administrators to charter management staff, is much whiter than it was before the storm. Though it may not have been policymakers' intention, the evisceration of UTNO and transformation of the school system was an explicitly anti-Black project. "The white community is satisfied," explains LaCour. "The majority of the whites in New Orleans don't have their kids in public school, but the ones that do for the most part, can get them into the better schools. So, it's working for them."[7] Jim Randels suggests that racial bias also influences how people view UTNO's legacy:

> There's a segment of the city that has and had a certain fear of Black
> folks developing more power and control. And I think almost all of white
> New Orleans had a fear of that, some more subconsciously and some
> more consciously. So I think UTNO was seen as a threat to white power
> in the city. . . . There are a lot of white folks who embraced it and said,
> "I want to support that." There are plenty of white folks who were also

like, "We should let democracy move forward." And there were probably a majority of white folks who in one form or another thought of it as a bad thing and some would justify it by saying, "Teachers are professionals, they don't need a union." They would cloak their racist biases in other language usually. But it's almost an exclusively racial divide in how UTNO is perceived.[8]

Post-Katrina critiques of the union that suggest it was corrupt, that its members did not care about the children they taught, or that UTNO primarily served to enforce arcane bureaucracy and protect bad teachers serve to justify the school transformations while denying the long civil rights history of the union and its central role in Black social life and politics. "What the teachers union provided was not just the economic stability of being a teacher, but they also had healthcare, and they were supportive of just about every major activity that was going on in the Black community," explains ya Salaam.[9]

UTNO's history offers lessons for organizers nationwide. The union demonstrates the deep connections between the civil rights movement and the labor movement and the power of uniting campaigns against racism with campaigns against economic exploitation. Its legacy shows the importance of working in collaboration with the larger community and expanding labor demands beyond the workplace to encompass larger social justice issues or the "common good." Above all, UTNO's history demonstrates the key role that union democracy plays in maintaining union energy, vibrancy, and power over time. UTNO prioritized strikes and disruption, but its members also had fun during their job actions, like when they baked a cake that read "Bury the Board" or released balloons at a school board meeting to emphasize how they felt board members were full of hot air. These activities inspired high member participation and kept the union relevant in the city, even as organized labor lost battle after battle statewide. In the end, it took a major hurricane, forced evacuations, and an alliance between well-funded national, state, and local pro-reform advocates to defeat the union. Despite UTNO's diminished state today, its legacy speaks to what is possible for workers in the Deep South and to the key role education organizing plays in bolstering progressive causes amid a politically conservative environment.

It is unclear what role UTNO will continue to play in the school system. Randels believes the union still works to promote teacher voice and encourage collaboration and democracy:

We have a role to play in a democracy of people who are in the workplace. . . . There's always a need for people with inside access to be able to feel confident and comfortable and secure in speaking out, particularly when it involves children and public education. . . . And we think educators can help administrators and board members make better decisions about education quality, about everything related to public education: curriculum, instruction, funding, everything. They can make better decisions if they do it in partnership with their workforce and with the families and students in the schools than if they do it in isolation. So our role is always to be to hold hands and be in partnership with the people who have power in this most precious public institution.[10]

Yet in a fragmented district in which the union must organize each campus separately and develop contracts tailored to each individual school, UTNO's ability to create meaningful partnerships and increase democracy and transparency is limited.

Though the New Orleans school transformation is complete, at least for now, the privatization of education continues in other major cities across the country. The UTNO story demands that reformers ask themselves—and also the educators, parents, students, and members of the community in which they work—are test scores and graduation rates the only metrics that matter when we evaluate education? Or, do we also care about democracy, active community participation, workers' rights, and a system that builds brighter futures for everyone involved in the educational project? Policymakers continue to present neoliberal solutions, such as privatization, increased data and testing, and school choice and competition as the only options to improve struggling districts, often using the New Orleans school reforms to justify their proposals. Yet as education scholar Jean Anyon argues, "We need to reconsider what counts as education policy. The elimination of economic, housing, and other public policies responsible for urban poverty and segregation must become companion goals of urban educational reform."[11] Unions across the education sector could potentially play a large role in setting a more holistic agenda for school reform, one that centers racial and economic justice beyond the classroom. UTNO, despite its flaws, provides one example of what is possible.

Background, Positionality, and Methodology

I got my first taste of the New Orleans charter system on a visit to the city in the spring of 2010. A friend was teaching at Pride College Prep charter school, and she invited me to spend a day with her and assist in her classroom. We arrived at the school around 7:00 a.m., just before the day started, and joined a circle of mostly white, young teachers by the entrance to Pride's portable classrooms, in the shadow of the unoccupied Gregory school that had flooded after Hurricane Katrina. The principal, Michael Richard, gave daily announcements and then asked for shout-outs for faculty and students who were "on the PATH" (Perseverance, Achievement, Teamwork, and Healthy Living). Teachers stood around awkwardly in silence, looking down, as their colleagues debated whether to contribute. Minutes passed until the group achieved their required three shout-outs, and the exercise ended with the collective daily chant: "Our Pride, Our Vision, Together We Are on a Mission!" By the time of my visit in 2010, UTNO had been officially without a contract for four years; they had never gained much traction in RSD–run charter schools like Pride. That meant that Richard could set the work hours and work routines—including mandatory daily team building—however he liked, without any union or district constraints.

Wendy Kopp, the founder of TFA, visited Pride around the same time that I did, and what she saw was progressive education reform: "As I toured Pride College Prep and Akili Academy with their respective principals, I realized that both of these hard-driving school leaders were drawn to the role because of the unprecedented 'room to maneuver' they'd been given.... I saw and met mission-driven teachers drawn into the New Orleans school system by the promise of autonomy to innovate and by the city's explicit appeal to those who want to prove to the country that a truly exceptional urban school district is in fact possible."[1]

Today, the New Orleans charter school district is a national model for figures like Kopp, who advocate for a radical transformation of urban public education. The educational philosophies of Kopp and Richard, a TFA-alum, lie at the heart of debates about what types of schools work best for working-class children of color—and for their communities. Yet what, I wondered, is working in those schools like for educators?

The RSD revoked Pride's charter in 2013, due to low performance, and the school closed that June.[2] The building was taken over by a new Charter Management Organization (CMO), Arise Academy, and is currently rated "F" by the state.[3] My experience visiting Pride, as well as during the two years I later spent working in various charter schools throughout the city as an arts educator (2013–15), led me to think more deeply about the school system that had existed before the storm, the one that Pride, and Arise, and the revolving door of young teachers and administrators had helped to erase. What was lost when the school system was dismantled? I also began to reflect on the role that teachers' unions play in improving salary and working conditions, in giving teachers voice in school policies and decision-making, and in increasing faculty retention to create more stable schools. Though I was automatically a member, I had taken the union for granted during the five years I had taught in New York City public schools. Perks such as a duty-free forty-minute lunch break, getting paid to cover classes during my prep periods, and a fixed start and end time to the day seemed like normal benefits for a professional job. Those benefits are also key to retaining older, more experienced teachers and teachers with children of their own, who need a regular schedule in order to arrange childcare and spend time with their families. Notably, in the 2012–13 school year, 91 percent of Pride's teachers had zero to one years of experience in the classroom.[4]

I began to wonder: What happened to the teachers who had worked in the school system before the storm, who knew the children and had experienced the destruction of the hurricane themselves? After the storm, when the school employees were all fired and new crops of young, alternatively certified teachers arrived to take their place, veteran educators were demonized by reformers. Two post-storm TFA members said they had been told the pre-Katrina schools were "completely dysfunctional" and that "teachers didn't care."[5] Narratives like these served to justify the district's mass terminations and its move toward employing a younger and whiter workforce, which was seen by reformers as more professional. "[Teachers] were being blamed before the storm, and even after the storm, they were being blamed," argues teacher Joe DeRose.[6] Those images of "nightmarish"[7] schools and dysfunctional teachers were perhaps in *Chicago Tribune* columnist Kristen McQueary's mind when she wrote, on the tenth anniversary of Hurricane Katrina, that she wished a similar disaster would strike Chicago: "That's what it took to hit the reset button in New Orleans. Chaos. Tragedy. Heartbreak. . . . An underperforming public school system saw a complete makeover. A new schools chief, Paul Vallas, designed a school system with the flexibility of an entrepreneur. No restrictive mandates from the city or the state. No demands from teacher unions to abide. Instead, he created the nation's first free-market education system. Hurricane Katrina gave a great American city a rebirth."[8] There has been much debate about the relative successes and failures of the new school system, but there have been far fewer careful studies of what was lost, both in terms of the educators and leaders who never returned and in terms of the conditions for creative and sustainable teaching that disappeared from many of New Orleans's schools along with the union's contract.

At first, I set out to study the role UTNO played immediately before and after Hurricane Katrina. However, the more I learned about the union, the more I realized the story had to start much earlier. Though the remaking of the school system and the dismissal of educators happened rather quickly following the storm, the battle over what education should look like started years prior. In truth, I could have started in 1937, when Black educators first chartered Local 527. However, to limit the scope of my project, I decided to begin when the local launched its collective bargaining campaign, in 1965, situating it as part of the wave of public sector organizing that took place throughout the 1960s and 1970s. The union defied stereotypes. It was a powerful Black-led and intentionally integrated union at a time when the AFT was mostly making headlines for its strikes against community control in Brooklyn, New York, and its militant strikes throughout the Midwest and Northeast that were widely perceived as prioritizing the interests of middle-class white teachers over Black and Latino students.[9] UTNO was a strong, influential union that held significant local and statewide clout in a conservative southern state for more than thirty years. And its complete evisceration after Hurricane Katrina—the dismissal of 7,500 mostly Black educators—is typically framed as collateral damage in the quest to improve education in the district.

To investigate the history of the union and the role it played in determining the contours of New Orleans's education landscape, I conducted fifty-one semistructured interviews and analyzed publicly available archival data as well as personal documents and photographs provided to me by interviewees. To find subjects, I first contacted current UTNO leaders and then, using a snowball method, asked them to refer me to others they recommended I speak with. Stakeholders included union leaders and staff, teachers, clerical workers, paraprofessionals, district employees, principals, and superintendents. These interviews were conducted in person between 2018 and 2020, and each interview lasted one to two hours. Following each interview, I took extensive notes and wrote a memo, transcribed the interview, coded it using the program Dedoose, and then analyzed common themes.[10] I am especially indebted to former UTNO presidents Jim Randels and Nat LaCour, who were generous with their time and expertise and who also made a special effort to connect me to other knowledgeable stakeholders.

Though I tried to make my sample of interviewees representational, I ended up with an overrepresentation of white people, men, teachers, and individuals who supported UTNO (see table A.1). I attribute these biases to various factors. First, white people and, to a lesser extent, men, tend to be less skeptical of the research process, especially in post-Katrina New Orleans, where residents have "research fatigue" and the stories of Black storm survivors have been regularly fetishized in the media.[11] Additionally, I always identified myself as a graduate student at Tulane when requesting an interview, and many educators were wary of Tulane, particularly because of the role that then-president Scott Cowen played in the post-Katrina school transformations.[12] White residents also tend to be more supportive of the school reforms than Black residents.[13] Further, my identity as a white woman likely made me less threatening to white respondents, who may have believed I would identify more with their perspective.

In terms of the overrepresentation of teachers: first, there were always significantly more teachers working in the system than paraprofessionals or clerical workers. Second, clerical workers as a group tended to be less loyal to the union because they worked closely with school administrators; in addition, there were generally only one or two assigned per school.[14] Third, paraprofessionals and clerical workers were working-class employees, most of whom were Black, and thus they faced significant barriers to returning to New Orleans after the storm. Teacher Billie Dolce returned to learn the paraprofessional she had worked closely with had perished in the flood waters.[15] When I asked community activist Beth Butler about Geraldine Bell, a paraprofessional who had been active in Louisiana ACORN, Butler told me, "She passed away at an untimely death at the age of 55."[16] Race and poverty all too often limit life expectancy and determine health outcomes,[17] and I struggled to find clerical workers and paraprofessionals to interview. One paraprofessional I called several times was never able to find a time to speak to me due to his schedule; he was working two jobs and caring for an elderly relative. Finally, my lack of access to paraprofessionals and clerical workers also speaks to a divide in the union. While most teachers were happy to suggest a list of other teachers whom I could interview and passed along their phone numbers, they rarely were still in contact with paraprofessionals or clerical workers, nor could they think of names of individuals I might search for. Though the union worked to create a united front across barriers of race and class, that does not appear to have resulted in large numbers of cross-class friendships that transcended the storm and UTNO's evisceration.

Table A.1. Interviewee demographics

	RACE			GENDER		UNION ORIENTATION	
	Black	White	Latino	Women	Men	Pro-union	Mixed/ anti-union*
Teachers	17	15	1	21	12	25	8
Paraprofessionals and clerical workers	4	0	0	4	0	4	0
Other stakeholders	2	12	0	5	9	10	4
Total	**23**	**27**	**1**	**30**	**21**	**39**	**12**

* "Mixed/anti-union" indicates that the individual was either explicitly anti-union, they joined the union and then later ended their membership, or they initially opposed the union and then changed their mind after the storm.

As my research question focused on the internal workings of the union as well as on its role in the larger school system, I sought out more supporters of the union than opponents. My primary contacts were former and current UTNO presidents, who pointed me toward educators who had leadership roles within the union or nuanced perspectives on union activity. Further, the educators I spoke with who did not join the union, the majority of whom were white, generally knew little about the union or its role in the system. Most educators who did not join made that decision because they did not see the benefit to themselves, not because they felt vehemently opposed to the union or the positions it took. I found these interviews less fruitful and, thus, did not pursue contacts who fell into this category. I reached out to several prominent individuals involved in the post-Katrina charterizations, but they declined to speak with me, perhaps because I explained the project as a history of UTNO. I did speak to two school district employees who very clearly articulated their opposition to UTNO and ways they believed UTNO limited educational success in the district, and in my work, I tried to weave in those perspectives regularly to highlight the diversity of perspectives on UTNO.

In addition to the fifty-one individuals I interviewed for this project, I supplemented the epilogue with five interviews I conducted as part of another project examining why teachers choose to organize unions in charter schools. These interviews were conducted in fall 2017 and spring 2018 under the direction of Dr. Huriya Jabbar at the University of Texas at Austin. Due to the stipulations of that project, all these interviews are anonymous and therefore are not included in my larger list of interviewees. These final five interviews helped me explore the difficulties of union organizing in the charter landscape. Reflecting the new educator demographics in New Orleans, the interviews were mostly with white teachers, who make up a majority of the mostly higher-performing schools where teachers have sought unionization.

In addition to the interviews, I conducted extensive archival research for this project. I reviewed the *Times Picayune* and the *Louisiana Weekly* to analyze the perspectives of both the white and Black press, respectively. Using a keyword search, I read and coded every article in the *Times Picayune* that mentioned UTNO, the LFT, or union leaders from 1965 to 2008. Because the *Louisiana Weekly* is not digitized, I went through that newspaper's archives on microfilm, focusing on dates when major union activity occurred. I cite the *Times Picayune* more often than the *Louisiana Weekly* because the articles were easier to search, it was published more frequently, and it provided more comprehensive reporting in the years leading up to and after the storm. This speaks to ongoing disparities in funding for Black-led journalism. In addition to the newspapers, I reviewed the UTNO and OPSB archives held at the University of New Orleans Earl K. Long Library, the AFT archives held at Wayne State University, and various New Orleans mayors' papers held at the Amistad Research Center and the New Orleans Public Library Special Collections. Finally, UTNO graciously made available to me their uncatalogued archives, held at a local storage unit, which I digitized and organized; they are now available for public access at the Earl K. Long Library.

Though charter advocates advertise their schools as data-driven and accountable, there is a clear issue with transparency in the district. As a favor to the union, I agreed to submit public records requests to check that the charter schools had implemented an educator pay raise passed by Governor Edwards in 2019. The union suspected that, due to secrecy around salaries, some charter networks may have just applied the pay raises to administrative costs or otherwise diverted them from educators. Because of the decentralized nature of the district, I had to send Freedom of Information Act (FOIA) requests to forty-six separate charter management organizations (CMOs). Some of these CMOs listed the custodian of records on their websites, as they are legally required to do, but others failed to list the custodian or gave the email address of the person responsible for providing student transcripts, who was unfamiliar with FOIA requests. I followed up by phone and responses slowly trickled in. Eventually, I reached out to the OPSB, and they encouraged schools who had still not submitted their documents to comply. One CMO administrator told me that the documents did not exist (I was asking for educator salaries for the prior and current school year). One school never sent anything. Another school CEO discussed with me (unprompted) how other schools were poaching her teachers, allegedly by offering higher salaries, and asked how much teachers at other top-tier schools were making. I passed along a document with teacher salaries, which this CEO did not know were public records. The whole process took over six months. Issues like this plague the school district and create barriers to information both for community members and for researchers. They also discourage public oversight and participation in school district affairs. An activist educator approached me after the #BlackLives-Matter protests in summer 2020 to ask for help finding information about how many police officers work in New Orleans charter schools. When I described the FOIA process, he gave up.

Though I made an effort to find sources that reflect the demographics of UTNO, in the end I am a white researcher, over-relying on white sources, telling a story about an integrated and Black union. I am sure that this has led to some errors; still, I hope that I did the story justice. I am especially indebted to Nat LaCour, who generously line-edited a draft of each chapter and helped me sharpen my analysis. As an example of his influence, in an earlier draft I described Victor Schiro, mayor of New Orleans from 1961 to 1970, as a "segregationist." In one of our phone conversations, Mr. LaCour explained to me that the Black community would not have referred to Schiro as a "segregationist," a term that was used for virulently racist individuals. Though Schiro did nothing to dismantle the segregationist status quo in the city, Mr. LaCour explained, he really was not that bad compared to some of his peers. I am humbled by the attention to detail and care that Mr. LaCour dedicated to the manuscript as well as by the insights he shared with me. I believe his work has made the piece significantly stronger overall, and I hope that former UTNO members, across races, will see their experiences reflected in the final text.

After finishing this project, I believe even more deeply in the importance of teacher unions in schools and the crucial task of nurturing and protecting Black educators. I do not believe that what I observed at Pride reflects a successful model as it does not foster teacher creativity, autonomy, or voice. Career teachers, especially teachers who come from the community in which they are teaching, are key to creating high-quality, stable schools in which children are educated holistically and lovingly. In the words of former UTNO president Jim Randels: "I think [the charter system] ends up providing a testing approach to education that most white folks in the city would not want their kids to attend or experience. Most people in the middle and professional class in the country don't want a test-driven education. But the perception of how do we make things better for poor, Black, young children in New Orleans—and I think sometimes with really good motives—ends up being not quite what's needed."[18] I hope that this project leads to deeper discussions of what constitutes quality education for children and how to build a larger educational landscape that supports communities, both in New Orleans and across the country.

NOTES

ABBREVIATIONS

LSA Louisiana State Archives, Baton Rouge, LA
LSC Louisiana and Special Collections, Earl K. Long Library,
     University of New Orleans, New Orleans, LA
WPR Walter P. Reuther Library, Archives of Labor and Urban
     Affairs, Wayne State University, Detroit, MI

INTRODUCTION

1. Paraprofessionals, clerical workers, social workers, educational diagnosticians, and administrators also lost their jobs in the layoffs. Garda, "Politics of Education Reform"; Buras, "Mass Termination."

2. Barrett and Harris, "Significant Changes."

3. Barrett and Harris, "Significant Changes."

4. Barrett, Strunk, and Lincove, "When Tenure Ends."

5. Steve Ritea, "Teachers Union Contract in Jeopardy—School Board Refuses 45-Day Extension," *Times Picayune*, June 15, 2006; Steve Ritea, "Teachers Union Left without Contract—School Board Lets Pact Expire, Era End," *Times Picayune*, July 1, 2006.

6. Hudson and Holmes, "Missing Teachers, Impaired Communities."

7. Erickson, *Making the Unequal Metropolis.*

8. US Department of Health, Education, and Welfare, *Displacement of Black Educators.*

9. Reardon and Owens, "60 Years after *Brown.*"

10. "NEA Hits Desegregation in All La. School Districts," *Louisiana Weekly*, April 11, 1970.

11. Middleton, "The Louisiana Education Association."

12. Allison Plyer and Lamar Gardere, "The New Orleans Prosperity Index: Tricentennial Edition." The Data Center, 2018, https://s3.amazonaws.com/gnocdc/reports/ProsperityIndex.pdf/.

13. Devore and Logsdon. *Crescent City Schools.*

14. Emile Lafourcade, "School Board Is Blamed in Statement by Selden," *Times Picayune*, November 14, 1970.

15. Grace Lomba (teacher), interview by the author, February 15, 2019.

16. Similarly, Lane Windham argues that scholars have misinterpreted the decline of private sector collective bargaining agreements in the 1970s to indicate workers' reduced interest in unionizing. Instead, she demonstrates that workers continued organizing at similar rates—they just became much less likely to win collective bargaining. Windham, *Knocking on Labor's Door.*

17. Hall, "The Long Civil Rights Movement."

18. Conway, "Beyond 1968."

19. Smith, "Mississippi's First Statewide Teachers' Strike"; Miller and Canak, "From 'Porkchoppers' to 'Lambchoppers.'"

20. Windham, *Knocking on Labor's Door.*

21. Kahlenberg, *Tough Liberal.*

22. Kahlenberg, *Tough Liberal*; Podair, *Strike That Changed New York.*

23. Deslippe, *Protesting Affirmative Action.*

24. Perlstein, *Justice, Justice.*

25. Shelton, *Teacher Strike!* One of the only examples of anti-racist, progressive teacher organizing held up before the 1990s is the Teachers Union in New York City, which was destroyed by the communist purges of the 1950s and supplanted by the less radical Teachers Guild, precursor to the United Federation of Teachers. See Taylor, *Reds at the Blackboard.*

26. Golin, *Newark Teacher Strikes*; Westbrook, *Fair and Forward Union.*

27. Korstad, *Civil Rights Unionism.* See also Hall, "The Long Civil Rights Movement"; Honey, *Southern Labor*; Jones, "Simple Truths of Democracy"; Kelley, *Hammer and Hoe*; Korstad and Lichtenstein, "Opportunities Found and Lost."

28. Korstad and Lichtenstein, "Opportunities Found and Lost."

29. Honey, *Going Down Jericho Road.*

30. Isaac and Christiansen, "How the Civil Rights Movement Revitalized"; Jones, *March on Washington.*

31. Johnston, *Success while Others Fail*; Moody, *US Labor.*

32. Michael Burke, "LA Teachers' Union Leader Says 2019 Strike Sparked Local and Statewide Change," *Ed Source*, January 17, 2020, https://edsource.org/2020/la-teachers-union-leader-says-2019-strike-sparked-local-and-statewide-change/622498; Uetricht, *Strike for America.*

33. McCartin, Sneiderman, and BP-Weeks, "Combustible Convergence"; Cory Turner, Clare Lombardo, and Erin Logan. "Teacher Walkouts: A State by State Guide," *NPR*, April 25, 2018, www.npr.org/sections/ed/2018/04/25/602859780/teacher-walkouts-a-state-by-state-guide. Andrew Van Dam, "Teacher Strikes Made 2018 the Biggest Year for Worker Protest in a Generation," *Washington Post*, February 14, 2019, www.washingtonpost.com/us-policy/2019/02/14/with-teachers-lead-more-workers-went-strike-than-any-year-since.

34. Ransby, *Ella Baker*; Polletta, *Freedom Is an Endless Meeting*; Charron, *Freedom's Teacher.*

35. Polletta, *Freedom Is an Endless Meeting*; Ransby, *Ella Baker.*

36. Gwendolyn Adams (teacher), interview by the author, June 13, 2019.

37. Mike Stone (teacher), interview by the author, May 30, 2019; Patti Reynolds (teacher), interview by the author, May 30, 2019; Connie Goodly (teacher and UTNO staffer), interview by the author, May 31, 2019; Joe DeRose (teacher and UTNO staffer), interview by the author, April 10, 2019; Katrena Ndang (teacher and UTNO staffer), interview by the author, June 18, 2019.

38. Shelton, *Teacher Strike*; Podair, *Strike That Changed New York*; Golin, *Newark Teacher Strikes.*

39. Clawson and Clawson, "What Has Happened to the US Labor Movement?"; Moody, *US Labor*.

40. McCartin, *Collision Course*; Moody, *US Labor*; MacLean, *Freedom Is Not Enough*.

41. Dixon and Martin, "Can the Labor Movement Succeed?"

42. Littice Bacon-Blood, "Education Debate—Pay Raise Will Come, Foster Tells Teachers—6,000 School Workers Rally at State Capitol," *Times Picayune*, May 1, 1997.

43. Brian Thevenot, "School Takeover Plan Makes Rounds," *Times Picayune*, April 6, 2003.

44. See, for example, A. Reed, *Stirrings in the Jug*; Hopkins and McCabe, "After It's Too Late."

45. Brian Thevenot, "Teachers Give F's to Amato and Board—250 Union Members Protest at Meeting," *Times Picayune*, March 1, 2005.

46. Stone interview; Reynolds interview; Goodly interview.

47. Kalamu ya Salaam (community activist), interview by the author, November 22, 2019; Hightower, "Campaign for a Living Wage."

48. Pattillo, *Black on the Block*; Connolly, *A World More Concrete*; Forman, *Locking up Our Own*.

49. Anonymous (teacher), interview by the author, August 29, 2019.

50. Pattillo, *Black Picket Fences*.

51. Shelton, *Teacher Strike*.

52. Iris Kelso, "LaCour on the School Tax Proposal," *Times Picayune*, August 10, 1986.

53. Leoance Williams (teacher), interview by the author, August 22, 2019.

54. See, for example, Lipman, *New Political Economy*; Slater, "Education as Recovery"; Saltman, "Neoliberalism and Corporate School Reform"; Todd-Breland, *A Political Education*; Watkins, *Assault on Public Education*; Au and Ferrare, "Sponsors of Policy."

55. Many Black parents have divested from public schools for good reason—because they have promoted racism and have a poor history of educating Black children. For a nuanced discussion of this, see Stulberg, *Race, Schools, and Hope*.

56. Friedman, *Capitalism and Freedom*, 87.

57. Melamed, *Represent and Destroy*.

58. Schneider and Berkshire, *Wolf at the Schoolhouse Door*, xv.

59. Lipman, *New Political Economy*.

60. Stern, *Race and Education in New Orleans*.

61. Lipman, *New Political Economy*.

62. Kahlenberg, *Tough Liberal*.

63. Schneider and Berkshire, *Wolf at the Schoolhouse Door*.

64. Ehrenfeucht and Nelson, "Young Professionals as Ambivalent Change Agents"; Buras, *Charter Schools, Race, and Urban Space*.

65. Rhonda Mckendall, "Test to Graduate Will Begin in 1989," *Times Picayune*, April 29, 1988; Kim Chatelain, "The Cost of Choice: How Louisiana's Voucher Program Steered Families into D and F Private Schools," *WWNO*, May 7, 2019, www.wwno.org/post/cost-choice-how-louisianas-voucher-program-steered-families-d-and-f-private-schools.

66. UTNO and LFT, "Charter Schools in Louisiana," ca. 2004, uncatalogued UTNO office documents.

67. Doug Myers. "Group Critical of Education Plan," *Baton Rouge Advocate*, December 15, 1994. Louisiana Federation of Teachers, Phil Kugler, email to Gene Didier and enclosed press clippings, December 27, 1994, AFT Southern Regional Office Records, box 7, folder 12, WPR.

68. Aesha Rasheed, "BESE Seizure of Schools Going to Vote—Dramatic Reform Needed to Step Academic Failings, Supporters Say," *Times Picayune*, September 21, 2003.

69. Fred Skelton, "Union Explains Problems with Takeover Plan," *Times Picayune*, April 19, 2003.

70. Skelton, "Union Explains"; Morel, *Takeover*.

71. Boyd, "The Politics of Privatization in American Education."

72. Woods, *Development Drowned and Reborn*; MacLean, "Southern Dominance in Borrowed Language," 22.

73. The AFT suspended New Orleans's white local in 1956 and then expelled them in 1958 for refusing to integrate. Parr, *A Will of Her Own*.

74. Piven and Cloward, *Poor People's Movements*.

75. Kahlenberg, *Tough Liberal*; Murphy, *Blackboard Unions*; Perrillo, *Uncivil Rights*.

76. Deslippe, *Protesting Affirmative Action*; Wilson *Truly Disadvantaged*.

77. Perrillo, *Uncivil Rights*; Bell, "*Brown v. Board*."

78. Shelton, *Teacher Strike*; Podair, *Strike That Changed New York*; Perlstein, *Justice*.

79. Sukarieh and Tannock, "American Federation of Teachers."

80. Though "participatory democracy" is similar to "rank-and-file unionism," I use the former term to denote the ways in which UTNO also opened up democratic potential for union members as well as for the broader community through its political work and interactions with the school board. "Participatory democracy" also emphasizes the way in which UTNO borrowed the strategy from the civil rights movement and the labor movement. Finally, I argue that one of the big losses of the post-Katrina charterization is the foreclosure of possibilities for democratic participation and oversight. The destruction of the union played a significant part in this loss.

81. "N.O. Teachers Threaten 'Work Stoppage,'" *Louisiana Weekly*, February 5, 1966; "Picket Lines of AFT Local to Be Honored, Rally Told," *Times Picayune*, February 10, 1966; "School Board Meeting Ends in Disruption," *Louisiana Weekly*, February 1, 1969; "Statement of Executive Board Local 527," May 29, 1968, United Teachers of New Orleans, Local 527 Collection (MSS 135), box no. 10, LSC.

82. Until Jim Randels became president in 2018, UTNO's presidents had been exclusively Black—with the exception of Eugene Didier, who was president from 1969 to 1971.

83. Adam Fairclough quoted in Rubio, *There's Always Work at the Post Office*, 4.

84. Taylor, "The Long History of Attacking Teachers' Unions."

85. Ya Salaam interview.

86. Ya Salaam interview.

87. Plyer and Gardere, "Prosperity Index," 49.

88. Tyler Bridges, "Public Officials Opt for Private Schools for Their Children," *Times Picayune*, March 26, 1989.

89. Logsdon and DeVore, *Crescent City*.

90. Moody, *US Labor*; Melamed, *Represent and Destroy*.

91. Jessop, "Hollowing Out the 'Nation-State.'"

92. Ritea, "Teachers Union Left."

93. Woods, *Development Drowned*.

94. Woods, *Development Arrested*, 2.

1. Local 527 would change its name to UTNO in 1972 after it merged with the NEA local, OEA.

2. Veronica B. Hill, interviewed by Al Kennedy, Harvey, LA, 1994. Videotape provided to the author by UTNO.

3. This was not unique to New Orleans. All the white locals in the South refused to integrate, and the AFT lost approximately 14 percent of its total membership. Dewing, "American Federation of Teachers"; Parr, *A Will of Her Own*.

4. "N.O. Teachers Will Back Strike, Say Union Officials," *Times Picayune*, March 9, 1966.

5. Parr, *A Will of Her Own*.

6. DeVore and Logsdon, *Crescent City Schools*.

7. DeVore and Logsdon, *Crescent City Schools*.

8. DeVore and Logsdon, *Crescent City Schools*. By 1970, the public schools were 69.6 percent Black, and by 1980 they were 85 percent Black.

9. "School Board Will Study 'Implications' of Request," *Times Picayune*, May 11, 1965.

10. Charles Cogen, "AFT Leads the Revolution in Education" (transcript of speech), November 24, 1965, Walter P. Reuther Library, http://reuther.wayne.edu/node/6911. Cogen's support for the New Orleans local does not indicate a radical stance on Black rights. Both Cogen (1964–68) and his successor, Dave Selden (1968–74), emerged from the Teachers Guild in New York City, the more moderate of the two large locals there. The more radical Teachers Union prioritized grassroots activism and coalitions with Black parents and community members, whereas Cogen critiqued Black families and blamed them for their children's educational struggles. However, both Cogen and Selden supported civil rights, including the 1963 March on Washington. Selden voiced more concern for Black teachers and community members than Al Shanker, who assumed the presidency of the AFT in 1974, though Selden was Shanker's mentor. See also Jonna Perrillo, *Uncivil Rights*; Kahlenberg, *Tough Liberal*; Selden, *Teacher Rebellion*; Taylor, *Reds at the Blackboard*.

11. Lyons, "American Federation of Teachers."

12. "Teacher Group Demands Vote," *Times Picayune*, December 12, 1965; Nat LaCour (teacher and UTNO president 1971–99), interview by the author, March 21, 2019.

13. Several newspaper articles around this time describe Local 527's membership as 80 percent Black. However, a white organizer sent by the AFT to work in New Orleans in 1971 told me that when he arrived "they had 1,493 members, six of whom were white." Fred Skelton (UTNO staffer and LFT president), interview by the author, March 28, 2019. See also "AFT Teachers Support Work Stoppage," 1966; "Picket Lines of AFT Local," 1966; "Two-Thirds of City's Teachers," 1966.

14. "N.O. Teachers Threaten 'Work Stoppage.'" *Louisiana Weekly*, February 5, 1966; "Picket Lines of AFT Local to Be Honored, Rally Told," *Times Picayune*, February 10, 1966.

15. Joe Darby, "LFT Plans Strike Unless Board Meets 5 Demands," *Times Picayune*, January 25, 1966.

16. "NAACP Supports Teachers Petition to School Board," *Louisiana Weekly*, February 5, 1966. Though the NAACP would later come out in support of Affirmative Action and ratios or quotas more broadly, at this time the organization saw quotas as "a sugar-coated form of segregation." Deslippe, *Protesting Affirmative Action*.

17. "Picket Lines of AFT Local to Be Honored, Rally Told," *Times Picayune*, February 10, 1966.

18. New Orleans would not have a Black superintendent until Everett Williams assumed the position in 1985.

19. Joe Darby, "Real Issue Not Racial—Dolce," *Times Picayune*, January 26, 1966.

20. Joe Darby, "LFT Plans Strike Unless Board Meets 5 Demands," *Times Picayune*, January 25, 1966.

21. Darby, "Real Issue Not Racial—Dolce."

22. "AFT Local 527 States Position on Sales Tax," *Louisiana Weekly*, February 12, 1966. "Teachers Local Conditions Aid," *Times Picayune*, February 5, 1966.

23. "Backing Given Orleans Board," *Times Picayune*, January 28, 1966; Urban, *Gender, Race, and the National Education Association*.

24. "Pierce Accuses Teacher Union," *Times Picayune*, February 15, 1966.

25. Joe Darby, "Real Issue Not Racial—Dolce."

26. "N.O. Teachers Threaten 'Work Stoppage'"; "Backing Given Orleans Board."

27. "AFT Rally Set for Thursday," *Louisiana Weekly*, March 5, 1966.

28. Associated Press, "Longtime La. Labor Leader Victor Bussie Dead at 92," September 4, 2011, www.dailycomet.com/news/20110904/longtime-la-labor-leader-victor-bussie -dead-at-92.

29. Diana Brown (teacher and librarian), interview by the author, August 27, 2019.

30. Michael Martin, "Violence, Vetoes and Votes," *64 Parishes*, 2020, https://64parishes .org/violence-vetoes-and-votes.

31. "AFT Teachers Support Work Stoppage," *Louisiana Weekly*, March 12, 1966.

32. "Conference of Executive Board Local 527," January 15, 1969, Louisiana State Federation of Teachers, United Teachers of New Orleans, Local 527 Collection (MSS 135), box 9, folder 2, LSC.

33. Joe Darby, "AFT Local to Stage School Strike Today," *Times Picayune*, March 11, 1966; "Teachers Vote to Back Strike," *Times Picayune*, March 4, 1966.

34. The only school where classes were disrupted was Samuel J. Green—the school where union president Veronica Hill taught. "Don't Use Aides in Strike—AFT," *Times Picayune*, March 13, 1966.

35. "Fruitless 'Strike,'" *Times Picayune*, March 12, 1966.

36. "Don't Use Aides in Strike—AFT."

37. Joe Darby, "Union Votes to Continue Orleans School Walkout," *Times Picayune*, March 14, 1966; Joe Darby, "Back to Classrooms, Union Tells Teachers," *Times Picayune*, March 16, 1966.

38. Hill, interviewed by Al Kennedy. Darby, "Union Votes to Continue"; Barbara Perry, "UTNO Mourns the Passing of Veronica Hill," March 31, 1999, AFT Secretary-Treasurer's Office Records, CLOSED, WPR.

39. Joe Darby, "Back to Classrooms, Union Tells Teachers."

40. Charles Cogen [telegram], March 17, 1966. Louisiana Federation of Teachers, AFT State Federations Records, box 8, folder 4, WPR.

41. Hill, interviewed by Al Kennedy.

42. "Cong. Conyers Praises Teachers Strike Effort," *Louisiana Weekly*, April 9, 1966; "Two-Thirds of City's Teachers Anti-Strike," *Times Picayune*, March 10, 1966.

43. Joe Darby, "AFT Strike Idles 507 N.O. Teachers," *Times Picayune*, March 12, 1966.

44. Susie Beard (paraprofessional), interview by the author, October 1, 2019.

45. Joe Darby, "Union Votes to Continue Orleans School Walkout," *Times Picayune*, March 14, 1966.

46. See also Shelton, *Teacher Strike!*

47. Clarence Doucet, "Part of Proposed Levy Earmarked for Salaries," *Times Picayune*, April 19, 1966; Local 527 [advertisement], *Times Picayune*, May 12, 1966.

48. "AFT Local 527 Elects Officers," *Louisiana Weekly*, May 28, 1966.

49. "State Labor Confab Urges End to Grant-in-Aid; Opposes Sales Tax," *Louisiana Weekly*, April 16, 1966.

50. DeVore and Logsdon, *Crescent City Schools*.

51. Cortez, "The Faculty Integration of New Orleans Public Schools"; DeVore and Logsdon, *Crescent City Schools*.

52. "Significant Recommendations by PAR," *Louisiana Weekly*, March 8, 1969.

53. Mack Spears [advertisement], *Times Picayune*, November 7, 1968.

54. "AFT Local Has No Endorsement," *Times Picayune*, November 19, 1968.

55. "Rittiner and Spears," *Times Picayune*, October 19, 1968.

56. "Parents Charge Principal with Bias at Wilson," *Louisiana Weekly*, May 18, 1968; "Irate Parents Charge Board with Brushoff," *Louisiana Weekly*, June 8, 1968.

57. "Pickets Hinted in Board Issue," *Times Picayune*, June 9, 1968; "Teacher Union Assails Board," *Times Picayune*, May 30, 1968.

58. "Parents Want Open Hearing on 'Issue,'" *Louisiana Weekly*, June 15, 1968.

59. "Statement of the Executive Board," May 29, 1968, Misc. (created), United Teachers of New Orleans, Local 527 Collection (MSS 135), box 10, LSC.

60. Germany, *New Orleans after the Promises*.

61. Fairclough, *Race and Democracy*.

62. Parr, *Will of Her Own*; V. Hill, "History of Teacher Salary Equalization," ca. 1967, Misc. (created), United Teachers of New Orleans, Local 527 Collection (MSS 135), box 10, LSC.

63. Buras, *Charter Schools*; Middleton, "The Louisiana Education Association."

64. Germany, *New Orleans after the Promises*.

65. Brenda Mitchell (teacher and UTNO president 1999–2008), interview by the author, September 3, 2019.

66. Rubio, *There's Always Work at the Post Office*.

67. Emile Lafourcade, "Principal Shift Voted by Board," *Times Picayune*, August 13, 1968.

68. Emile Lafourcade, "N.O. School Board Deals with Variety of Matters," *Times Picayune*, March 12, 1968; "Teachers Union Is Aiming at N.O.," *Times Picayune*, November 28, 1967.

69. Robert C. Smith to Veronica Hill, May 14, 1968, Correspondence OPSB (in-out), United Teachers of New Orleans, Local 527 Collection (MSS 135), box 4, LSC.

70. Carl J. Dolce, OPSB Propaganda to Teachers, March 22, 1968, United Teachers of New Orleans, Local 527 Collection (MSS 135), box 11, LSC.

71. "Union Is Rapped by NEA Official," *Times Picayune*, October 17, 1968.

72. Charles Cogen to Veronica Hill, March 20, 1968, Louisiana Correspondence, AFT Office of the President (1965–71) Records, box 17, folder 6, WPR.

73. Reggie Zeringue to George Darensbourg, December 2, 1968, AFT Organizing Department Records, box 68, folder 16, WPR; James E. Mundy to Veronica Hill, October 3, 1968, AFT Organizing Department Records, box 65, folder 7, WPR.

74. "Conference of Executive Board Local 527."

75. "Louisiana Locals," January 9, 1969, LA State Fed of Teachers, United Teachers of New Orleans, Local 527 Collection (MSS 135), box 9, folder 1, LSC.

76. By 1972, Fontaine had left the state organization and become president of the Jefferson Parish Federation of Teachers (JFT). "LFT Correspondence," 1969–71, AFT Organizing Department Records, box 68, folder 16, WPR.

77. "Arrest 54 at Fortier 'Confrontation,'" *Louisiana Weekly*, January 25, 1969; "School Board Meeting Ends in Disruption," *Louisiana Weekly*, February 1, 1969.

78. The NAACP backed the students' demands with the exception of their desire for a Black student union because they saw that demand as promoting segregation.

79. Veronica B. Hill, "Fortier 1969," January 29, 1969, United Teachers of New Orleans, Local 527 Collection (MSS 135), box 6, LSC.

80. "8 Students Suspended at Fortier," *Louisiana Weekly*, February 15, 1969.

81. "School Board Meeting Ends in Disruption," *Louisiana Weekly*, February 1, 1969.

82. Allan Katz, "Fortier Boycott Blamed on 'Outside Influence,'" *States-Item*, February 4, 1969.

83. Emile Lafourcade, "Board Member Doubts Effect of Teacher Strike," *Times Picayune*, March 25, 1969.

84. Lafourcade, "Board Member Doubts Effect."

85. Anderson, *Education of Blacks*. Litwack, *Trouble in Mind*. Perry, "Up from the Parched Earth."

86. Shelton, *Teacher Strike!*

87. Vincent Lee, "Teacher Strike Prospect Told," *Times Picayune*, March 27, 1969.

88. Emile Lafourcade, "Group Seeking Sanction of Collective Bargaining," *Times Picayune*, April 2, 1969.

89. "OEA Anti-CB & Anti-Strike Literature" [broadside], ca. 1969, United Teachers of New Orleans, Local 527 Collection (MSS 135), box 11, LSC.

90. "Is Union for Our School System?," *States-Item* (New Orleans, LA), March 1969; "OEA Anti-CB & Anti-Strike Literature" [broadside].

91. "Bargaining Concept Is OK'd by HRC," *Louisiana Weekly*, April 5, 1969; Emile Lafourcade, "29 Schools Closed; Strike Begins Today," *Times Picayune*, April 3, 1969; "Strike Nearing, Says AFT Aide," *Times Picayune*, March 29, 1969; "Teachers' Strike Erupts in Incident of Violence," *Times Picayune*, April 10, 1969.

92. "Black Council Calls for City-Wide Gen'l Strike," *Louisiana Weekly*, April 5, 1969.

93. Kalamu ya Salaam (community activist), interview by the author, November 22, 2019.

94. "Committee Finds 'No Clear Overt Act of Bias' at Fortier School," *Louisiana Weekly*, April 5, 1969.

95. Gerald Glaser, "Strike's Delay Proposed Here," *Times Picayune*, March 30, 1969.

96. LaCour interview.

97. Lee, "Teacher Strike Prospect."

98. Emile Lafourcade, "Group Seeking Sanction of Collective Bargaining," *Times Picayune*, April 2, 1969.

99. "AFT Sets Teachers' Strike for Thursday," *Louisiana Weekly*, April 5, 1969.

100. "Teacher Strike Continues as Replacements Are Sought," *Louisiana Weekly*, April 12, 1969.

101. Lafourcade, "29 Schools Closed; Strike Begins Today."

102. Emile Lafourcade, "Striking Teachers May Be Replaced," *Times Picayune*, April 8, 1969.

103. Robert Pack, "Dolce, Teachers' Union Exchange Angry Blasts," *Times Picayune*, April 6, 1969.

104. Paul Atkinson, "Geisert to Beef Up Security Forces," *Times Picayune*, September 1, 1978.

105. The strike began on Thursday, April 3, one day before the Easter holiday (and the anniversary of Dr. King's assassination). The AFT often called strikes for the day before

a holiday in order to drum up support without teachers missing school and losing pay. Therefore, the second day on which teachers were out was Monday, April 7.

106. Lafourcade, "Striking Teachers May Be Replaced."

107. Emile Lafourcade, "Board to Seek New Teachers," *Times Picayune*, April 9, 1969.

108. "Schools Work Way to Normalcy," *Times Picayune*, April 9, 1969.

109. "What Happens to the Children?," *Louisiana Weekly*, April 12, 1969.

110. Arend, *Showdown in Desire*.

111. "Teachers' Strike Erupts in Incident of Violence," *Times Picayune*, April 10, 1969.

112. "Teachers Point of View," *Louisiana Weekly*, April 12, 1969.

113. Emile Lafourcade, "Schools Fully Open by Wednesday—Dolce," *Times Picayune*, April 11, 1969.

114. "Strikers Fake Dolce Debate," *Times Picayune*, April 12, 1969.

115. 1969 Strike Video (1969), filmmaker unknown, provided to the author by the AFT.

116. "1,500 New Orleans Teachers go on Strike for Right to Vote," American Teacher 53 (May 1969), American Federation of Teachers Publications Collection, WPR.

117. "Board Offices Again Picketed," *Times Picayune*, April 14, 1969.

118. Emile Lafourcade, "Teacher Strike Number Drops," *Times Picayune*, April 15, 1969.

119. Rev. Davis was a civil rights leader in New Orleans who, in 1975, became the first Black person to sit on the city council after he was appointed to fill a vacancy. He then ran for that city council seat in 1976 and won.

120. Lafourcade, "Teacher Strike Number Drops."

121. "End of Walkout Announced by Federation of Teachers," *Times Picayune*, April 17, 1969.

122. "End of Walkout Announced."

123. Hasket Derby, "To: Mrs. Veronica B. Hill, President, Local 527, AFT, AFL-CIO, and Members of the Executive Board," *Louisiana Weekly*, May 17, 1969. Hasket Derby to Charles Miller, June 13, 1969, Agreement-LFT, United Teachers of New Orleans, Local 527 Collection (MSS 135), box 1, LSC.

124. Emile Lafourcade, "Public Schools Back at Work," *Times Picayune*, April 18, 1969.

125. Emile Lafourcade, "School Board Dismisses 14 Temporary Teachers," *Times Picayune*, April 29, 1969.

126. Mike Johnson (teacher), interview by the author, October 31, 2019.

127. Mitchell interview.

128. Connie Goodly (teacher and UTNO staffer), interview by the author, May 31, 2019.

129. Grace Lomba (teacher), interview by the author, February 15, 2019.

130. Lafourcade, "School Board Dismisses 14 Temporary Teachers."

131. "Board to Delay Teacher Hiring," *Times Picayune*, April 29, 1969.

132. Derby to Charles Miller.

133. "29 Teachers Lose Fight for Former Assignment," *Louisiana Weekly*, May 17, 1969.

134. Derby, "To: Mrs. Veronica B. Hill, President."

135. Veronica B. Hill [letter on dismissal of Hasket Derby], ca. 1969, Agreement-LFT, United Teachers of New Orleans, Local 527 Collection (MSS 135), box 5, LSC.

136. Emile Lafourcade, "Secretary Is Dismissed by Teacher Union Local," *Times Picayune*, June 5, 1969.

137. Hill was required to retire by a Louisiana law that mandated that teachers retire at 65 years old. She went on to become a vice president for the national AFT.

138. "Green School Lauds Teacher," *Times Picayune*, June 5, 1969. Lafourcade, "Secretary Is Dismissed."

139. "Didier Knocks School Board," *Times Picayune*, June 6, 1969.

140. Lafourcade, "School Board Dismisses 14 Temporary Teachers."

141. Edward Fontaine to Dave Selden, June 13, 1969, AFT Office of the President Records, series 1, box 1, folder 82, WPR.

142. Fontaine to Dave Selden.

143. A. P. Stoddard to Dave Selden, June 13, 1969, AFT Office of the President Records, series 1, box 1, folder 18, WPR.

144. Victor Bussie to Kenneth Miesen, June 12, 1969, AFT Office of the President Records, series 1, box 1, folder 82, WPR.

145. Veronica B. Hill (1969), Report of Vice President, Veronica Hill Papers, unprocessed, Amistad Research Center, Tulane University, New Orleans, LA.

146. Dave Selden, "LA AFL-CIO Correspondence," June 19, 1969, AFT Office of the President Records, series 1, box 1, folder 82, WPR.

147. Mitchell interview.

148. LaCour interview.

149. "Didier Knocks."

150. Louise Alford, "How AFT Won Collective Bargaining in New Orleans," 1984, AFT Southern Regional Office Records, box 2, folder 22, WPR.

151. "What Is the Lesson?," *Louisiana Weekly*, April 26, 1969.

152. "1,500 New Orleans Teachers go on Strike."

153. Lamar Smith, "The Plight of the Black Teacher in New Orleans," ca. 1969, United Teachers of New Orleans, Local 527 Collection (MSS 135), box 15, LSC.

154. Germany, *New Orleans after the Promises*.

155. Cortez, "The Faculty Integration of New Orleans Public Schools."

156. Emile Lafourcade, "Orleans Board Approves Faculty, Staff Mixing Plan," *Times Picayune*, March 3, 1970.

157. "527 Speaks," 1970, United Teachers of New Orleans, Local 527 Collection (MSS 135), box 6, LSC.

158. "527 Speaks."

159. Harold T. Porter, memorandum to Alton Cowan, March 19, 1970, Hiawatha Street Staff Deseg, United Teachers of New Orleans, Local 527 Collection (MSS 135), box 6, LSC.

160. "NEA Hits Desegregation in All La. School Districts," *Louisiana Weekly*, April 11, 1970.

161. "NEA Hits Desegregation in 2 Southern States; Cites Widespread Racial Bias," *Louisiana Weekly*, November 21, 1970.

162. "NEA Files Suit to Stop Phazing Out Teachers," Louisiana Weekly, March 27, 1971.

163. Emile Lafourcade, "School Board Is Blamed in Statement by Selden," *Times Picayune*, November 14, 1970.

164. Cortez, "The Faculty Integration."

165. "800 Teachers to Be Shifted," *Times Picayune*, July 26, 1972.

166. "Teacher Groups Differ on N.O. Faculty 'Mix,'" *Louisiana Weekly*, September 2, 1972.

167. Goodly interview.

168. Lomba interview.

169. Laverne Kappel (teacher), interview by the author, September 27, 2019.

170. Wilson Boveland (teacher and UTNO staffer), interview by the author, April 25, 2019.

171. Beard interview.

172. Skelton interview.

173. LaCour interview; Bruce Nolan, "Teacher Transfer Policy Causing Many Problems," *Times Picayune*, October 13, 1972.

174. "Teachers' Organizations to Vote on Merger Plan," *Times Picayune*, May 20, 1972.

175. "Teachers Overwhelmingly Ratify OEA-AFT Merger," *Louisiana Weekly*, June 10, 1972.

176. Urban, *Gender, Race, and the NEA.*

177. Emile Lafourcade, "N.O. Teachers Approve Merger," *Times Picayune*, June 6, 1972.

178. Ken Ducote (teacher and district employee), interview by the author, September 6, 2019.

179. Didier then moved to the AFT's Southern Regional Office.

180. "Teachers Overwhelmingly Ratify."

181. "OEA Anti-CB & Anti-Strike Literature" [broadside].

182. LaCour interview.

183. Mitchell interview.

184. LaCour interview.

185. Bob Crowley (OEA, UTNO, and LFT staffer), interview by the author, March 10, 2020.

186. Crowley interview.

187. Mauney, "Consciousness and Activism of Atlanta Teachers."

188. LaCour interview.

189. "Informational Report."

190. Ducote interview.

191. Kappel interview.

192. Mitchell interview.

193. Billie Dolce (teacher), interview by the author, August 29, 2019.

194. Williams interview.

195. Ducote interview.

196. Alton Cowan replaced Superintendent Dolce in May 1969, shortly after the unsuccessful strike. However, he resigned in June 1971.

197. "Dr. Spears for Superintendent," *Louisiana Weekly*, August 21, 1971; "Dr. Spears Is Top Choice for Superintendent's Job," *Louisiana Weekly*, August 21, 1971.

198. "Says Racism Guides School Superintendent Selection," *Louisiana Weekly*, September 18, 1971.

199. "Says Racism."

200. Emile Lafourcade, "Dr. Geisert Is Approved as School Superintendent," *Times Picayune*, September 28, 1971.

201. Geisert interview. Lafourcade, "Dr. Geisert Is Approved."

202. Lafourcade, "Dr. Geisert Is Approved."

203. Skelton interview.

204. Geisert, "Mr. Nobody."

205. Geisert interview.

206. Alford, "How AFT Won."

207. Ed Anderson, "6,000 Strike Port Anew as Nixon's Freeze Ends," *Times Picayune*, November 15, 1971; James Gillies, "Strike Freezes Trash Services," *Times Picayune*, January 21, 1969; J. Douglas Murphy, "Transit Strike Called against NOPSI Tuesday," *Times Picayune*, December 14, 1974.

208. Urban, *Gender, Race, and the NEA.*

209. Bob Crowley, "Milestones in LFT History," ca. 1994, AFT Southern Regional Office Records, box 7, folder 13, WPR.

210. Skelton interview.

211. Alford, "How AFT Won."

212. LaCour interview.

213. Alford, "How AFT Won"; Photograph. (ca. 1974), United Teachers of New Orleans, Local 527 Collection (MSS 135), box 13, LSC.

214. "Teachers' Strike Ahead?," *Times Picayune*, February 25, 1974.

215. Alford, "How AFT Won."

216. "Collective Bargaining Is Necessary," *Louisiana Weekly*, March 23, 1974.

217. Alford, "How AFT Won."

218. Goodly interview.

219. Newton Renfro, "Megal Doubts Teacher Tieup," *Times Picayune*, March 28, 1974.

220. Brent Manley, "A&P Rejects Union Bid for Lettuce Boycott Aid," *Times Picayune*, June 20, 1973.

221. Alford, "How AFT Won."

222. Skelton interview.

223. Alford, "How AFT Won"; Newton Renfro, "Teamsters Leader Gives Backing to N.O. Teachers," *Times Picayune*, April 3, 1974.

224. UTNO, "History of UTNO," ca. 1982, provided to the author by UTNO.

225. Alford, "How AFT Won."

226. Gene Geisert (OPSB superintendent 1971–80), interview by the author, June 14, 2019.

227. Newton Renfro, "Unionism among Teachers Issue Subject of Controversy," *Times Picayune*, January 20, 1974.

228. Geisert interview.

229. Renfro, "Unionism among Teachers."

230. "Teacher Groups Differ."

231. Newton Renfro, "UTNO to Seek Teacher Vote," *Times Picayune*, January 14, 1974.

232. Renfro, "Unionism among Teachers."

233. Renfro, "Unionism among Teachers."

234. Skelton interview.

235. Newton Renfro, "Safety Guards Leave Schools," *Times Picayune*, February 12, 1974.

236. Renfro, "Safety Guards Leave Schools."

237. DeVore and Logsdon. *Crescent City Schools.*

238. Golin, *Newark Teacher Strikes.* Podair, *Strike That Changed New York.*

239. Golin, *Newark Teacher Strikes.*

240. Shelton, *Teacher Strike.*

241. Crowley interview.

242. Newton Renfro, "Picketing Teachers Begin Collective Bargaining Try," *Times Picayune*, March 12, 1974; "Teachers Wage Fight for Recognition," *Louisiana Weekly*, March 16, 1974.

243. "Teachers Wage Fight."

244. Johnston, *Success while Others Fail.*

245. Newton Renfro, "4,000 Teachers Sign Call for Collective Bargaining," *Times Picayune*, March 26, 1974.

246. Alford, "How AFT Won."

247. "UTNO Petition Is Challenged," *Times Picayune*, April 6, 1974.

248. Skelton interview.

249. Alford, "How AFT Won."

250. Skelton interview.

251. Newton Renfro, "Guste Opinion: 'Bargaining OK,'" *Times Picayune*, April 10, 1974; Newton Renfro, "An Analysis: Will There Be a Teachers' Strike?," *Times Picayune*, April 14, 1974.

252. For context, today five states prohibit public employee collective bargaining altogether: Georgia, North Carolina, South Carolina, Texas, and Virginia. Winkler, Scull, and Zeehandelaar, "How Strong Are U.S. Teacher Unions?"

253. Anthony, "Public Employee Collective Bargaining in Louisiana."

254. Newton Renfro, "Election OK'd for Teachers," *Times Picayune*, April 16, 1974; "UTNO Request to Be Answered," *Times Picayune*, April 15, 1974.

255. Renfro, "Election OK'd for Teachers."

256. Not a single teacher, principal, or school board employee I spoke with had a single negative thing to say about LaCour. Teacher Mike Stone recalled that his principal's wife, a school board employee, once said to him, "The best spokesman for public education in New Orleans is Nat LaCour, the union guy, and I hate it."

257. "Board Concedes Union Vote," *Times Picayune*, April 17, 1974.

258. "Tribute to a Legend: Nat LaCour," June 18, 1999, AFT Organizing Department Records, box 107, folder 28, WPR.

259. "Tribute to a Legend"; Nat LaCour (teacher and UTNO president 1971–99), interview by the author, March 21, 2019.

260. LaCour interview.

261. Lomba interview.

262. Geisert interview.

263. Skelton interview.

264. Leoance Williams (teacher), interview by the author, October 22, 2019.

265. Several students at Southern held desegregation sit-ins at Baton Rouge lunch counters and department stores and then were expelled by the university administration. Governor Earl K. Long was unsympathetic to the protesters: "I don't think the colored people of this state have anything fundamentally to complain about," he told a reporter. "I would suggest those who are not satisfied—like the seven at the lunch counter—return to their native Africa." LaCour became involved in the student demonstrations that followed, protesting the expulsions, which became known as "The Cause." See also James M'Lean, "Sitdown Move Is Hit by Long," *Times Picayune*, March 29, 1960.

266. LaCour interview; Gwendolyn Adams (teacher), interview by the author, June 13, 2019.

267. Newton Renfro, "UTNO Scores a Coup on House Education Bill," *Times Picayune*, June 12, 1974; Newton Renfro, "Teacher Bill Apparently Beaten by Labor Forces," *Times Picayune*, July 5, 1974.

268. Newton Renfro, "Teachers' Election OK'd on Collective Bargaining," *Times Picayune*, September 24, 1974.

269. "Bargain Agent Vote Approved," *Times Picayune*, November 10, 1974; "Court Okays N.O. Teachers Election," *Times Picayune*, November 1, 1974; "Election Halt Sought by LTA," *Times Picayune*, October 23, 1974; Newton Renfro, "LTA Tries to Block Election," *Times Picayune*, October 9, 1974.

270. Thirty years later in the wake of Hurricane Katrina, the *Times Picayune* wholeheartedly supported the state takeover of the school system, a move that vastly reduced

OPSB's power and eliminated any real "voice of the people" in the Orleans school district. "Teachers' Bargaining Vote," *Times Picayune*, November 12, 1974.

Newton Renfro, "Teacher Unit Wins Election," *Times Picayune*, November 13, 1974.

272. Renfro, "Teacher Unit Wins Election."

273. Newton Renfro, "Teamsters to Represent N.O. School Custodians," *Times Picayune*, November 20, 1974; Newton Renfro, "Federation Given Right to Represent Custodians," *Times Picayune*, December 4, 1974; Newton Renfro, "Education Board Delays Vote Issue," *Times Picayune*, December 18, 1974; Newton Renfro, "Funding Okayed for CAB," *Times Picayune*, March 4, 1975.

274. LaCour interview.

275. "Victory in New Orleans Cheers Southern Teachers," *American Teacher* 59 (November 1974), American Federation of Teachers Publications Collection, WPR.

276. Conway, "Beyond 1968."

277. McHugh, "The Florida Experience in Public Employee Collective Bargaining"; Miller and Canak, "From 'Porkchoppers' to 'Lambchoppers.'"

278. Winkler, et al., *How Strong Are U.S. Teacher Unions?*; Steve Flowers, "The Day Paul Hubbert Took on George Wallace," *The Blount Countian*, July 15, 2015, www.blountcountian.com/articles/the-day-paul-hubbert-took-on-george-wallace/.

279. Smith, "Mississippi's First Statewide Teachers' Strike."

280. Windham, *Knocking on Labor's Door*.

CHAPTER 2

1. Susie Beard (paraprofessional), interview by the author, October 1, 2019.

2. Beard interview.

3. Korstad, *Civil Rights Unionism*; Honey, *Southern Labor*.

4. Hall, "The Long Civil Rights Movement," 1259.

5. Ransby, *Ella Baker*.

6. Polletta, *Freedom Is an Endless Meeting*.

7. McAlevey, *No Shortcuts*, 90.

8. Beard interview. Beard lived in the Desire Housing Development when the Black Panther Party had its showdown with the New Orleans Police Department in 1970. On that subject, she remembered, "They had a breakfast program for feeding the children who were low income and they were there a good while until the city didn't want them there anymore. It was a good program."

9. See Collins, *Black Feminist Thought*; Woods, *Development Arrested*.

10. Beard interview.

11. Connie Goodly (teacher and UTNO staffer), interview by the author, May 31, 2019.

12. DeVore and Logsdon, *Crescent City Schools*, 264.

13. Rogers, *Righteous Lives*.

14. US Census Bureau, *Profile of General Demographic Characteristics: Race and Hispanic Origin*, Decennial Census: 1950, 1960, 1970, 1980, 1990, 2000, 2010, https://data.census.gov/.

15. Fairclough, *Race and Democracy*.

16. DeVore and Logsdon, *Crescent City Schools*.

17. Jim Randels (teacher and UTNO president 2016–19), interview by the author, November 13, 2018.

18. Gene Geisert (OPSB superintendent 1971–80), interview by the author, June 14, 2019.

| *Notes to Chapter 2*

19. G. Geisert interview. Geisert also extensively recruited teachers from France, who would give a two-year commitment much like the Teach for America program requires today: "And then we got the idea of going to France because France has a law that when you graduate from French colleges, you have to serve two years of community service. So I talked to the French government. I said, 'Have them serve their two years with me,' and we'll basically fill our slots with white French teachers. And they did. They said yes. . . . They kept the ratio of white teachers to the minority teacher pretty close to 50/50."

20. "Study of Faculty and Staff Attitudes toward the New Orleans Public Schools," (Report by Louis, Bowles and Grace, Inc., 1973), Orleans Parish School Board (MSS 147), Geisert, box 2, folder 5, LSC.

21. The plaintiff in the case that allowed Black students to attend LSU law was Charles Hatfield, a Local 527 activist.

22. Kalamu ya Salaam (community activist), interview by the author, November 22, 2019; Hirsch, "Fade to Black."

23. Piliawsky and Stekler, "From Black Politics to Blacks in the Mainstream."

24. Perkins, "Failing the Race."

25. A. Reed, *Stirrings in the Jug*, 49.

26. Stanley Taylor (postal worker and NALC member), interview by the author, December 23, 2019. Wade Rathke (union organizer, ACORN), interview by the author, December 16, 2019.

27. Newton Renfro, "Teamsters to Represent N.O. School Custodians," *Times Picayune*, November 20, 1974; Newton Renfro, "Federation Given Right to Represent Custodians," *Times Picayune*, December 4, 1974.

28. Joseph McCartin, "A Wagner Act for Public Employees."

29. Renfro, "Teamsters to Represent."

30. Newton Renfro, "Education Board Delays Vote Issue," *Times Picayune*, December 18, 1974.

31. Jacqueline Johnson (paraprofessional), interview by the author, January 14, 2020.

32. Newton Renfro, "UTNO Scores Victory," *Times Picayune*, March 19, 1975.

33. "United Teachers of New Orleans Paraprofessional Contract," ca. 1977, uncatalogued UTNO office documents.

34. "UTNO Update," vol. 6, no. 4, October 5, 1977, uncatalogued UTNO office documents.

35. Nancy Weldon, "AFSCME Named Bargaining Agent by Orleans School Food Workers," *Times Picayune*, January 27, 1976.

36. Western and Rosenfeld, "Unions, Norms, and the Rise in U.S. Wage Inequality."

37. Jan Skelton (JFT president), interview by the author, November 4, 2019.

38. Newton Renfro, "Jeff Teachers to Drive for Bargaining Election," *Times Picayune*, December 5, 1974.

39. Editorial Board, "Public Unions Grow," *Times Picayune*, April 12, 1975.

40. Rathke, "Labor's Failure in the South."

41. Newton Renfro, "UTNO Pact Okay Predicted," *Times Picayune*, December 11, 1974.

42. Fred Skelton (UTNO staffer and LFT president), interview by the author, March 28, 2019.

43. Editorial Board, "Teachers' Contract Demands," *Times Picayune*, March 27, 1975.

44. Karen Walk Geisert (teacher), interview by the author, June 14, 2019.

45. Nancy Weldon, "Orleans Teachers Decide to Strike If No Contract," *Times Picayune*, May 15, 1975.

46. Dwight Ott, "Strike Vote Effect Argued," *Times Picayune*, May 16, 1975.

47. Editorial Board, "Teacher Strike Vote," *Times Picayune*, May 11, 1975.

48. See, for example, Rogers, *Righteous Lives*; Fairclough, *Race and Democracy*; Arend, *Showdown in Desire*.

49. F. Skelton interview.

50. Patti Reynolds (teacher), interview by the author, May 30, 2019.

51. ACORN worked on various community-driven campaigns, for example, around police violence, and also organized service workers into Local 100 in the 1980s. Local 100 later became an SEIU-affiliate. For more on ACORN, see Atlas, *Seeds of Change*.

52. Beth Butler (community activist), interview by the author, December 16, 2019.

53. Frank Fudesco (principal and OPSB negotiator), interview by the author, November 20, 2019.

54. Polletta and Gardner, "The Forms of Deliberative Communication."

55. Joe DeRose (teacher and UTNO staffer), interview by the author, April 10, 2019.

56. Mike Stone (teacher), interview by the author, May 30, 2019.

57. Jo Anna Russo (UTNO staffer), interview by the author, May 24, 2019.

58. Juanita Bailey (teacher and UTNO staffer), interview by the author, May 30, 2019.

59. Parker and Gruelle, *Democracy Is Power*, 15.

60. Merikaye Presley, "Talks Are Called 'Unsatisfactory,'" *Times Picayune*, June 14, 1975.

61. Nat LaCour (teacher and UTNO president 1971–99), interview by the author, March 21, 2019.

62. UTNO, "A View from the Classroom," *Times Picayune*, June 28, 1977; DeVore and Logsdon, *Crescent City Schools*, 271.

63. Brenda Mitchell (teacher and UTNO president 1999–2008), interview by the author, September 3, 2019.

64. G. Geisert interview.

65. Editorial Board, "School Budget Dilemma," *Times Picayune*, June 18, 1975.

66. Ed Anderson, "Lacour: Pay Hike Not Only Big Item," *Times Picayune*, June 19, 1975.

67. Ed Anderson, "Orleans School Budget OK'd," *Times Picayune*, June 19, 1975.

68. John Rousseau, "Local Teachers Gird for Strike," *Louisiana Weekly*, June 7, 1975.

69. "UTNO–School Board Fail to Agree; Need Mediator," *Louisiana Weekly*, June 28, 1975.

70. Nancy Weldon, "Teacher Bargaining Stalled, Strike Said 'Almost Certain,'" *Times Picayune*, August 9, 1975.

71. Earl Lawless, "Teacher Strike Almost a Certainty—Lacour," *Louisiana Weekly*, August 16, 1975; Bill Mongelluzzo, "Teachers, Board Negotiations Slow," *Times Picayune*, August 14, 1975.

72. Editorial Board, "Strike Talk Elicits Yawns," *Times Picayune*, August 18, 1975.

73. Editorial Board, "Schools on Perilous Course," *Times Picayune*, August 23, 1975.

74. Merikaye Presley, "Board, Teamsters Sign Contract," *Times Picayune*, August 16, 1975.

75. "Public Schools Will Open Wednesday, Geisert Says," *Louisiana Weekly*, August 23, 1975.

76. Millie Ball and Nancy Weldon, "Strike Now Hours Away," *Times Picayune*, August 24, 1975.

77. Newton Renfro, "Strike Was Prevented by Backroom Intrigue," *Times Picayune*, August 28, 1975.

78. Newton Renfro, "Teacher Strike Off; Board Meets Demands," *Times Picayune*, August 25, 1975.

79. Nancy Weldon, "Teachers Ratify Contract," *Times Picayune*, August 30, 1975.

80. "UTNO, School Bd. Reach Accord; Strike Is Averted," *Louisiana Weekly*, August 30, 1975.

81. Newton Renfro, "Pupils and the Community Can Still Have a Voice," *Times Picayune*, September 2, 1975.

82. F. Skelton interview.

83. "Parents Charge Principal with Bias at Wilson," *Louisiana Weekly*, May 18, 1968; "Arrest 54 at Fortier 'Confrontation,'" *Louisiana Weekly*, January 25, 1969; "School Board Meeting Ends in Disruption," *Louisiana Weekly*, February 1, 1969.

84. Nancy Weldon, "No School Pay Offer," *Times Picayune*, May 25, 1975.

85. Newton Renfro, "Veto Power over Experimental Programs Is Demanded," *Times Picayune*, March 25, 1975.

86. Faue, "Battle for the Classroom."

87. LaCour interview.

88. Nancy Weldon, "School Board Okays Teacher Pact," *Times Picayune*, September 4, 1975.

89. Forman, *Locking Up Our Own*. See also Meiners, *Right to Be Hostile*.

90. Maryrose Hughes, "Schools Undisciplined" [letter to the editor], *Times Picayune*, March 6, 1975.

91. "Study of Faculty and Staff Attitudes toward the New Orleans Public Schools."

92. Faue, "Battle for the Classroom."

93. Coming full circle, some of the leftist caucuses in major unions today have made eliminating zero tolerance policies—as well as addressing systemic racism more broadly—one of their bargaining priorities. They call this framework, "bargaining for the common good." See Faue, "Battle for the Classroom."

94. F. Skelton interview.

95. Clancy DuBos, "Teacher Pay Action Asked," *Times Picayune*, August 23, 1976.

96. Clancy DuBos, "Board, UTNO at Odds," *Times Picayune*, September 21, 1976.

97. Newton Renfro, "Teachers' Discipline No Better Than Pupils'," *Times Picayune*, September 26, 1976.

98. "UTNO Vows to Postpone Strike Vote," *Times Picayune*, September 23, 1976.

99. Clancy DuBos, "Orleans Public Schools Take a Step Forward," *Times Picayune*, January 30, 1977; Clancy DuBos, "Millage Election Asked," *Times Picayune*, March 8, 1977.

100. DuBos, "Millage Election Asked."

101. Clancy DuBos, "Orleans Teacher on Food Stamps," *Times Picayune*, May 15, 1977.

102. "A View from the Classroom: A Teacher Speaks to the People of New Orleans," *Times Picayune*, May 24, 1977.

103. "A View from the Classroom: A Teacher Talks about 'Accountability,'" *Times Picayune*, May 31, 1977.

104. "A View from the Classroom: Please . . . We Need Your Help!" *Times Picayune*, July 5, 1977.

105. Jay Wilkinson, "School Board Plans Hearings on Budget," *Times Picayune*, June 23, 1977.

106. Clancy DuBos, "Teachers Stage March," *Times Picayune*, August 11, 1977; Sandra Barbier, "Teachers Negotiate Past Strike Deadline," *Times Picayune*, August 22, 1977.

107. Editorial Board, "Peace in the Classrooms," *Times Picayune*, September 10, 1977.

108. "Ratification of Teacher Pact Seen," *Times Picayune*, August 23, 1977.

109. Frank Washington, "Survey Says Voters against Schools Aid with Tax Hike," *Times Picayune*, August 24, 1977.

110. Merger talks between the AFT and NEA have occurred periodically. Proponents argue that teachers would have more power if they were united under one union and wouldn't have to dedicate time and resources to competing with one another for members and resources. However, the two groups have never been able to reach an agreement. A national merger was last attempted in 1998. The AFT voted in favor, but the NEA turned down the proposal. When AFT Local 527 and the OEA (local) merged to form UTNO in 1972, it appeared that a merger was likely on a national level. By the late 1970s, that no longer seemed like a possibility, and UTNO members were saddled with paying dues to two separate nationals for little reason. Richard Cooper, "NEA Teachers Reject Merger with Old Rivals," *Los Angeles Times*, July 6, 1998; Therese Mitchell, "Substitute Teachers Get Pay Increase," *Times Picayune*, March 14, 1978; Therese Mitchell, "Orleans Teachers' Union Breaks with LAE, NEA," *Times Picayune*, April 27, 1978.

111. Gene Geisert, "A Lot Is Happening in Public Education," *Times Picayune*, August 21, 1977.

112. "Carter's Urban Policy Should Be Analyzed, Black Assembly Told," *Times Picayune*, April 2, 1978.

113. Therese Mitchell, "Schools Told to Use Funds Wisely," *Times Picayune*, April 4, 1978.

114. Editorial Board, "Get Teacher Talks Moving," *Times Picayune*, August 17, 1978.

115. F. Skelton interview.

116. Andrea Stahl, "N.O. School Negotiations 'Hopeless,'" *Times Picayune*, August 28, 1978.

117. G. Geisert interview.

118. G. Geisert interview.

119. Joyce Robinson, "Teachers' Strike Effort Has Failed, Geisert Says," *Times Picayune*, August 31, 1978.

120. Therese Mitchell, "Drivers to Join Teachers' Strike," *Times Picayune*, August 31, 1978.

121. Paul Atkinson, "Geisert to Beef Up Security Forces," *Times Picayune*, September 1, 1978.

122. K. W. Geisert interview.

123. Atkinson, "Geisert to Beef Up Security Forces."

124. Wilson Boveland (teacher and UTNO staffer), interview by the author, April 25, 2019.

125. Therese Mitchell, "Teachers Abused for Years—LaCour," *Times Picayune*, September 1, 1978.

126. Ken Ducote (teacher and district employee), interview by the author, September 6, 2019; "Worker Suspensions Protested to Geisert," *Times Picayune*, September 2, 1978.

127. Ducote interview.

128. "School Board UTNO Still without Solution," *Louisiana Weekly*, September 9, 1978.

129. Ed Anderson, "Parents Picket against 'Sitters,'" *Times Picayune*, September 2, 1978.

130. Joyce Robinson, "Petition May Be Circulated for School Board Recall," *Times Picayune*, September 6, 1978.

131. Boveland interview.

132. G. Geisert interview.

133. Goodly interview.

134. Diego Gonzalez-Grande (teacher), interview by the author, April 9, 2019.

135. Ed Anderson, "Student Coalition Calls for Walkouts, Picketing," *Times Picayune*, September 7, 1978.

136. Beard interview.

137. Mitchell interview.

138. Boveland interview.

139. Fudesco interview.

140. DeRose interview.

141. Frank D. Fudesco, "The Rationale of Nonstriking Teachers—A Modified Delphi Technique" (PhD diss., Vanderbilt University, 1981).

142. G. Geisert interview.

143. Alan Guma (principal), interview by the author, September 17, 2019.

144. Paul Atkinson and Ed Anderson, "Board Offer Lowered by $1.5 Million," *Times Picayune*, September 7, 1978.

145. "City Fund Offer Was Refused," *Times Picayune*, September 7, 1978.

146. "City Fund Offer Was Refused."

147. Ed Anderson and Paul Atkinson, "Negotiators Summoned for Weekend," *Times Picayune*, September 8, 1978.

148. "LaCour Sees No Quick End," *Times Picayune*, September 9, 1978.

149. "Parent-Student Coalition Pickets," *Times Picayune*, September 8, 1978.

150. Grace Lomba (teacher), interview by the author, February 15, 2019.

151. J. Johnson interview.

152. Butler interview.

153. Reynolds interview.

154. Lomba interview.

155. Lomba interview; Boveland interview.

156. Steve Cannizaro and Bill Mongelluzzo, "School Talks to Resume Today," *Times Picayune*, September 10, 1978.

157. Paul Atkinson, "The Turning Point That Broke Strike," *Times Picayune*, September 12, 1978.

158. Boveland interview.

159. Cindy Robinson (teacher and librarian), interview by the author, March 14, 2019.

160. Linda Pichon (paraprofessional), interview by the author, January 17, 2020.

161. F. Skelton interview.

162. Paul Atkinson and Ed Anderson, "Orleans Schools Back to Normal," *Times Picayune*, September 12, 1978.

163. Ava Roussell, "Strike Over, School Bd. Meets Demands," *Louisiana Weekly*, September 16, 1978.

164. G. Geisert interview.

165. William Reeves, "Anatomy of the Teachers' Strike," *Times Picayune*, September 21, 1978.

166. Dan Bennett, "Teachers to Start Union," *Times Picayune*, October 19, 1978. Atkinson, "The Turning Point."

167. Atkinson and Anderson, "Orleans Schools Back to Normal."

168. G. Geisert interview.

169. Joyce Robinson, "4 Schools to Close," *Times Picayune*, September 12, 1978.

170. Ava Roussell, "Board Votes to Close Schools," *Louisiana Weekly*, October 14, 1978.

171. Molly Moore, "School Budget Cuts Tentatively OK'd," *Times Picayune*, September 13, 1978.

172. Atkinson and Anderson, "Orleans Schools Back to Normal." Laverne Kappel (teacher), interview by the author, September 27, 2019.

173. Beard interview.

174. Dolce interview.

175. Ducote interview.

176. Beard interview.

177. Guma interview.

178. Reynolds interview.

179. Mitchell interview.

180. Molly Moore, "School Year Was One of Controversy," *Times Picayune*, January 28, 1979. Molly Moore and Kim Chatelain, "Geisert Voted Out by Orleans Board," *Times Picayune*, October 4, 1979.

181. G. Geisert interview.

182. "A Clerical Victory" [clerical campaign flyers], ca. 1981, Southern Regional Office, box 10, folder 14, WPR.

183. Donisia Wise (clerical worker), interview by the author, September 24, 2019.

184. Molly Moore, "Board Delays Decision on School Union Election," *Times Picayune*, February 24, 1981.

185. Laurie Hays, "School Union, Workers Protest Talks Deadlock," *Times Picayune*, March 23, 1982. Joan Treadway, "Teachers May Join if Secretaries Strike," *Times Picayune*, April 25, 1982.

186. "Clerks OK Contract with N.O. Schools," *Times Picayune*, September 25, 1982.

187. "Teachers End Strike without Bargaining," *Times Picayune*, March 31, 1979.

188. J. Skelton interview. Molly Moore, "Jeff Holds Firm on Teacher Offer," *Times Picayune*, September 4, 1979.

189. J. Skelton interview.

190. J. Skelton interview.

191. J. Skelton interview.

192. "Teachers Help Each Other at N.O. Center," *Times Picayune*, February 17, 1980.

193. Mitchell interview.

194. Mitchell interview.

195. LaCour interview.

196. Katrena Ndang (teacher and UTNO staffer), interview by the author, June 18, 2019.

197. Louise Mouton Johnson (art teacher), interview by the author, April 19, 2019.

198. Russo interview.

199. Diana Brown (teacher and librarian), interview by the author, August 27, 2019.

200. Russo interview.

201. "Ratification of Teacher Pact Seen," *Times Picayune*, August 23, 1977.

202. "State Funds to Aid Teacher Benefits," *Times Picayune*, January 22, 1980.

203. Sheila Grissett-Welsh, "Orleans Teacher Pay Linked to Tax Vote," *Times Picayune*, September 25, 1985.

204. LaCour interview.

205. Joel Behrman (teacher), interview by the author, March 8, 2019.

206. Mike Johnson (teacher), interview by the author, October 31, 2019.

207. "Tribute to a Legend: Nat LaCour," June 18, 1999. AFT Organizing Department Records, box 107, folder 28, WPR.

208. K. W. Geisert interview.

209. "UTNO's Public Trust," *Times Picayune*, May 7, 1976. "Teachers to Discuss Finances, Other Issues," *Times Picayune*, April 17, 1986.

1. Patti Reynolds (teacher), interview by the author, May 30, 2019.

2. Reynolds interview.

3. Mike Stone (teacher), interview by the author, May 30, 2019.

4. See Bonilla-Silva, *Racism without Racists*; Omi and Winant, *Racial Formation*.

5. Nat LaCour (teacher and UTNO president 1971–99), interview by the author, March 21, 2019.

6. Connie Goodly (teacher and UTNO staffer), interview by the author, May 31, 2019.

7. Brenner and Theodore, "Cities and the Geographies"; Friedman, *Capitalism and Freedom*; Harvey, *Brief History of Neoliberalism*.

8. Or, within the housing sector, reformers tear down large public housing projects and replace them with smaller, mixed-income developments. Arena, *Driven from New Orleans*; Hackworth, *Neoliberal City*; Pattillo, *Black on the Block*.

9. Lipman, *New Political Economy*.

10. MacLean, "Southern Dominance in Borrowed Language."

11. Dixon and Martin, "Can the Labor Movement Succeed without the Strike?"; McCartin, *Collision Course*.

12. Fones-Wolf, *Selling Free Enterprise*; Phillips-Fein, *Invisible Hands*; Windham, *Knocking on Labor's Door*.

13. Kahlenberg, *Tough Liberal*.

14. LaCour interview; Ott, D. "Public Schools—as Usual—Today," *Times Picayune*, August 27, 1975.

15. Editorial Board, "Teachers and Job Freedom," *Times Picayune*, May 31, 1976.

16. Nat LaCour to Al Shanker, 1992, President's Office: Shanker, box 17, folder 527, WPR.

17. McCartin, "A Wagner Act for Public Employees."

18. Nicholas Foster, "Jumpstarting a Stalled Economy: Business and Rhetoric in Louisiana's 1976 Right-to-Work Campaign" (master's thesis, Tulane University, 2017).

19. Foster, "Jumpstarting a Stalled Economy."

20. Therese Mitchell, "'Work Right' Law Rapped," *Times Picayune*, May 15, 1976.

21. Foster, "Jumpstarting a Stalled Economy."

22. Buras, *Charter Schools, Race, and Urban Space*; Saltman, "Neoliberalism and Corporate School Reform"; Slater, "Education as Recovery."

23. Melamed, *Represent and Destroy*.

24. Clancy DuBos, "N.O. Tenured Teachers to Be Evaluated," *Times Picayune*, August 21, 1976; Clancy DuBos, "Teachers Willing to 'Wait, See,'" *Times Picayune*, August 25, 1976.

25. Newton Renfro, "Sweet and Sticky Teacher Evaluations," *Times Picayune*, September 12, 1976.

26. Billie Dolce (teacher), interview by the author, August 29, 2019; Ken Ducote (teacher and district employee), interview by the author, September 6, 2019.

27. Shelton, *Teacher Strike!*

28. Molly Moore, "Teacher Evaluation Law Not Helping, Koppel Says," *Times Picayune*, October 22, 1978; Connie Goodly (teacher and UTNO staffer), interview by the author, May 31, 2019; Russo interview.

29. Shelton, *Teacher Strike!*

30. Moore, "Teacher Evaluation Law Not Helping."

31. Mitchell interview.

32. Molly Moore, "Nix's Proposal to Abolish Tenure Laws Is Blasted," *Times Picayune*, November 7, 1978.

33. "NTA Test Culturally Biased Declares LEA," *Louisiana Weekly*, January 7, 1978; "LAE Charges Nix with Professional Illiteracy," *Louisiana Weekly*, November 11, 1978.

34. David Crosby, "Legislator Defends Teachers," *Times Picayune*, April 29, 1979.

35. Molly Moore, "School System Has Few Answers for Bad Teachers," *Times Picayune*, April 6, 1981.

36. Rhonda McKendall, "New Standards Set for Teachers Taking NTE," *Times Picayune*, July 23, 1983.

37. Rhonda McKendall, "School Leaders Go to National Meet," *Times Picayune*, December 5, 1983.

38. Gregory Belanger, "Union Chief: Input Needed on Tests," *Times Picayune*, May 1, 1988.

39. Bob Crowley (OEA, UTNO, and LFT staffer), interview by the author, March 10, 2020.

40. Ed Anderson, "Teacher Evaluation Law Is Overturned," *Times Picayune*, February 9, 1991.

41. Jack Wardlaw, "Teacher Evaluations Will Stay—For Now," *Times Picayune*, February 28, 1991. Rhonda Nabonne, "90 percent of Teachers Make the Grade on State Test," *Times Picayune*, March 28, 1991. Lisa Frazier, "Teachers Declare War on Program," *Times Picayune*, May 7, 1991.

42. Crowley interview.

43. Nat LaCour, "Union Chief: Evaluation Plan Riddled with Flaws," *Times Picayune*, March 14, 1991. Lisa Frazier, "Teacher Evaluations Suspended," *Times Picayune*, June 25, 1991.

44. Ed Anderson, "Business Lobbyist Talks Tough on Teacher Testing," *Times Picayune*, March 19, 1991.

45. "Lawmakers Rip School Reforms" [editorial], *Times Picayune*, June 14, 1991.

46. Joe DeRose (teacher and UTNO staffer), interview by the author, April 10, 2019.

47. Rhonda Nabonne, "Leaders: Proposal to Dilute Spending," *Times Picayune*, October 19, 1991.

48. Rhonda Nabonne, "Agency Backs Three Tax Issues—School Board in N.O. Faulted," *Times Picayune*, April 18, 1998.

49. Rhonda McKendall, "Merit Pay Program for La.'s Teachers Is Supported by Nix," *Times Picayune*, June 30, 1983; Rhonda McKendall, "N.O. Teachers' Leader Faults Merit Pay Idea," *Times Picayune*, August 31, 1983.

50. Rhonda McKendall, "Don't Base Teachers' Salaries on Kids' Scores, Union Chief Says," *Times Picayune*, May 20, 1984.

51. Harvey, *Brief History of Neoliberalism*.

52. Kahlenberg, *Tough Liberal*.

53. Kahlenberg, *Tough Liberal*.

54. Ron Thibodeaux, "Pay: Green Pastures Lure Teachers," *Times Picayune*, October 29, 1985.

55. Anne Veigle, "School Reform a Threat to Blacks, Caucus Told," *Times Picayune*, November 16, 1986.

56. Cole, "The Black Educator: An Endangered Species."

57. Rhonda McKendall, "Learning Problems Next Project for Business Leaders," *Times Picayune*, May 25, 1983.

58. Kabacoff was later a member of the OPSB and is most famous for his post-Katrina work as a largescale real estate developer in the city.

59. Rhonda McKendall, "Civic Leaders Pound the Drum for Education," *Times Picayune*, August 24, 1983.

60. Rhonda McKendall, "N.O. Teachers' Leader Faults Merit Pay Idea," *Times Picayune*, August 31, 1983.

61. Rhonda McKendall, "School Board Salaries Make Biggest Jump," *Times Picayune*, September 14, 1983.

62. Rhonda McKendall, "Don't Base Teachers' Salaries on Kids' Scores, Union Chief Says," *Times Picayune*, May 20, 1984.

63. Rhonda McKendall, "Teacher Unions Propose Method to Pay for Raises," *Times Picayune*, June 7, 1984.

64. James Hodge, "School Debate Focuses on Fate of Tenure Plan," *Times Picayune*, September 18, 1984.

65. Rhonda McKendall, "Tougher Curriculum Plan Running into Resistance," *Times Picayune*, December 16, 1983.

66. Lovell Beaulieu and James Hodge, "Curriculum Is Toughened in Orleans," *Times Picayune*, February 14, 1984.

67. Rhonda McKendall, "Haste Hurting Education, Union Says," *Times Picayune*, April 24, 1984.

68. Rhonda McKendall, "Budget Cuts Too Deep, Lacour Says," *Times Picayune*, September 7, 1985.

69. Johnston, *Success while Others Fail*; McCartin, "Bargaining for the Common Good."

70. "UTNO Seeks Veto Override," *Times Picayune*, September 7, 1975; Clancy DuBos, "Carter Tells Concern for Schools," *Times Picayune*, July 8, 1977.

71. "A View from the Classroom—A Teacher Talks about Student Achievement," *Times Picayune*, June 14, 1977; "A View from the Classroom: Please . . . We Need Your Help!" *Times Picayune*, July 5, 1977.

72. Reagan cut the federal share of total education spending in half during his eight-year tenure, from 12 percent to 6 percent. Clabaugh, "The Educational Legacy of Ronald Reagan."

73. Leoance Williams (teacher), interview by the author, October 22, 2019.

74. Bill Scott (teacher), interview by the author, March 20, 2019.

75. Editorial Board, "UTNO and the Money Tree," *Times Picayune*, September 28, 1976.

76. Frank Fudesco (principal and OPSB negotiator), interview by the author, November 20, 2019.

77. Charles Hargroder, "Panel Defeats Bill Using Mineral Fund to Build Schools," *Times Picayune*, June 16, 1981.

78. Iris Kelso, "LaCour on the School Tax Proposal," *Times Picayune*, August 10, 1986.

79. Morel, *Takeover*.

80. Rhonda McKendall, "N.O. Teachers Undaunted by Jeff Tax Failures," *Times Picayune*, October 28, 1985.

81. Molly Moore, "School Budget Accepted," *Times Picayune*, November 27, 1979.

82. Rhonda McKendall, "Tax Rise Sought to Help Schools," *Times Picayune*, September 10, 1985; Rhonda McKendall, "N.O. Teachers Undaunted by Jeff Tax Failures," *Times Picayune*, October 28, 1985.

83. Rhonda McKendall, "Tax Boost Sought for Schools, Raises," *Times Picayune*, April 20, 1986.

84. McKendall, "Tax Boost Sought."

85. Ted Lewis, "Coaches Mobilizing to Rescue Programs," *Times Picayune*, June 28, 1986.

86. Rhonda McKendall, "Schools May Hire Companies for Many Jobs," *Times Picayune*, July 2, 1986.

87. McKendall, "Schools May Hire Companies."

88. McKendall, "Schools May Hire Companies."

89. Ted Lewis, "Public Schools Get Two-Week Extension on Football Insurance," *Times Picayune*, July 31, 1986; Jo Yeager, "Millage and Jobs" [letter to the editor], *Times Picayune*, July 29, 1986.

90. Iris Kelso, "LaCour on the School Tax Proposal," *Times Picayune*, August 10, 1986; Rhonda McKendall, "School Pay Plan Questioned," *Times Picayune*, September 19, 1986.

91. Kelso, "LaCour on the School Tax Proposal."

92. Campanella, *New Orleans: A Timeline of Economic History.*

93. Walt Philbin, "One-Third of Fire Stations to Close Sunday," *Times Picayune*, October 4, 1986; Rhonda McKendall, "School Board Cancels Its November Tax Election," *Times Picayune*, October 7, 1986.

94. MacLean, "Southern Dominance in Borrowed Language."

95. Brenda Mitchell (teacher and UTNO president 1999–2008), interview by the author, September 3, 2019.

96. Williams interview.

97. These connections were not without controversy. Some of the big Black political organizations in New Orleans (such as SOUL, COUP, BOLD, LIFE, and the Progressive Democrats) had made questionable alliances and were not always accountable to the working-class Black community. Political scientist Adolph Reed argues that organizations such as these focused on racial equity at the expense of a genuine redistributive agenda, thus acquiescing to neoliberal reforms as long as they included Black stakeholders. A. Reed, "The Post-1965 Trajectory of Race, Class, and Urban Politics." Perkins, "Failing the Race."

98. Violet Johnson (district employee), interview by the author, October 31, 2019.

99. Joel Behrman (teacher), interview by the author, March 8, 2019.

100. Grace Lomba (teacher), interview by the author, February 15, 2019.

101. DeRose interview.

102. Goodly interview.

103. Stanley Taylor (postal worker and NALC member), interview by the author, December 23, 2019.

104. Wade Rathke (union organizer, ACORN), interview by the author, December 16, 2019.

105. Rathke interview.

106. UTNO also had an outsized voice in the AFL-CIO because the AFT requires that members pay per capita dues for 100 percent of their members. Thus, not only did UTNO have the most members in the state but they paid for all of them, whereas other unions would not pay "on a fair count." For example, they might have 500 members but then only pay dues to the AFL-CIO on 100 of them to save money. Rathke recalls, "Because the building trades were half-assed, they'd pay for some, whatever. And that's part of why they had to deal with unions like ours and the AFT."

107. Rathke interview.

108. Williams interview.

109. LaCour interview.

110. Juanita Bailey (teacher and UTNO staffer), interview by the author, May 30, 2019.

111. Wanda Richard (teacher and UTNO president 2019–2022), interview by the author, November 25, 2019.

112. Lomba interview.

113. Beth Butler (community activist), interview by the author, December 16, 2019.

114. Williams interview.

115. Donisia Wise (clerical worker), interview by the author, September 24, 2019.

116. Jo Anna Russo (UTNO staffer), interview by the author, May 24, 2019.

117. Rathke interview.

118. LaCour interview. Leslie Williams, "3 Reformers Win School Board Seats," *Times Picayune*, November 4, 1992.

119. Laverne Kappel (teacher), interview by the author, September 27, 2019.

120. Bailey interview.

121. Richard interview.

122. Gwendolyn Adams (teacher), interview by the author, June 13, 2019.

123. Taylor interview.

124. LaCour interview.

125. LaCour interview.

126. Joy Van Buskirk (UTNO and LFT lobbyist), interview by the author, April 21, 2020.

127. Van Buskirk interview.

128. Van Buskirk interview.

129. LaCour interview.

130. Though the AFT had locals at 14 universities in Louisiana, none of these locals won collective bargaining.

131. Crowley interview.

132. Crowley interview.

133. LaCour interview.

134. Fred Skelton (UTNO staffer and LFT president), interview by the author, March 28, 2019.

135. Rhonda Nabonne, "Rally Might Close Schools in N.O.," *Times Picayune*, April 29, 1997.

136. Littice Bacon-Blood, "Education Debate—Pay Raise Will Come, Foster Tells Teachers—6,000 School Workers Rally at State Capitol," *Times Picayune*, May 1, 1997.

137. James Gill, "Teachers Rally, but Did They Sway Their Public?," *Times Picayune*, May 4, 1997.

138. Williams interview.

139. Larry Samuel (UTNO and LFT lawyer), interview by the author, May 14, 2019.

140. Skelton, F. interview.

141. Stone interview.

142. Goodly interview.

143. Nat LaCour, "Union Chief: Gill's Teacher Attack Unwarranted" [letter to the editor], *Times Picayune*, May 25, 1997.

144. Stone interview.

145. "Vote for Edwards," *UTNO Newsletter*, November 13, 1991, uncatalogued UTNO office documents.

146. Goodly interview.

147. LaCour interview.

148. LaCour interview.

149. Ed Anderson, "School Employees Ratify 3-Year Contracts," *Times Picayune*, December 12, 1987.

150. Rhonda McKendall, "N.O. Schools to Ask Voters for 19.4-mill Increase in Taxes," *Times Picayune*, February 9, 1988.

151. Lee Gary, "Gary Opposed to Millage Hike for School Board" [letter to the editor], *Times Picayune*, April 13, 1988; Rhonda McKendall, "Panel to Unify Taxing Bodies is Proposed by N.O. Assessor," *Times Picayune*, April 13, 1988; "Schools Build Our Future: VOTE April 16" [advertisement], *Times Picayune*, April 14, 1988.

152. Rhonda McKendall, "Schools Win 4 of 5 Tax Issues," *Times Picayune*, April 17, 1988.

153. Rhonda McKendall, "School Millage Backers Still Soaring from Win," *Times Picayune*, April 18, 1988. The 1954 property tax for the schools was not, in fact, a tax increase, but rather a constitutional amendment that transferred mills from the levee board to the school board. This measure was passed in the same election in which Louisiana enshrined school segregation in the state constitution in response to *Brown v. Board of Education*. See "Measures Added to Constitution," *Times Picayune*, December 11, 1954.

154. DeRose interview.

155. LaCour interview.

156. LaCour interview.

157. At this time, per the UTNO contract, the board covered 80 percent of educators' health care premiums and 50 percent of their premiums for dependents.

158. Rhonda McKendall, "Pay Raise Is Mandatory, Teachers' Leader Says," *Times Picayune*, April 30, 1990.

159. Tyler Bridges, "Union Pay, Clout Fall with LA. Economy," *Times Picayune*, September 4, 1989.

160. Scott interview.

161. Rhonda Nabonne, "N.O. Teachers Reject Strike, Start School—Board Is Given Raise Deadline," *Times Picayune*, September 5, 1990.

162. Rhonda Nabonne, "City School Staff among Top-Paid," *Times Picayune*, September 5, 1990.

163. Nabonne, "N.O. Teachers Reject Strike."

164. Rhonda Nabonne, "Teachers Ready to Bargain, Set to Strike," *Times Picayune*, September 13, 1990.

165. Rhonda Nabonne, "Strike Won't Shut Down Schools, Board Vows," *Times Picayune*, September 17, 1990.

166. DeRose interview.

167. Goodly interview.

168. Stone interview.

169. LaCour interview.

170. Nabonne, "Strike Won't Shut Down Schools."

171. Long, "Complicating the Narrative."

172. "Tribute to a Legend: Nat LaCour," June 18, 1999, AFT Organizing Department Records, box 107, folder 28, WPR.

173. Rhonda Nabonne, "Board Makes New Offer of 3 Percent Raise This Year," *Times Picayune*, October 6, 1990; Rhonda Nabonne, "Strike to Last to Bitter End, Teachers Vow," *Times Picayune*, September 18, 1990.

174. Phyllis Krzyzek, "School Board Insensitive to Teachers' Needs" [letter to the editor], *Times Picayune*, September 18, 1990; Ronald Parent, "Teachers Strike a Travesty" [letter to the editor], *Times Picayune*, October 6, 1990; Reynolds interview.

175. Ducote interview.

176. US Census Bureau, *Numbers of Families Below the Poverty Level and Poverty Rate*, Decennial Census: 1980, 1990, https://data.census.gov/.

177. Diego Gonzalez-Grande (teacher), interview by the author, April 9, 2019.

178. Williams interview.

179. Cindy Robinson (teacher and librarian), interview by the author, March 14, 2019.

180. Robinson interview.

181. Samantha Turner (teacher), interview by the author, April 18, 2019.

182. Mitchell interview.

183. F. Skelton interview.

184. Gonzalez-Grande interview.

185. Susie Beard (paraprofessional), interview by the author, October 1, 2019.

186. Louise Mouton Johnson (art teacher), interview by the author, April 19, 2019.

187. Mouton Johnson interview.

188. Marta Bivens (theater teacher), interview by the author, March 19, 2019.

189. Rhonda Nabonne, "Anger Hardens Resolve of N.O. Teachers on Strike—Pickets: It's More Than Pay," *Times Picayune*, September 20, 1990.

190. Gonzalez-Grande interview.

191. Beard interview.

192. Gonzalez-Grande interview.

193. Behrman interview.

194. Gonzalez-Grande interview.

195. V. Johnson interview.

196. Wise interview.

197. Wise interview.

198. Scott interview.

199. Alorea Gilyot (teacher), interview by the author, April 25, 2019.

200. Gonzalez-Grande interview.

201. Linda Pichon (paraprofessional), interview by the author, January 17, 2020.

202. Robinson interview.

203. Lomba interview.

204. Scott interview.

205. Katrena Ndang (teacher and UTNO staffer), interview by the author, June 18, 2019.

206. Rhonda Nabonne, "Teachers, Board May Talk Today," *Times Picayune*, September 22, 1990.

207. Jacqueline Johnson (paraprofessional), interview by the author, January 14, 2020.

208. Adams interview; DeRose interview; Ndang interview; Jim Randels (teacher and UTNO president 2016–19), interview by the author, November 13, 2018.

209. Williams interview.

210. Diana Brown (teacher and librarian), interview by the author, August 27, 2019.

211. Brown interview.

212. Beard interview.

213. Frank Fudesco (principal and OPSB negotiator), interview by the author, November 20, 2019.

214. Podair, *Strike That Changed New York*; Shelton, *Teacher Strike!*

215. Stone interview.

216. Adams interview.

217. Stone interview.

218. Fudesco interview.

219. Beard interview.

220. Ducote interview.

221. Rhonda Nabonne, "Talks at Standstill while School Board Debates Service Cuts," *Times Picayune*, September 27, 1990.

222. Fudesco interview.

223. Rhonda Nabonne, "Talks Resume; Board Has Stormy Session," *Times Picayune*, September 29, 1990.

224. James Hodge, "School Board Meeting Over in Two Minutes and $75,000," *Times Picayune*, October 2, 1990.

225. Christy Harrison, "Name-Calling Gets Louder on Picket Lines at Schools," *Times Picayune*, September 21, 1990; Mary Harrison, "Quit Passing the Buck" [letter to the editor], *Times Picayune*, November 18, 1990.

226. Stone interview.

227. Nabonne, "Board Makes New Offer of 3 Percent Raise This Year."

228. Rhonda Nabonne, "Union, Board Differ on Using Mediator," *Times Picayune*, October 4, 1990.

229. Ed Anderson, "Mediator Doherty Is 'Whip-Cracker,'" *Times Picayune*, September 10, 1978.

230. Nabonne, "Board Makes New Offer of 3 Percent Raise This Year."

231. Rhonda Nabonne, "Teachers Ready to Roll on Recall Drive," *Times Picayune*, October 3, 1990.

232. Rhonda Nabonne, "School's In as Teachers Accept Pact," *Times Picayune*, October 8, 1990.

233. Stone interview.

234. Nabonne. "School's In as Teachers Accept Pact."

235. Fudesco interview.

236. Stone interview.

237. Nabonne. "School's In as Teachers Accept Pact."

238. Rhonda Nabonne, "Teachers Union OKs Contract, Drops Recall," *Times Picayune*, October 19, 1990; Rhonda Nabonne, "School Strike, Mistrust Prod Parents into Action," *Times Picayune*, October 28, 1990.

239. Frank Donze, "Citizens Unveil Reform Ticket—Change Sought in School Board," *Times Picayune*, September 12, 1990.

240. Nabonne. "School's In as Teachers Accept Pact."

241. Stone interview.

242. Melamed, *Represent and Destroy*.

243. Manuel Roig-Franzia, "Recent Grads Fill in Holes—Teach in Places Others Wouldn't," *Times Picayune*, March 27, 1995.

244. Bivens interview.

245. It is unclear why McMain would have had TFA teachers placed there, since the magnet school would have had no trouble recruiting a highly qualified and certified teaching staff.

246. Reynolds interview.

247. Harris, *Charter School City*.

248. Rhonda Nabonne, "Classrooms, Paychecks Top Teachers' List—Union Will Bring Wish List to Legislature," *Times Picayune*, November 26, 1996.

249. Behrman interview.

250. Butler interview.

251. See, for example, Piven and Cloward, *Poor People's Movements*; A. Reed, *Stirrings in the Jug*. For counterexamples, see Lipset, Trow, and Coleman, *Union Democracy*; Voss and Sherman, "Breaking the Iron Law of Oligarchy."

CHAPTER 4

1. Jessop, "Hollowing Out the 'Nation-State.'"

2. Brenda Mitchell (teacher and UTNO president 1999–2008), interview by the author, September 3, 2019.

3. Mitchell interview.

4. Jo Anna Russo (UTNO staffer), interview by the author, May 24, 2019.

5. Nat LaCour (teacher and UTNO president 1971–99), interview by the author, March 21, 2019.

6. Bernard McGhee, "Teachers' Union Picks New President—LaCour Replaced After 27 Years as N.O. Chief," *Times Picayune*, May 29, 1999.

7. Fred Skelton (UTNO staffer and LFT president), interview by the author, March 28, 2019.

8. Crenshaw, "Mapping the Margins," 1241.

9. Mitchell interview.

10. Veronica Hill retired in 1969.

11. Mitchell interview.

12. Mitchell interview.

13. Larry Carter (teacher, UTNO president 2008–16, and LFT president 2016–present), interview by the author, December 8, 2019.

14. Joy Van Buskirk (UTNO and LFT lobbyist), interview by the author, April 21, 2020.

15. Mike Stone (teacher), interview by the author, May 30, 2019.

16. Wilson Boveland (teacher and UTNO staffer), interview by the author, April 25, 2019.

17. Boveland interview.

18. Joe DeRose (teacher and UTNO staffer), interview by the author, April 10, 2019.

19. Leoance Williams (teacher), interview by the author, October 22, 2019.

20. Williams interview.

21. Juanita Bailey (teacher and UTNO staffer), interview by the author, May 30, 2019.

22. Mitchell interview.

23. Wade Rathke (union organizer, ACORN), interview by the author, December 16, 2019.

24. Boveland interview.

25. Steve Ritea, "Teachers Union Loses Its Force in Storm's Wake—When State Took Over Schools, Collective Bargaining Diminished," *Times Picayune*, March 6, 2006.

26. Kahlenberg, *Tough Liberal*.

27. Kahlenberg, *Tough Liberal*, 352.

28. See, for example, Honey, *Southern Labor*; Korstad, *Civil Rights Unionism*; Moody, *US Labor*.

29. Jim Randels (teacher and UTNO president 2016–19), interview by the author, November 13, 2018.

30. Mitchell interview.

31. Brenda Mitchell to Al Shanker, 1993, President's Office: Shanker, box 17, folder 527, WPR.

32. Mitchell interview.

33. Fraser and Brenner, "What Is Progressive Neoliberalism?"

34. Stein, *Pivotal Decade*; Fraser and Brenner, "What Is Progressive Neoliberalism?"

35. Fraser and Brenner, "What Is Progressive Neoliberalism?," 131.

36. Melamed, *Represent and Destroy.*

37. Hale, "The Making of the New Democrats"; Morgan, "Jimmy Carter, Bill Clinton, and the New Democratic Economics"; Atkins, "Forging a New Democratic Party."

38. Atkins, "Forging a New Democratic Party"; Hadderman, "Charter Schools"; Betts and Atkinson, "Better Research Needed."

39. See, for example, "Fight the Power" [editorial], *Times Picayune*, April 26, 2003; "Keep on Pushing" [editorial], *Times Picayune*, July 27, 2003; Brenda Mitchell, "Union Isn't Tied to Status Quo" [letter to the editor], *Times Picayune*, August 3, 2003; Beabout, "Stakeholder Organizations."

40. Piven and Cloward, *Poor People's Movements.* Others have argued that protest and mobilization are not incompatible with formal organization. See, for example, J. Jenkins, "Resource Mobilization Theory"; Minkoff, "From Service Provision to Institutional Advocacy."

41. Lipset, Trow, and Coleman, *Union Democracy*; Michels, *Political Parties*; Tolbert and Hiatt, "On Organizations and Oligarchies." Legal scholar Matthew Dimick argues that this is particularly the case in the United States due to the nature of US labor law. Dimick, "Revitalizing Union Democracy." To read a refutation of Michels' theory, see Diefenbach, "Why Michels' 'Iron Law of Oligarchy' Is Not an Iron Law."

42. Voss and Sherman, "Breaking the Iron Law of Oligarchy"; Windham, *Knocking on Labor's Door.* However, scholars, including Voss and Sherman, also argue that labor unions can reverse patterns of institutionalization and bureaucratization, primarily through engaging in democratic decision-making, organizing new members, welcoming fresh leadership, building coalitions with groups outside the workplace, and generally promoting "social movement unionism" that looks to organize workers beyond just the workplace. See Fantasia and Voss, *Hard Work*; Moody, *US Labor.*

43. See, for example, Pattillo, Delale-O'Connor, and Butts, "High-Stakes Choosing"; Saltman, "Neoliberalism and Corporate School Reform"; Cooper, "School Choice as 'Motherwork.'"

44. Anand Vaishnav, "State Ratings Herald Era of Reform," *Times Picayune*, September 24, 1999.

45. Anand Vaishnav, "Foster to Teachers: Focus on Literacy," *Times Picayune*, November 24, 1998.

46. "Putting BESE in Better Hands" [editorial], *Times Picayune*, January 1, 1996; Nat LaCour, "Don't Shut Union-Member Teachers Out of BESE" [letter to the editor], *Times Picayune*, January 22, 1996.

47. Jacobs and her brother, Stephen Rosenthal, ran the Rosenthal Agency, the largest private insurance agency in Louisiana, which they sold to Hibernia National Bank for more than $22.3 million. Brian Thevenot, "Jacobs Stirs up System and Dishes Out Results," *Times Picayune*, October 23, 2000.

48. Thevenot, "Jacobs Stirs Up System."

49. Thevenot, "Jacobs Stirs Up System."

50. Thevenot, "Jacobs Stirs Up System"; K. Coleman, "Panel Oks First Charter School in City," *Times Picayune*, June 4, 1998.

51. Anand Vaishnav, "3 More Charter Schools to Open," *Times Picayune*, August 2, 1999; Lynne Jensen, "Charter School to Offer Global Curricula," *Times Picayune*, June 18, 2000.

52. Buras, *Charter Schools, Race, and Urban Space*; Vergari, "Charter School Authorizers."

53. Schneider and Berkshire, *Wolf at the Schoolhouse Door*. Even charter schools that focus on social justice can uphold a framework of anti-Blackness, as Savannah Shange demonstrates in *Progressive Dystopia*.

54. Manuel Roig-Franzia, "Parents, Community Get Chance in Charter Schools," *Times Picayune*, August 2, 1995.

55. Van Buskirk interview.

56. Van Buskirk interview.

57. Van Buskirk interview.

58. Brian Thevenot, "UTNO Offers to Run 10 Schools—Charter District Could Try Out Reform Ideas," *Times Picayune*, June 23, 2001.

59. Brian Thevenot, "Paige Makes Charter-Schools Pitch," *Times Picayune*, May 2, 2001. Though New Orleans Charter Middle was officially not a magnet school, since it did not require particular test scores for admission, it did require that parents participate in a lottery and visit the school in order to enroll, thus self-selecting some of the more motivated families in the district.

60. Michelle Krupa, "4 Schools Reject Takeover by UNO," *Times Picayune*, June 5, 2002.

61. Kahlenberg, *Tough Liberal*; Mitchell interview; LaCour interview; Joel Behrman (teacher), interview by the author, March 8, 2019; Randels interview.

62. Bailey interview.

63. Russo interview.

64. Krupa, "4 Schools Reject Takeover by UNO."

65. Boveland interview.

66. Aesha Rasheed, "UNO Cancels School Takeover," *Times Picayune*, August 30, 2002.

67. "Keep on Pushing" [editorial], *Times Picayune*, July 27, 2003.

68. Bruce Alpert, "Voucher Plans Slow to Catch On Nationally," *Times Picayune*, August 23, 2003.

69. LaCour interview.

70. Russo interview.

71. Laura Maggi, "House Panel Oks Voucher Plan," *Times Picayune*, June 8, 2005.

72. Laura Maggi, "Political Landscape Tipping toward School Vouchers," *Times Picayune*, March 23, 2003.

73. Laura Maggi, "Foster Offers Voucher Plan with Mandatory Testing," *Times Picayune*, March 29, 2003.

74. Abdulkadiroglu, Pathak, and Walters, *School Vouchers and Student Achievement*.

75. Ken Ducote (teacher and district employee), interview by the author, September 6, 2019.

76. Ducote interview; James Gill, "Bond Proposal May Let School Board Avoid Bids," *Times Picayune*, April 21, 1989.

77. Ducote interview.

78. Brian Thevenot, "Pair Set to Plead Guilty to Bribe Scheme," *Times Picayune*, February 18, 2004; Brian Thevenot, "Schools Sweep Indicts 11 More," *Times Picayune*, December 17, 2004.

79. Brian Thevenot, "New Probe of N.O. Schools Is Launched," *Times Picayune*, April 20, 2004; Gordon Russell, "Ex-school Official Admits Bribes," *Times Picayune*, June 20, 2004.

80. Frank Fudesco (principal and OPSB negotiator), interview by the author, November 20, 2019.

81. Williams interview.

82. "Examples of Problems Affecting School Buildings," ca. 1992, UTNO Office Documents. Provided to the author by UTNO.

83. For example, students and parents sued Kennedy High's charter group for "gross mismanagement" after a series of grade-changing scandals as well as for graduating students who were ineligible for state diplomas. One year later, Kennedy's charter network, New Beginnings, voted to dissolve. Marta Jewson, "'Gross Mismanagement' at Kennedy HS Leads Lawyer to Expand Lawsuit to Include All Students," *The Lens*, August 29, 2019. Officials accused Sci Tech Charter of cheating on exams and overenrolling students in special education to make up their budget deficit. Similarly, the state accused Lagniappe Academies of telling students with special needs to enroll elsewhere, resulting in the school losing its charter and closing. Andrew Vanacore, "Officials Say New Orleans Charter School Tried to Cheat on Exams, Funding Formula," *Times Picayune*, January 31, 2016. Landry-Walker High fired several employees following a cheating scandal there. "Cheating Scandal Rocks Algiers High School," *WWL-TV*, February 16, 2016. In December 2019, a city investigation found that only 58 percent of buses used by charter schools had proper licensure; by February 2020, four schools had still not properly licensed their buses. Della Hasselle, "Four New Orleans Charter Schools Still Have Unlicensed Buses," *Times Picayune*, February 20, 2020. In 2016, the New Orleans NAACP called for a moratorium on charter schools due to ongoing issues around fraud, mismanagement, and lack of transparency. Bill Quigley, "Major Weaknesses of New Orleans Charter Schools Have Been Laid Bare," *Salon*, April 29, 2017.

84. Wanda Richard (teacher and UTNO president 2019–22), interview by the author, November 25, 2019.

85. Chris Gray, "Pay Glitches Frustrate School Workers," *Times Picayune*, December 18, 1999.

86. Brian Thevenot, "School Board Agrees to Payroll Changes," *Times Picayune*, January 23, 2001.

87. Karen Walk Geisert (teacher), interview by the author, June 14, 2019.

88. "Return to Sender" [editorial], *Times Picayune*, March 23, 2002.

89. Ducote interview; Mike Johnson (teacher), interview by the author, October 31, 2019.

90. Steve Ritea, "N.O. Schools Are Righting Financial Ship," *Times Picayune*, July 19, 2006.

91. Brian Thevenot, "School Paycheck Errors Rampant," *Times Picayune*, September 10, 2004.

92. Fudesco interview.

93. Carter interview.

94. Mitchell interview.

95. Beth Butler (community activist), interview by the author, December 16, 2019.

96. Anand Vaishnav, "Marine Will Command N.O. School System," *Times Picayune*, May 25, 1999.

97. Brian Thevenot, "'It's Time': Schools Chief Davis to Leave," *Times Picayune*, June 14, 2002; Lisa Fine, "State Probes La. District on Overtime," *Education Week*, June 12, 2002.

98. DeRose interview. Former mayor Ray Nagin was convicted of corruption in 2014 and sentenced to ten years in prison.

99. Brian Thevenot and Aesha Rasheed, "Nagin Offers to Help Schools," *Times Picayune*, February 5, 2004.

100. Thevenot and Rasheed, "Nagin Offers to Help Schools."

101. Krist, "Mayoral Control of Schools."

102. Diane Cardwell, "School Control Nears Reality for Bloomberg," *New York Times*, June 8, 2002.

103. Brian Thevenot, "Besieged Amato Calls It Quits," *Times Picayune*, April 13, 2005.

104. Bailey interview.

105. Cindy Robinson (teacher and librarian), interview by the author, March 14, 2019.

106. Luetta Stewart (teacher), interview by the author, March 15, 2019. After Katrina, the legislature ruled that only 15 of Orleans Parish's 117 schools were performing highly enough to exempt them from state takeover.

107. Laura Maggi, "Lawmakers Propose BESE Take Over Schools," *Times Picayune*, March 23, 2003.

108. Brian Thevenot, "School Takeover Plan Makes Rounds," *Times Picayune*, April 6, 2003.

109. Maggi, "Lawmakers Propose BESE Take Over Schools."

110. Thevenot, "School Takeover Plan Makes Rounds."

111. Laura Maggi, "House Committee Backs Bill on Taking Control of Schools," *Times Picayune*, April 17, 2003.

112. "Fight the Power" [editorial], *Times Picayune*, April 26, 2003.

113. Aesha Rasheed, "Panel Debates School Takeover Plan," *Times Picayune*, September 24, 2003; Aesha Rasheed, "School Takeover Backers Celebrate," *Times Picayune*, October 7, 2003.

114. US Census Bureau, *Profile of General Demographic Characteristics: Race and Hispanic Origin*, Decennial Census: 2000, https://data.census.gov/; Rasheed, "School Takeover Backers Celebrate."

115. Rasheed, "School Take Over Backers Celebrate."

116. Van Buskirk interview.

117. Williams interview.

118. Matthew Brown, "BESE Backs Capdau Takeover," *Times Picayune*, May 19, 2004.

119. Aesha Rasheed, "Transformed School Builds Parents' Hopes," *Times Picayune*, October 11, 2004.

120. Rasheed, "Transformed School Builds Parents' Hopes."

121. Joan Treadway, "UNO, SUNO, Three Nonprofits Submit Their Turnaround Plans," *Times Picayune*, February 21, 2005.

122. LaCour interview.

123. Aesha Rasheed, "Move May Be Afoot to Fire Amato," *Times Picayune*, June 4, 2004.

124. Brian Thevenot, "Details of State Takeover Cloudy," *Times Picayune*, June 6, 2004.

125. Laura Maggi and Aesha Rasheed, "School Board Bill Goes to Blanco," *Times Picayune*, June 10, 2004; Aesha Rasheed, "It's Back to Business for School Board, Amato," *Times Picayune*, June 13, 2004.

126. Morel, *Takeover*.

127. Morel, *Takeover*.

128. Morel, *Takeover*.

129. Coleman Warner and Susan Finch, "Feds Put Ball in State's Court," *Times Picayune*, February 17, 2005.

130. Lynne Jensen, "Amato Pledges to Meet Teacher Payroll," *Times Picayune*, April 7, 2005.

131. Brian Thevenot, "La. Asks N.O. School Board to Cede Reins," *Times Picayune*, April 8, 2005.

132. Brian Thevenot, "Besieged Amato Calls It Quits," *Times Picayune*, April 13, 2005; Mark Schleifstein, "Panel Backs Taking Over Schools," *Times Picayune*, April 21, 2005.

133. Brian Thevenot, "Schools Give Up Financial Reins," *Times Picayune*, May 24, 2005.

134. Thevenot, "Schools Give Up Financial Reins."

135. Stephanie Grace, "School Board Chief Makes Matters Worse," *Times Picayune*, June 2, 2005.

136. Sanders, *Coup d'État*.

137. Thevenot, "Schools Give Up Financial Reins."

138. Brian Thevenot, "School Finance Deal Alters Roles," *Times Picayune*, May 25, 2005.

139. Steve Ritea, "'This Is a Mess'—The Company Hired to Turn Around the Orleans Parish Public School District's Finances Discovers an Accounting System in Chaos," *Times Picayune*, July 24, 2005.

140. Ritea, "'This Is a Mess.'"

141. Williams interview.

142. Bill Scott (teacher), interview by the author, March 20, 2019.

143. Scott interview.

144. Richard interview.

145. Diana Brown (teacher and librarian), interview by the author, August 27, 2019.

146. Brown interview.

147. Mitchell interview.

148. Steve Ritea and Brian Thevenot, "School Board Facing Up to Layoffs," *Times Picayune*, August 10, 2005.

149. Ritea and Thevenot, "School Board Facing Up to Layoffs."

150. Carter interview.

151. Carter interview.

152. Brian Thevenot, "Audit Finds Profuse Payroll Abuse," *Times Picayune*, August 26, 2005.

153. Scott interview.

154. Hackworth, *Neoliberal City*; Coates, "The Case for Reparations"; Harvey, *Brief History of Neoliberalism*.

155. Raynard Sanders argues that this fiscal crisis was manufactured by state superintendent Cecil Picard and his allies to justify taking over the district. Sanders, *Coup d'État*.

156. Brenner and Theodore, "Cities and the Geographies of 'Actually Existing Neoliberalism.'"

157. See, for example, Moe, *Special Interest*; Hoxby, "How Teachers' Unions Affect Education Production"; Lindsey Burke and Corey DeAngelis, "Defund the Police? How About Defund Teachers Unions," *National Interest*, June 21, 2020.

158. Barrett and Harris, "Significant Changes."

159. Violet Johnson (district employee), interview by the author, October 31, 2019.

160. Ducote interview.

161. Larry Samuel (UTNO and LFT lawyer), interview by the author, May 14, 2019.

162. Samuel interview.

163. Fudesco interview.

164. Carter interview.

165. Bailey interview.

166. Boveland interview.

167. V. Johnson interview.

168. Alan Guma (principal), interview by the author, September 17, 2019.

169. Diego Gonzalez-Grande (teacher), interview by the author, April 9, 2019.

170. LaCour interview.

171. LaCour interview.

172. C. Robinson interview.

173. C. Robinson interview.

174. Ducote interview.

175. M. Johnson interview.

176. V. Johnson interview.

177. Ducote interview.

178. DeRose interview.

179. Mitchell interview.

180. "Teachers Union Chief Re-elected," *Times Picayune*, May 25, 2004.

181. Laverne Kappel (teacher), interview by the author, September 27, 2019.

182. Gonzalez-Grande interview.

183. C. Robinson interview.

184. Carter interview.

185. Billie Dolce (teacher), interview by the author, August 29, 2019.

186. Susie Beard (paraprofessional), interview by the author, October 1, 2019.

187. Linda Pichon (paraprofessional), interview by the author, January 17, 2020.

188. Behrman interview.

189. Kappel interview.

190. Stone interview.

191. Van Buskirk interview.

192. Voss and Sherman, "Breaking the Iron Law of Oligarchy."

193. Voss and Sherman, "Breaking the Iron Law of Oligarchy."

194. Uetricht, *Strike for America*; McAlevey, *No Shortcuts*.

195. Randels interview.

196. Mark Waller, "Test Scores Show Mixed Results," *Times Picayune*, May 13, 2005.

197. Gwendolyn Adams (teacher), interview by the author, June 13, 2019.

198. Shelly McAlister (teacher and ASL interpreter), interview by the author, September 9, 2019.

199. Samantha Turner (teacher), interview by the author, April 18, 2019.

CHAPTER 5

1. Newton Renfro, "Most Groups to Support 'Magnet' Prep School," *Times Picayune*, April 28, 1974.

2. Alan Guma (principal), interview by the author, September 17, 2019.

3. Maude Harris (teacher), interview by the author, February 22, 2019.

4. Luetta Stewart (teacher), interview by the author, March 15, 2019.

5. Marta Bivens (theater teacher), interview by the author, March 19, 2019.

6. Laverne Kappel (teacher), interview by the author, September 27, 2019.

7. Harris interview.

8. Melamed, *Represent and Destroy*.

9. Hacker and Pierson, *Winner-Take-All Politics*; Harvey, *Brief History of Neoliberalism*; Windham, *Knocking on Labor's Door*.

10. Bonilla-Silva, *Racism without Racists*.

11. MacLean, *Freedom Is Not Enough*.

12. Sondel, "Raising Citizens or Raising Test Scores?," 291.

13. See Buras, *Charter Schools, Race, and Urban Space*; Carr, *Hope against Hope*; Jabbar, "Drenched in the Past"; Sondel, "Raising Citizens or Raising Test Scores?"

14. Bullard and Wright. *Race, Place, and Environmental Justice.*

15. Billie Dolce (teacher), interview by the author, August 29, 2019.

16. Susie Beard (paraprofessional), interview by the author, October 1, 2019.

17. Leoance Williams (teacher), interview by the author, October 22, 2019.

18. Diana Brown (teacher and librarian), interview by the author, August 27, 2019.

19. Klein, *Shock Doctrine*; Saltman, "Neoliberalism and Corporate School Reform."

20. Linda Johnson, "BESE Annual Report 2005–2006," P-2008-029 BESE Board Annual Reports 2005–7, LSA.

21. Harvey, *Brief History of Neoliberalism.*

22. Arena, *Driven from New Orleans*; Berlin, "Historic Partnership"; Buras, "Race, Charter Schools, and Conscious Capitalism"; Glustrom, *Big Charity*; Gotham and Greenberg, *Crisis Cities*; Long, "Poverty Is the New Prostitution."

23. Frank Donze and Gordon Russell, "4 Months to Decide: Nagin Panel Says Hardest-Hit Areas Must Prove Viability," *Times Picayune*, January 11, 2006.

24. Adams, *Markets of Sorrow, Labors of Faith*, 7; Arena, *Driven from New Orleans*; Craemer, "Evaluating Racial Disparities"; P. D. Reed, "From the Freedmen's Bureau to FEMA."

25. Lori Rodriguez and Zeke Minaya, "New Orleans' Racial Makeup in the Air," *Houston Chronicle*, September 2, 2005.

26. Gary Rivlin, "Why New Orleans's Black Residents Are Still Underwater after Katrina," *New York Times*, August 18, 2015.

27. To read more critiques of teachers' unions, especially in charter schools, see Moe, *Special Interest*; Vergari, "The Politics of Charter Schools"; Strunk, "Are Teachers' Unions Really to Blame?"

28. Buras, "Mass Termination."

29. Larry Abramson, "For Charter Schools, New Orleans Is Citywide Lab," *Morning Edition*, NPR, October 3, 2006; Della Hasselle, "Now an All-Charter District, New Orleans Schools Experiment Still Faces Questions," *Times Picayune*, August 12, 2019; Emily Langhorne, "Following New Orleans's Lead on Charter School Education," *Washington Post*, July 1, 2018.

30. Steve Ritea, "Orleans Board Makes 13 Schools Charters," *Times Picayune*, October 8, 2005.

31. Steve Ritea, "School Board Politics Emerge Intact," *Times Picayune*, October 3, 2005.

32. Ritea, "School Board Politics Emerge Intact."

33. Laura Maggi and Steve Ritea, "State May Take Over 104 N.O. Schools," *Times Picayune*, November 4, 2005.

34. Laura Maggi, "Legislature Oks School Takeover," *Times Picayune*, November 15, 2005; Laura Maggi, "Orleans School State-Takeover Plan Advances," *Times Picayune*, November 18, 2005. See also Garda, "Politics of Education Reform."

35. Ritea, "Orleans Board Makes 13 Schools Charters."

36. BESE Minutes, November 9, 2005, P-2016-022 BESE/BOR Packets 2005–7, LSA.

37. Mark Waller, Lynne Jensen, and Rob Nelson, "$2.4 Billion Sought for Teacher Pay," *Times Picayune*, September 13, 2005.

38. Mike Stone (teacher), interview by the author, May 30, 2019.

39. Wanda Richard (teacher and UTNO president 2019–present), interview by the author, November 25, 2019.

40. Brian Thevenot, "Schools Give Up Financial Reins," *Times Picayune*, May 24, 2005.

41. Williams interview.

42. Wilson Boveland (teacher and UTNO staffer), interview by the author, April 25, 2019.

43. See also Jabbar, "Drenched in the Past."

44. Lipman, *New Political Economy*; Todd-Breland, *A Political Education*; Uetricht, *Strike for America*.

45. Jabbar et al., "Teacher Power"; Kate Zernike, "A Sea of Charter Schools in Detroit Leaves Students Adrift," *New York Times*, June 28, 2016.

46. Mikhail Zinshteyn, "Beyond Higher Pay and Smaller Class Sizes, Charter Debate Is Undercurrent of Teachers Strike in Los Angeles," *EdSource*, January 16, 2019; Alia Wong, "L.A.'s Teachers Got What They Wanted—For Their Students," *The Atlantic*, January 25, 2019.

47. Rebecca David and Kevin Hesla, "Estimated Public Charter School Enrollment, 2017–2018," *National Alliance for Public Charter Schools*, March 2018.

48. According to the National Association for Public Charter Schools, in 2018–19, there were 718 unionized charter schools in the country, representing 10.4 percent of all charter schools. Over half are bound by state law or district policy to participate in collective bargaining. National Association for Public Charter Schools, "Unionized Charter Schools: Data from 2018–2019," www.publiccharters.org/sites/default/files/documents/2018-02/Unionized%20Charter%20Schools%202016-17_0.pdf. See also, Jabbar et al, "Teacher Power"; Lavery and Jochim, "Why Charter Teachers Unionize."

49. For example, see Hill, Angel, and Christensen, "Charter School Achievement Studies"; Zimmer, et al., "Examining Charter Student Achievement Effects." Harris, *Charter School City*.

50. Burian-Fitzgerald, Luekens, and Strizek, "Less Red Tape or More Green Teachers"; Cannata and Penaloza, "Who Are Charter-School Teachers?"; Podgursky and Ballou, *Personnel Policy in Charter Schools*; Torres and Oluwole, "Teacher Satisfaction and Turnover in Charter Schools"; Torres, "Is This Work Sustainable?"

51. Barrett and Harris. "Significant Changes."

52. Buras, "Mass Termination"; Henry, "Discursive Violence."

53. For a detailed breakdown of these steps, see Garda, "Politics of Education Reform."

54. "A Painful Unfinished Journey: Chronology of an Educational Experiment," 2007, UTNO-LFT-AFT, AFT Secretary-Treasurer's Office, CLOSED, WPR.

55. BESE Board Minutes, October 20, 2005, P-2016-022 BESE/BOR Packets, 2005–6, LSA.

56. Steve Ritea, "N.O. School to Debut on Nov. 28," *Times Picayune*, November 19, 2005; Larry Samuel, Wilson Boveland, and David J. Strom, "Update on the New Orleans Situation and the State's Effort to Take Over and Restructure the New Orleans School System," 2006, AFT Secretary-Treasurer's Office—Chief of Staff, CLOSED, WPR.

57. Brenda Mitchell (teacher and UTNO president 1999–2008), interview by the author, September 3, 2019.

58. Williams interview.

59. Lomba interview.

60. Glustrom, *Big Charity*.

61. Buras, "Race, Charter Schools, and Conscious Capitalism."

62. Susan Finch, "Orleans Public Schools Plan Gradual Reopening," *Times Picayune*, September 15, 2005.

63. Susan Finch, "Some Orleans Schools to Open on West Bank," *Times Picayune*, September 17, 2005.

64. Juanita Bailey (teacher and UTNO staffer), interview by the author, May 30, 2019.

65. Ken Ducote (teacher and district employee), interview by the author, September 6, 2019.

66. Violet Johnson (district employee), interview by the author, October 31, 2019.

67. Bailey interview.

68. Williams interview.

69. Jo Anna Russo (UTNO staffer), interview by the author, May 24, 2019.

70. Russo interview.

71. Mitchell interview.

72. Larry Carter (teacher, UTNO president 2008–16, and LFT president 2016–present), interview by the author, December 8, 2019.

73. Beth Butler (community activist), interview by the author, December 16, 2019.

74. Butler interview. Nat LaCour (teacher and UTNO president 1971–99), interview by the author, February 3, 2020.

75. Harris, *Charter School City*, 61.

76. Beabout, "Stakeholder Organizations."

77. Gwendolyn Adams (teacher), interview by the author, June 13, 2019.

78. Chris Fusco, "The Watchdogs: How Chicago Teachers Union Spends Its Money," *Chicago Sun Times*, January 30, 2017.

79. Harris, *Charter School City*.

80. Harris, *Charter School City*, 54.

81. Harris interview.

82. Cowen and Seifter, *Inevitable City*, 10.

83. Walter Isaacson, "Foreword," in Cowen and Seifter, *Inevitable City*, xii.

84. Harris, *Charter School City*.

85. Samantha Turner (teacher), interview by the author, April 18, 2019.

86. Stewart interview.

87. Joy Van Buskirk (UTNO and LFT lobbyist), interview by the author, April 21, 2020.

88. Jacqueline Johnson (paraprofessional), interview by the author, January 14, 2020.

89. Mitchell interview.

90. Shelly McAlister (teacher and ASL interpreter), interview by the author, September 9, 2019.

91. Coleman Cowan, "A Turnaround Ace for New Orleans," *Business Week*, April 3, 2006.

92. Harris, *Charter School City*, 53. Though the New Orleans reforms have been touted as "innovative," at least half the schools in New Orleans today are cookie-cutter replicas of the "no excuses" model popularized by international charter management organizations such as KIPP.

93. Morel, *Takeover*.

94. Brian Thevenot, "Schools Give Up Financial Reins," *Times Picayune*, May 24, 2005.

95. James Gill, "Sorry to See UTNO Go? We Didn't Think So," *Times Picayune*, November 20, 2005.

96. Moe, *Politics of Institutional Reform*, 42.

97. Peter Cook, "Going Backwards: A Year in the Old New Orleans Public Schools," *Peter Cook* (blog), 2015, https://peterccook.com/2015/08/18/going-backwards.

98. Cowen and Seifter, *Inevitable City*. 19.

99. Buras, "Race, Charter Schools, and Conscious Capitalism," 297.

100. Steve Ritea, "Absent School Employees Face Ax," *Times Picayune*, December 1, 2005.

101. Bailey interview.

102. Prior to Katrina and in fall 2005, OPSB provided employees with health insurance through Coventry, an oft maligned insurance agency. In 2002, the board extended the contract "despite concerns over the company's shaky financial rating, an outside consultant's endorsement of another company and objections by the teachers union over rising premiums and poor service." In January 2006, Coventry dropped the OPSB, forcing them to move onto a self-insured plan, because the shift in demographics to so many retirees and so few active employees "scared away all major companies who were invited to insure the district." Brian Thevenot, "School Board Insures Its Own Workers," *Times Picayune*, January 13, 2006; Brian Thevenot, "School Panel Oks Old Health Insurer," *Times Picayune*, March 23, 2002.

103. See, for example, Lipman, *New Political Economy*; Saltman, "Neoliberalism and Corporate School Reform"; Todd-Breland, *Political Education*.

104. Scott interview.

105. Turner interview.

106. Adams interview.

107. Frank Fudesco (principal and OPSB negotiator), interview by the author, November 20, 2019.

108. Jim Randels (teacher and UTNO president 2016–19), interview by the author, November 13, 2018.

109. Williams interview.

110. Cindy Robinson (teacher and librarian), interview by the author, March 14, 2019.

111. Katrena Ndang (teacher and UTNO staffer), interview by the author, June 18, 2019.

112. Jennifer Tiller (librarian), interview by the author, March 7, 2019.

113. Louise Mouton Johnson (art teacher), interview by the author, April 19, 2019.

114. Boveland interview.

115. Steve Ritea, "School Health Coverage Revamped," *Times Picayune*, October 15, 2005.

116. Ndang interview.

117. Joe DeRose (teacher and UTNO staffer), interview by the author, April 10, 2019.

118. Thevenot, "School Board Insures Its Own Workers."

119. DeRose interview.

120. Donisia Wise (secretary), interview by the author, September 24, 2019.

121. Williams interview.

122. "Briefing Book—News and Views from the Louisiana Capitol," *Times Picayune*, June 18, 2010.

123. Joel Behrman (teacher), interview by the author, March 8, 2019.

124. DeRose interview.

125. Diana Brown (teacher and librarian), interview by the author, August 27, 2019.

126. Steve Ritea, "Teachers Union Loses Its Force in Storm's Wake," *Times Picayune*, March 6, 2006.

127. Fudesco interview.

128. Ritea, "Teachers Union Loses Its Force."

129. Buras, "Mass Termination"; BESE Minutes, April 20, 2006, P-2016-022 BESE/BOR Packets 2005–7, LSA.

130. Tiller interview.

131. Harris, *Charter School City*.

132. Buras, "Mass Termination."

133. Kretchmar, Sondel, and Ferrare, "Mapping the Terrain."

134. Kari Harden, "Group Forms in Protest of Teach for America," *Louisiana Weekly*, September 23, 2013.

135. Kretchmar, Sondel, and Ferrare, "Mapping the Terrain."

136. Terrenda White, "Teach for America's Paradoxical Diversity Initiative."

137. Williams interview.

138. Harden, "Group Forms in Protest of Teach for America."

139. Schneider and Berkshire, *Wolf at the Schoolhouse Door*.

140. Melamed, *Represent and Destroy*; Shange, *Progressive Dystopia*.

141. Adams interview.

142. Lomba interview.

143. Mitchell interview.

144. Piven and Cloward, *Poor People's Movements*.

145. "Report on UTNO/LFT/AFT Efforts in the Wake of Katrina," May 14, 2006, AFT Secretary-Treasurer's Office—Chief of Staff, CLOSED, WPR.

146. "Report on UTNO/LFT/AFT Efforts in the Wake of Katrina."

147. "Post-Katrina Lawsuits and Grievances Filed by UTNO," April 5, 2007, AFT Secretary-Treasurer's Office—Chief of Staff, CLOSED, WPR.

148. "Post-Katrina Lawsuits and Grievances Filed by UTNO"; *United Teachers of New Orleans v. State Bd. Of Elementary . . .*, 985 So.2d 184 (2008).

149. *Oliver v. Orleans Parish School Bd.*, 133 So.3d 38 (2014).

150. Ndang interview.

151. Dolce interview.

152. Laura Maggi, "Legislature Oks School Takeover," *Times Picayune*, November 15, 2005.

153. Harris interview.

154. "Report on UTNO/LFT/AFT Efforts in the Wake of Katrina."

155. Ed McElroy, "Where We Stand: It's Just the Beginning for New Orleans," *American Teacher* 90, no. 7 (May/June 2006), AFT Publications (B7), WPR.

156. "Draft AFT/UTNO Organizing Plan," February 26, 2007, AFT Secretary-Treasurer's Office—Chief of Staff, CLOSED, WPR.

157. Steve Ritea, "Teachers Union Contract in Jeopardy," *Times Picayune*, June 15, 2006.

158. Jewell Gould and Lynne Mingarelli, "Thoughts on Contract Negotiations," AFT Secretary-Treasurer's Office—Chief of Staff, CLOSED, WPR.

159. Ritea, "Teachers Union Contract in Jeopardy."

160. Ritea, "Teachers Union Contract in Jeopardy."

161. Steve Ritea, "Teachers Union Left without Contract," *Times Picayune*, July 1, 2006.

162. Ritea, "Teachers Union Left without Contract."

163. Harris, *Charter School City*.

164. Carter interview.

165. Carter interview.

166. "AFT Union Summer Program: Talking Points for Ed McElroy," ca. 2007, AFT Secretary-Treasurer's Office—Chief of Staff, CLOSED, WPR.

167. "We're Fighting for You!" *American Teacher* 91, no. 2 (October 2006), AFT Publications (B7), WPR.

168. Lomba interview.

169. Behrman interview.

170. Behrman interview.

171. Bailey interview.

172. Robinson interview.

173. Bailey interview.

174. Williams interview.

175. Bivens interview.

176. DeRose interview.

177. Mouton Johnson interview.

178. "Revised RSD Proposal in Brief," January 26, 2007, AFT Secretary-Treasurer's Office—Chief of Staff, CLOSED, WPR.

179. Kalamu ya Salaam (community activist), interview by the author, November 22, 2019.

180. Ndang interview.

181. Ndang interview.

182. Mitchell interview.

183. DeRose interview.

184. David Strom and D. McNeil, "Roadmap for UTNO Referral Service," May 9, 2006, AFT Secretary-Treasurer's Office—Chief of Staff, CLOSED, WPR.

185. Behrman interview.

186. Bailey interview.

187. Pattillo, *Black Picket Fences*.

188. Russo interview.

189. Buerger and Harris, "How Did the New Orleans School Reforms Influence School Spending?"

190. Schneider and Berkshire, *Wolf at the Schoolhouse Door*.

191. Dolce interview.

192. Barrett, et al., "When the Walls Come Down."

193. Sondel, "Raising Citizens or Raising Test Scores?"

194. Randels interview.

195. Randels interview.

196. Randels interview.

197. Klein, *Shock Doctrine*.

198. Friedman, *Capitalism and Freedom*.

199. *Moore v. Tangipahoa Parish Sch. Bd.*, 843 F.3d 198, 202 (5th Cir. 2016).

200. Brown interview.

201. Nat LaCour, "People's Rally to Rebuild Louisiana Right," October 29, 2005, AFT Secretary-Treasurer's Records, Part II, box 211, folder 4, WPR.

202. Mitchell interview.

203. Moody, *US Labor*; Hacker and Pierson, *Winner-Take-All Politics*.

204. McCartin, *Collision Course*.

205. Behrman interview.

206. Carter interview.

CONCLUSION

1. Katrena Ndang (teacher and UTNO staffer), interview by the author, June 18, 2019.

2. Danielle Dreilinger, "Miller-McCoy Academy Principal Leaves after One Year, Replaced by Interim," *Times Picayune*, September 9, 2014.

3. Danielle Dreilinger, "Miller-McCoy Academy to Close in the Summer," *Times Picayune*, December 18, 2014.

4. For a more comprehensive breakdown of these reforms, see Garda, "Politics of Education Reform; Jabbar, "'Drenched in the Past.'"

5. Danielle Dreilinger, "Should New Orleans Have Closed So Many Schools?," *Times Picayune*, October 17, 2016; "2020–2021 New Orleans Public Schools Governance Chart," *Cowen Institute*, www.coweninstitute.org/resources-H3B0W/governance-chart-19-20-86w87.

6. Harris, *Charter School City*.

7. Della Hasselle, "Nearly Half of New Orleans' All-Charter District Schools Got D or F Grades," *Times Picayune*, November 23, 2019.

8. Harris, *Charter School City*.

9. Harris, *Charter School City*.

10. Harris, *Charter School City*, 93.

11. Harris, *Charter School City*, 17.

12. Lindsay and Hart, "Teacher Race and School Discipline"; Ananat et al., "Children Left Behind."

13. Harvey, "The Right to the City."

14. Jabbar, "Selling Schools."

15. Lincove, Barrett, and Strunk, *Lessons from Hurricane Katrina*.

16. Barrett and Harris, "Significant Changes."

17. Joel Behrman (teacher), interview by the author, March 8, 2019.

18. Charter School Teacher 1, interview by the author, October 9, 2017.

19. Morel, *Takeover*.

20. Connie Goodly (teacher and UTNO staffer), interview by the author, March 21, 2019.

21. Windham, *Knocking on Labor's Door*; Clawson and Clawson, "What Has Happened to the US Labor Movement?"

22. Logan, "Consultants, Lawyers, and the 'Union Free' Movement"; Windham, *Knocking on Labor's Door*; Bronfenbrenner, "We'll Close!"

23. "Unfair Labor Practice Cases Involving United Teachers of New Orleans (Local 527)," Data from NxGen: Cases Filed from October 1, 2010, to June 1, 2018, Freedom of Information Act request to the National Labor Relations Board.

24. Charter School Teacher 1 interview.

25. Jabbar et al., "Teacher Power."

26. Bill Scott (teacher), interview by the author, March 20, 2019.

27. Behrman interview.

28. Behrman interview.

29. Alorea Gilyot (teacher), interview by the author, April 25, 2019.

30. Gilyot interview.

31. Katelyn Umholtz, "After Losing Charter, Mary D. Coghill School Gets New Operator for 2021–2022 School Year," *Times Picayune*, August 12, 2020.

32. Jabbar et al., "Teacher Power."

33. Grace Lomba (teacher), interview by the author, February 15, 2019.

34. Nat LaCour (teacher and UTNO President 1971–99), interview by the author, February 3, 2020.

35. Lomba interview.

36. Jabbar et al., "Teacher Power."

37. Juanita Bailey (teacher and UTNO staffer), interview by the author, May 30, 2019.

38. Ni, "Teacher Working Conditions in Charter Schools"; Roch and Sai, "Charter School Teacher Job Satisfaction"; Stuit and Smith, "Explaining the Gap in Charter and Traditional Public School"; Torres and Oluwole, "Teacher Satisfaction and Turnover"; Torres, "Is This Work Sustainable?"

39. Beabout and Gill, "Why Here and Why Now?"; Jabbar et al., "Teacher Power."

40. Jennifer Tiller (librarian), interview by the author, March 7, 2019.

41. Diego Gonzalez-Grande (teacher), interview by the author, April 9, 2019.

42. Gonzalez-Grande interview.

43. Weixler, Harris, and Barrett, "Teachers' Perspectives on the Learning and Work Environments."

44. Carter interview.

45. Behrman interview.

46. Lomba interview.

47. Cook and Dixson, "Writing Critical Race Theory and Method."

48. Kate Babuneau, Arpi Karapetyan, and Vincent Rossmeier, "What Do Parents Think? A Poll of New Orleans Public School Parents," *Cowen Institute*, October 2019, www.coweninstitute.org/resources-H3B0W/poll2019.

49. Lomba interview.

50. Joe DeRose (teacher and UTNO staffer), interview by the author, April 10, 2019.

51. Behrman interview.

52. Sarah Gamard, "Most Charter Boards Didn't Comply with or Know about Open-Meetings Law," *The Lens*, August 19, 2016.

53. Bailey interview.

54. Scott interview.

55. De la Torre and Gwynne, *When Schools Close*.

56. Alan Guma (principal), interview by the author, September 17, 2019.

57. Marta Jewson, "Five Years after Settlement in Citywide Special Education Suit, Some New Orleans Families Still Struggle for Services," *The Lens*, December 10, 2019.

58. Gene Geisert (OPSB superintendent 1971–80), interview by the author, June 14, 2019.

59. Billie Dolce (teacher), interview by the author, August 29, 2019.

60. Louise Mouton Johnson (art teacher), interview by the author, April 19, 2019.

61. Mallory Falk, "Charter School Group Accused of Violating Students' Civil Rights," *WWNO*, April 16, 2014.

62. LaCour interview, February 3, 2020.

63. Louisiana Department of Education, "Multiple Statistics by School System for Total Public Students," accessed March 1, 2021, www.louisianabelieves.com/resources/library /school-system-attributes.

64. Jacqueline Johnson (paraprofessional), interview by the author, January 14, 2020.

65. LaCour interview, February 3, 2020.

66. Jo Anna Russo (UTNO staffer), interview by the author, May 24, 2019.

67. Behrman interview.

68. Lincove and Valant, *New Orleans Students' Commute Times by Car*.

69. Wanda Richard (teacher and UTNO president 2019–present), interview by the author, November 25, 2019.

70. Connie Goodly (teacher and UTNO staffer), interview by the author, May 31, 2019.

71. Gwendolyn Adams (teacher), interview by the author, June 13, 2019.

72. Luetta Stewart (teacher), interview by the author, March 15, 2019.

73. "Early Childhood Program," *Audubon Charter School*, accessed March 1, 2021, www
.auduboncharter.org/pre-kla4application.aspx; "Lower School Admissions Process," *Lusher
Charter School*, accessed March 10, 2021, www.lusherschool.org/admissions/lower-school;
Della Hasselle, "New Hynes Charter School on UNO Campus to Reserve Some Seats for
University Employees," *Times Picayune*, February 19, 2019.

74. Richard interview.

75. Della Hasselle, "OneApp Results Are In—See the Hardest New Orleans Public
Schools to Get Into This Year," *Times Picayune*, April 25, 2019.

76. Behrman interview.

77. Buerger and Harris, "How Did the New Orleans School Reforms Influence School
Spending?"

78. Tiller interview.

79. Leoance Williams (teacher), interview by the author, October 22, 2019.

80. Bailey interview.

81. LaCour interview, February 3, 2020.

82. Della Hasselle, "New Study Outlines Why New Orleans Teachers Leave, and Provides
a Plan to Get Them to Stay," *Times Picayune*, October 26, 2019.

83. Bailey interview.

84. Barrett, Carlson, Harris, and Lincove, "Do Charter Schools Keep Their Best
Teachers?"

85. Carter interview.

86. Violet Johnson (district employee), interview by the author, October 31, 2019.

87. Joy Van Buskirk (UTNO and LFT lobbyist), interview by the author, April 21, 2020.

88. Van Buskirk interview.

89. Cindy Robinson (teacher and librarian), interview by the author, March 14, 2019.

EPILOGUE

1. Brenda Mitchell (teacher and UTNO president 1999–2008), interview by the author,
September 3, 2019.

2. Stern, *Race and Education in New Orleans*.

3. Kalamu ya Salaam (community activist), interview by the author, November 22, 2019.

4. Allison Plyer and Lamar Gardere, "Median Household Income by Race and Ethnicity,"
The New Orleans Prosperity Index: Tricentennial Edition, Data Center, April 11, 2018, www
.datacenterresearch.org/reports_analysis/prosperity-index/.

5. Patti Reynolds (teacher), interview by the author, May 30, 2019.

6. A. Reed, "The Post-1965 Trajectory of Race, Class, and Urban Politics," 268.

7. LaCour interview, February 3, 2020.

8. Jim Randels (teacher and UTNO president 2016–19), interview by the author, November 13, 2018.

9. Ya Salaam interview.

10. Randels interview.

11. Anyon, *Radical Possibilities*, 12.

1. Kopp, *A Chance to Make History*, 95.

2. Marta Jewson, "Pride College Prep Leaders Prepare to Release Control to New Hands," *The Lens*, December 13, 2012.

3. "Arise Academy: K-12 Report Card Grade," *Louisiana Department of Education*, accessed April 1, 2021, https://louisianaschools.com/schools/373001/academic-performance#overall _performance.

4. "Pride College Prep Academy Financial Statements: For the Year Ended June 30, 2013," 17, https://app.lla.state.la.us/PublicReports.nsf/164D23651548FF5886257C84004C65B8 /$FILE/00037C8C.pdf.

5. Tompkins, "There's No Such Thing as a Bad Teacher," 215.

6. Joe DeRose (teacher and UTNO staffer), interview by the author, April 10, 2019.

7. Tompkins, "There's No Such Thing as a Bad Teacher," 215.

8. Kristen McQueary, "Chicago, New Orleans, and Rebirth," *Chicago Tribune*, August 13, 2015.

9. Podair, *Strike That Changed New York*; Shelton, *Teacher Strike!*

10. Maxwell, *Qualitative Research Design*; Spradley, *Ethnographic Interview*.

11. See, for example, Robinson and Gruber, "Feasibility of Neighborhood Surveys in Post-Katrina New Orleans"; Ashley, "Accounting for Research Fatigue in Research Ethics."

12. Cowen and Seifter, *Inevitable City*.

13. Morel and Nuamah, "Who Governs?"

14. Donisia Wise (clerical worker), interview by the author, September 24, 2019.

15. Billie Dolce (teacher), interview by the author, August 29, 2019.

16. Beth Butler (community activist), interview by the author, December 16, 2019.

17. See Zonderman et al., "Race and Poverty Status as a Risk."

18. Jim Randels (teacher and UTNO president 2016–19), interview by the author, November 13, 2018.

BIBLIOGRAPHY

MANUSCRIPT AND ARCHIVAL COLLECTIONS

American Federation of Teachers Archives. Walter P. Reuther Library, Archives of Labor and Urban Affairs, Wayne State University, Detroit, MI.

Board of Elementary and Secondary Education (BESE). Papers. Louisiana State Archives, Baton Rouge.

Hill, Veronica Brown. Papers. Amistad Research Center, Tulane University, New Orleans, LA.

Morial, Marc. Papers. Amistad Research Center, Tulane University, New Orleans, LA.

Nagin, Ray. Papers. City Archives and Special Collections, New Orleans Public Library, LA.

Orleans Parish School Board Collection. Louisiana and Special Collections, Earl K. Long Library, University of New Orleans, LA.

United Teachers of New Orleans, Local 527 Collection. Louisiana and Special Collections, Earl K. Long Library, University of New Orleans, LA.

PERIODICALS

American Teacher	*The Lens*	*New Orleans Times Picayune*
Atlantic	*Louisiana Weekly*	*New York Times*
EdSource	*New Orleans States-Item*	

INTERVIEWS

Unless otherwise noted, all interviews were conducted in person by the author and were recorded. Entries followed by an asterisk are pseudonyms.

Gwendolyn Adams. Teacher. June 13, 2019.

Juanita Bailey. Teacher and UTNO staffer. May 30, 2019.

Susie Beard. Paraprofessional. October 1, 2019.

Joel Behrman. Teacher. March 8, 2019.*

Marta Bivens. Theater teacher. March 19, 2019.

Wilson Boveland. Teacher and UTNO staffer. April 25, 2019.

Diana Brown. Teacher and librarian. August 27, 2019.*

Beth Butler. Community activist, ACORN. December 16, 2019.

Larry Carter. Teacher and UTNO president (2008–16) and LFT president (2016–present). December 8, 2019.

Bob Crowley. OEA, UTNO, and LFT staffer. March 10, 2020.

Joe DeRose. Teacher and UTNO staffer. April 10, 2019.

Billie Dolce. Teacher. August 29, 2019.

Kenneth Ducote. Teacher and district employee. September 6, 2019.

Frank Fudesco. Principal and OPSB negotiator. November 20, 2019.

Gene Geisert. OPSB superintendent (1971–80). June 14, 2019.

Karen Walk Geisert. Teacher. June 14, 2019.

Alorea Gilyot. Teacher. April 25, 2019.

Diego Gonzalez-Grande. Teacher. April 9, 2019.

Connie Goodly. Teacher and UTNO staffer. May 31, 2019.

Alan Guma. Principal. September 17, 2019.

Maude Harris. Teacher. February 22, 2019.*

Jacqueline Johnson. Paraprofessional. January 14, 2020.

Louise Mouton Johnson. Art teacher. April 19, 2019.

Mike Johnson. Teacher. October 31, 2019.*

Violet Johnson. District employee. October 31, 2019.*

Laverne Kappel. Teacher. September 27, 2019.

Nat LaCour. Teacher and UTNO president (1971–98). March 21, 2019, and February 3, 2020.

Grace Lomba. Teacher. February 15, 2019.

Shelly McAlister. Teacher and American Sign Language interpreter. September 9, 2019.

Brenda Mitchell. Teacher and UTNO president (1999–2008). September 3, 2019.

Katrena Ndang. Teacher and UTNO staffer. June 18, 2019.

Linda Pichon. Paraprofessional. January 17, 2020.

Jim Randels. Teacher and UTNO president (2016–19). November 13, 2018.

Wade Rathke. Union organizer, ACORN. December 16, 2019.

Patti Reynolds. Teacher. May 30, 2019.

Wanda Richard. Teacher and UTNO president (2019–22). November 25, 2019.

Cindy Robinson. Teacher and librarian. March 14, 2019.*

Jo Anna Russo. UTNO staffer. May 24, 2019.

Kalamu ya Salaam. Community activist. November 22, 2019.

Larry Samuel. UTNO and LFT lawyer. May 14, 2019.

Bill Scott. Teacher. March 20, 2019.*

Fred Skelton. UTNO staffer and LFT president. March 28, 2019.

Jan Skelton. JFT president (1977–88). November 4, 2019 (phone interview).

Luetta Stewart. Teacher. March 15, 2019.

Mike Stone. Teacher. May 30, 2019.

Stanley Taylor. Postal worker and NALC member. December 23, 2019.

Jennifer Tiller. Librarian. March 7, 2019.*

Samantha Turner. Teacher. April 18, 2019.*

Joy Van Buskirk. UTNO and LFT lobbyist. April 21, 2020 (phone interview).

Leoance Williams. Teacher. October 22, 2019.

Donisia Wise. Clerical worker. September 24, 2019.

Abdulkadiroglu, Atila, Parag Pathak, and Christopher Walters. *School Vouchers and Student Achievement: Evidence from the Louisiana Scholarship Program*. Cambridge, MA: National Bureau of Economic Research, 2015.

Adams, Vincanne. *Markets of Sorrow, Labors of Faith: New Orleans in the wake of Katrina*. Duke University Press, 2013.

Ananat, Elizabeth Oltmans, Anna Gassman-Pines, Dania V. Francis, and Christina M. Gibson-Davis. "Children Left Behind: The Effects of Statewide Job Loss on Student Achievement." Working paper 17104. National Bureau of Economic Research, Cambridge, MA, 2011. www.nber.org/papers/w17104.

Anderson, James D. *The Education of Blacks in the South, 1860–1935*. Chapel Hill: University of North Carolina Press, 1988.

Anderson, Madeline. *I Am Somebody*. Icarus Films, 1970. DVD.

Anthony, Susan Weeks. "Public Employee Collective Bargaining in Louisiana." *Louisiana Law Review* 34, no. 1 (1973–74): 56–68.

Anyon, Jean. *Radical Possibilities: Public Policy, Urban Education, and a New Social movement*, 2nd ed. New York: Routledge, 2014.

Arena, John. *Driven from New Orleans: How Nonprofits Betray Public Housing and Promote Privatization*. Minneapolis: University of Minnesota Press, 2012.

Arend, Orissa. *Showdown in Desire: The Black Panthers Take a Stand in New Orleans*. Fayetteville: University of Arkansas Press, 2010.

Ashley, Florence. "Accounting for Research Fatigue in Research Ethics." *Bioethics* 35, no. 3 (2021): 270–76.

Atkins, Curtis. "Forging a New Democratic Party: The Politics of the Third Way from Clinton to Obama." PhD diss., York University, 2015.

Atlas, John. *Seeds of Change: The Story of ACORN, America's Most Controversial Antipoverty Community Organizing Group*. Nashville: Vanderbilt University Press, 2010.

Au, Wayne, and Joseph J. Ferrare. "Sponsors of Policy: A Network Analysis of Wealthy Elites, Their Affiliated Philanthropies, and Charter School Reform in Washington State." *Teachers College Record* 116, no. 8 (2014): 1–24.

Barrett, Nathan, Deven Carlson, Douglas Harris, and Jane Lincove. "When the Walls Come Down: Evidence on Charter Schools' Ability to Keep Their Best Teachers without Unions and Certification Rules." *Education Research Alliance*, 2020.

Barrett, Nathan, and Douglas Harris. "Significant Changes in the New Orleans Teacher Workforce." *Education Research Alliance*, August 24, 2015.

Barrett, Nathan, Katharine O. Strunk, and Jane Lincove. "When Tenure Ends: The Short-Run Effects of the Elimination of Louisiana's Teacher Employment Protections on Teacher Exit and Retirement." *Educational Economics* 29, no. 6 (2021): 559–79.

Beabout, Brian. "Stakeholder Organizations: Hurricane Katrina and the New Orleans Public Schools." *Multicultural Education* 15, no. 2 (2007): 43–49.

Beabout, Brian, and Ivan Gill. "Why Here and Why Now? Teacher Motivations for Unionizing in a New Orleans Charter School." *Journal of School Choice* 9, no. 4 (2015): 486–502.

Bell, Derrick. "*Brown v. Board of Education* and the Interest-Convergence Dilemma." *Harvard Law Review* 93, no. 3 (1980): 518–33.

Berlin, Susan. "A Historic Partnership: Veolia and New Orleans RTA." *Passenger Transport* 67, no. 19 (2009): 8.

Betts, Julian, and Richard Atkinson. "Better Research Needed on the Impact of Charter Schools." *Science* 335, no. 6065 (2012): 171–72.

Bonilla-Silva, Eduardo. *Racism without Racists: Color-Blind Racism and the Persistence of Racial Inequality in the United States*. Lanham: Rowman and Littlefield, 2006.

Boyd, William. "The Politics of Privatization in American Education." *Educational Policy* 21, no. 1 (2007): 7–14.

Brenner, Neil, and Nik Theodore. "Cities and the Geographies of 'Actually Existing Neo-liberalism.'" *Antipode* 34, no. 3 (2002): 349–79.

Bronfenbrenner, Kate. "We'll Close! Plant Closings, Plant-Closing Threats, Union Organizing and NAFTA." *Multinational Monitor* 18, no. 3 (1997): 8–13.

Buerger, Christian, and Douglas Harris. "How Did the New Orleans School Reforms Influence School Spending?" *Education Research Alliance*, January 2017.

Bullard, Robert, and Beverly Wright. *Race, Place, and Environmental Justice after Hurricane Katrina: Struggles to Reclaim, Rebuild, and Revitalize New Orleans and the Gulf Coast*. New York: Perseus Books, 2009.

Buras, Kristen. *Charter Schools, Race, and Urban Space: Where the Market Meets Grassroots Resistance*. New York: Routledge, 2014.

———. "The Mass Termination of Black Veteran Teachers in New Orleans: Cultural Politics, the Education Market, and Its Consequences." In *The Educational Forum* 80, no. 2 (2016): 154–70.

———. "Race, Charter Schools, and Conscious Capitalism: On the Spatial Politics of Whiteness as Property (and the Unconscionable Assault on Black New Orleans)." *Harvard Educational Review* 81, no. 2 (2011): 296–331.

Burian-Fitzgerald, Marisa, Michael Luekens, and Gregory Strizek. "Less Red Tape or More Green Teachers: Charter-School Autonomy and Teacher Qualifications." In *Taking Account of Charter Schools: What's Happened and What's Next*, edited by Katrina Bulkley and Priscilla Wohlstetter, 11–31. New York: Teachers College Press, 2004.

Campanella, Richard. *New Orleans: A Timeline of Economic History*. New Orleans New Opportunities–New Orleans Business Alliance, 2012.

Cannata, Marissa A., and Roberto Penaloza. "Who Are Charter-School Teachers? Comparing Teacher Characteristics, Job Choices, and Job Preferences." *Education Policy Analysis Archives* 20, no. 29 (2012): 1–25.

Carr, Sarah. *Hope against Hope: Three Schools, One City, and the Struggle to Educate America's Children*. New York: Bloomsbury, 2014.

Charron, Katherine Mellen. *Freedom's Teacher: The Life of Septima Clark*. Chapel Hill: University of North Carolina Press, 2009.

Clabaugh, Gary K. "The Educational Legacy of Ronald Reagan." *Educational Horizons* 82, no. 4 (2004): 256–59.

Clawson, Dan, and Mary Ann Clawson. "What Has Happened to the US Labor Movement? Union Decline and Renewal." *Annual Review of Sociology* 25, no. 1 (1999): 95–119.

Coates, Ta-Nehisi. "The Case for Reparations." *The Atlantic* 313, no. 5 (2014): 54–71.

Cole, Beverly P. "The Black Educator: An Endangered Species." *Journal of Negro Education* 55, no. 3 (1986): 326–34.

Collins, Patricia Hill. *Black Feminist Thought: Knowledge, Consciousness, and the Politics of Empowerment*. New York: Routledge, 2002.

Connolly, Nathan D. B. *A World More Concrete: Real Estate and the Remaking of Jim Crow South Florida*. Chicago: University of Chicago Press, 2014.

Conway, James. "Beyond 1968: The 1969 Black Monday Protest in Memphis." In *An Unseen Light: Black Struggles for Freedom in Memphis, Tennessee*, edited by Adam Goudsouzian and Charles W. McKinney Jr., 306–29. Lexington: University Press of Kentucky, 2018.

Cook, Danielle Ann, and Adrienne D. Dixson, "Writing Critical Race Theory and Method: A Composite Counterstory on the Experiences of Black Teachers in New Orleans Post-Katrina." *International Journal of Qualitative Studies in Education* 26, no. 10 (2013): 1238–58.

Cooper, Camille W. "School Choice as 'Motherwork': Valuing African-American Women's Educational Advocacy and Resistance." *International Journal of Qualitative Studies in Education* 20, no. 5 (2007): 491–512.

Cortez, Mark. "The Faculty Integration of New Orleans Public Schools, 1972." *Louisiana History* 37, no. 4 (1996): 405–34. www.jstor.org/stable/4233340.

Cowen, Scott, and Betsy Seifter. *The Inevitable City: The Resurgence of New Orleans and the Future of Urban America*. New York: Macmillan, 2014.

Craemer, Thomas. "Evaluating Racial Disparities in Hurricane Katrina Relief Using Direct Trailer Counts in New Orleans and FEMA Records." *Public Administration Review* 70, no. 3 (2010): 367–77.

Crenshaw, Kimberle. "Mapping the Margins: Intersectionality, Identity Politics, and Violence against Women of Color." *Stanford Law Review* 43, no. 6 (1990): 1241–99.

De la Torre, Marisa, and Julia Gwynne. *When Schools Close: Effects on Displaced Students in Chicago Public Schools*. Research Report. Consortium on Chicago School Research, 2009.

Deslippe, Dennis. *Protesting Affirmative Action: The Struggle over Equality after the Civil Rights Revolution*. Baltimore, MD: John Hopkins Press, 2012.

Devore, Donald E., and Joseph Logsdon. *Crescent City Schools: Public Education in New Orleans, 1841–1991*. Lafayette: Center for Louisiana Studies, University of Southwestern Louisiana, 1991.

Dewing, Rolland. "The American Federation of Teachers and Desegregation." *Journal of Negro Education* 42, no. 1 (1973): 79–92.

Diefenbach, Thomas. "Why Michels' 'Iron Law of Oligarchy' Is Not an Iron Law—and How Democratic Organisations Can Stay 'Oligarchy-Free.'" *Organization Studies* 40, no. 4 (2019): 545–62.

Dimick, Matthew. "Revitalizing Union Democracy: Labor Law, Bureaucracy, and Workplace Association." *Denver University Law Review* 88, no. 1 (2010). https://digitalcommons.law .buffalo.edu/journal_articles/84.

Dixon, Marc, and Andrew Martin. "Can the Labor Movement Succeed without the Strike?" *Contexts* 6, no. 2 (2007): 36–39.

Dudziak, Mary L. "Desegregation as a Cold War Imperative." *Stanford Law Review* 41, no. 1 (1988): 61–120.

Ehrenfeucht, Renia, and Marla Nelson. "Young Professionals as Ambivalent Change Agents in New Orleans after the 2005 Hurricanes." *Urban Studies* 50, no. 4 (2013): 825–41.

Erickson, Ansley T. *Making the Unequal Metropolis: School Desegregation and Its Limits*. Chicago: University of Chicago Press, 2016.

Fairclough, Adam. *Race and Democracy: The Civil Rights Movement in Louisiana, 1915–1972*. Athens: University of Georgia Press, 1995.

Fantasia, Rick, and Kim Voss. *Hard Work: Remaking the American Labor Movement*. Berkeley: University of California Press, 2004.

Faue, Elizabeth. "Battle for or in the Classroom: Teachers' Strikes in the Context of the 'Epidemic' of School Violence and the Working Environment." In *Strike for the Common Good: Fighting for the Future of Public Education*, edited by Rebecca Kolins Givan and Amy Schrager Lang, 36–49. Ann Arbor: University of Michigan Press, 2020.

Fones-Wolf, Elizabeth A. *Selling Free Enterprise: The Business Assault on Labor and Liberalism, 1945–60.* Chicago: University of Illinois Press, 1994.

Forman, James Jr. *Locking Up Our Own: Crime and Punishment in Black America.* New York: Farrar, Straus and Giroux, 2017.

Fraser, Nancy, and Johanna Brenner. "What Is Progressive Neoliberalism? A Debate." *Dissent* 64, no. 2 (2017): 130–40.

Friedman, Milton. *Capitalism and Freedom.* 40th anniv. ed. Chicago: University of Chicago Press, 2009.

Fudesco, Frank D. "The Rationale of Nonstriking Teachers—A Modified Delphi Technique." PhD diss., Vanderbilt University, 1981.

Garda, Robert. "The Politics of Education Reform: Lessons from New Orleans." *Journal of Law and Education* 40, no. 1 (2011): 1–42.

Geisert, G. "Mr. Nobody." *The Phi Delta Kappan* 48, no. 4 (1966): 158–59.

Germany, Kent B. *New Orleans after the Promises: Poverty, Citizenship, and the Search for the Great Society.* Athens: University of Georgia Press, 2007.

Glustrom, Alexander, dir. *Big Charity: The Death of America's Oldest Hospital.* 2014. Film.

Golin, Steve. *The Newark Teacher Strikes: Hopes on the Line.* New Brunswick, NJ: Rutgers University Press, 2002.

Gotham, Kevin Fox, and Miriam Greenberg. *Crisis Cities: Disaster and Redevelopment in New York and New Orleans.* New York: Oxford University Press, 2014.

Hacker, Jacob S., and Paul Pierson. *Winner-Take-All Politics: How Washington Made the Rich Richer—and Turned Its Back on the Middle Class.* New York: Simon and Schuster, 2010.

Hackworth, Jason. *The Neoliberal City: Governance, Ideology, and Development in American Urbanism.* Ithaca: Cornell University Press, 2007.

Hadderman, Margaret. "Charter Schools." *ERIC Digest*, no. 118 (1998): 1–5. https://files.eric .ed.gov/fulltext/ED422600.pdf.

Hale, Jon. "The Making of the New Democrats." *Political Science Quarterly* 110, no. 2 (1995): 207–32.

Hall, Jacquelyn Dowd. "The Long Civil Rights Movement and the Political Uses of the Past." *Journal of American History* 91, no. 4 (2005): 1233–63.

Harris, Douglas. *Charter School City: What the End of Traditional Public Schools in New Orleans Means for American Education.* Chicago: University of Chicago Press, 2020.

Harvey, David. "The Right to the City." *City Reader* 6, no. 1 (2008): 23–40.

———. *A Brief History of Neoliberalism.* New York: Oxford University Press, 2007.

Henry, Kevin, "Discursive Violence and Economic Retrenchment: Chartering the Sacrifice of Black Educators in Post-Katrina New Orleans." In *The Charter School Solution: Distinguishing Fact from Rhetoric*, edited by Jamel Donnor and Tara Affolter, 80–98. New York: Routledge, 2016.

Hightower, Jim. "Campaign for a Living Wage." *Journal of Public Health Policy* 23, no. 3 (2002): 265–67.

Hill, Paul, Lawrence Angel, and Jon Christensen. "Charter School Achievement Studies." *Education Finance and Policy* 1, no. 1 (2006): 139–50.

Hirsch, Arnold R. "Fade to Black: Hurricane Katrina and the Disappearance of Creole New Orleans." *Journal of American History* 94, no. 3 (2007): 752–61.

Honey, Michael K. *Going Down Jericho Road: The Memphis Strike, Martin Luther King's Last Campaign.* New York: W. W. Norton, 2011.

———. *Southern Labor and Black Civil Rights: Organizing Memphis Workers.* Chicago: University of Illinois Press, 1993.

Hopkins, Daniel J., and Katherine T. McCabe. "After It's Too Late: Estimating the Policy Impacts of Black Mayoralties in U.S. Cities." *American Politics Research* 40, no. 4 (2012): 665–700.

Hoxby, Caroline Minter. "How Teachers' Unions Affect Education Production." *Quarterly Journal of Economics* 111, no. 3 (1996): 671–718.

Hudson, Mildred J., and Barbara J. Holmes. "Missing Teachers, Impaired Communities: The Unanticipated Consequences of *Brown v. Board of Education* on the African American Teaching Force at the Precollegiate Level." *Journal of Negro Education* 63, no. 3 (1994): 388–93.

Isaac, Larry, and Lars Christiansen. "How the Civil Rights Movement Revitalized Labor Militancy." *American Sociological Review* 67, no. 5 (2002): 722–46.

Jabbar, Huriya. "'Drenched in the Past': The Evolution of Market-Oriented Reforms in New Orleans." *Journal of Education Policy* 30, no. 6 (2015): 751–72.

———. "Selling Schools: Marketing and Recruitment Strategies in New Orleans." *Peabody Journal of Education* 91, no. 1 (2016): 4–23.

Jabbar, Huriya, Jesse Chanin, Jamie Haynes, and Sara Slaughter. "Teacher Power and the Politics of Union Organizing in the Charter Sector." *Educational Policy* 34, no. 1 (2020): 211–38.

Jenkins, J. Craig. "Resource Mobilization Theory and the Study of Social Movements." *Annual Review of Sociology* 9 (1983): 527–53.

Jessop, Bob. "Hollowing Out the 'Nation-State' and Multi-level Governance." In *A Handbook of Comparative Social Policy*, 2nd ed. Cheltenham, UK: Edward Elgar, 2013.

Johnston, Paul. *Success while Others Fail: Social Movement Unionism and the Public Workplace.* Ithaca, NY: Cornell University Press, 1994.

Jones, William P. *The March on Washington: Jobs, Freedom, and the Forgotten History of Civil Rights.* New York: W. W. Norton, 2013.

———. "Simple Truths of Democracy: African Americans and Organized Labor in the Post–World War II South." In *The Black Worker: Race, Labor, and Civil Rights since Emancipation*, edited by Eric Arnesen, 250–70. Chicago: University of Illinois Press, 2007.

Kahlenberg, Richard D. *Tough Liberal: Albert Shanker and the Battle over Schools, Unions, Race, and Democracy.* New York: Columbia University Press, 2007.

Kelley, Robin D. G. *Hammer and Hoe: Alabama Communists during the Great Depression.* Chapel Hill: University of North Carolina Press, 2015.

Kessler-Harris, Alice. *Out to Work: A History of Wage-Earning Women in the United States.* New York: Oxford University Press, 2003.

Klein, Naomi. *The Shock Doctrine: The Rise of Disaster Capitalism.* New York: Macmillan, 2007.

Kopp, Wendy. *A Chance to Make History: What Works and What Doesn't in Providing an Excellent Education for All.* New York: Public Affairs, 2012.

Korstad, Robert. *Civil Rights Unionism: Tobacco Workers and the Struggle for Democracy in the Mid-Twentieth Century South.* Chapel Hill: University of North Carolina Press, 2003.

Korstad, Robert, and Nelson Lichtenstein. "Opportunities Found and Lost: Labor, Radicals, and the Early Civil Rights Movement." *Journal of American History* 75, no. 3 (1988): 786–811.

Kretchmar, Kerry, Beth Sondel, and Joseph Ferrare. "Mapping the Terrain: Teach for America, Charter School Reform, and Corporate Sponsorship." *Journal of Education Policy* 29, no. 6 (2014): 742–59.

Krist, Michael. "Mayoral Control of Schools: Politics, Trade-Offs, and Outcomes." In *When Mayors Take Charge: School Governance in the City*, edited by Joseph P. Viteritti, 46–63. Washington, DC: Brookings Institute Press, 2009.

Lavery, Lesley, and Ashley Jochim. "Why Charter Teachers Unionize." *Educational Policy* 37, no. 5 (2022): 1217–40.

Lincove, Jane, Nathan Barrett, and Katherine O. Strunk. *Lessons from Hurricane Katrina: The Employment Effects of the Mass Dismissal of New Orleans Teachers*. Education Research Alliance of New Orleans, 2017. https://educationresearchalliancenola.org/files/publications/120517-Lincove-Barrett-Strunk-Lessons-from-Hurricane-Katrina.pdf.

Lincove, Jane, and Jon Valant. *New Orleans Students' Commute Times by Car, Public Transit, and School Bus*. Urban Institute, September 2018. https://educationresearchalliancenola.org/files/publications/new_orleans_students_commute_times_by_car_public_transit_and_school_bus.pdf.

Lindsay, Constance A., and Cassandra M. D. Hart. "Teacher Race and School Discipline: Are Students Suspended Less Often When They Have a Teacher of the Same Race?" *Education Next* 17, no. 1 (2017): 72–79.

Lipman, Pauline. *The New Political Economy of Urban Education: Neoliberalism, Race, and the Right to the City*. New York: Routledge, 2011.

Lipset, Seymour M., Martin Trow, and James Coleman. *Union Democracy: The Internal Politics of the International Typographical Union*. New York: Anchor Books, 1956.

Litwack, Leon F. *Trouble in Mind: Black Southerners in the Age of Jim Crow*. New York: Vintage, 1999.

Logan, John. "Consultants, Lawyers, and the 'Union Free' Movement in the USA since the 1970s." *Industrial Relations Journal* 33, no. 3 (2002): 197–214.

Long, Alecia P. "Poverty Is the New Prostitution: Race, Poverty, and Public Housing in Post-Katrina New Orleans." *Journal of American History* 94, no. 3 (2007): 795–803.

Long, Emma. "Complicating the Narrative: Labor, Feminism, and Civil Rights in the United Teachers of New Orleans Strike of 1990." Master's thesis, University of New Orleans, 2016.

MacLean, Nancy. *Freedom Is Not Enough: The Opening of the American Workplace*. Boston: Harvard University Press, 2008.

———. "Southern Dominance in Borrowed Language: The American Origins of Neoliberalism." In *New Landscapes of Inequality: Neoliberalism and the Erosion of Democracy in America*, edited by Jane Collins, Brett Williams, and Micaela di Leonardo, 21–37. Santa Fe, NM: School for Advanced Research Press, 2008.

Mauney, Margaret Ann, "Consciousness and Activism of Atlanta Teachers: Unionization and Desegregation, 1960–1990." PhD diss., Emory University, 1997.

Maxwell, Joseph A. *Qualitative Research Design: An Interactive Approach*, 3rd ed. Applied Social Research Methods, vol. 41. Thousand Oaks: Sage Publications, 2012.

McAlevey, Jane. *No Shortcuts: Organizing for Power in the New Gilded Age*. New York: Oxford University Press, 2016.

McCartin, Joseph A. "Bargaining for the Common Good." *Dissent* 63, no. 2 (2016): 128–35.

———. *Collision Course: Ronald Reagan, the Air Traffic Controllers, and the Strike That Changed America*. New York: Oxford University Press, 2011.

———. "A Wagner Act for Public Employees: Labor's Deferred Dream and the Rise of Conservatism, 1970–1976." *Journal of American History* 95, no. 1 (2008): 123–48.

McCartin, Joseph A., Marilyn Sneiderman, and Maurice BP-Weeks. "Combustible Convergence: Bargaining for the Common Good and the# RedforEd Uprisings of 2018." *Labor Studies Journal* 45, no. 1 (2020): 97–113.

McHugh, William F. "The Florida Experience in Public Employee Collective Bargaining, 1974–1978: Bellwether for the South." *Florida State University Law Review* 6, no. 2 (1978): 263–356.

Meiners, Erica R. *Right to be Hostile: Schools, Prisons, and the Making of Public Enemies.* New York: Routledge, 2010.

Melamed, Jodi. *Represent and Destroy: Rationalizing Violence in the New Racial Capitalism.* Minneapolis: University of Minnesota Press, 2011.

Michels, Robert. *Political Parties: A Sociological Study of the Oligarchical Tendencies of Modern Democracy.* New York: Hearst's International Library, 1915.

Middleton, Ernest J. "The Louisiana Education Association, 1901–1970." *Journal of Negro Education* 47, no. 4 (1978): 363–78.

Miller, Berkeley, and William Canak. "From 'Porkchoppers' to 'Lambchoppers': The Passage of Florida's Public Employee Relations Act." *Industrial and Labor Relations Review* 44, no. 2 (1991): 349–66.

Minkoff, Debra C. "From Service Provision to Institutional Advocacy: The Shifting Legitimacy of Organizational Forms." *Social Forces* 72, no. 4 (1994): 943–69.

Moe, Terry M. *The Politics of Institutional Reform: Katrina, Education, and the Second Face of Power.* Cambridge, UK: Cambridge University Press, 2019.

———. *Special Interest: Teachers Unions and America's Public Schools.* Washington, DC: Brookings Institution Press, 2011.

Moody, Kim. *US Labor in Trouble and Transition: The Failure of Reform from Above, the Promise of Revival from Below.* London: Verso Books, 2007.

Morel, Domingo. *Takeover: Race, Education, and American Democracy.* New York: Oxford University Press, 2018.

Morel, Domingo, and Sally Nuamah. "Who Governs? How Shifts in Political Power Shape Perceptions of Local Government Services." *Urban Affairs Review* 56, no. 3 (2019): 1503–28.

Morgan, Iwan. "Jimmy Carter, Bill Clinton, and the New Democratic Economics." *Historical Journal* 47, no. 4 (2004): 1015–39.

Murphy, Marjorie. *Blackboard Unions: The AFT and the NEA, 1900–1980.* Ithaca, NY: Cornell University Press, 1990.

Ni, Yongmei. "Teacher Working Conditions in Charter Schools and Traditional Public Schools: A Comparative Study." *Teachers College Record* 114, no. 3 (2012): 1–26.

Omi, Michael, and Howard Winant. *Racial Formation in the United States.* New York: Routledge, 2014.

Parker, Mike, and Martha Gruelle. *Democracy Is Power: Rebuilding Unions from the Bottom Up.* Detroit: Labor Education and Research Project, 1999.

Parr, Leslie G. *A Will of Her Own: Sarah Towles Reed and the Pursuit of Democracy in Southern Public Education.* Athens: University of Georgia Press, 2010.

Pattillo, Mary. *Black on the Block: The Politics of Race and Class in the City.* Chicago: University of Chicago Press, 2010.

———. *Black Picket Fences: Privilege and Peril among the Black Middle Class.* Chicago, University of Chicago Press, 2013.

Pattillo, Mary, Lori Delale-O'Connor, and Felicia Butts. "High-Stakes Choosing: Race and Place in Chicago School Reform." In *Choosing Homes, Choosing Schools*, edited by Annette Lareau and Kimberly Goyette, 237–67. New York: Russell Sage Foundation, 2014.

Perkins, Lyle K. "Failing the Race: A Historical Assessment of New Orleans Mayor Sidney Barthelemy, 1986–1994." Master's thesis, Louisiana State University, 2005.

Perlstein, Daniel H. *Justice, Justice: School Politics and the Eclipse of Liberalism*. New York: Peter Lang, 2004.

Perrillo, Jonna. *Uncivil Rights: Teachers, Unions, and Race in the Battle for School Equity*. Chicago: University of Chicago Press, 2012.

Perry, Theresa. "Up From the Parched Earth." *Young, Gifted, and Black: Promoting High Achievement among African-American Students*. New York: Beacon Press, 2003.

Phillips-Fein, Kim. *Invisible Hands: The Businessmen's Crusade against the New Deal*. New York: W. W. Norton, 2010.

Piliawsky, Monte, and Paul Stekler. "From Black Politics to Blacks in the Mainstream: The 1986 New Orleans Mayoral Election." *Western Journal of Black Studies* 15, no. 2 (1991): 114–22.

Piven, Frances Fox, and Richard Cloward. *Poor People's Movements: Why They Succeed, How They Fail*. New York: Vintage, 2012.

Podair, Jerald E. *The Strike That Changed New York: Blacks, Whites, and the Ocean Hill-Brownsville Crisis*. New Haven: Yale University Press, 2008.

Podgursky, Michael, and Dale Ballou. *Personnel Policy in Charter Schools*. Washington, DC: Thomas B. Fordham Foundation, 2001.

Polletta, Francesca. *Freedom Is an Endless Meeting: Democracy in American Social Movements*. Chicago: University of Chicago Press, 2002.

Polletta, Francesca, and Beth Gardner. "The Forms of Deliberative Communication." In *The Oxford Handbook of Deliberative Democracy*, edited by André Bächtinger, John S. Dryzek, Jane J. Mansbridge, and Mark Warren, 70–85. Oxford, UK: Oxford University Press, 2018.

Ransby, Barbara. *Ella Baker and the Black Freedom Movement: A Radical Democratic Vision*. Chapel Hill: University of North Carolina Press, 2003.

Rathke, Wade. "Labor's Failure in the South." In *American Crisis, Southern Solutions: From Where We Stand, Peril and Promise*, edited by Anthony Dunbar, 169–89. Montgomery: NewSouth Books, 2008.

Ray, Victor. "A Theory of Racialized Organizations." *American Sociological Review* 84, no. 1 (2019): 26–53.

Reardon, Sean F., and Ann Owens. "60 Years after Brown: Trends and Consequences of School Segregation." *Annual Review of Sociology* 40 (2014), 199–218.

Reed, Adolph, Jr. "The Post-1965 Trajectory of Race, Class, and Urban Politics in the United States Reconsidered." *Labor Studies Journal*. 41 no. 3 (2016) 260–91.

———. *Stirrings in the Jug: Black Politics in the Post-Segregation Era*. Minneapolis: University of Minnesota Press, 1999.

Reed, Pamela D. "From the Freedmen's Bureau to FEMA: A Post-Katrina Historical, Journalistic, and Literary Analysis." *Journal of Black Studies* 37, no. 4 (2007): 555–67.

Robinson, William T., and DeAnn Gruber. "Feasibility of Neighborhood Surveys in Post-Katrina New Orleans: Development of a Systematic Social Observation Tool." Paper presented at the American Statistical Association Surveying Hard to Reach Population conference, October 31–November 3, 2012, New Orleans, LA. www.asasrms.org

/Proceedings/H2R2012/Feasibility_of_Neighborhood_Surveys_in_Post-Katrina_New
_Orleans_Development_of_a_Systematic_Social_.pdf.

Roch, Christine H., and Na Sai. "Charter School Teacher Job Satisfaction." *Educational Policy* 31, no. 7 (2017): 951–91.

Rogers, Kim Lacy. *Righteous Lives: Narratives of the New Orleans Civil Rights Movement*. New York: New York University Press, 1993.

Rubio, Philip F. *There's Always Work at the Post Office: African American Postal Workers and the Fight for Jobs, Justice, and Equality*. Chapel Hill: University of North Carolina Press, 2010.

Saltman, Kenneth J. "Neoliberalism and Corporate School Reform: 'Failure' and 'Creative Destruction.'" *Review of Education, Pedagogy, and Cultural Studies* 36, no. 4 (2014): 249–59.

Sanders, Raynard. *The Coup d'État of the New Orleans Public School District: Money, Power, and the Illegal Takeover of a Public School System*. New York: Peter Lang, 2018.

Schneider, Jack, and Jennifer Berkshire. *A Wolf at the Schoolhouse Door: The Dismantling of Public Education and the Future of School*. Cambridge, MA: The New Press of Harvard University Press, 2020.

Selden, David. *The Teacher Rebellion*. Washington, DC: Howard University Press, 1985.

Shange, Savannah. *Progressive Dystopia: Abolition, Antiblackness, and Schooling in San Francisco*. Durham, NC: Duke University Press, 2019.

Shelton, Jon. *Teacher Strike! Public Education and the Making of a New American Political Order*. Chicago: University of Illinois Press, 2017.

Slater, Graham B. "Education as Recovery: Neoliberalism, School Reform, and the Politics of Crisis." *Journal of Education Policy* 30, no. 1 (2015): 1–20.

Smith, Emily D. "Mississippi's First Statewide Teachers' Strike." Master's thesis, University of Southern Mississippi, 2018.

Sondel, Beth. "Raising Citizens or Raising Test Scores? Teach for America, 'No Excuses' Charters, and the Development of the Neoliberal Citizen." *Theory and Research in Social Education* 43, no. 3 (2015): 289–313.

Spradley, James P. *The Ethnographic Interview*. Long Grove, IL: Waveland Press, 2016.

Stein, Judith. *Pivotal Decade: How the United States Traded Factories for Finance in the Seventies*. New Haven: Yale University Press, 2010.

Stern, Walter. *Race and Education in New Orleans: Creating the Segregated City, 1764–1960*. Baton Rouge: Louisiana State University Press, 2018.

Strunk, Katharine O. "Are Teachers' Unions Really to Blame? Collective Bargaining Agreements and Their Relationships with District Resource Allocation and Student Performance in California." *Education Finance and Policy* 6, no. 3 (2011): 354–98.

Stuit, David A., and Thomas M. Smith. "Explaining the Gap in Charter and Traditional Public School Teacher Turnover Rates." *Economics of Education Review* 31, no. 2 (2012): 268–79.

Stulberg, Lisa M. *Race, Schools, and Hope: African Americans and School Choice after Brown*. New York: Teachers College Press, 2008.

Sukarieh, Mayssoun, and Stuart Tannock. "The American Federation of Teachers in the Middle East: Teacher Training as Labor Imperialism." *Labor Studies Journal* 35, no. 2 (2010): 181–97.

Taylor, Clarence. "The Long History of Attacking Teachers' Unions and Public Education." In *Strike for the Common Good: Fighting for the Future of Public Education*, edited by Rebecca Kolins Givan and Amy Schrager Lang, 76–90. Ann Arbor: University of Michigan Press, 2020.

————. *Reds at the Blackboard: Communism, Civil Rights, and the New York City Teachers Union*. New York: Columbia University Press, 2011.

Todd-Breland, Elizabeth. *A Political Education: Black Politics and Education Reform in Chicago since the 1960s*. Chapel Hill: University of North Carolina Press, 2018.

Tolbert, Pamela S., and Shon R. Hiatt. "On Organizations and Oligarchies: Michels in the Twenty-First Century." In *The Oxford Handbook of Sociology and Organization Studies*, edited by Paul Adler, 174–99. New York: Oxford University Press, 2009.

Tompkins, Christien. "There's No Such Thing as a Bad Teacher: Reconfiguring Race and Talent in Post-Katrina Charter Schools." *Souls* 17, no. 3–4 (2015): 211–30.

Torres, A. Chris. "Is This Work Sustainable? Teacher Turnover and Perceptions of Workload in Charter Management Organizations." *Urban Education* 51, no. 8 (2016): 891–914.

Torres, A. Chris, and Joseph Oluwole. "Teacher Satisfaction and Turnover in Charter Schools: Examining the Variations and Possibilities for Collective Bargaining in State Laws." *Journal of School Choice* 9, no. 4 (2015): 503–28.

Turner, Lowell, and Richard Hurd. "Building Social Movement Unionism." In *Rekindling the Movement: Labor's Quest for Relevance in the Twenty-First Century*, edited by Lowell Turner, Harry Katz, and Richard Hurd, 9–26. Ithaca, NY: ILR Press, 2001.

Uetricht, Micah. *Strike for America: Chicago Teachers against austerity*. New York: Verso, 2014.

Urban, Wayne J. *Gender, Race, and the National Education Association: Professionalism and its Limitations*. New York: Taylor and Francis, 2000.

US Department of Education, National Center for Education Statistics, and Schools and Staffing Survey. "Public School Teacher Data File." 2011–12.

US Department of Health, Education, and Welfare. *Displacement of Black Educators in Desegregating Public Schools*. Washington, DC: Government Printing Office, 1972.

Vergari, Sandra. "Charter School Authorizers: Public Agents for Holding Charter Schools Accountable." *Education and Urban Society* 33, no. 2 (2001): 129–40.

————. "The Politics of Charter Schools." *Educational Policy* 21, no. 1 (2007): 15–39.

Voss, Kim, and Rachel Sherman. "Breaking the Iron Law of Oligarchy: Union Revitalization in the American Labor Movement." *American Journal of Sociology* 106, no. 2 (2000): 303–49.

Watkins, William. *The Assault on Public Education: Confronting the Politics of Corporate School Reform*. New York: Teachers College Press, 2015.

Weixler, Lindsay Bell, Douglas N. Harris, and Nathan Barrett. "Teachers' Perspectives on the Learning and Work Environments under the New Orleans School Reforms." *Educational Researcher* 47, no. 8 (2018): 502–15.

Westbrook, Kyle, "A Fair and Forward Union: Black Teachers and the Chicago Teachers Union 1963–1987." PhD diss., University of Chicago, 2020.

Western, Bruce, and Jake Rosenfeld. "Unions, Norms, and the Rise in U.S. Wage Inequality." *American Sociological Review* 76, no. 4 (2011): 513–37.

White, Terrenda. "Teach for America's Paradoxical Diversity Initiative: Race, Policy, and Black Teacher Displacement in Urban Public Schools." *Education Policy Analysis Archives* 24, no. 16 (2016): 1–42.

Wilson, William Julius. *The Truly Disadvantaged: The Inner City, the Underclass, and Public Policy*. Chicago: University of Chicago Press, 2012.

Windham, Lane. *Knocking on Labor's Door: Union Organizing in the 1970s and the Roots of a New Economic Divide*. Chapel Hill: University of North Carolina Press, 2017.

Winkler, Amber M., Janie Scull, and Dara Zeehandelaar. *How Strong Are U.S. Teacher Unions? A State-by-State Comparison*. Thomas B. Fordham Institute, October 2012.

Woods, Clyde. *Development Arrested: From the Plantation Era to the Katrina Crisis in the Mississippi Delta*. New York: Verso, 2010.

―――. *Development Drowned and Reborn: The Blues and Bourbon Restorations in Post-Katrina New Orleans*. Athens: University of Georgia Press, 2017.

Zimmer, Ron, Brian Gill, Kevin Booker, Stephanie Lavertu, and John Witte. "Examining Charter Student Achievement Effects Across Seven States." *Economics of Education Review* 31, no. 2 (2012): 213–24.

Zonderman, Alan B., Nicolle A. Mode, Ngozi Ejiogu, and Michele K. Evans. "Race and Poverty Status as a Risk for Overall Mortality in Community-Dwelling Middle-Aged Adults." *JAMA Internal Medicine* 176, no. 9 (2016): 1394–95.

INDEX

Page numbers in italics refer to illustrations.

Minimum Foundation Program (MFP) money, 154

Mississippi: statewide strikes in, 60; wildcat teachers' strike in, 6

Mitchell, Brenda: on accountability movement, 107; background of, 32, 145–46; on collective bargaining, 74; on Didier's election, 41; as director of teacher center, 94–95; experiences of racial and gender discrimination, 48; on Hurricane Katrina, immediate aftermath, 187, 189–90, 192, 193, 200; leadership post-Katrina of, 207; leadership style of, 12–13, 144–45, 146–49, 149, 175, 177; on NEA-AFT merger, 46; political connections of, 149–51; and QuEST, 96; reelection of, 173; on school reform, 155–56; on school strikes, 39, 85–86; on takeover of New Orleans schools, 164–65, 166; UTNO's political power, 115, 128; on UTNO's legacy, 212, 231; working class alliances of, 150

Morel, Domingo, 164, 178, 217; *Takeover*, 178

Morial, Dutch, 69, 81; strike of 1978, 86–87, 89

Morial, Marc, 157, 160

NAACP (National Association for the Advancement of Colored People), 27, 206

Nagin, Ray, 160, 190, 192, 211

National Association of Letter Carriers (NALC), 30, 116, 119, 178, 206

National Coalition for Black Civic Participation, 207

National Education Association (NEA): criticism of AFT of, 33; on desegregation in Louisiana, 43–44; opposition to strikes of, 28; possible merger with AFT, 264n110; report on segregation by, 2–3

National Labor Relations Board (NLRB), 217

National Teacher Examination (NTE), 107

Nation at Risk, A (1983), 16, 20, 106, 108, 110

Ndang, Katrena, 95, 134, 196, 202, 207, 214–15, 224

neighborhood canvassing, 117, 204–6

neighborhood schools, 22, 189; loss of, 215, 222, 225–26

neoliberal education reform: and business model for education, 106–9; and color blindness, 13–16, 59–60, 101, 107–8, 179–80; as creative destruction, 110, 167, 182–83, 216; despair as change motivator in, 167; failure of, 13–16, 98; history and overview of, 102–5; multiculturalism in, 14, 151, 200; resistance to, 140–41, 151; role of, in UTNO's evisceration, 207–8; school reform agenda, 209; and union losses, 103–4; unions' opposition to, 232, 235; and voucher programs, 156. *See also* No Child Left Behind (2001)

Newark, NJ, 6, 164

New Orleans: Black City Council, 36; Black political power in, 68–69; Black support for UTNO in, 11; Business Task Force on Education, 110–11, 113, 114, 124; Charity Hospital, 56, 183, 188, 211; class stratification in, 11–12; fiscal crisis in, 114–15; green dot plan for rebuilding, 211; neighborhood catchment zones post-Katrina in, 215; one-cent sales tax in, 28, 30; public attitudes toward public education in, 81–82; Urban League, 110; white flight in, 63, 67, 68, 178, 233

New Orleans Center for Creative Arts (NOCCA), 68, 129–30, 131

New Orleans Charter Middle School, 153, 154

New Orleans Classroom Teachers Federation (NOCTF), 24

New Orleans public school system: administration funding of, 228; Alvarez and Marsal's control of, 164–67; desegregation efforts in, 31; facility maintenance of, 112–14, 157–58, 176; faculty desegregation in, 43–46, 47–48, 49, 67; payroll issues in, 158–59; pre-Katrina, 175–77; post-Katrina displacement of teachers in,

New Orleans public school system
(*continued*)

184–85; push for all-charter district of,
183–84; school board 1968 elections,
31; segregation in, 24–25, *26*; state
takeover of, 161–67; superintendents
of, *159*, 159–60; Support and Appraisal
in, *130*; white flight from, 53–54
New Orleans Public School Teachers
Association, 24
New York City teachers' unions, 6, 78,
248n25
Nix, Kelly, 107
No Child Left Behind (2001), 144, 152–53
No Shortcuts (McAlevey), 99

Obama, Barack, 186
O'Dwyer, Avra, 137
OEA (Orleans Education Association),
35, 46
O'Keefe, Michael, 119
OneApp system, 227
open-meetings laws, 222–23
OPSB. *See* Orleans Parish School Board
(OPSB)
Orleans Educators Association (OEA),
35, 46
Orleans Parish School Board (OPSB):
budget cuts of, post-1978 strike,
90–91; budget negotiations of, 75;
charter schools in, post-Katrina,
184–85; contract agreement of,
76–77; corruption in, criticized for,
156–61; FBI investigation of, 157; fiscal
difficulties of, 98; Geisert's contact
with, 93; lottery system in, 226–27;
redesign of, after Hurricane Katrina,
1–2, 3–4; reduction in influence of,
post-Katrina, 204; reopening delays
of, post-Katrina, 187; sales tax in,
28, 30; school takeovers of, 155–56;
security during 1990 strike of, 137;
superintendent search for, 49–50;
teacher tenure in, 106; and UTNO
collective bargaining campaign, 52–56;
UTNO's recall campaign against,
135–36, 137–39, 140
Orleans Principals Association, 49

Paige, Rod, 154
PANOPSI (Professional Administrators of
New Orleans Public Schools), 206
paraprofessionals: and collective
bargaining, 58; marginalization of, 70;
and negotiation skills, 73; 1990 UTNO
strike and, 128–29; raises for, 7; union
involvement of, 65–66, 242; and union
leadership, 87; UTNO involvement of,
51; wages of, 124–25
parent conferences, 77
Parents for Educational Justice, 153
Parker, Mike, 62; *Democracy Is Power*, 62
participatory decision-making, 73–74
participatory democracy, 64–65, 97–98,
250n80
Pattillo, Mary, 12, 209
Picard, Cecil, 164, 189–90
Pichon, Linda, 89, 133, 173
picketing. *See* strikes
Pierce, Don, 30
Piven, Frances Fox, 16, 201
Polletta, Francesca, 64–65
poverty, 109, 162–63, 175, 209, 224–25,
242
Pride College Prep charter school,
239–40
privatization, 102–3, 110, 114; and disaster
recovery post-Katrina, 234–35; as
post-Katrina agenda, 182–83, 193–94,
202, 210–11. *See also* charter school
movement; charter schools; school
choice movement
public opinion: on conflict with UTNO,
90–91; on school restructuring
post-Katrina, 191; support of, for 1978
strike, 84–85, 87

QuEST (Quality Educational Standards in
Teaching), 96–97, 146

racism: in AFT Local 527, 27–28,
31–33, 40–48, 49, 59; in charter
school movement, 235–36; during
post-Katrina turmoil, 185–86, 208–9,
212, 234–35; during strike of 1978,
89; during strike of 1990, 129–30,
133–34; in Fortier High School, 34;

314 | *Index*

Winters, Chuck, 52
Wise, Donisia, 93, 117–18, 132–33, 197
Woods, Clyde, 22
Wurf, Jerry, 69

Xavier University, 49

ya Salaam, Kalamu, 1, 17–18, 36, 207, 234, 236

Zanders, Willie, 191, 192, 201